AF575461

Both easy to read and well-documented, this commentary will benefit students, pastors, and scholars. Rarely does one find a commentary that is both so clearly written and erudite.

—JAMES D. NOGALSKI,
W. Marshall & Lulie Craig Professor of Old Testament, Baylor University

Dennis Tucker's thorough and judicious use of scholarship illuminates the message of Malachi as Christian Scripture. It is a valuable resource for all who seek to read this prophetic book with understanding and insight.

—BARRY JONES,
professor of Old Testament and Hebrew, Campbell University Divinity School

Insightful and compelling, Tucker offers a fresh reading of Malachi helpful to pastors, scholars, and interested readers alike. Tucker interweaves clear exegetical insights with theological depth as he examines Malachi's themes such as God's kingship, rededication to worship, and a clarion call to faithfulness. In his commentary, Tucker shows how the message of Malachi continues to connect meaningfully to the challenges we face today.

—BETH STOVELL,
professor of Old Testament and chair general theological studies,
Ambrose Seminary, Ambrose University

Prepare yourself for a fresh encounter with the Hebrew text of Malachi, faithfully explicated with attention to linguistic structure as well as historical context. Be assured that the theological horizon is not ignored as this commentary provides pathways for the text to enter into the lives of contemporary readers and hearers of this often-neglected prophetic book.

—MARK J. BODA,
professor of Old Testament, McMaster Divinity School

This excellent commentary on the book of Malachi balances two strengths that are often perceived to be in conflict. On the one hand, Tucker's analysis is based on rigorous textual, literary, and linguistic analysis and on helpful interaction with other scholars. On the other hand, everything is explained and presented so clearly that it doesn't feel too technical. The author is appropriately selective of the most important issues and provides the kind of guidance that will be very helpful for pastors, including identification of the main idea of each section and relevant theological observations. Tucker proves to be an expert guide to this important prophetic book.

—ERIC J. TULLY,
professor of Old Testament and Semitic languages, Trinity International University

Zondervan Exegetical Commentary on the Old Testament

MALACHI
Fidelity to the Great King

ZONDERVAN
Exegetical Commentary
ON THE
Old Testament
A DISCOURSE ANALYSIS OF THE HEBREW BIBLE

W. DENNIS TUCKER JR.

DANIEL I. BLOCK
General Editor

ZONDERVAN ACADEMIC

Malachi

Published in Grand Rapids, Michigan, by Zondervan. Zondervan is a registered trademark of The Zondervan Corporation, L.L.C., a wholly owned subsidiary of HarperCollins Christian Publishing, Inc.

Requests for information should be addressed to customercare@harpercollins.com.

Zondervan titles may be purchased in bulk for educational, business, fundraising, or sales promotional use. For information, please email SpecialMarkets@Zondervan.com.

Library of Congress Cataloging-in-Publication Data

Names: Tucker, W. Dennis, Jr., author.
Title: Malachi : a discourse analysis of the Hebrew Bible / W. Dennis Tucker, Jr.
Other titles: Zondervan exegetical commentary on the Old Testament
Description: Grand Rapids : Zondervan, 2024. | Series: Zondervan exegetical commentary on the Old Testament | Includes bibliographical references and index.
Identifiers: LCCN 2023016755 | ISBN 9780310283003 (hardcover)
Subjects: LCSH: Bible Malachi--Commentaries. | Hebrew Bible--Discourse analysis.
Classification: LCC BS1675.53 .T83 2024 | DDC 224/.9907--dc23/eng/20230927
LC record available at https://lccn.loc.gov/2023016755

The Hebrew text is from Deuteronomy 31:11–13, which highlights the importance of "hearing" the voice of Scripture:

> When all Israel comes to appear before יהוה your God at the place he will choose, you shall read this torah before them in their hearing. Assemble the people—men, women and children, and the foreigners residing in your towns—so they can *listen* and learn to fear יהוה your God and follow carefully all the words of this Torah. Their children, who do not know this Torah, must *hear* it and learn to fear יהוה your God as long as you live in the land you are crossing the Jordan to possess. (NIV, modified)

Cover design: Tammy Johnson
Interior design: Beth Shagene

Printed in the United States of America

23 24 25 26 27 28 29 30 31 32 33 34 35 /TRM/ 18 17 16 15 14 13 12 11 10 9 8 7 6 5 4 3 2 1

To Letitia

אֵשֶׁת נְעוּרַי

Contents

Series Introduction

Prospectus

Modern audiences are often taken in by the oratorical skill and creativity of preachers and teachers. However, they tend to forget that the authority of proclamation is directly related to the correspondence of the key points of the sermon to the message the biblical authors were trying to communicate. Since we confess that "all Scripture [including the entirety of the OT] is God-breathed and is useful for teaching, rebuking, correcting and training in righteousness, so that [all God's people] may be thoroughly equipped for every good work" (2 Tim 3:16–17 NIV), it seems essential that those who proclaim its message should pay close attention to the rhetorical agendas of biblical authors. Too often modern readers, including preachers, are either baffled by OT texts, or they simply get out of them that for which they are looking. Many commentaries available to pastors and teachers try to resolve the dilemma either through word-by-word and verse-by-verse analysis or synthetic theological reflections on the text without careful attention to the flow and argument of that text.

The commentators in this series recognize that too little attention has been paid to biblical authors as rhetoricians, to their larger rhetorical and theological agendas, and especially to the means by which they tried to achieve their goals. Like effective communicators in every age, biblical authors were driven by a passion to communicate a message. So we must inquire not only what that message was, but also what strategies they used to impress their message on their hearers' ears. This reference to "hearers" rather than to readers is intentional, since the biblical texts were written to be heard. Not only were the Hebrew and Christian Scriptures composed to be heard in the public gathering of God's people but also before the invention of moveable type, and few would have had access to their own copies of the Scriptures. While the contributors to this series acknowledge with Paul that every Scripture—that is, every passage in the Hebrew Bible—is God-breathed, we also recognize that the inspired authors possessed a vast repertoire of rhetorical and literary strategies. These included not only the special use of words and figures of speech, but also the deliberate selection, arrangement, and shaping of ideas.

The primary goal of this commentary series is to help serious students of

Scripture, as well as those charged with preaching and teaching the Word of God, to hear the messages of Scripture as biblical authors intended them to be heard. While we recognize the timelessness of the biblical message, the validity of our interpretation and the authority with which we teach the Scriptures are related directly to the extent to which we have grasped the message intended by the author in the first place. Accordingly, when dealing with specific texts, the authors of the commentaries in this series are concerned with three principal questions: (1) What are the principal theological points the biblical writers are making? (2) How do biblical writers make those points? (3) What significance does the message of the present text have for understanding the message of the biblical book within which it is embedded and the message of the Scriptures as a whole? The achievement of these goals requires careful attention to the way ideas are expressed in the OT, including the selection and arrangement of materials and the syntactical shaping of the text.

To most readers syntax operates primarily at the sentence level. But recent developments in biblical study, particularly advances in rhetorical and discourse analysis, have alerted us to the fact that syntax operates also at the levels of the paragraph, the literary unit being analyzed, and the composition as a whole. Discourse analysis, also called macrosyntax, studies the text beyond the level of the sentence (sentence syntax), where the paragraph serves as the basic unit of thought. Those contributing to this series recognize that this type of study may be pursued in a variety of ways. Some will prefer a more bottom-up approach, where clause connectors and transitional features play a dominant role in analysis. Others will pursue a more top-down approach, where genre or literary form begins the discussion. However, we all understand that both approaches are required to understand fully the method and the message of the text. For this reason, the ultimate value of discourse analysis is that it allows the text to set the agenda in biblical interpretation.

One of the distinctive goals for this series is to engage the biblical text using some form of discourse analysis to understand not only what the text says, but also how it says it. While attention to words or phrases is still essential, contributors to this commentary series will concentrate on the flow of thought in the biblical writings, both at the macroscopic level of entire compositions and at the microscopic level of individual text units. In so doing we hope to help other readers of Scripture grasp both the message and the rhetorical force of OT texts. When we hear the message of Scripture, we gain access to the mind of God.

Format of the Commentary

The format of this series is designed to achieve the goals summarized above. Accordingly, each volume in the series will begin with an introduction to the book being explored. In addition to answering the usual questions of date, authorship, and provenance of the composition, commentators will highlight what they consider to be the main theological themes of the book and then discuss broadly how the style and structure of the book develop those themes. This discussion will include a coherent outline of the contents of the book, demonstrating the contribution each part makes to the development of the principal themes.

The commentaries on individual text units that follow will repeat this process in greater detail. Although complex literary units will be broken down further, the commentators will address the following issues.

1. **Main Idea of the Passage:** A one- or two-sentence summary of the key ideas the biblical author seeks to communicate.
2. **Literary Context:** A brief discussion of the relationship of the specific text to the book as a whole and to its place within the broader arguments.
3. **Translation and Exegetical Outline:** Commentators will provide their own translations of each text, formatted to highlight the discourse structure of the text and accompanied by a coherent outline that reflects the flow and argument of the text.
4. **Structure and Literary Form:** An introductory survey of the literary structure and rhetorical style adopted by the biblical author, highlighting how these features contribute to the communication of the main idea of the passage.
5. **Explanation of the Text:** A detailed commentary on the passage, paying particular attention to how the biblical authors select and arrange their materials and how they work with words, phrases, and syntax to communicate their messages. This will take up the bulk of most commentaries.
6. **Canonical and Theological Significance:** The commentary on each unit will conclude by building bridges between the world of the biblical author and other biblical authors and with reflections on the contribution made by this unit to the development of broader issues in biblical theology—particularly on how later OT and NT authors have adapted and reused the motifs in question. The discussion will also include brief reflections on the significance of the message of the passage for readers today.

The way this series treats biblical books will be uneven. Commentators on smaller books will have sufficient scope to answer fully each of the issues listed above on each unit of text. However, limitations of space preclude full treatment of every text for the larger books. Instead, commentators will guide readers through #1–4 and 6 for every literary unit, but full Explanation of the Text (#5) will be selective, generally limited to twelve to fifteen literary units deemed most critical for hearing the message of the book.

In addition to these general introductory comments, we should alert readers of this series to several conventions that we follow. First, the divine name in the OT is presented as YHWH. The form of the name—represented by the Tetragrammaton, יהוה—is a particular problem for scholars. The practice of rendering the divine name in Greek as κύριος (=Heb. אֲדֹנָי, "Adonay") is carried over into English translations as "Lord," which represents Hebrew יהוה and distinguishes it from "Lord," which represents Hebrew אֲדֹנָי. But this creates interpretive problems, for the connotations and implications of referring to someone by name or by title are quite different. When rendering the word as a name, English translations have traditionally vocalized יהוה as "Jehovah," which seems to combine the consonants of יהוה with the vowels of אֲדֹנָי. However, today non-Jewish scholars often render the name as "Yahweh," recognizing that "Jehovah" is an artificial construct.

Second, frequently the verse numbers in the Hebrew Bible differ from those in our English translations. Since the commentaries in this series are based on the Hebrew text, the Hebrew numbers will be the default numbers. Where the English numbers differ, they will be provided in square brackets (e.g., Joel 4:12[3:12]).

Third, when discussing specific biblical words or phrases, these will be represented in Hebrew font and in translation, except where the transliterated form is used in place of an English term, either because no single English expression captures the Hebrew word's wide range meaning (e.g., *ḥesed* for חֶסֶד, rather than "lovingkindness"), or when it functions as a title or technical expression not readily captured in English (e.g., *gōʾēl* for גֹּאֵל, rather than "kinsman-redeemer").

Daniel I. Block, general editor

Author's Preface and Acknowledgments

The book of Malachi occupies the final position in the Protestant canon of the Old Testament. Despite its significant location, the book itself remains relatively obscure to most readers of Scripture. Of course, there are texts commonly cited from the book (e.g., divorce [2:16], tithing [3:10]), but most of the book remains largely absent from our preaching and teaching—to our own detriment. Even those texts commonly cited are not always examples of our best exegetical work. At first glance, the book seems so foreign to the modern reader. References to temple worship, sacrifices, priestly instruction, and "daughters of a foreign god," not to mention a coming messenger, may challenge our homiletical skills in allowing this text to be the word of God for the people of God—but indeed it is. A careful reading of the Hebrew text coupled with thoughtful theological construction positions us well to ensure that this biblical book receives a new hearing in and among our congregations.

I am grateful to Daniel Block for the initial invitation to write in this series, and even more so, for the generous latitude he extended to each author in utilizing different approaches for examining the discourse that is present in each biblical book. Both Daniel Block, general editor, and Miles van Pelt, associate editor, have been sources of encouragement throughout the writing process, for which I am most grateful.

In the Series Introduction to the *Zondervan Exegetical Commentary on the Old Testament*, Block contends that "too little attention has been paid to biblical authors as rhetoricians, to their larger rhetorical and theological agendas, and especially to the means by which they tried to achieve those goals." In what follows, I have sought to take seriously this critique. To that end, I have attempted to consider not only what the text means but "how the text means," i.e., how does the structure of the clauses and sentences serve to create meaning, and more importantly, how then do those same clauses and sentences contribute to the larger argument being constructed in the discourse itself. Rather than utilizing the more formal features of discourse analysis as employed by Robert Longacre and others, my approach will be a much more "bottom-up approach," one that focuses on grammatical structure as a means for analyzing the discourse in the text. As evidenced in the commentary, such an analysis can prove fruitful for understanding the author's argumentation. To aid in this analysis, some of the concepts associated with generative grammar have been utilized. Throughout the commentary, definitions, explanations, and references to specific methodological issues appear in the footnotes, while leaving the commentary section itself to attend to the specifics of the biblical text.

The writing of a commentary is never done in isolation. Authors are buoyed along by the support, friendship, and collegiality of others. The faculty, staff, and administration at Baylor University's George W. Truett Theological Seminary are stellar colleagues who share a common commitment to formative theological education. Their collegiality and friendship have enriched my life and the writing of this commentary. I also wish to thank Dr. Robert Holmstedt and Dr. John Cook, both exemplary scholars in Hebrew linguistics and both deep persons of faith. They were kind enough to read selected sections of the volume and to respond to my thoughts on particularly challenging linguistic questions.

Lastly, I am grateful for my three daughters, Hannah, Sarah, and Hope for the joy they bring to my life in countless ways. This commentary is dedicated to my wife, Letitia Campbell Tucker, the "wife of my youth," אֵשֶׁת נְעוּרַי. After more than thirty years of marriage, she remains my cherished companion (2:14).

W. Dennis Tucker Jr.
Eastertide 2022

Abbreviations

Abbreviations for books of the Bible, pseudepigrapha, rabbinic works, papyri, classical works, and the like are readily available in sources such as the *SBL Handbook of Style* and are not included here.

ABD	*Anchor Yale Bible Dictionary*. Edited by D. N. Freedman. 6 vols. New York: Doubleday, 1992
ABRL	Anchor Bible Reference Library
AYBC	Anchor Yale Bible Commentary
BASOR	*Bulletin of the American Schools of Oriental Research*
BHHB	Baylor Handbook on the Hebrew Bible
BHK	*Biblia Hebraica (Kittel)*, 3rd ed., 1937
BHQ	*Biblia Hebraica Quinta*. Edited by Adrian Schrenker, et. al. Stuttgart: Deutsche Bibelgesellschaft, 2004–
BHRG	Van der Merwe, Christo H. J., et al. *A Biblical Hebrew Reference Grammar*. 2nd ed. London: Bloomsbury T&T Clark, 2017
BHS	*Biblia Hebraica Stuttgartensia*. Edited by K. Ellinger and W. Rudolph. Stuttgart: Deutsche Bibelgesellschaft, 1983
BKAT	Biblischer Kommentar, Altes Testament
BT	*The Bible Translator*
BTB	*Biblical Theology Bulletin*
BZAW	Beihefte zur Zeitschrift für die alttestamentliche Wissenschaft
CBQ	*Catholic Biblical Quarterly*
CBSC	Cambridge Bible for Schools and Colleges
ConBOT	Coniectanea Biblica: Old Testament Studies
CR:BS	*Currents in Research: Biblical Studies*
DD	Direct Discourse
EKKNT	Evangelisch-Katholischer Kommentar zum Neuen Testament
ESV	English Standard Version
EvT	*Evangelische Theologie*
FOTL	Forms of Old Testament Literature
FRLANT	Forschungen zur Religion und Literatur des Alten und Neuen Testament

GKC	*Gesenius' Hebrew Grammar.* Edited by E. Kautzsch. Translated by A. E. Cowley. 2nd ed. Oxford: Clarendon, 1910
GTJ	*Grace Theological Journal*
HALOT	*The Hebrew and Aramaic Lexicon of the Old Testament*. L. Koehler, W. Baumgartner, and J. J. Stamm. Translated and edited under the supervision of M. E. J. Richardson. 4 vols. Leiden: Brill, 1994–1999
HAR	*Harvard Annual Review*
HCOT	Historical Commentary on the Old Testament
HCSB	Holman Christian Standard Bible
HSM	Harvard Semitic Monographs
HThKAT	Herders Theologische Kommentar zum Alten Testament
HTS Theological Studie	*Hervormde Teologiese Studies Theological Studies*
IBHS	Waltke, Bruce K. and Michael O'Connor. *An Introduction to Biblical Hebrew Syntax.* Winona Lake: Eisenbrauns, 1990
ICC	International Critical Commentary
IEKAT	Internationaler Exegetischer Kommentar zum Alten Testament
ITC	International Theological Commentary
JAOS	*Journal of the American Oriental Society*
JBL	*Journal of Biblical Literature*
JBT	Jahrbuch für Biblische Theologie
JETS	*Journal of the Evangelical Theological Society*
JHS	*Journal of Hellenic Studies*
JM	Paul Joüon and Takamitsu Muraoka. *A Grammar of Biblical Hebrew.* SBS 27. 2nd edition. Rome: Gregorian and Biblical Press, 2016
JNSL	*Journal of Northwest Semitic Languages*
JPS	Jewish Publication Society
JQR	*Jewish Quarterly Review*
JSOTSup	Journal for the Study of the Old Testament Supplement Series
JSS	*Journal of Semitic Studies*
JTI	*Journal of Theological Interpretation*
KAT	Kommentar zum Alten Testament
KUSATU	*Kleine Untersuchung zur Sprache des Alten Testaments und seiner Umwelt*
LHBOTS	Library of Hebrew Bible/ Old Testament Studies
LXX	Septuagint
MT	Masoretic Text
NAB	New American Bible
NAC	New American Commentary
NASB	New American Standard Bible
NCBC	New Century Bible Commentary

NET	New English Translation
NIBC	New International Bible Commentary
NICOT	New International Commentary on the Old Testament
NIDOTTE	*New International Dictionary of Old Testament Theology and Exegesis.* Edited by W. A. VanGemeren. 5 vols. Grand Rapids: Zondervan, 1997
NIV	New International Version
NKJV	New King James Version
NLT	New Living Translation
NRSV	New Revised Standard Version
NRSVUE	New Revised Standard Version Updated Edition
OBO	Orbis Biblicus et Orientalis
OTE	*Old Testament Essays*
OTL	Old Testament Library
OTS	Old Testament Studies
RevExp	*Review and Expositor*
SBLDS	Society of Biblical Literature Dissertation Series
SBS	Stuttgarter Bibelstudien
SHBC	Smyth & Helwys Bible Commentary
SP	Samaritan Pentateuch
STDJ	Studies on the Texts of the Deserts of Judah
StPB	Studia Post-Biblica
TDOT	*Theological Dictionary of the Old Testament.* Edited by G. J. Botterweck, H. Ringgren and H.-J. Fabry. Translated by J. T. Willis et. al. 15 vols. Grand Rapids: Eerdmans 1974–2006
TOTC	Tyndale Old Testament Commentaries
UBC	Understanding the Bible Commentary Series
VT	*Vetus Testamentum*
VTSup	Vetus Testamentum Supplement
WBC	Word Biblical Commentary
ZAW	*Zeitschrift für die alttestamentliche Wissenschaft*
ZBKAT	Zürcher Bibelkommentare Altes Testament
ZCINT	Zondervan Critical Introductions to the New Testament
ZECOT	Zondervan Exegetical Commentary on the Old Testament

Select Bibliography

Baldwin, Joyce G. *Haggai, Zechariah, Malachi*. TOTC. London: Tyndale, 1972.

Berquist, Jon L. *Judaism in Persia's Shadow: A Social and Cultural Approach*. Philadelphia: Fortress, 1995.

Briant, Pierre. *From Cyrus to Alexander: A History of the Persian Period*. Translated by Peter T. Daniels. Winona Lake, IN: Eisenbrauns, 2002.

Cook, John. "The Hebrew Participle and Stative in Typological Perspective." *JNSL* 34 (2008): 1–19.

________. "Verbal Valency: The Intersection of Syntax and Semantics." Pages 53–86 in *Contemporary Examinations of Classical Languages (Hebrew, Aramaic, Syriac, and Greek): Valency, Lexicography, Grammar, and Manuscripts*. Perspectives in Linguistics and Ancient Languages 8. Edited by Timothy Martin Lewis, Alison G. Salvesen, Beryl Turner. Piscataway, NJ: Gorgias, 2016.

Crystal, David. *A Dictionary of Linguistics and Phonetics*. 6th ed. Oxford: Blackwell, 2008.

Feldmeier, Reinhard and Hermann Spieckermann. *God of the Living: A Biblical Theology*. Waco, TX: Baylor University Press, 2011.

Fischer, James A. "Notes on the Literary Form and Message of Malachi." *CBQ* 34 (1972): 315–20.

Floyd, Michael H. "The MAŚŚĀ' as a Type of Prophetic Book." *JBL* 121 (2002): 401–22.

________. *Minor Prophets, Part 2*. FOTL 22. Grand Rapids: Eerdmans, 2000.

Fuller, Russell. "Text-Critical Problems in Malachi 2:10–16." *JBL* 10 (1991): 47–57.

Gibson, Jonathan. *Covenant Continuity and Fidelity: A Study of Innerbiblical Allusion and Exegesis in Malachi*. LHBOTS 625. New York: Bloomsbury, 2016.

________. "Cutting off 'Kith and Kin,' 'Er and Onan'? Interpreting an Obscure Phrase in Malachi 2:12." *JBL* 133 (2014): 519–37.

Glazier-McDonald, Beth. *Malachi: The Divine Messenger*. SBLDS 98. Atlanta: Scholars, 1987.

Graffy, Adrian. *A Prophet Confronts His People*. Analecta Biblica 104. Rome: Biblical Institute Press, 1984.

Hays, Nathan. "Malachi as a Response to Its Interlocutors." PhD diss., Baylor University, 2017.

Hill, Andrew E. *Malachi*. AYBC 25D. New York: Doubleday, 1998.

Holmstedt, Robert D. "Critical at the Margins: Edge Constituents in Biblical Hebrew." *KUSATU* 17 (2014): 110–58.

________. *The Relative Clause in Biblical Hebrew*. Eisenbrauns: Winona Lake, 2016.

Holmstedt, Robert D. and Andrew R. Jones, "Apposition in Biblical Hebrew: Structure and Function." *Kleine Untersuchung zur Sprache des Alten Testaments und seiner Umwelt* 22 (2017): 21–51.

Hugenberger, Gordon P. *Marriage as a Covenant: Biblical Law and Ethics as Developed from Malachi*. VTSup 52. Leiden: Brill, 1994.

Jacobs, Mignon. *The Books of Haggai and Malachi*. NICOT. Grand Rapids: Eerdmans, 2017.

Kaiser, Walter J., Jr. "The Promise of the Arrival of Elijah in Malachi and the Gospels," *GTJ* 3 (1982): 221–33.

Kessler, Rainer. *Maleachi*. HThKAT: Herder, 2011.

Körting, Corinna "Marriage and Divorce as a Matter of Social Justice in Mal 2:10–16." *Canon and Culture* 10 (2016): 205–25.

Kuhrt, Amélie. *The Persian Empire: A Corpus of Sources from the Achaemenid Empire*. London: Routledge, 2007.

Lear, Sheree. *Scribal Composition: Malachi as a Test Case*. FRLANT 270. Göttingen: Vandenhoeck & Ruprecht, 2018.

Longman Tremper, III, and Daniel G. Reid. *God Is a Warrior*. Studies in Old Testament Biblical Theology. Grand Rapids: Eerdmans, 1995.

McKenzie, Steven L. and Howard N. Wallace. "Covenant Themes in Malachi." *CBQ* 45 (1983): 549–63.

Meier, Samuel A. *Speaking of Speaking: Marking Direct Discourse in the Hebrew Bible*. VTSup 46. Leiden: Brill, 1992.

Meinhold, Arndt "Dialogische Strukturen in den Streitreden des Buches Maleachi." *ZAW* 102 (1990): 194–212.

_______. *Maleachi*. BKAT 14. Neukirchen-Vluyn: Neukirchener, 2006.

Meyers, Eric M. and Carol L. Meyers, *Zechariah 9–14: A New Translation with Introduction and Commentary*. AYBC 25C. New Haven: Yale University Press, 1998.

Miller-Naudé, Cynthia. "Vocative Syntax in Biblical Hebrew Prose and Poetry." *JSS* 55 (2010): 347–64.

Nogalski, James D. *The Book of the Twelve: Micah–Malachi*. SHBC. Macon, GA: Smyth & Helwys, 2011.

_______. *Interpreting Prophetic Literature: Historical and Exegetical Tools for Reading the Prophets*. Louisville: Westminster John Knox, 2015.

_______. "Intertextuality and the Twelve." Pages 102–24 in *Forming Prophetic Literature: Essays on Isaiah and the Twelve in Honor of James D. W. Watts*. JSOTSup 235. Edited by James W. Watts and Paul R. House. Sheffield: Sheffield Academic, 1996.

_______. *Redactional Processes in the Book of the Twelve*. BZAW 218. Berlin: De Gruyter, 1993.

O'Brien, Julia M. "Malachi in Recent Research." *CR: BS* 3 (1995): 81–94.

_______. *Priest and Levite in Malachi*. SBLDS 121. Atlanta: Scholars Press, 1990.

Ogden, Graham S. and Richard R. Deutsch. *Joel and Malachi*. ITC. Grand Rapids: Eerdmans, 1987.

Petersen, David L. *Zechariah 9–14 and Malachi*, OTL. Louisville: Westminster John Knox, 1995.

Pfeiffer, Egon. "Die Disputationsworte im Buch Maleachi." *EvT* 19 (1959): 546–68.

Redditt, Paul. "The Book of Malachi in Its Social Setting." *CBQ* 56 (2006): 240–55.

_______. *Haggai, Zechariah and Malachi*. NCBC. Grand Rapids: Eerdmans, 1995.

Reventlow, H. G. *Die Propheten Haggai, Sacharja und Malachi*. Das Alte Testament Deutsch. Göttingen: Vandenhoeck & Ruprecht, 1993.

Rudolph, Wilhelm. *Haggai, Sacharja 1–8, Sacharja 9–14, Maleachi*. KAT 13, 4. Gütersloh: Mohn, 1976.

Scalise, Pamela J. "Malachi." Pages 315–66 in *Minor Prophets II*. UBC. Peabody, MA: Hendrickson, 2009.

_______. "Malachi 3:13–4:3: A Book of Remembrance for Godfearers." *RevExp* 95 (1998): 571–81.

_______. "To Fear or Not to Fear: Questions of Reward and Punishment in Malachi 2:17–4:3." *Review and Expositor* 84 (1987): 409–18.

Schart, Aaron. *Maleachi*. IEKAT. Stuttgart: Kohlhammer, 2020.

_______. "Putting the Eschatological Visions of Zechariah in Their Place: Malachi as a Hermeneutical Guide for the Last Section of the Book of the Twelve." Pages 333–43 in *Bringing out the Treasure: Inner Biblical Allusions in Zechariah 9–14*. JSOTSup 370. Edited by Mark J. Boda and Michael H. Floyd. Sheffield: Sheffield Academic Press, 2003.

Schmid, Konrad. "Himmelsgott, Weltgott, und Schöpfer: 'Gott' und der 'Himmel' in der Literatur der Zeit des Zweiten Tempels." Pages 111–48 in *Der Himmel*. Edited by Martin Ebner and Irmtraud Fischer. JBT 20. Neukirchen-Vluyn: Neukirchener, 2005.

Shields, Martin A. "Syncretism and Divorce in Malachi 2,10–16." *ZAW* 111 (1999): 68–86.

Smith, J. M. P. "Malachi." Pages 3–88 in Hinckley G. Mitchell, John Merlin Powis Smith, and Julius A. Brewer, *Critical and Exegetical Commentary on Haggai, Zechariah, Malachi and Jonah*. ICC. Edinburgh: T&T Clark, 1912.

Smith, Ralph L. *Micah–Malachi*. WBC 32. Waco, TX: Word, 1984.

Snyman, S. D. "Antithesis in Malachi 1:2–5." *ZAW* 98 (1986): 436–438.

________. *Malachi*. HCOT. Leuven: Peeters, 2015.

________. "Malachi 4:4–6 (Heb 3:22–24) as a Point of Convergence in the Old Testament or Hebrew Bible: A Consideration of the Intra and Intertextual Relationships." *HTS Theological Studies* 68 (2012): 1–6.

Taylor, Richard A. and E. Ray Clendenen. *Haggai, Malachi*. New American Commentary 21A. Nashville: Broadman & Holman, 2004.

Verhoef, Pieter A. *The Books of Haggai and Malachi*. NICOT. Grand Rapids: Eerdmans, 1976.

Weyde, Karl W. *Prophecy and Teaching: Prophetic Authority, Form Problems and the Use of Traditions in the Book of Malachi*. BZAW 288. Berlin: De Gruyter, 2000.

Zehnder, Markus. "A Fresh Look at Malachi II 13–16." *VT* 53 (2003): 224–59.

Translation of Malachi

Malachi 1

1 An oracle. The word of YHWH [that came] to Israel by the hand of Malachi.
2 "I have chosen you," says YHWH. "But you say, 'In what way have you chosen
us?' Is not Esau a brother of Jacob?" utterance of YHWH. "I chose Jacob, 3 but Esau,
I did not choose. I have made his mountains a desolation and his inheritance for
the jackals of the wilderness. 4 If Edom should say, 'We are shattered so let us rebuild
the ruins,'" thus says YHWH Sabaoth, "They may build, but I will destroy. And they
shall call them a wicked territory, the people with whom YHWH is angry forever.
5 Your eyes shall see and you shall say, 'Great is YHWH beyond the borders of Israel.'
6 "'A son honors his father; and a servant [honors] his master.' If I am a father, then
where is the honor due me? And if I am a master, then where is the fear due me?"
says YHWH Sabaoth to you, O priests who despise my name. "But you say, 'How
have we despised your name?' 7 By presenting defiled food upon my altar. But you
say, 'How have we defiled you?' When you say, 'The table of YHWH, it is despised.'
8 And when you present blind [animals] in order to sacrifice, [you say] 'There is no
defect.' And when you present lame and sick [animals], [you say] 'There is no defect.'
Offer that to your governor. Will he accept you or regard you?" says YHWH Sabaoth.
9 "So now, entreat the face of God so that he may be gracious to us. This is from your
hand. Will he regard you?" says YHWH Sabaoth. 10 "Who among you would shut the
doors and not light my altar in vain? I take no delight in you," says YHWH Sabaoth,
"and I will not accept offerings from your hands. 11 From the rising of the sun until its
setting, great is my name among the nations. In every place, incense is being offered
up to my name—a pure offering. Indeed, great is my name among the nations," says
YHWH Sabaoth. 12 "And you are polluting it when you say, 'The table of the Lord, it is
treated as defiled. And its fruit—its food—is despised.' 13 And you say, 'Behold what a
hardship!' Yet you ignite it," says YHWH Sabaoth. "And you bring the stolen, the lame
and the sick, and you bring them as an offering. Shall I accept it from your hand?"
says YHWH. 14 "Cursed is the deceiver and there is a male in his flock. He vows yet

sacrifices a blemished animal to the Lord. For I am the Great King," says YHWH
Sabaoth, "And my name is feared among the nations."

Malachi 2

1"And now to you, O priests, this commandment: 2If you do not listen and take
[it] to heart to give honor to my name," says YHWH Sabaoth, "then I will send
on you the curse, and I will curse your blessings. Indeed, I have already cursed it
because you did not take it to heart. 3Behold, I am about to rebuke your offspring,
and I will spread dung on your faces, the dung of your festivals, and someone will
carry you to it. 4And then you will know that I sent this commandment to you so
that my covenant with Levi will continue," says YHWH Sabaoth. 5"My covenant,
one of life and peace, was with him. And I gave them to him, along with fear, and he
feared me. Before my name, he was dismayed. 6True instruction was in his mouth
and deceit could not be found on his lips. In peace and in uprightness, he walked
with me and he turned many from iniquity. 7Because the lips of the priest should
preserve knowledge, they should seek torah from his mouth, for he is the messenger
of YHWH Sabaoth. 8But you have turned aside from the way. You have caused many
to stumble through your instruction. You have corrupted the covenant of Levi,"
says YHWH Sabaoth. 9"I, in turn, will make you despised and humiliated before all
the people, in as much as you are not keeping my ways and [you are not] properly
regarding matters of torah."

10Do we not have one father? Did not one God create us? Why then does each
act faithlessly against his brother, thereby profaning the covenant of our ancestors?
11Judah has acted faithlessly; that is, an abomination has been committed in Israel
and in Jerusalem, because Judah has profaned the holy [people] of YHWH, whom
he loves, and married the daughter of a foreign god. 12May YHWH cut off from the
man who does it offspring from the tents of Jacob, although he brings an offering to
YHWH Sabaoth.

13And another thing you do: [You] cover the altar of YHWH with tears, weeping
and wailing, because he no longer regards the offering or accepts it favorably from
you. 14But you say, "Why?" Because YHWH was a witness between you and the
wife of your youth with whom you dealt treacherously. She is your companion and
the wife of your covenant. 15No one does [it] and has a remnant of the spirit in
him. What is that one seeking? Godly offspring. So guard your spirit and do not act
treacherously against the wife of your youth. 16"If a man hates [and] divorces [his
wife]," says YHWH, the God of Israel, "then he covers his garment in violence," says
YHWH Sabaoth. So guard your spirits and do not act treacherously.

17"You have wearied YHWH with your words. But you say, 'How have we wearied

[him]?' When you say, 'All who do evil are good in the eyes of YHWH and in them he delights.' Or [when you say], 'Where is the God of justice.'

Malachi 3

[1]Behold, I am about to send my messenger and he will prepare a way before me. And suddenly, he will come into his temple, the Lord whom you are seeking and the messenger of the covenant, for whom you long, behold he is coming," says YHWH Sabaoth. [2]"Who will be able to endure the day of his coming? And who will be able to stand when he appears because he is like a refiner's fire and a launder's soap? [3]And he will act as one who refines and purifies silver. And he will purify the sons of Levi and refine them like gold and silver so that they might be the ones who present proper offerings to YHWH. [4]The offering of Judah and Jerusalem will be pleasing to YHWH as in the days of old and the former years. [5]And then I will draw near to you for judgment and I will be a swift witness against sorcerers, against adulterers, against those who swear falsely, and those who oppress hired workers, [and those who oppress] the widow, the orphan, and those who turn aside the sojourner—they did not show me fear," says YHWH Sabaoth.

[6] "Because I, YHWH, have not changed, you, O sons of Jacob, have not come to an end. [7]From the days of your ancestors, you have turned aside from my statutes and you have not kept [them]. Return to me so that I may return to you," says YHWH Sabaoth. "But you say, 'In what sense should we return?' [8]Can a person rob God, yet you are robbing me. But you say, 'In what sense are we robbing you?' [9]Tithes and offerings. With the curse, you are being cursed and you are robbing me, the entire nation. [10]Bring the full tithe into the storehouse so that there will be food in my house. And test me in this, I pray," says YHWH Sabaoth. "Surely I will open for you the windows of heaven and pour out for you blessings until there is no more need. [11]Then I will rebuke for you the devourer so that it will no longer destroy the fruit of the ground that belongs to you. The vine in the field will no longer drop its fruit prematurely," says YHWH Sabaoth. [12]"And all nations shall call you blessed because you will be a land of delight," says YHWH Sabaoth.

[13]"Your words have been strong against me," says YHWH. "But you say, 'What have we said among ourselves against you?' [14]You say, 'To serve God is futile,' and 'What gain is there because we have kept his requirements and because we walk as mourners before YHWH Sabaoth? [15]Now we pronounce the arrogant blessed. Not only have those who have done wickedness been built up but they have tested God and escaped.'"

[16]Then those who fear YHWH spoke among themselves, each with his neighbor. YHWH listened attentively and he heard. And then a book of remembrance was

written before him for those who fear YHWH and those who respect his name.
17“They will belong to me,” says YHWH Sabaoth, “on the day that I act, a special
possession. And I will have compassion upon them as a man has compassion upon
his son who serves him. 18Then you will once more distinguish between the just and
the wicked, between those serving God and those who do not serve God.

19[4:1]“For behold, the day is coming, burning like an oven. All the arrogant and
all the workers of wickedness shall be stubble and the coming day shall set them
ablaze,” says YHWH Sabaoth, “which shall not leave them root or branch. 20[4:2]A sun
of righteousness shall rise for you who fear my name, and healing will be in its wings.
You shall go out and you shall skip as calves from the stall. 21[4:3]You shall trample the
wicked ones because they shall be ashes under the soles of your feet on the day that
I will act,” says YHWH Sabaoth.

22[4:4]“Remember the Torah of Moses, my servant, that I commanded him on
Horeb for all Israel—the statutes and judgments. 23[4:5]Behold I am sending to you
Elijah the prophet before the coming of the great and awesome Day of YHWH. 24[4:6]
And he will turn the hearts of fathers to children and the hearts of children to fathers
lest I come and strike the land with utter destruction.

Introduction to Malachi

Fidelity to the Great King

The book of Malachi reflects the challenge of faith in an age of despair for the post-exilic community in and around Jerusalem. The troubling social, political, and historical circumstances, coupled with their seemingly dashed hope for a fully restored community, led them to consider the unthinkable, i.e., that faithfulness to YHWH was futile (3:14). The actions of the community suggest that such cynicism manifested itself both in their love of God and of one another. Devotion to worship had devolved into meaningless activity, while commitment and solidarity within the community threatened to collapse under the weight of injustice. Into such a challenging context, the prophet calls the community back to faithfulness to the God who had created them (2:10); he calls them to fidelity to the great King (1:14).

Author and Date

Author

The meaning and function of the term "Malachi," מַלְאָכִי, in verse 1 remains a matter of some debate. Scholarship remains divided on whether מַלְאָכִי functions as a title or whether it is simply a name, and if so, what is the meaning of the proper noun. This question is not new, however. From the early textual witnesses, translations differed. The Septuagint, for example, understood the name as a title, having translated מַלְאָכִי as ἀγγέλου αὐτου, "his messenger" instead of a proper noun. The shift from first person (i.e., "*my* messenger") to third person ("*his* messenger") further accentuates the presumed titular nature of the term in the LXX. Some manuscripts of Tg. Mal. 1:1 add "whose name was Ezra the scribe," clearly assuming that מַלְאָכִי is meant to function as a title rather than a proper noun.[1]

1. For the targumic textual evidence, see Alexander Sperber, *The Bible in Aramaic* (Leiden: Brill, 1962), 3:500, whose base text does not include the identification of Ezra. More recently Odil Hannes Steck has revived the possible connection between

There remain, however, compelling reasons for understanding מַלְאָכִי, "Malachi," as a proper noun. First, in the superscriptions of other prophetic books, there is no indication that the names provided are titular in nature (cf. Isa; Jer; Hos, Joel, Amos, Obad, Mic, Nah, Hab, Hag, Zech), but instead are actually proper nouns. Further, the collocation "X + בְּיַד" ("by the hand of X") which appears in Mal 1:1 also appears in Hag 1:1, 3; 2:1 where it clearly refers to the prophet. Second, although the Septuagint appears to render the term as a title, other ancient witnesses consider the term as a name, including Theodotion, Symmachus, as well as the Peshitta and Vulgate. Third, some have rejected the claim that מַלְאָכִי, "Malachi," could be a proper noun on the grounds that no parent would call a child "my messenger." Hill and Gibson, among others, have suggested that the *hireq*, which appears at the end of the name, may suggest a hypocoristic (i.e., augmented) pattern with מַלְאָכִי being "the shortest form in a series of successively shortened names": מלאכיהוה ("messenger of YHWH"), מלאכיהו ("messenger of Yahu"), מלאכיה ("messenger of Yah").[2] Thus מַלְאָכִי is better rendered as a construct relationship between the two elements (i.e., messenger; YHWH) in the name and not a noun with a first-person-pronoun suffix.[3] Understood this way, מַלְאָכִי is properly understood as a theophoric name similar to other prophetic figures (e.g., Isaiah, Jeremiah, Ezekiel).

Although the name of the prophet appears in the superscription to the book (1:1), nothing more is said explicitly of Malachi, either in the book itself or the larger canon.[4] What little can be known about Malachi is based on the content of the disputations in the book. Malachi has considerable familiarity with the temple and the activities associated with the temple (e.g., sacrifice, tithing) as well as familiarity with the priesthood. Although Hill suggests that the prophet operates as "one observing the system from the *outside*," the evidence seems to point to the reverse.[5] Redditt notes four indicators that the prophet was likely part of the priesthood: (1) he held a high view of the Levitical calling (2:4–7); (2) he was familiar with earlier traditions;

מַלְאָכִי and Ezra by noting the chronological sequence of figures in the book of Ezra: Haggai, Zechariah, and Ezra (5:1; 6:14; 7:1–6). Steck (*Der Abschluß der Prophetie im Alten Testament. Ein Versuch zur Frage Vorgeschichte des Kanons* [Neukirchen-Vluyn: Neukirchener Verlag, 1991], 131–32.) notes a similar chronological sequence in the Book of the Twelve with Haggai, Zechariah, and Malachi, leading Steck to suggest that Ezra may have been understood as the messenger from the creation of the book.

2. Jonathan Gibson, *Covenant Continuity and Fidelity: A Study of Innerbiblical Allusion and Exegesis in Malachi*, LHBOTS 625 (New York: Bloomsbury, 2016), 27n15.

3. Gibson, *Covenant Continuity and Fidelity*, 27n15. For a similar view, see also Andrew E. Hill, *Malachi*, AYBC 25D (New York: Doubleday, 1998), 16–18. Wilhelm Rudolph argued this philological point two decades earlier (Rudolph, *Haggai, Sacharja 1-8, Sacharja 9-14, Maleachi*, KAT 13, 4 [Gütersloh: Mohn, 1976], 237). On the construct form, see *IBHS* §9.5.1b, c.

4. Although the name מַלְאָכִי appears again in 3:1, clearly the figure in 3:1 is not the same. As Beth Glazier-McDonald surmises, "Such an identification wreaks havoc with the book's message, furnishing the text with a confused, almost unintelligible meaning, especially since the role of the messenger in Mal 3:1 is characterized as a future one" (*Malachi: The Divine Messenger*, SBLDS 98 [Atlanta: Scholars, 1987], 29).

5. Hill, *Malachi*, 18, emphasis added.

(3) he was concerned with cultic purity; and (4) he never advocated replacing the priesthood.[6] In further support that Malachi may have been part of the priesthood, Weyde noted that in the book of Chronicles, the Levites and priests have both prophetic and scribal functions and are often described in prophetic categories (e.g., 2 Chr 19:8–11; 24:20–22).[7] Clearly the book of Malachi reflects some form of scribalism, thus buttressing Redditt's initial claim.[8]

In the post-exilic period, there were two classifications of priests: the Zadokites, who traced their lineage to Aaron, and the Levites. Some have suggested that Malachi was a Levite who was attempting to critique the more powerful Zadokites, but as Scalise and O'Brien rightly observe, the book of Malachi does not distinguish between the two groups of priests, but instead "between present priests and a personification of the ideal priest who faithfully discharged the wide range of priestly duties in the past."[9] This distinction is made most forcefully in 2:1–9 where the ideal priest, Levi, functions as a foil to the failed priesthood of Malachi's generation.

Date

Without exception, scholars assign the book of Malachi to the post-exilic period, a rather complex period within Israel's history that was filled, in part, with unmet expectations and an uncertain future. The assignment of Malachi to this period in Israel's history is predicated upon several indicators in the book. First, the reference to the devastation of Edom in 1:4 locates the book some time after the Babylonian campaign of Nabonidus in 552 BCE, a campaign that swept through the southern Transjordan region, sacking regions including Edom. Second, the references to the temple in the book provide an additional clue as to its possible dating. In 1:10, for example, the doors (דְּלָתַיִם) of the temple are mentioned.[10] The temple is mentioned yet again in 3:1 and 3:10. Together these texts suggest an operational temple at the time of the book. Even though some of those in exile in Babylon returned to Yehud in 538 BCE and others in subsequent waves, the restoration of the temple did not begin

6. Paul Redditt, "The Book of Malachi in Its Social Setting," *CBQ* 56 (2006): 240–55, esp. 252.

7. Karl W. Weyde, *Prophecy and Teaching: Prophetic Authority, Form Problems and the Use of Traditions in the Book of Malachi*, BZAW 288 (Berlin: de Gruyter, 2000), 63–64. On scribalism in Malachi, see most recently Sheree Lear, *Scribal Composition: Malachi as a Test Case*, FRLANT 270 (Göttingen: Vandenhoeck & Ruprecht, 2018).

8. On the question of Malachi's identity *within* the priesthood, see the review of scholarship in Julia M. O'Brien, *Priest and Levite in Malachi*, SBLDS 121 (Atlanta: Scholars, 1990), 15–26.

9. Pamela J. Scalise, "Malachi," in John Goldingay and Pamela J. Scalise, *Minor Prophets II*, UBC (Grand Rapids: BakerBooks, 2009), 323; O'Brien, *Priest and Levite in Malachi*, 144–48.

10. Most English translations read similar to the NIV, "Oh that one of you would shut the temple doors." Even though the word "temple" actually does not appear in v. 10, the doors (דְּלָתַיִם) mentioned are clearly understood as those of the temple.

until 520 BCE (cf. Hag 1:12–15a) and was not completed until 515 BCE (Ezra 6:15). As a result, most scholars assign the *terminus a quo* for the book to 515 BCE but, given the assumption in these texts that the temple had been fully operational for some time, even this date is likely too early. A third indicator is the reference (1:8) to one of the civil officials in Yehud as a פֶּחָה or "governor," a term used to reference a government official in the Persian empire.[11] A fourth indicator concerns the selected themes present in the book of Malachi and the similarity of those themes with themes present in the Ezra-Nehemiah complex. Two matters are of particular importance. Both Malachi and the Ezra-Nehemiah complex refer to the presence of cultic abuses, including sacrifices and tithing, in the post-exilic community (Mal 1:6–2:9; 3:6–12; Neh 10:1–39). In addition, the issue of exogamy, or marriage outside the clan or tribe, prompted concern in both writings (cf. Mal 2:10–16; Ezra 9:1–4; 10:1–17; Neh 13:23–28).

While the *terminus a quo* can be fairly well established, as suggested above, the *terminus ad quem*, or latest possible date, proves more difficult to locate with absolute certainty. Although scholars frequently cite the affinities between Malachi and the Ezra-Nehemiah complex as evidence for a precise date, they often deviate in opinion as to whether Malachi came prior to the visits of Ezra and Nehemiah or after their visits.[12] And others, such as Michael Floyd argue that such precision is simply not possible.[13] This commentary takes the position that Malachi was likely written prior to the visits of Ezra and Nehemiah, based in part upon the linguistic dating provided by Hill and the events that unfolded under Persian rule in Yehud.

11. Lexically, there are two other possible Persian influences: סֵפֶר זִכָּרוֹן in 3:16 (cf. Ezra 6:1–2; Est 2:23; 6:1–3) and שֶׁמֶשׁ צְדָקָה in 3:20[4:2].

12. The view that Malachi precedes Ezra and Nehemiah remains the dominant view among interpreters, with some offering rather precise dates. For example, Glazier-McDonald assigns the book to 460–450 BCE (*Malachi*, 17), as do S. D. Snyman (*Malachi*, HCOT [Leuven: Peeters, 2015], 2) and H. G. Reventlow (*Die Propheten Haggai, Sacharja und Malachi*, Das Alte Testament Deutsch 25/2 [Göttingen: Vandenhoeck & Ruprecht, 1993], 130). Each of them notes the considerable congruity with Ezra and Nehemiah in assigning this date. Others, however, simply refer more generally to the first half of the fifth century BCE. See Jon L. Berquist, *Judaism in Persia's Shadow: A Social and Cultural Approach* (Philadelphia: Fortress, 1995); Hill, *Malachi*, 80–84; E. Ray Clendenden, "Malachi," in Richard A. Taylor and E. Ray Clendenen, *Haggai, Malachi*, NAC 21A (Nashville: Broadman & Holman, 2004), 204–6; Scalise, "Malachi," 320–22; Mignon Jacobs, *The Books of Haggai and Malachi*, NICOT (Grand Rapids: Eerdmans, 2017), 132. Examples of later dating include Pieter A.Verhoef who suggests a date between the two visits of Nehemiah, after 433 BCE (*The Book of Haggai and Malachi*, NICOT [Grand Rapids: Eerdmans, 1976], 156–60) and Rainer Kessler who argues for a fourth century BCE dating based on the assumption that the author of Malachi had the Pentateuch and selected prophetic books "right in front of him" (*Maleachi*, HThKAT [Freiburg: Herder, 2011], 77).

13. Michael H. Floyd, *Minor Prophets, Part 2*, FOTL 22 (Grand Rapids: Eerdmans, 2000), 575. For similar assessment, see James D. Nogalski, *Redactional Processes in the Book of the Twelve*, BZAW 218 (Berlin: de Gruyter, 1993), 186–87.

Historical Analysis

Historical Context

Although the book of Malachi comes from the fifth century BCE, the historical context that figures into the background of the book begins much earlier and under a different empire, that of the Babylonians. As a result of an attempted rebellion against Babylon by king Zedekiah of Judah, King Nebuchadnezzar and his Babylonian forces laid siege to Jerusalem in 586 BCE (2 Kgs 24:20b–25:21). As the siege waned on and food gave out, a breach was made in the city wall, allowing Zedekiah and his soldiers to escape, only later to be captured by the Babylonians. Zedekiah's family was executed, he was taken into exile in Babylon and the city of Jerusalem was decimated. The temple was razed to the ground and the gold, silver and bronze fixtures associated with the temple complex were carried off into exile. In addition to the king and the temple treasures, many of the leaders in Jerusalem were also carried off into exile, with "the poorest people of the land" left to till the soil (25:12).

For the Jewish community exiled in Babylon, there seemed little hope that the Babylonian imperial juggernaut would be overcome and that they would return home. Yet stirring in the eastern corner of the empire was Cyrus II. In 559 BCE, he rose to power as "king of Anšan," an Elamite city and nearly a decade later (550 BCE), he engaged in battle with the Medes led by Astyages. Cyrus proved victorious and captured the Median capital of Ecbtana. From there, Cyrus unleashed his military might upon Asia Minor where additional victories were secured, including a victory over the legendary wealthy Lydian king Croesus. Cyrus then turned his sights on King Nabonidus and the massive Babylonian empire. The Nabonidus Chronicle recounts that on October 12, 539 BCE, Cyrus's army, led by the military commander Ugbaru, "without battle entered Babylon" and secured a decisive victory for Cyrus, in effect, bringing the Babylonian empire to an end and ushering in the Achaemenid empire.[14]

Although space does not allow for a full recounting of the history of the Achaemenid empire, there are particular aspects of the empire that are worthy of note, given the date assigned to the book of Malachi above.[15]

14. See Amélie Kuhrt, *The Persian Empire: A Corpus of Sources from the Achaemenid Empire* (London: Routledge, 2007), 47–53.

15. On the history of the Persian empire, see Pierre Briant, *From Cyrus to Alexander: A History of the Persian Period*, trans. Peter T. Daniels (Winona Lake, IN: Eisenbrauns, 2002), 507; Muhammed A. Dandamaev, *A Political History of the Achaemenid Empire* (Leiden: Brill, 1989); Peter Frei and Klaus Koch, *Reichsidee und Reichsorganisation im Persereich*, OBO 55 (Göttingen: Vandenhoeck & Ruprecht, 1996); Richard N. Frye, *The History of Ancient Iran* (Münich: Beck, 1984); and Amélie Kuhrt, *Persian Empire*. Treatments on the rise of the Persian empire and its influence within the more narrowly confined context of Yehud are likewise extensive. Representative

Cyrus's Edict

The book of Ezra recounts that shortly after conquering Babylon, Cyrus issued an edict (Ezra 1:2–4 [in Hebrew]; 6:3–5 [in Aramaic]) that permitted those in captivity to return to their homeland and to rebuild the temple in Jerusalem (2 Chr 36:20–23). Although earlier interpreters envisioned Cyrus as a great liberator and champion of religious tolerance, more recent scholarship has argued otherwise. As Pierre Briant has explained, "Contrary to what has often been said Cyrus had no special status for Yahwism. He acted with respect to the Yahwistic cult as he had acted with respect to the Babylonian temples . . . : while it was a decisive episode for the Judeans themselves, at the same time it was a common and banal event for the Persian political establishment."[16] The decision to return exiles to their homeland so that they might rebuild their temples was clearly meant to benefit the empire. Whereas the Babylonians brought exiles back to Babylon, to the center of the empire as it were, the Persians moved exiles to the peripheries of the empire.[17] In so doing, the borders of the empire were populated and strengthened, thus allowing for the possibility of territorial expansion. By having a robust population at the border, there was sufficient support for imperial forces as they moved through the empire and into new regions. The rebuilding of temples in the peripheral regions also served the larger interests of the Persian empire; the sites functioned as the official locale for the collection of taxes and tributes (in addition to the traditional cultic activity).

Although the edict of Cyrus permitted both the return of the exiles and the rebuilding of the temple, very little activity seems to have taken place in the region of Yehud during the rule of Cyrus and even to some degree, under Cambyses.[18] Significant change, both in administrative organization and in infrastructure, did not occur until the reign of Darius I.

Darius I (522–486 BCE)

Although Cyrus and Cambyses had expanded the Achaemenid empire, it was Darius who provided administrative structure to the empire. Briant argues that while Darius continued the work of Cyrus and Cambyses, it is only with Darius that one

examples include: Jon Berquist, *Judaism in Persia's Shadow*, 3–127; Lester L. Grabbe, *Yehud: A History of the Persian Province of Judah* (New York: T&T Clark, 2004), 263–349; and Erhard Gerstenberger, *Israel in the Persian Period: The Fifth and Fourth Centuries BCE*, Biblical Encyclopedia, trans. Siegfried S. Schatzmann (Atlanta: SBL Press, 2011), 45–76. See also the collections of essays in Oded Lipschits and Manfred Oeming, eds., *Judah and the Judeans in the Persian Period* (Winona Lake, IN: Eisenbrauns, 2006); and Jon L. Berquist, ed., *Approaching Yehud: New Approaches to the Study of the Persian Period*, Semeia Studies 50 (Atlanta: SBL, 2007).

16. Pierre Briant, "Persian Empire," *ABD* 5:238.

17. Berquist, *Judaism in Persia's Shadow*, 27–29.

18. John Kessler, *The Book of Haggai: Prophecy and Society in Early Persian Yehud*, VTSup 91 (Leiden: Brill, 2002), 85–87; Berquist, *Judaism in Persia's Shadow*, 29.

may speak of "an imperial enterprise in the fullest sense of the word."[19] In particular, for Briant, Darius's "imperial enterprise" was rooted in his capacity to create an empire that maintained a strongly unified identity amid the diversity of its conquered people groups. Arguably this can be attributed to the imperial ideology that permeated all elements of the empire, both at the center and the periphery. To this end, Darius sought ways to solidify his imperial hold over the expansive Achaemenid empire. The Greek historian Herodotus records that Darius organized the empire into twenty satrapies, with a Persian appointed governor to rule over each (*Hist.* 3:88–95). Each satrap represented a large regional area within the empire. For example, the book of Ezra (4:10; 8:36) and Nehemiah (2:7, 9) report that Palestine was part of the satrap labeled עֵבֶר הַנָּהָר, the region "Beyond the River" (i.e., Euphrates), and Ezra 6 records that Tattenai was the governor during the reign of Darius. Each satrap was further divided into provinces with there being nineteen provinces in the "Beyond the River" satrap, one of which was Yehud with Zerubbabel serving as a provincial leader during the reign of Darius.[20] Surrounding Yehud in the region Beyond the River were the provinces of Samaria to the north, Idumea to the south, with Moab and Ammon to the east, presumably each with their own provincial ruler that was answerable to the Achaemenid powers.

Although Cyrus allowed the exiles to return home and even permitted them to rebuild their temples and religious buildings (Ezra 1:3–4), reconstruction did not commence until the reign of Darius and his mandate that all provinces have a temple. The newly constructed temple complex would provide a centralized location for imperial government, financial administration and the worship of regional deities. Many in Yehud may have wondered if this moment was not the time for which they had yearned. Haggai and Zechariah called for the rebuilding of the temple in this period, and the people responded with unusual compliance and haste to the prophetic word. With a temple in place, those in Yehud may have wondered if a new era was about to unfold. As evidence of this expectation, the book of Haggai concludes with the following oracle:

> Speak to Zerubbabel, governor of Judah, saying, "I am about to shake the heavens and the earth, and to overthrow the throne of kingdoms; I am about to destroy the strength of the kingdoms of the nations and overthrow the chariots and their riders; and the horses and their riders shall fall, every one by the sword of a comrade. On that day," says YHWH of hosts, "I will take you O Zerubbabel my servant, son of Shieltiel," says YHWH, "and make you a signet ring." (2:21–23, author's translation)

19. Pierre Briant, *From Cyrus to Alexander*, 507.

20. See Eric M. Meyers and Carol L. Meyers, *Haggai, Zechariah 1–8: A New Translation, with Introduction and Commentary*, AYBC 25B (New York: Doubleday, 1987), 13–16.

These events did not unfold as anticipated, likely contributing to the type of skepticism reflected later in the attitudes of the priests and laity in the book of Malachi. The anguish of an unrealized future caused the people of Judah to consider the unthinkable in the book of Malachi: God no longer had concern for his people (1:2–5).

Xerxes and Declining Temple Support

Under the reign of Darius, the Persian empire funded a number of temples for the reasons outlined above. With the death of Darius and the accession of his son Xerxes to the throne (486 BCE), imperial policy shifted. Xerxes withheld funds from the construction and maintenance of temples, and in some cases, destroyed temples in an effort to squelch rising sentiments of nationalism among the satrapies.[21] The temple in Yehud, while not destroyed, was stripped of its imperial funding. The lack of aid, coupled with oppressive taxation, likely created economic pressures in Yehud. These pressures are likely reflected in the book of Malachi. For example, the practice of intermarriage between provinces, a practice roundly rejected by Malachi (2:10–16), was likely borne out of financial necessity. In addition, the references to tithes and offerings in the book of Malachi (3:6–12) seem to suggest that such giving had all but disappeared, once more a reflection of the economic pressures of that period.

Literary Analysis

Prior to analyzing the larger structure of the book of Malachi, careful attention to its form merits attention.

Form

Across the prophetic corpus, direct discourse (i.e., speech) contributes significantly to the rhetorical strategy of each book and this is no less true for the book of Malachi. In fact, by virtue of its very form (see discussion below), attention to direct discourse (DD) is paramount for the interpreter.

Generally speaking, DD is either "marked" or "unmarked" in Hebrew.[22] In marked discourses, a wide range of verbs (e.g., אמר, דבר, ענה, שבע) can function as

21. Berquist, *Judaism in Persia's Shadow*, 88–93. Briant provides a slightly different reading of the evidence, suggesting that Xerxes's action does not represent as radical a break in policy and in execution from his predecessors (*From Cyrus to Alexander*, 543–49).

22. This is not to suggest that "unmarked" texts are not "internally marked." Conventions of language such as the vocative, imperative, and cohortative, along with pronoun shifting, can signal that a text is dialogic.

a quotative frame and serve to introduce speech.[23] These markers may point to a short response such as, "Then YHWH said (אמר) to me, 'Amos, what do you see?'" (Amos 7:8), or they may introduce a lengthy speech, especially a divine speech (e.g., Ezek 17:3–10). Other prophetic books, however, contain *unmarked* DD, meaning that even though these texts do not include a quotative frame, they are clearly speech (DD) uttered by someone or something. For example, Isa 5 (the song of the unfruitful vineyard) does not include a quotative frame, yet the first-person perspective leaves little doubt that this is direct speech. Unmarked speech is not limited to one figure in a story alone. In Isa 63:1–3, for example, YHWH responds to a series of questions posed by the prophet:

> Who is this, robed in splendor,
> striding forward in the greatness of his strength?
>
> "It is I, proclaiming victory,
> mighty to save."
>
> Why are your garments red,
> like those of one treading the winepress?
>
> "I have trodden the winepress alone
> from the nations no one was with me
> I trampled them in my anger
> and trod them down in my wrath . . ." (NIV)

Although there are no quotative frames, the dialogical nature of the text itself makes it comprehensible to the reader. In other texts, marked and unmarked DD appear adjacent to one another, and thus require the reader to remain vigilant in observing the shifts in speech. For example, a quotative frame כֹּה אָמַר יְהוָה ("thus says YHWH") begins a divine speech in Jer 10:2–5.[24] The response which follows in verses 6–10 is clearly DD, but absent any type of quotative frame (i.e., unmarked DD). The unobservant reader may assume that the continued DD is associated with the previous speaker (i.e., YHWH), given that there is no quotative frame present. To reduce the

23. This would include most notably, the phrase כֹּה אָמַר יְהוָה ("thus says the Lord") and נְאֻם יְהוָה, "utterance of the Lord," among other Hebrew verbs. Regarding speech in the prophetic literature, see James D. Nogalski, *Interpreting Prophetic Literature: Historical and Exegetical Tools for Reading the Prophets* (Louisville: Westminster John Knox, 2015), 24–35.

24. This quotative frame, also labeled a "messenger formula," serves "as a strong indicator that a new speech is beginning" (Nogalski, *Interpreting Prophetic Literature*, 17). See also Floyd, *Minor Prophets, Part 2*, 650.

possibility of this type of confusion, the NET inserts "I said" at the start of verse 6 even though it is absent in the Hebrew.

In his analysis of DD across the Hebrew Bible, Samuel Meier observed that the first seven prophetic books in the Book of the Twelve remain rather reserved in their use of discourse markers, despite the fact that they are replete with divine speeches.[25] For example, the book of Hosea contains 197 verses but only 22 occurrences of the verb אמר, with all but one usage marking DD.[26] The bulk of the book, chapters 4–11, contains divine speeches but the verb אמר, "to say," occurs only seven times.[27] Strikingly, the verb is never used to mark DD by YHWH in those texts; all divine speech remains unmarked.

The book of Malachi differs considerably not just from Hosea but also from other prophetic books in its extensive use of DD markers. By way of contrast with Hosea, in the book of Malachi the verb אמר occurs forty times in only fifty-five verses, with the verb marking out the DD of *both* YHWH and the priests or people. Even more striking is the position of the verb in each instance. Whenever others speak (i.e., Edom, the priests, the laity), the verb introduces the DD. Most famously in the book of Malachi are the adversative formulas, i.e., "but you say" (וַאֲמַרְתֶּם), which mark the speech uttered by the priest and people in response to the claims of YHWH.[28] When YHWH speaks, however, the DD marker is non-initial, typically appearing mid-sentence.[29] Meier concludes that Malachi's preference for a non-initial אָמַר יְהוָה creates a "unique configuration of divine DD marking in the Bible."[30] Constructed in this way, the DD of YHWH precedes the quotative frame thereby drawing attention to the divine speech. These features (i.e., divine DD followed by the adversative formula) typically appear adjacent to one another, as in Mal 1:2.

> "I have chosen you," says YHWH (אָמַר יְהוָה),
> But you say (וַאֲמַרְתֶּם), "In what way have you chosen us?"

For similar constructions, see also 1:6h/1:6i–j; 2:17a/2:17b; 3:7c/3:7f–g; 3:8a–b/3:8c–d; and 3:13a–b/3:13c–d.

The dominance of DD in Malachi has long garnered the attention of scholars. In considering the form of the book, earlier scholars recognized the function of DD in the book of Malachi, and in particular, the dialogic nature of the book.[31] More recent

25. Samuel A. Meier, *Speaking of Speaking: Marking Direct Discourse in the Hebrew Bible*, VTSup 46 (Leiden: Brill, 1992).

26. The scarcity of discourse markers in Hosea is also evident with the phrase נְאֻם־יְהוָה, "utterance of the LORD," occurring only four times to mark divine DD.

27. The verb also occurs in 7:2, but not as a marker of DD.

28. 1:2, 6, 7, 13; 2:14, 17; 3:7; 3:8, 13.

29. 1:2, 6, 8, 9, 10, 11, 13a, 13b, 14; 2:2, 4, 8, 16a, 16b; 3:1, 5, 7, 10, 11, 13, 17, 19. In two instances the DD closes the speech (3:12, 21).

30. Meier, *Speaking of Speaking*, 230.

31. For a review of scholarship in the 19th century, with a particular emphasis on the dialogical nature of the book, see Karl W. Weyde, *Prophecy and Teaching*, esp. 14–17. See also

discussions on the dialogic features of Malachi have been largely in reaction to the work of Egon Pfeiffer in the middle of the twentieth century.[32] Setting aside the superscription (1:1) and the appendix (3:22–24[4:4–6]), Pfeiffer argued that Malachi was comprised of six units that he labeled "disputations": 1:2–5; 1:6–2:9; 2:10–16; 2:17–3:5; 3:6–12; and 3:13–21[3:13–4:3]. According to Pfeiffer, the disputation (as present in Malachi) opens with a statement, or more precisely, an affirmation, spoken by YHWH (e.g., 1:2a) or the prophet (e.g., 2:17a), which is then followed by an objection (i.e., adversative formula, וַאֲמַרְתֶּם, "but you say") spoken by the priests or the people. Pfeiffer argued that a response, which often includes admonitions and accusations, follows when the central idea (*Kernstück*) is articulated.[33]

Not all scholars have been convinced of Pfeiffer's description of the disputation speech more broadly or his analysis of the form in the book of Malachi, more specifically. In response to Pfeiffer's work, Adrian Graffy provided a far more restrictive view of the disputation speech across the prophetic corpus, contending that a disputation speech proper consisted of only two components: the prophet's quotation of the other speaker and the prophet's refutation of that claim.[34] As noted by Pfeiffer, however, the disputation form in Malachi begins with a statement, followed by a question by the people or priests, only then to be refuted by God or the prophet. As a result of this incongruity between his definition of the disputation form and what appears in Malachi, Graffy contended that the pericopes identified by Pfeiffer in Malachi are not disputation speeches at all, but instead a different genre altogether.[35] Based on this revised definition, Graffy concludes that the chief aim of the form in Malachi "is to convince the listeners of the initial stated point, not to reject the listener's

Julia O'Brien, "Malachi in Recent Research," *CR:BS* 3 (1995): 81–94.

32. Egon Pfeiffer, "Die Disputationsworte im Buch Maleachi," *EvT* 19 (1959): 546–68.

33. Pfeiffer, "Die Disputationsworte," 555. According to Pfeiffer, although disputations appear in earlier texts (Amos 5:18–20; Isa 40:27–31), the book of Malachi exhibits the most developed form, leading him to conclude that while the form of the disputation is late, it is not a new form altogether ("Die Disputationsworte," 568).

34. Adrian Graffy, *A Prophet Confronts His People*, Analecta Biblica 104 (Rome: Biblical Institute Press, 1984), 107–10. Based upon his more narrowly defined understanding of a disputation speech, Graffy's list of this form in the prophetic corpus includes: Isa 28:14–19; 40:27–31; 49:14–25; Jer 8:8–9; 31:29–30; 33:23–26; Ezek 11:2–12; 11:14–17; 12:21–25; 12:26–28; 18:1–20; 20:32–44; 33:10–20; 33:23–29; 37:11b–13; Hag 1:2, 4–11.

35. Graffy, *A Prophet Confronts His People*, 22. See also Floyd, *Minor Prophets: Part 2*, 562–74, who abandons any sense of "stylistic consistency" in the book of Malachi based upon the statement-objection-response form due to the considerable irregularity of the form in each discrete unit (567). The notion of "identical units" is replaced by a "generically varied configuration of somewhat differently differentiated units" (567–68). Floyd, *Minor Prophets: Part 2*, 568, explains that

> after an introduction (1:2–5) that may still be called a prophetic disputation, the rest of the book (1:6–3:24) divides into two sections. The first section (1:6–2:16) consists of two speeches, one addressed to the priests (1:6–2:9) and the other to the people (2:10–16), regarding practices that profane the cult. The speech to the priests and the speech to the people are structurally parallel in form. Both begin with a prophecy of punishment (1:6–14; 2:10–12) announcing the penalty that is already in effect (1:10–14; 2:12) for a practice that profanes the cult (1:6–9; 2:10–11). Both conclude with a prophetic call to repentance (2:1–9, 13–16) urging the addressees to behave in a way that avoids profanation of the cult.

quoted opinion."[36] Subsequent interpreters have also noted this type of catechetical quality in Malachi.[37]

Others have accepted the division of the book predicated upon the three-fold disputation form (statement—objection—response) but differ from Pfeiffer as to the disputation form's function. Rather than arguing that each pericope stands on its own as a disputation speech, Julia O'Brien argues that each unit functions as an integral part of a covenant lawsuit levied by YHWH against the priests and people.[38] The first pericope (1:2–5) serves as the prologue, with five accusations to follow (1:6–2:9; 2:10–16; 2:17–3:5; 3:6–12; 3:13–21[3:13–4:3]). The lawsuit concludes with an admonition in 3:22[4:4] and a final ultimatum in 3:23–24[4:5–6].[39] While O'Brien's proposal rightly highlights the role of covenant in the book of Malachi, a number of the typical features associated with the covenant lawsuit are noticeably absent (e.g., an opening imperative ["Hear"], the call for nature to serve as witnesses, cf. Mic 6:1–2).[40] Similar to O'Brien, David L. Petersen agrees largely with Pfeiffer's identification of pericopes within Malachi and even affirms Pfeiffer's claim that Malachi contains a distinctive literary style, but he breaks with Pfeiffer, however, by rejecting the label "disputation speech," arguing instead that the Hellenistic form "diatribe" is more descriptive.[41] Regarding the problematic nature of Petersen's proposal, see the critique offered by Floyd.[42]

Although minor quibbles exist concerning the form of the disputation itself, most treatments of Malachi recognize this form as central to the organization of the book.[43] Although each disputation unit follows a similar structure, as Pfeiffer observed, notable differences do remain. The units vary in length with the shortest being four verses and the longest, eighteen. Some units follow the statement—question—response

36. Floyd, *Minor Prophets: Part 2*, 568.

37. See James A. Fischer, "Notes on the Literary Form and Message of Malachi," *CBQ* 34 (1972): 315–20. Similarly, Hill, while recognizing the disputation form of the pericopes, suggests that the book serves as "a catechism on covenant relationship with YHWH" (*Malachi*, 37).

38. Julia M. O'Brien, *Priest and Levite*.

39. O'Brien, *Priest and Levite*, 57–84.

40. See also Hill's assessment of O'Brien's proposal (*Malachi*, 32–33).

41. David L. Petersen, *Zechariah 9–14 and Malachi*, OTL (Louisville: Westminster John Knox, 1995), 31–4.

42. Floyd, *Minor Prophets: Part 2*, 566–67. Other proposals have been set forward. For example, diverging considerably from Pfeiffer, Clendenen contends that "rather than interpreting Malachi in terms of a certain culture-specific genre [i.e., disputation speech] which is highly debatable," a linguistic approach focused on universal discourse types, as developed by R. A. Longacre, is preferable (E. Ray Clendenen, "Malachi," in Richard A. Taylor and E. Ray Clendenen, *Haggai, Malachi*, NAC 21A [Nashville: Broadman and Holman, 2004], 221). Clendenen understands Malachi as a form of hortatory discourse. Rather than understanding the book as a series of six disputation speeches (plus introductory and concluding material) as Pfeiffer argued, Clendenen suggests that the book is comprised of three lengthy exhortations (1:2–2:9; 2:10–3:6; 3:7–24), with a command (i.e., exhortation) at the center of the first two units (1:10; 2:15c–16). He argues that the commands in the third unit open and close the unit (3:7–10b; 3:22–24[4:4–6]).

43. A notable exception is Floyd, *Minor Prophets, Part 2*, 571–73. He rejects the claim that Malachi consists of a series of units that are all of the same genre (i.e., disputation). For Floyd, the variations between and among the different units is too great to consider them "generically homogenous" (573).

form, while others also include what Meinhold has termed a "theological preamble" (e.g., 3:6).[44] In some units, the speech of God dominates (e.g., 1:2–5), while in others, the prophet's voice moves to the fore (e.g., 2:10–16). Some units contain criticism and rebuke, while others exhort the audience to a particular behavior (e.g., 3:6–12). Some units simply begin with a statement (1:2; 2:17; 3:6, 13) while others begin with a rhetorical question (1:6; 2:10). Others still adopt a more complex argumentative structure, employing a second statement—question—response. For example, in the second disputation unit (1:6–2:9), the statement—objection—response format appears in 1:6h–7a:

Statement/YHWH: "O Priests, who despise my name."
Objection/Priests: "But you say, 'How have we despised your name?"
Response/YHWH: "By presenting defiled food on my altar."

The exchange between YHWH and the priests continues with the response of YHWH in 7a now functioning as the initial statement for the subsequent exchange.

Statement/YHWH: "By presenting defiled food on my altar."
Objection/Priests: "But you say, how have we defiled you?"
Response/YHWH: "When you say, 'The table of YHWH, it is despised.'"

The additional questions and answers serve to advance the argument, and in the case of this disputation, actually introduce the primary matter of contention.[45]

Structure

Although there is some variation as to form within each of the units identified by Pfeiffer, this does not require the interpreter to jettison the notion of a disputation form in Malachi.[46] Rather the disputation, even in a form that deviates from earlier disputation forms (as noted by Graffy), remains the dominant form in the book. That said the book of Malachi remains best understood as a collection of disputations that have been arranged meaningfully in the creation of the book. In attempting to identify the intentional structure of the book, Rainer Kessler has proposed that the book has both a linear and concentric structure, as represented in the graphic below:[47]

44. Arndt Meinhold, "Dialogische Strukturen in den Streitreden des Buches Maleachi," *ZAW* 102 (1990): 194–212.

45. James D. Nogalski, *The Book of the Twelve: Micah-Malachi*, SHBC (Macon, GA: Smyth & Helwys, 2011), 995.

46. Nogalski contends that while the question and response form dominate the book of Malachi, "the style is not fixed as an absolute pattern without deviation" (*Redactional Processes in the Book of the Twelve*, 182–83).

47. Adapted from Kessler, *Maleachi*, 53.

Foundation	Critique		Future		Purpose
I. 1:2–5	II. 1:6–2:9	III. 2:10–16	IV. 2:17–3:5	V. 3:6–12	VI. 3:13–21
• YHWH speaks to addressees • Addressees speak to YHWH	• YHWH speaks to addressees • Addressees speak to YHWH • Two objections raised • Emphasis on the temple cult	• Malachi speaks to addressees • The addressees do not identify their audience[48] • Directed to Judah and Jerusalem (2:11)	• Malachi speaks to addressees • The addressees do not identify their audience • Directed to Judah and Jerusalem (3:4)	• YHWH speaks to addressees • Addressees speak to YHWH • Two objections raised • Emphasis on the temple cult	• YHWH speaks to addressees • Addressees speak to YHWH

The book moves logically in linear fashion. The opening disputation (1:2–5), with its emphasis on YHWH's covenant fidelity, rightly functions as the "programmatic introduction" to the entire book.[49] The second and third disputations levy critiques against the temple personnel in the first instance and then to the larger population in the latter regarding current violations. Beginning with the fourth disputation, however, the orientation of the book shifts. As Nogalski has rightly observed, "what has not been as frequently noted is the extent to which the focus shifts from the present to the future with the introduction of the day of YHWH" in the fourth disputation (3:1).[50] The fifth disputation continues the future orientation with a call to repentance and a promise of blessing. The linear orientation of the book remains evident in the last disputation with the reference to the coming day (3:19[4:1]), a day in which the wicked, evildoers, and arrogant will be judged and the righteous will experience deliverance.

In addition to the linear orientation of the book, Kessler notes that the book also has a concentric orientation.[51] In the first and last disputations, the people have challenged YHWH for being a derelict covenant partner who has apparently abandoned his people. In response, YHWH affirms that his covenantal commitment to his people remains valid, and further, that some are not the beneficiaries of that commitment (i.e., Edom, the wicked). The second and fifth disputations focus on the activities associated with the temple cult, or temple worship. Malachi 1:6–2:9 deals exclusively with the abusive practices of priests as it pertains to the sacrificial system at the temple. Although the disputation in 3:6–12 is directed at the nation (3:6, "children of Jacob"), the issue at hand concerns temple activity, namely the

48. Kessler contends that in the third and fourth disputations, the prophet delivers his critique ("statement"), but in the objection by the people no addressee, neither the prophet nor YHWH, is identified (*Maleachi*, 53).

49. Arnt Meinhold, *Maleachi*, BKAT XIV/8 (Neukirchen-Vluyn: Neukirchener, 2006), 24.

50. Nogalski, *Redactional Processes in the Book of the Twelve*, 183.

51. For a similar analysis, see Ernst Wendland, "Linear and Concentric Patterns in Malachi," *BT* 36 (1985):108–21.

giving of tithes and offerings. The two inner most disputations (2:10–16; 2:17–3:5) include charges brought by the prophet against those in Judah and Jerusalem for their own covenant failures, as evident in ethical lapses within the community. The concentric structure of the book reflects the close connection between "right worship and right action" in the book of Malachi.[52]

Poetry versus Prose

One last literary issue that demands a brief word is whether the book of Malachi should be understood as poetry or prose. Certain texts within the book certainly suggest a poetic quality to the book. For example, parallelism seems to be clearly at work in the second disputation in 1:6a–g:

> "A son honors a father;
>   and a servant [honors] his master."
> If I am a father,
>   then where is the honor due me?
> If I am a master,
>   where is the fear due me.

Both *BHS* and *BHQ*, as well as the earlier *BHK*, have all formatted the book in poetic fashion, thus confirming the suspicions of some as it pertains to the poetic nature of the book itself. Evidence may suggest otherwise. Andersen and Freedman have observed that three particles occur with considerable regularity in prose texts, while the converse is true of poetic texts: אֲשֶׁר (the relative), ה (the article), and אֵת (the accusative particle).[53] Based on their statistical analysis, Andersen and Freedman observed that prose texts consist of 15 percent or more of these three particles, whereas poetic texts consist of 5 percent or less. When applied to a seemingly well-known poetic text, such as Jonah 2, application of the metrics identified by Andersen and Freedman appears to confirm the poetic nature of the text. The Song of Thanksgiving in Jonah (2:3–10) contains a total of eighty-one words with only one occurrence of אֲשֶׁר (v. 10), one occurrence of the definite article (v. 7), and one occurrence of the accusative particle אֵת (v. 8). Statistically, these particles comprise only 3.7 percent (3/81) of the song of Jonah, falling well below the threshold established for a poetic text by Andersen and Freedman.

52. Thomas Hieke, *Kult und Ethos. Die Verschmelzung von rechtem Gottesdienst und gerechtem Handeln im Lesevorgang der Maleachischrift*, SBS 208 (Stuttgart: Katholisches Bibelwerk, 2006), 78. See also Snyman, *Malachi*, 11–12.

53. Francis I. Andersen and David Noel Freedman, *Hosea*, AYBC 24 (New York: Doubleday, 1980), 57–66.

Andrew Hill applied these same metrics to the book of Malachi. According to Hill, 24 of the 210 words (11.4 percent) in chapter 1 are contained in the prose-particle set identified by Andersen and Freedman. In chapter 2, the percentage increases with 37 of the 241 words (15.4 percent) falling within the set and in chapter 3, the number increases yet again to 67 of 328 (20.4 percent).[54] Taken together, the prose-particle frequency for the entire book is 16.4 percent (128 of the 779 words), suggesting that the book is more prosaic than poetic. That said, however, the book contains a number of poetic forms, including, for example, parallelism (1:6), chiasm (1:2; 3:11), ellipsis (1:6), synecdoche (2:11), metonymy (1:2, 3), and rhetorical questions (1:2, 13), thus complicating the question further. In the end, Hill's final determination of the book as "oracular prose" seems a fitting label that attempts to adjudicate the evidence fairly. According to Hill, "the literary texture of Malachi is a combination of prosaic and rhetorical features approaching poetic discourse but distinctive of prophetic style."[55] In the commentary to follow, careful attention will be given to both the poetic and prosaic features of the text but also their contribution to the rhetorical strategy of the book as a whole.

The Theological Message of Malachi

Despite its relative brevity, the book of Malachi touches upon a number of theological themes. The theological claims that are foundational to the book are a response, in part, to the social, historical, and theological crises experienced by those in Yehud. Beyond that, these themes also represent an appropriation and an extension of earlier theological reflection found in selected biblical texts, most notably Deuteronomy. In other words, the author of Malachi sought a new and renewed articulation of the community's faith amid ever-new and ever-changing circumstances.

YHWH as the Central Confession

From beginning to end, YHWH is the central confession of the book of Malachi. The book is, as Hill rightly suggests, "theological testimony" in its fullest sense.[56] Although the reader of Malachi may be tempted to place considerable emphasis on the waywardness of the community throughout the book, these accusations must

54. Hill, *Malachi*, 23–24. For a similar assessment, see Kessler, *Maleachi*, 55–57.

55. Hill, *Malachi*, 26. In her analysis of Malachi, Glazier-McDonald notes the highly stylized language of Malachi and the frequent use of poetic forms and concludes that the book was indeed poetry. She suggests that while the poetry of Malachi differs considerably from other poetic texts (i.e., psalms) that "should not be a stumbling block in the way of viewing the work as poetry" (*Malachi: The Divine Messenger*, 4). Consequently, she attempts to a render the Hebrew text and English translation in poetic form throughout her book.

56. Hill, *Malachi*, 48.

always be heard in light of the book's core confession about Israel's covenant God. What makes the community's waywardness so scandalous is the character and nature of the God that they claim to serve.

In the opening line of the first disputation, YHWH makes known his covenantal commitment by declaring, "I have chosen you" (1:2). In the very next disputation, YHWH announces that he is a God worthy of fear and honor (1:6) because he is the great king (1:14). Elsewhere in the book, YHWH is described as the God who has created his people and the one who stands over them as "father" (2:10).[57] And despite the community's claims to the contrary (2:17; 3:14–15), YHWH declares that he does not change (3:6).

In addition to these claims, the book of Malachi recalls another theme rehearsed throughout the prophetic corpus. This God, Israel's God, is the one who calls people back to himself, waywardness notwithstanding. "Return (שׁוּבוּ) to me so that I may return (וְאָשׁוּבָה) to you," YHWH declares in 3:7. This invitation echoes that of a similar invitation found in the opening prophetic text in the Book of the Twelve. Hosea declares, "Return (שׁוּבוּ) to YHWH your God, for you have stumbled because of your iniquity" (14:1). In both books, the iniquity of the community is clearly on display, yet so too is the redemptive disposition of Israel's covenant God. Although judgment occupies an important place within the overall theology of Malachi, and rightly so (2:9; 3:2–5; 3:19[4:1]), these declarations of impending judgment only serve to reinforce the shocking fidelity of YHWH as made evident through his invitation to return.

The final confession concerns the coming Day of YHWH (3:1–5, 3:17 and 3:23[4:5]). Like the other elements in the book mentioned above, this too is a confession about YHWH. In the fourth and sixth disputations (2:17–3:5; 3:13–21[3:13–4:3]), the people challenge the justice of God and assert that the expected norms of covenantal blessings and curses no longer seems operative. Based on such observations, the community is left to conclude that YHWH has ceased to act in accordance with the covenant, and worse yet, that YHWH's favor seems to have fallen on the arrogant evildoers. The announcement of the coming day of YHWH, however, jettisons such claims. On the Day of YHWH, God will distinguish between the righteous and the wicked, between those who serve God and those who do not (3:18). This declaration signals that YHWH has not abandoned his role as covenant partner nor has he reneged on his commitment to covenantal justice. To the contrary,

57. On the use of the title "father" in the Old and New Testaments, see Reinhard Feldmeier and Hermann Spieckermann, *God of the Living: A Biblical Theology* (Waco, TX: Baylor University Press, 2011), 51–91. Whereas the Tetragrammaton (יהוה) is used nearly seven thousand times in the Old Testament and *elohim* (אֱלֹהִים) nearly twenty-six hundred times, the language of God as "father" occurs a mere seventeen times. Feldmeier and Spieckermann suggest that the appropriation of this language in the post-exilic period was intended "to transform the suffering of God's remoteness into the experience of God's saving presence" (65). Cf. Isa 63:15–16, 19; 64:7–8, 11.

on that day, righteousness will rise like the sun and the righteous ones will skip like calves out of the stall (3:20[4:2]).

Primacy of Covenantal Themes

Covenantal language with its related imagery dominates the book of Malachi and represents a foundational claim in the book. From the first disputation to the last, and even in the two appendices, references to covenant are readily evident.[58] The dialogical nature of the book itself even underscores the covenantal relationship between YHWH and his people in Yehud.

The actual term "covenant" (בְּרִית) appears only six times in the book. Three times in reference to the covenant of Levi (2:4, 5, 8), once in reference to the covenant with the ancestors (2:10), once in reference to marriage (2:14), and once in reference to the coming of YHWH (3:1). The relative infrequency of the term itself, however, is not indicative of the importance of the idea for the entirety of the book, as suggested above. Additional vocabulary and imagery appear regularly and serve to reinforce the centrality of the theme. The opening disputation illustrates this vividly. In many translations of 1:2, YHWH declares, "I have loved you," to which the community responds, "How have you loved us?" (NIV). The notion of "love" (אהב) is not necessarily an emotive term, but rather one that is rooted in treaty or covenant language.[59] Understood this way, the question is not whether YHWH has feelings for those in Yehud, but whether YHWH remains committed to the community by way of the covenant, a claim the community repeatedly disputes. The emphasis on covenant in the opening disputation signals the significance of this theme for the remainder of the book.

In addition to the use of "covenant" (בְּרִית) and "love" (אהב), other language associated with covenant appears. Repeatedly the prophet appropriates language from other biblical traditions, especially Deuteronomy, in an attempt to connect the prophetic critique with covenantal expectations. Examples of this kind of appropriation are explored more fully in the commentary section to follow. Beyond particular terms or allusive references, the prophetic rhetoric includes imagistic language intended to invoke covenantal overtones. For example, the father-son metaphor and the lord-servant imagery employed in 1:6 is clearly intended to invoke covenantal relations.[60]

58. Verhoef refers to covenant as the "systematic principle" of the dialogues and "the fundamental presupposition of his message" (*The Books of Haggai and Malachi*, 180). See also the extended assessment of this theme in Steven L. McKenzie and Howard N. Wallace, "Covenant Themes in Malachi," *CBQ* 45 (1983): 549–63; Steven L. McKenzie, *Covenant*, Understanding Biblical Themes (St. Louis: Chalice, 2000).

59. On the background of this term, see the classic treatment in William L. Moran, "The Ancient Near Eastern Background of Love of God in the Book of Deuteronomy," *CBQ* 25 (1963), 77–87. The use of the verb "to hate" (שׂנא) in Mal 1:3 functions similarly with strong covenantal overtones (82).

60. See the earlier study of F. C. Fensham, "Father and Son as Terminology for Treaty and Covenant," in *Near Eastern Studies in Honor of William F. Albright*, ed. Hans Goedicke (Baltimore: Johns Hopkins Press, 1971), 121–35.

In many ways, the various disputations in Malachi highlight the primacy of covenant by rehearsing the community's failure in abiding by the very stipulations of that covenant. The offering of improper sacrifices in 1:6–14 and the foregoing of the tithe (3:6–12) exemplify serious violations of covenantal norms. The abomination created by marrying the daughters of foreign gods (2:11) reflects the community's willingness to sidestep covenantal demands in favor of personal and communal security. Further, the community's treatment of its more vulnerable members (2:16; 3:5) garners the attention of YHWH. They are grave acts of injustice that are symptomatic of a community that has jettisoned its commitment to the covenant and the repeated claims therein to care for the socially insecure.

Although the opening disputation reaffirms the covenantal faithfulness of YHWH, such a claim does not appear to fully persuade the community. In subsequent disputations, questions concerning God's justice occupy the thoughts of the community (2:17; 3:14–15). These questions are not rooted in some general sense of fairness and equity, but rather, in a particular expectation that is predicated upon YHWH's covenantal faithfulness. The complaints issued in the fourth and sixth disputations challenge such divine faithfulness by alleging that YHWH has apparently abandoned his covenantal commitments and thereby undercut the covenantal expectations of blessings and curses. To such a claim, YHWH responds by announcing that he will come as the "messenger of the covenant" (3:1) and that on the day in which he acts, justice will be meted out (3:17–18). The announcement of an impending arrival is meant to serve as confirmation of divine faithfulness. Thus, even as the small book of Malachi opens with the covenant in view so in the same manner does it close. From beginning to end, YHWH declares his faithfulness and fidelity to a people who struggle to reciprocate the same.

The Necessity of Worship

The opening disputation reinforces the centrality of YHWH and the primacy of covenant for the book of Malachi. The second disputation (1:6–2:9) turns to consider the proper human response to those claims: reverence and fear. The problem, as YHWH notes, is that such responses appear altogether lacking in the community.[61] This lack of fear is most clearly on display in the community's practice of offering deficient sacrifices and unworthy worship. More troubling is that when such offerings are presented, the priests declare "there is no defect" (1:8). The irony is worth noting. The one who is the Great King (1:14) receives that which would be unacceptable even

61. The reference to "fear" in 1:6g appears again in the concluding verses of the book 3:16a, 20a[4:2a], but with a notable difference. In the first instance, the entire community *lacks* an appropriate reverent response to YHWH, whereas in the final verses, a smaller subset within the community is marked out specifically because of their posture of piety (i.e., fear).

to a human governor (1:8). YHWH takes no pleasure in such worship (1:10) and suggests that it is offered in vain (חִנָּם). The issue, however, is not the immoderate and outrageous demands of the Divine, but instead, the seeming audacity of the community to engage in worship as though YHWH remains continually inattentive.

Lest one think otherwise, the book of Malachi is not about the necessity of correct ritual and sacrifice, but instead, about the necessity of worshipping the one who merits our fear and reverence, the Great King. The abhorrent behavior reported throughout the book is the result of the community's failure to acknowledge the first two claims (centrality of YHWH and primacy of the covenant), but also their failure to engage in unadulterated worship of God. So long as YHWH is presumed to be inattentive at the altar, one can assume YHWH remains inattentive in all aspects of life, i.e., marriage (2:10–16), care of the most vulnerable (3:5), and even tithes (3:8).

The book of Malachi invites readers to give careful thought to the necessity of worship, and even more, the deleterious effects upon individuals and communities alike when such a posture of piety is altogether absent.

Outline of the Book of Malachi

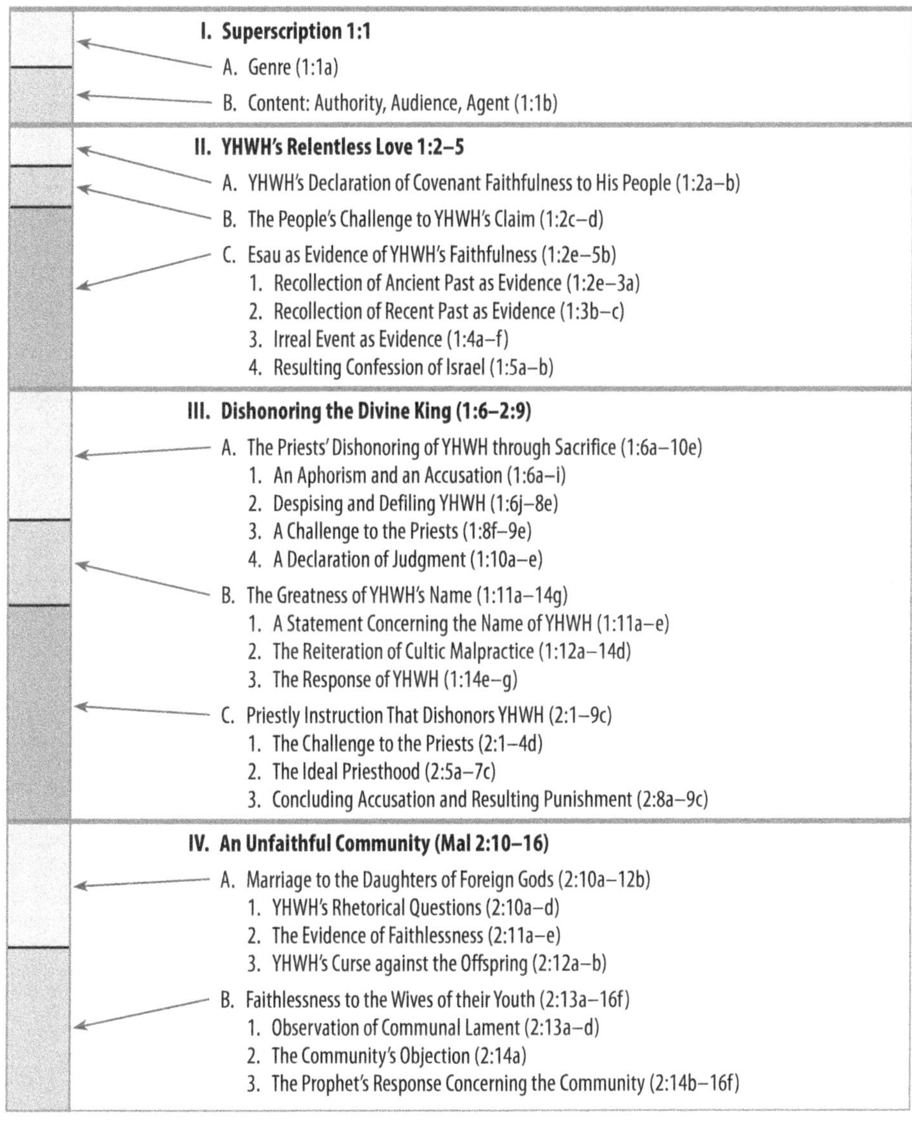

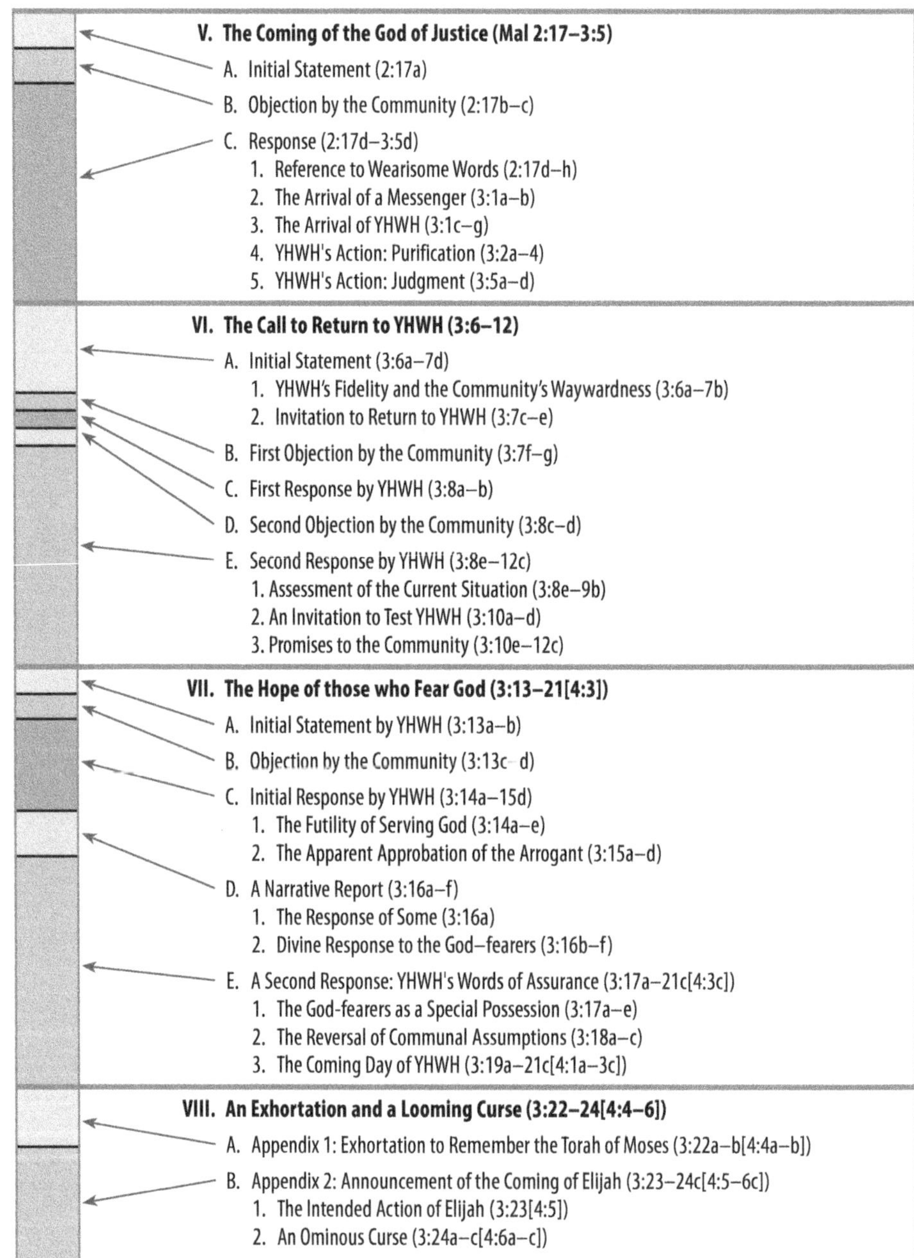

V. The Coming of the God of Justice (Mal 2:17–3:5)
A. Initial Statement (2:17a)
B. Objection by the Community (2:17b–c)
C. Response (2:17d–3:5d)
1. Reference to Wearisome Words (2:17d–h)
2. The Arrival of a Messenger (3:1a–b)
3. The Arrival of YHWH (3:1c–g)
4. YHWH's Action: Purification (3:2a–4)
5. YHWH's Action: Judgment (3:5a–d)
VI. The Call to Return to YHWH (3:6–12)
A. Initial Statement (3:6a–7d)
1. YHWH's Fidelity and the Community's Waywardness (3:6a–7b)
2. Invitation to Return to YHWH (3:7c–e)
B. First Objection by the Community (3:7f–g)
C. First Response by YHWH (3:8a–b)
D. Second Objection by the Community (3:8c–d)
E. Second Response by YHWH (3:8e–12c)
1. Assessment of the Current Situation (3:8e–9b)
2. An Invitation to Test YHWH (3:10a–d)
3. Promises to the Community (3:10e–12c)
VII. The Hope of those who Fear God (3:13–21[4:3])
A. Initial Statement by YHWH (3:13a–b)
B. Objection by the Community (3:13c–d)
C. Initial Response by YHWH (3:14a–15d)
1. The Futility of Serving God (3:14a–e)
2. The Apparent Approbation of the Arrogant (3:15a–d)
D. A Narrative Report (3:16a–f)
1. The Response of Some (3:16a)
2. Divine Response to the God–fearers (3:16b–f)
E. A Second Response: YHWH's Words of Assurance (3:17a–21c[4:3c])
1. The God-fearers as a Special Possession (3:17a–e)
2. The Reversal of Communal Assumptions (3:18a–c)
3. The Coming Day of YHWH (3:19a–21c[4:1a–3c])
VIII. An Exhortation and a Looming Curse (3:22–24[4:4–6])
A. Appendix 1: Exhortation to Remember the Torah of Moses (3:22a–b[4:4a–b])
B. Appendix 2: Announcement of the Coming of Elijah (3:23–24c[4:5–6c])
1. The Intended Action of Elijah (3:23[4:5])
2. An Ominous Curse (3:24a–c[4:6a–c])

CHAPTER 1

Malachi 1:1

I. Superscription

Main Idea of the Passage

Similar to other prophetic books, the book of Malachi opens with a superscription that identifies the form and content of the message, its designated audience, and the prophetic messenger.

Literary Context

While some prophetic books include a rather lengthy superscription in which various details are included (e.g., Isaiah, Jeremiah, Ezekiel, Amos, Hosea), others include a much more truncated superscription, as is the case with the book of Malachi (e.g., Joel, Nahum, Habakkuk). In this latter grouping, the superscription limits comments to the name of an individual associated with the book itself and to terms which signal that what follows is a divine utterance ("vision," חֲזוֹן; "word of YHWH," דְּבַר־יְהוָה; "oracle," מַשָּׂא). At times in the book of Malachi, the agent speaking is clearly YHWH (1:2–5), while in other disputations, the prophet himself seems to voice the critique (2:10–16). The superscription enshrines the notion that regardless of who issues the utterance, the entire book of Malachi has divine authorization and should be received as such.

➡ **I. Superscription (1:1)**
A. Genre (1:1a)
B. Content: Authority, Audience, Agent (1:1b)
II. YHWH's Relentless Love (1:2–5)
III. Dishonoring the Divine King (1:6–2:9)
IV. An Unfaithful Community (2:10–16)
V. The Coming of the God of Justice (2:17–3:5)
VI. The Call to Return to YHWH (3:6–12)
VII. The Hope of Those Who Fear God (3:13–21[4:3])
VIII. An Exhortation and a Looming Curse (3:22–24[4:4–6])

Translation and Exegetical Outline

(See page 29.)

Structure and Literary Form

The initial word in the superscription, מַשָּׂא is a nominal form derived from the root נָשָׂא, meaning "to lift," or "to carry." In nearly half of the noun's sixty-five occurrences, the meaning is quite apparent, referring to something that is literally carried or lifted up.[1] As a result, some have attempted to associate מַשָּׂא in the prophetic literature with the notion of "burden," perhaps with the understanding that the prophetic word was a burden for the prophet to deliver.[2] Rejecting that etymological explanation, others have linked the term with the phrase נָשָׂא קוֹל, "lift a voice," and thus rendered the term "pronouncement."[3] Michael Floyd, following the earlier work of Richard Weiss, has challenged both etymological explanations, and sought an alternative understanding of the term as it pertains to genre.[4]

1. E.g., Exod 23:5; Num 4:15, 19, 24; Deut 1:12; 2 Sam 15:33; 2 Kgs 5:17; Isa 22:25; Jer 17:21; Ezek 24:25; Hos 8:10; Ps 38:5; Job 7:20; Neh 13:15, 19; 2 Chr 17:11.

2. In his formal translation, Smith renders the term "burden," and argues that מַשָּׂא is best read here as 'burden' referring to something the prophet must accept, carry, and deliver to others" (Ralph L. Smith, *Micah-Malachi*, WBC 32 [Waco, TX: Word, 1984], 301n1a). Earlier, Henry Gehman suggested that as used in prophecy, the term carries within it the ideas of judgment and catastrophe, and contended that the term "suggests sublime ominousness," and hence a burden for the prophet ("The 'Burden' of the Prophets," *JQR* 31 [1940]: 110). Verhoef follows somewhat similarly (*The Books of Haggai and Malachi*, 188). Cf. JPS, ASV, NKJV.

3. See HALOT, "מַשָּׂא II," 639–40. Cf. NASB, HCSB.

4. Michael Floyd, "The MAŚŚĀ' as a Type of Prophetic Book," *JBL* 121 (2002): 401–22. Floyd focuses principally upon written (versus oral) forms of prophetic discourse, "It bears

Malachi 1:1

	Hebrew	Translation	Outline
			I. Superscription (1:1)
1a	מַשָּׂא	An oracle.	A. Genre (1:1a)
1b	דְּבַר יְהוָה אֶל יִשְׂרָאֵל בְּיַד מַלְאָכִי	The word of YHWH [that came] to Israel by the hand of Malachi.	B. Content: Authority, Audience, Agent (1:1b)

Because the term frequently appears as a superscription to the prophetic utterance that follows (Isa 13:1; 14:28; 15:1; 17:1; 19:1; 21:1, 11, 13; 22:1; 23:1; 30:6; Ezek 12:10; Nah 1:1; Hab 1:1; Zech 9:1; 12:1), Weiss argued that מַשָּׂא represented a distinct prophetic genre and suggested that the term is better understood as a "prophetic exposition of divine revelation."[5] Floyd explained that such a genre contained three elements.

> First, an assertion is made, directly or indirectly, about Yahweh's involvement in a particular historical situation or course of events. Second, this assertion clarifies the implications of a previous revelation from Yahweh that is alluded to, referred to, or quoted from. Third, this assertion also provides the basis for directives concerning appropriate reactions or responses to Yahweh's initiative, or for insights into how Yahweh's initiative affects the future.[6]

In the prophetic books that contain מַשָּׂא in the opening superscription (Nahum, Habakkuk, Zech 9 and 12, and Malachi), these features are present in varying degrees, but taken together, they confirm and validate the proposal of Weiss and Floyd. The book of Malachi, for example, confirms YHWH's involvement in Israel's history (e.g., 1:2–5; 3:6), alludes to previous revelation from YHWH (e.g., 1:6–2:9; 3:5–6) and provides "directives concerning appropriate reactions" (e.g., 3:9–10; 3:16–21[4:3]).[7] Thus in Mal 1:1, the opening word of the entire book indicates the genre of literature that is to follow, and as such, aids the reader in anticipating the rhetorical moves to be made in this brief prophetic book.

---

emphasizing that we are concerned with the definition of מַשָּׂא as a genre of prophetic literature, recognizing that it may well have been rooted in conventions of prophetic speech but not assuming that any מַשָּׂא text necessarily had oral antecedents or that such antecedents can be recovered" (407).

5. Richard Weiss, "Oracle," *ABD* 5:28–29.

6. Floyd, "The MAŚŚĀ' as a Type of Prophetic Book," 409. For a similar assessment of מַשָּׂא as a *terminus technicus* referring to a particular genre, see Kessler, *Maleachi*, 97–98. Similarly, Ina. Willi-Plein, "Wort, Last oder Auftrag? Zur Bedeutung von משא in Überschriften Prophetischer Texteinheiten," in *Die unwiderstehliche Wahrheit. Studien zur alttestamentlichen Prophetie. Festschrift für Arndt Meinhold*, eds. Rüdiger Lux und Ernst-Joachim Waschke; Arbeiten zur Bibel und ihrer Geschichte Band 23 (Leipzig: Evangelische Verlagsanstalt, 2006), 431–38.

7. On the role of traditions in the book of Malachi, see Karl W. Weyde, *Prophecy and Teaching*. Weyde contends that "the fact that there is no reference to vocation, to auditory or visionary experiences, suggest [*sic*] that Malachi contains a special kind of prophecy: its authority and message are founded on traditions, in which previously spoken divine words are recorded" (12).

Explanation of the Text

A. Genre (1:1a)

See Structure and Literary Form, p. 28, for a discussion of the genre.

B. Content: Authority, Audience, Agent (1:1b)

The remainder of the verse provides additional information about the disputations which follow. The phrase דְּבַר־יְהוָה, "the word of YHWH," immediately follows מַשָּׂא, but the proximity of the two constituents has not made their precise relationship any easier to determine. Generally, speaking, interpreters have followed one of three options. Because of the presence of the conjunctive accent (*mērəkā*) in the Masoretic text and the use of the genitive in the LXX (λόγου κυρίου), some translations have rendered the second constituent as a complement of the first, i.e., "an oracle of the word of YHWH" (cf., NASB, ESV).[8] Others have interpreted the second constituent as standing in apposition to the first. Understood in this manner, the noun-noun appositional phrase would be of the sortal type.[9] In such an arrangement, the lead term is a broad class term, while the second is a narrower term of the same type, as reflected in Smith's translation, "A burden (oracle), the word of the Yahweh . . . " (cf. NIV, HCSB).[10] The third option, and the one reflected in the translation above, keeps the two phrases separate, recognizing that the first word functions as a heading to the prophetic writing (NET, NRSV).[11] Understood this way the first term indicates the genre of literature, i.e., a prophetic book with particular rhetorical features (as explained above), while the second phrase indicates the content of the literature (i.e., "the word of YHWH").[12]

The phrase אֶל־יִשְׂרָאֵל בְּיַד מַלְאָכִי ("to Israel by the hand of Malachi") identifies both the audience and agent. Linguistically, the phrase is best understood as an unmarked relative clause with a verbless clause:

> the word of YHWH [that came] to Israel by the hand of Malachi.

Frequently the phrase דְּבַר־יְהוָה, "the word of YHWH," functions as the subject of the verb הָיָה, "to be," in prophetic superscriptions (cf. Jer 1:2; Ezek 1:3), but in those instances, the verb is included. An even closer parallel to Mal 1:1 appears in Hos 1:1; Joel 1:1; Mic 1:1; and Zeph 1:1, further justifying the identification of the clause in Mal 1:1 as an unmarked relative clause with a verbless clause:[13]

8. See also Joyce G. Baldwin, *Haggai, Zechariah, Malachi*, TOTC (London: Tyndale, 1972), 237, and Glazier-McDonald, *Malachi*, 24.

9. *IBHS* §12.3b.

10. Smith, *Micah–Malachi*, 301.

11. See also Snyman, *Malachi*, 22; Floyd, *Minor Prophets, Part 2*, 578–79.

12. Floyd, "The MAŚŚĀ' as a Type of Prophetic Book," 415.

13. In some linguistic studies, a verbless clause is labeled a "null copula" clause.

Hos 1:1 דְּבַר־יְהוָה אֲשֶׁר הָיָה אֶל
"The word of YHWH that came to . . ."

Joel 1:1 דְּבַר־יְהוָה אֲשֶׁר הָיָה אֶל
"The word of YHWH that came to . . ."

Mic 1:1 דְּבַר־יְהוָה אֲשֶׁר הָיָה אֶל
"The word of YHWH that came to . . ."

Zeph 1:1 דְּבַר־יְהוָה אֲשֶׁר הָיָה אֶל
"The word of YHWH that came to . . ."

Mal 1:1 דְּבַר־יְהוָה [אֲשֶׁר הָיָה] אֶל־
"The word of YHWH [that came] to . . ."

In all five instances, the relative clause is best understood as a restrictive relative clause, i.e., a clause that includes information necessary for the head, i.e., דְּבַר־יְהוָה ("the word of YHWH"), to be correctly identified from other possible referents. It is not simply the word of YHWH but "the word of YHWH *that came to X*."[14] What differentiates Malachi from the four preceding examples in the book of the Twelve, however, is the object of the preposition אֶל, "to." In Hosea, Joel, Micah, and Zephaniah, the object is the prophet himself (e.g., "the word of YHWH that came to *Hosea*"), but in Malachi, Israel functions as the object of the preposition ("the word YHWH that came to Israel"). Similar to the superscription in Haggai (1:1), the superscription in Malachi identifies an audience other than the prophet to whom the "oracle," מַשָּׂא, is directed. In Haggai, Zerubbabel and Joshua are named as the audience while in Malachi, it is Israel.

Although the political entity known as the Northern Kingdom, previously identified as "Israel," had fallen more than two centuries earlier, the word "Israel" remained an important designation within the nation's language of self-identification. Subsequent to the exile, the term was reassigned to the remnant of the nation that survived the Babylonian exile (cf., Jer 2:4; Ezek 3:1, 4). In the post-exilic period, this newly configured "Israel" was founded on the rebuilt temple, a reorganized Levitical priesthood, a restored temple liturgy, and an oath of covenant renewal.[15] Yet instead of being imbued with political overtones, the term morphed into an overarching theological interpretation of the community's identity. Verhoef explains that "irrespective of their numbers, failures, and sins, they still were the representatives of the people of God, the bearers of his promises, the mediators of his revelation."[16] Thus, even though some of the disputations are directed at the priests specifically (1:6–2:9; 3:3[17]), the book of Malachi *in toto* has the covenant nation in view.

14. Brevard Childs offered a different rationale for absence of the verb in Malachi suggesting that it "may indicate a theological development in which the mediatory role of that prophet had receded" (*Introduction to the Old Testament as Christian Scripture* [Philadelphia: Fortress, 1979], 492). Following Childs's lead, Weyde noted that while other prophetic texts record that the דְּבַר־יְהוָה "came" (הָיָה) to the prophet, there is no "reference of this kind to a revelation of the divine word" in Mal 1:1 (Weyde, *Prophecy and Teaching*, 58). Both Childs and Weyde place the weight of their argument on the absence of the verb, but the simplest explanation for its absence is that of ellipsis; there is ample evidence of unmarked relative clauses and null copula constructions in the Old Testament. This is not to discount, however, Childs's and Weyde's claim that the "mediatory role" of the prophet had receded in the book of Malachi. Clearly the fact that "the word of YHWH" came to Israel (and not the prophet) is evidence enough to warrant a claim that a "change of prophecy" had taken place with the book of Malachi (Weyde, *Prophecy and Teaching*, 68).

15. Hill, *Malachi*, 142.

16. Verhoef, *The Books of Haggai and Malachi*, 191. See also Snyman, *Malachi*, 24–25.

17. Although note that while the purification of the Levites is in view in 3:3, the purificatory work of YHWH extends to the community in 3:4.

The collocation "by the hand of X" appears repeatedly in the Old Testament, typically referring to the agent through whom YHWH has chosen to speak. In such instances, the prepositional phrase, "by the hand" (בְּיַד), precedes a proper name, providing further rationale for understanding מַלְאָכִי, "Malachi," as a proper noun (e.g., Exod 9:35; 35:29; Lev 8:36; Num 9:23; 1 Kgs 16:12; Isa 20:2; Jer 50:1; Hag 1:1, 3, 2:1; 2 Chr 10:15).[18]

Canonical and Theological Significance

The importance of the superscription should not be overlooked. More than simply an introduction to the book, the first verse affirms the significance of what follows; it is the word of YHWH for the people of God.

18. On the question of whether מַלְאָכִי is a proper noun or title, see the introduction.

CHAPTER 2

Malachi 1:2–5

II. YHWH's Relentless Love

Main Idea of the Passage

YHWH remains a faithful covenant partner with the people in Yehud despite their apparent claims that he had abandoned them. His dealings with Edom provide a reminder of YHWH's faithfulness to his people, which in turn, should produce a renewed confession (v. 5c).

Literary Context

Although Mal 1:2–5 stands as the first disputation, it appears quite distinct from the others in the book. In the opening verse, the verb אהב is mentioned twice and thematically appears to govern the entire first disputation, yet interestingly, the word fails to appear elsewhere in the book. Moreover, references to Jacob and Esau dominate this initial unit but attention to these figures remain confined to this section of the book alone. For example, Esau is mentioned by name in 1:2e–4a but nowhere else in the book.[1] Furthermore, much of the book concerns matters associated with sacrifice and community life yet those topics are not explicitly addressed here. Its differences notwithstanding, the opening disputation plays a critical role in the development of the book. The first disputation challenged the skepticism concerning YHWH's love for his people. This reaffirmation of YHWH's covenantal commitment to his people serves as the basis for a call to proper observation of Israel's cultic

1. James Nogalski appropriately refers to this first unit as the "Edom Pericope" (*Redactional Processes in the Book of the Twelve*, 193).

activity (1:6–2:9; 3:6–12) and as sufficient evidence to prevent any doubt regarding YHWH's justice (2:17–3:5; 3:13–21[3:13–4:3]).

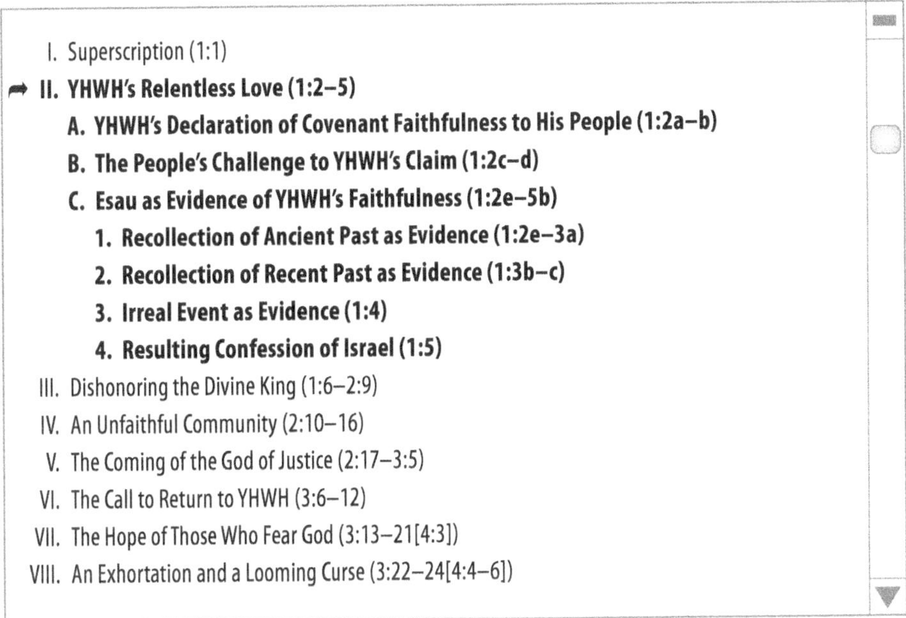
I. Superscription (1:1)
➡ **II. YHWH's Relentless Love (1:2–5)**
A. YHWH's Declaration of Covenant Faithfulness to His People (1:2a–b)
B. The People's Challenge to YHWH's Claim (1:2c–d)
C. Esau as Evidence of YHWH's Faithfulness (1:2e–5b)
1. Recollection of Ancient Past as Evidence (1:2e–3a)
2. Recollection of Recent Past as Evidence (1:3b–c)
3. Irreal Event as Evidence (1:4)
4. Resulting Confession of Israel (1:5)
III. Dishonoring the Divine King (1:6–2:9)
IV. An Unfaithful Community (2:10–16)
V. The Coming of the God of Justice (2:17–3:5)
VI. The Call to Return to YHWH (3:6–12)
VII. The Hope of Those Who Fear God (3:13–21[4:3])
VIII. An Exhortation and a Looming Curse (3:22–24[4:4–6])

Translation and Exegetical Outline

(See page 36.)

Structure and Literary Form

As noted in the introduction, each pericope in the book of Malachi is best understood as a disputation speech, yet variations in this form do occur across the six disputations. Although the briefest of the disputation speeches in the book, Mal 1:2–5 does contain all of the defining features of this form: statement (1:2a); objection (1:2c–d); and response (1:2e–5).[2]

2. Rainer Kessler gives particular attention to the communication structure formed in this disputation and its larger interpretative implications for the structure and meaning of the unit. Within this opening pericope, three figures are mentioned (YHWH; Jacob/Israel; Esau/Edom). YHWH and Jacob/Israel communicate directly with each other: "I have loved you," says the Lord (1:2a–b); "In what way have you loved us" (1:2c–d); "your eyes" and "you shall say" (1:5a). Although Edom does speak (1:4a–b), Edom does not direct her comments toward YHWH, and similarly, YHWH only speaks *about* Edom, but

Malachi 1:2–5

Verse	Hebrew	English	Outline
			II. YHWH's Relentless Love (1:2–5)
2a	אָהַבְתִּי אֶתְכֶם	"I have chosen you,"	A. YHWH's Declaration of Covenant Faithfulness to His
2b	אָמַר יְהוָה	says YHWH.	People (1:2a–b)
2c	וַאֲמַרְתֶּם	"But you say,	B. The People's Challenge to YHWH's Claim (1:2c–d)
2d	בַּמָּה אֲהַבְתָּנוּ	'In what way have you chosen us?'	
			C. Esau as Evidence of YHWH's Faithfulness (1:2e–5c)
2e	הֲלוֹא־אָח עֵשָׂו לְיַעֲקֹב	Is not Esau a brother of Jacob?'"	1. Recollection of Ancient Past as Evidence (1:2e–3a)
2f	נְאֻם־יְהוָה	utterance of YHWH.	
2g	וָאֹהַב אֶת־יַעֲקֹב׃	"I chose Jacob,	
3a	וְאֶת־עֵשָׂו שָׂנֵאתִי	but Esau, I did not choose.	
3b	וָאָשִׂים אֶת־הָרָיו שְׁמָמָה	I have made his mountains a desolation	2. Recollection of Recent Past as Evidence (1:3b–c)
3c	וְאֶת־נַחֲלָתוֹ לְתַנּוֹת מִדְבָּר	and his inheritance for the jackals of the wilderness.	
4a	כִּי־תֹאמַר אֱדוֹם	"If Edom should say,	3. Irreal Event as Evidence (1:4a–f)
4b	רֻשַּׁשְׁנוּ	'We are shattered	
4c	↑ וְנָשׁוּב וְנִבְנֶה חֳרָבוֹת	↑ so let us rebuild the ruins,'"	
4d	כֹּה אָמַר יְהוָה צְבָאוֹת ↓	thus says YHWH Sabaoth, ↓	
4e	הֵמָּה יִבְנוּ וַאֲנִי אֶהֱרוֹס	"They may build, but I will destroy.	
4f	וְקָרְאוּ לָהֶם גְּבוּל רִשְׁעָה וְהָעָם אֲשֶׁר־זָעַם יְהוָה עַד־עוֹלָם	And they shall call them a wicked territory, the people with whom YHWH is angry forever	
5a	וְעֵינֵיכֶם תִּרְאֶינָה	Your eyes shall see	4. Resulting Confession of Israel (1:5a–c)
5b	וְאַתֶּם תֹּאמְרוּ	and you shall say,	
5c	יִגְדַּל יְהוָה מֵעַל לִגְבוּל יִשְׂרָאֵל	'Great is YHWH beyond the borders of Israel.'"	

Embedded within the first disputation are a series of lines arranged in A/B/B′/A′ parallelism (chiasm). Together they create a tightly constructed arrangement that is meant to juxtapose a number of themes. Strikingly, each of the three involve contrast.[3]

1:2a–b "I have chosen you," says YHWH.
A B
1:2c–d But you say, "In what way have you chosen us."
B′ A′

1:2g I chose Jacob
A B
1:3a but Esau, I did not choose.
B′ A′

1:4b–c We are shattered so let us rebuild.
A B
1:4e They may build, but I will destroy.
B′ A′

These contrasts, or antithetical claims, serve to heighten the disputational nature of the opening section. While other prophetic books include lengthy narrations (c.f., Jeremiah, Ezekiel, Haggai), the book of Malachi is comprised primarily of speeches by various speakers. The dialogues oscillate between YHWH and the people and priests, as evident in the first and last examples above from the first disputation. Given this feature, i.e., the exchange of dialogues, Rainer Kessler has argued that the entire book of Malachi is a "dramatic text."[4] While the book of Malachi was not intended for performance, as some might suggest, features of the book do resemble something akin to a monologue in which one person is rehearsing the dialogues that take place between others.[5] Thus to appreciate the argumentation in the book, careful attention must be given to the speakers as well as to the content of their speeches.

---

not directly to her. Despite the kinship implied by the mention of Jacob and Esau by name, the two brothers/nations do not address each other. The dialogue in this first pericope does not focus on the verbal exchange between the two brothers/nations, as recounted elsewhere (Obadiah), but instead, the rhetoric is structured so as to draw attention to the strained YHWH-Jacob relationship (*Maleachi*, 108–9).

3. S. D. Snyman, "Antithesis in Malachi 1:2–5," *ZAW* 98 (1986): 436–38.

4. Kessler, *Maleachi*, 57.

5. On the possibility of dramatic performance, see Ina Willi-Plein, *Haggai, Sacharja, Maleachi*, ZBKAT (Zurich: Theologischer Verlag Zurich, 2007), 227.

Explanation of the Text

A. YHWH's Declaration of Covenant Faithfulness to His People (1:2a–b)

In the opening line of the disputation, YHWH declares his continual love (אהב) for his people.[6] The verb אהב occurs in a number of contexts in the Old Testament. In familial contexts, the term reflects the love between two persons, especially between a husband and wife (e.g., Jacob and Rachel, Gen 29:18, 20; Shechem and Dinah, Gen 34:3; Elkanah and Hannah, 1 Sam 1:5; David and Michal, 1 Sam 18:20), as well as love expressed in familial or near familial relationships (i.e., Ruth and Naomi [Ruth 4:15], David and Jonathan [1 Sam 18:1–3]). Beyond familial relationships, the verb appears repeatedly in reference to the divine-human relationship, especially in the book of Deuteronomy.[7] Although the term "love" typically invokes emotional connotations in English, the term's usage in reference to the divine-human relationship is an expression of a covenantal relationship, first and foremost.[8] This notion is reinforced in other texts where אהב stands in parallel construction with בחר ("to choose").[9] It is this latter context that informs the reading of Mal 1:2. The opening statement in the first disputation is a declaration of (continued) covenant fidelity by YHWH (e.g., "I have chosen you;" "I have covenanted with you").

The object of YHWH's love is referenced by the second-person-plural suffix attached to the definite direct object marker, "I have chosen you [אֶתְכֶם]." The use of the pronoun is an example of cataphora, meaning that the referent for the pronoun actually comes later in the discourse. In this instance, the referent is not clearly identified until 1:2g where אהב is repeated along with the proper noun, "Jacob" [יַעֲקֹב].[10]

אָהַבְתִּי אֶתְכֶם	I have chosen you . . . (v. 2a)
וָאֹהַב אֶת־יַעֲקֹב	Yet I chose Jacob (v. 2g)

The rhetorical intent is to bind the present generation ("you") with their eponymous ancestor ("Jacob") in an effort to confirm that the "chosenness" ("love") that was extended to the earlier generation remains intact for the present generation.

B. The People's Challenge to YHWH's Claim (1:2c–d)

The prophet reports the challenge of the people: "but you say" (וַאֲמַרְתֶּם). This verbal construction appears repeatedly in the objections uttered by the people and priests as reported elsewhere in the book (1:6, 7, 13; 2:14, 17; 3:7, 8, 13, 14). The quotation that follows introduces the chief complaint

6. The perfect form of the verb, אָהַבְתִּי, "I have loved," is best understood as a "durative stative perfective" (*IBHS* §30.5.3c). YHWH's decision to "love" Jacob represents a past activity that remains active into the present, a claim the community is prepared to challenge. Cf. Hill, *Malachi*, 147.

7. Cf. Deut 4:37–38; 7:8–9; 10:12, 14–15, 18–19; 11:1, 13, 22; 19:9; 23:6[5]; 30:16.

8. As Clendenen ("Malachi," 247) notes, "Although God certainly had affections for Israel, the focus here is on his repeated actions in accordance with a continuing relationship."

9. Cf. Deut 4:37; 10:15; Pss 47:5[4]; 78:68.

10. Mignon Jacobs (*The Books of Haggai and Malachi* [Grand Rapids: William B. Eerdmans Publishing, 2017], 157) argues that the antecedent of כֶם- is Israel in 1:1, an understandable assumption, given that the antecedent to most pronouns appears earlier (anaphoric reference). This understanding, however, fails to recognize the literary structure of the verse as suggested above. The parallel construction in v. 2a and 2g link the two lines together (verb [אהב] + object marker + complement).

or objection of the community, "In what way have you chosen us?" The reported speech of the people and priests throughout the book of Malachi reflects the *Zeitgeist* of Yehud during the post-exilic period. While their comments are not intended as exact quotes, they do attempt to capture the sentiments of the larger community.[11] As noted in the introduction, quoted objections are part of the disputation genre more broadly and play an important role in the rhetoric of the book. The confrontation between YHWH and the wayward community becomes much sharper because the objections are not simply *described* by the prophet but instead are placed in the mouths of the people and priests directly.

The objection posed by the people concerns the veracity of YHWH's initial claim, i.e., that God has chosen Jacob. The interrogative בַּמָּה (preposition + inanimate pronoun) can be rendered literally "in what (way)," but this should not be understood as a sincere request for information.[12] In fact, rhetorically the question operates in just the reverse, revealing the cynicism and doubt that plagued the people. Is it possible to identify the source of this cynicism and doubt? Although some might assume Judah's defeat at the hands of Babylonians, and the subsequent exile, would be the causal agent for such cynicism, such a cause seems unlikely given that some sixty to seventy years had passed since the return from Babylon. The context appears more immediate. The failure of the promises in Isa 40–55 to materialize and the firm grip of the Persians on Yehud coupled with the droughts and agricultural failures that plagued the community (e.g., Hag 1:10–11; Mal 3:10–11) likely contributed to a sense of cynicism that bordered on practical atheism (see Canonical and Theological Significance). All of these developments, and more besides, led the community to call into question God's faithfulness. As noted above, the verb אהב carries significant covenantal overtones, thus the initial objection posed by the people concerns whether God has actually remained faithful to his covenantal commitment with Israel.

C. Esau as Evidence of YHWH's Faithfulness (1:2e–5)

The remainder of the disputation provides a rebuttal to the challenge raised by the community. In response to their claim, YHWH offers three arguments that should result in a renewed confession by the community.

1. Recollection of Ancient Past as Evidence (1:2e–3a)

YHWH's response to the objection of the people includes a rhetorical question (v. 2d), followed by a claim (vv. 2g–3a); this claim is then substantiated by the evidence cited in verse 3b–c (i.e., the destruction of Edom). The rhetorical question begins with the combination of the interrogative *he* plus a particle of negation (הֲלוֹא). Typically, this construction functions as a double negative meant to yield an answer in the affirmative.[13] Most English translations render the question, "Was not [is not] Esau Jacob's brother?" (e.g., NIV, NRSV, NASB, ESV), with the presumed response, "yes." Beyond the rhetorical nature of the clause, as suggested by the interrogative, the word order itself

11. Kessler, *Maleachi*, 105.

12. Note here and in 2:17 בַּמָּה appears while in 1:6, 7; 3:7, 8 the final vowel is a *segol*. The presence of the aleph in the opening consonant in the subsequent word (cf. GKC §102.k) explains the use of the former form in 1:2.

13. *IBHS* §40.3b. הֲלוֹא occurs in one other verse in Malachi (2:10[2x]), but the rhetorical question posed there is not in response to an objection by the people/priests, as here, but instead functions as the initial statement in that unit posed by the prophet. In both instances, an affirmative answer is anticipated.

proves suggestive. The clause is a verbless clause (null copula clause). The basic constituent order for such clauses is subject—[null verb]—complement, but in some instances, as here, the nominal complement has been fronted for pragmatic reasons. The Hebrew reads הֲלוֹא־אָח עֵשָׂו לְיַעֲקֹב, literally, "Is not a brother Esau of Jacob?" with the noun אָח ("brother") fronted. The word order in traditional English translations places an emphasis on Esau (as the brother of Jacob), but in the Hebrew text, the emphasis falls on the noun אָח. YHWH's argument for his choice of Israel unfolds within the context of kinship—one family, two brothers—and yet YHWH's covenantal commitment remains focused on only one.[14]

Although the names of Jacob and Esau did function as ciphers for Israel and Edom respectively, interpreters should resist the temptation to move immediately to national symbolism. Given that the name "Esau" is used so sparingly in the Book of the Twelve (Obad 6, 8, 9, 18, 19, 21), the mere mention of his name alongside that of the eponymous ancestor of Israel likely has implications for the larger purposes of Malachi. These two are but one of several "brother pairs" that occur with great regularity in the book of Genesis (Cain and Abel, Ishmael and Isaac, Jacob and Esau, Joseph and the brothers).[15] The Jacob-Esau narrative appears in Gen 25–36 with the striking motif of the younger being the recipient of God's covenantal blessing, a theme repeated throughout the "brother pair" texts.

In response to the rhetorical question, YHWH makes a claim: he has chosen Jacob but not chosen Esau. Some have attempted to justify the selection of Jacob at the expense of Esau based on Esau's disregard for his birthright later in life and his marriage to foreign women, but such a rationale offers little explanatory power.[16] Before they were born, YHWH revealed to Rebekah that the older child would serve the younger (Gen 25:23), but no explanation for that decision is offered (cf. Rom 9:11). Malachi 1:2 simply affirms that YHWH chose, אהב, Jacob for a covenant relationship, but did not choose, שׂנא, Esau for the same.[17] The polemical—and rather stark—language of loving and hating found in most translations has prompted a number of attempts to justify, or perhaps soften, the rhetoric of the claim. For example, the language of love and hate does appear in other familial contexts in the Old Testament and is even present in the Jacob narrative. Genesis 29, for example, reports that Jacob had two wives and twice Leah is referred to as "hated," שׂנא (vv. 31, 33), and just prior to those verses, the narrator reports that Jacob "loved Rachel *more than* Leah" (Gen 29:30). Yet to apply this understanding to the text in Malachi suggests that love and hate operate on a

14. נְאֻם יְהוָה ("utterance of YHWH") appears immediately following the rhetorical question. BHS suggests omitting the clause because it disrupts the meter of the line, but of course, that decision presupposes Malachi is poetry, a claim challenged in the Introduction. Moreover, the LXX retains the language, albeit altering it to read λέγει κύριος, "says the Lord," presumably to match the subsequent messenger formula ("thus says YHWH Sabaoth") in v. 4d. Clendenen ("Malachi," 226) and Snyman (*Prophecy and Teaching*, 99–101) suggest that the primary purpose of נְאֻם יְהוָה is to confirm the source of the statement, but Weyde (*Prophecy and Teaching*, 99–101) considers the placement of this formula in light of the subject matter of the first disputation. Following the initial rhetorical question, נְאֻם יְהוָה marks the beginning of the judgment against Edom.

15. Johanna Erzberger, "Brüderpaare," in *Esau: Bruder und Feind*, ed. Gerhard Langer (Göttingen: Vandenhoeck & Ruprecht, 2009), 115–21.

16. D. J. Elazar, "Jacob and Esau and the Emergence of the Jewish People," *Judaism* 43 (1994): 294–301.

17. For a similar rendering of אהב and שׂנא, see Daniel I. Block, *Ruth*, ZECOT (Grand Rapids: Zondervan Academic, 2015), 108–9, 237–38.

continuum, i.e., God loves Israel *more than* God loves Edom. Such a reading may seem more palatable to the modern reader, but it does not appear to align with the larger argument in the disputation. Because the terms "love" and "hate" are emotionally charged terms in English, the two terms might be better rendered as "chosen" and "not chosen." God chose Jacob as his covenant people; God did not choose Esau. That said, a cautionary word is in order: Calvin's understanding of the predestining of the elect and the damned is foreign to this text (and to Gen 25–36), and should be jettisoned, as other interpreters have rightly noted.[18]

2. Recollection of Recent Past as Evidence (1:3b–c)

The initial claim invoked the name of the two eponymous figures as evidence of YHWH's faithfulness. In this section, the argument shifts from the individual to the nation (i.e., Israel and Edom) and from ancient stories to more recent events. The evidence supplied in these verses is intended to confirm that YHWH's decision to "hate, i.e., "not choose," Esau/Edom remains clearly on display.

Nogalski argues that Mal 1:2–5, and in particular, the references to Edom, appear to draw heavily from the book of Obadiah.[19] Examples of this dependence are many, including the mountains of Esau, which are mentioned only in Obad 8, 18 and Mal 1:3. Other examples include Edom's self-delusion regarding its own strength in both books (Obad 3; Mal 1:4). Further still, in Obadiah, Edom will be cut off forever (לְעוֹלָם) whereas in Malachi, God's anger against them will be "for forever," עַד־עוֹלָם. References to the territory (גְּבוּל) of each also appear to link the two texts together (Obad 7; Mal 1:4). Weyde, and more recently Gibson, however, have suggested that the writer of Malachi may actually have been drawing from a wider array of prophetic texts in which a judgment against Edom is issued.[20] For example, in Mal 1:3b, YHWH promises to make Edom a desolation (שְׁמָמָה), a term that recalls Ezek 35 where the term appears repeatedly in reference to the future of Edom, and in 35:9, Edom is said to become a "perpetual (עוֹלָם) desolation." Joel 4:19[3:19] announces that Edom will become a "desert wasteland" (מִדְבַּר שְׁמָמָה), terms also employed for Edom in Mal 1:3. In Isa 34:6, Edom is depicted as becoming a haunt for jackals, paralleling the language in Mal 1:3.[21] In these earlier prophetic texts, the fate of Edom remained in the future, an impending judgement awaiting fulfillment. In Mal 1:3, however, the presence of the *wayyiqtol* (וָאָשִׂים) signals that the anticipated events mentioned by earlier prophets have come to pass. Identification of the precise event or events that seem in view in Mal 1:3 remains elusive. Scholars have traditionally associated the downfall

18. Kessler, *Maleachi*, 113–15, Hill, *Malachi*, 164–65; Verhoef, *The Books of Haggai and Malachi*, 201–2.

19. Nogalski, *Redactional Processes in the Book of the Twelve*, 191–93.

20. Weyde, *Prophecy and Teaching*, 85–87; Jonathan Gibson, *Covenant Continuity and Fidelity*, 45–74.

21. The word תַנּוֹת, "jackal," is problematic because it appears here as a feminine plural, but elsewhere always in the masculine. The LXX reads εἰς δόματα ἐρήμου, "to desert dwellings." *BHS* suggests an alternate reading, נְוֹת, meaning "dwellings," "abodes" or even "pasturage." Although the MT does prove irregular, it is not nonsensical and should be retained. Likely, "jackals" functions as a noun that can be plural in both genders. For recent commentators who argued for maintaining the MT, see Snyman, *Malachi*, 38; Jacobs, *The Books of Haggai and Malachi*, 156; Hill, *Malachi*, 155; Verhoef, *The Books of Haggai and Malachi*, 203, among others. Jackals are mentioned fourteen times in the Old Testament, typically as part of a curse, perhaps further justification for maintaining the MT (Gibson, *Covenant Continuity and Fidelity*, 54).

of Edom with the Arabian campaign of Nabonidus in 552 BCE, perhaps followed by some form of Nabatean incursion.[22] McCarter notes that while the precise date for the demise of the Edomites is difficult to determine, "archaeological evidence, still regrettably meager, shows that the last part of the [sixth] century to have been a period of general collapse in Edomite culture."[23] To be sure, Edom was not "emptied out" following the campaign of Nabonidus based on the archaeological evidence in Buseirah and Tel el-Kheleifah; finds there suggest that modest occupation continued in those areas.[24] The rebuilding that apparently took place in that region may be what prompted the subsequent question in verse 4.

For the book of Malachi, the events associated with the devastation of Edom are understood through the lens of prior prophecy, and thus provide evidence for YHWH's earlier claim in Mal 1:3, i.e., "Esau, I have not chosen." Further still, the subtle allusions to earlier prophecy and its apparent fulfillment were also likely meant to highlight YHWH's faithfulness to his commitments, a fact that should not be lost upon Israel, a people that he has chosen (אהב).

3. Irreal Event as Evidence (1:4a–f)

Beginning in verse 4, the argument as it pertains to Edom shifts from the real to the irreal. To suggest that a statement is irreal is to suggest that although something is not real yet, or not known to exist, it remains possible based on circumstances. As suggested above, the *wayyiqtol* form in v. 3b narrates an event in the past. Following this recollection of Edom's demise, YHWH places a potential statement on the lips of Edom.[25] The particle כִּי begins the sentence and marks the *irreal* or conditional nature of the claim: "*If* Edom should say, 'We are shattered so let us rebuild the ruins.'"[26] Both Jacobs and Hill understand the particle כִּי ("if") as introducing the protasis of this conditional statement with כֹּה ("thus") introducing the apodosis. However, this does not appear to accurately reflect the structure of the text.[27] כֹּה normally either introduces a messenger formula (e.g., כֹּה אָמַר יְהוָה צְבָאוֹת) or it stands at the head of the clause, often functioning as a complement to the verb.[28] Rather than understanding כֹּה as a marker of the apodosis, the term is better understood simply as part of the messenger formula itself. The actual apodosis, then, appears after the messenger formula, absent any formal marker.

Protasis:	If Edom should say, "We are shattered, so let us rebuild the ruins,"
Messenger formula:	thus says YHWH Sabaoth,
Apodosis:	[then] they may build but I will destroy.

22. Cf. John R. Bartlett, *Edom and the Edomites*, JSOTSup 77 (Sheffield: JSOT, 1989), and John R. Bartlett, "Edom (Place) (Edom in History)," *ABD* 2:287–95. On the role the Nabateans may have played in the resettlement of Edom, see Jacob M. Myers, "Edom and Judah in the Sixth-Fifth Centuries," in *Near Eastern Studies in Honor of William Foxwell Albright*, ed. Hans Goedicke (Baltimore: Johns Hopkins University Press, 1971), 377–92. On the history of Edom and the surrounding region, more generally, see Joel S. Burnett, "Transjordan: The Ammonites, Moabites and Edomites," in *The World Around the Old Testament: The People and Places of the Ancient Near East*, ed. Bill T. Arnold and Brent A. Strawn (Grand Rapids: Baker Academic, 2016), 309–52.

23. "Obadiah 7 and the Fall of Edom," *BASOR* 221 (1976): 89.

24. Glazier-McDonald, *Malachi*, 37–41.

25. On the use of כִּי to introduce an *irreal* supposition, see JM §167i.

26. Some interpreters and translations (e.g., NIV, NET) understand the particle כִּי to introduce a concessive clause, i.e., "even though . . ." See Glazier-McDonald, *Malachi*, 31; Gibson, *Covenant Continuity and Fidelity*, 45.

27. Jacobs, *The Books of Haggai and Malachi*, 166; Hill, *Malachi*, 156.

28. Cf. Ruth 1:17, "May YHWH do thus to me" (כֹּה יַעֲשֶׂה יְהוָה לִי). The NIV understands the messenger formula of Mal 1:4 as the start of a new paragraph, but in doing so, the linguistic connections, including chiasm, with v. 4a are obscured.

Although the entire "if . . . then" clause is spoken by YHWH, the placement of כֹּה אָמַר יְהוָה צְבָאוֹת does not come until midpoint in the conditional claim. Typically, the messenger formula precedes the oracle, as in Hag 1:2, but here the formula appears embedded within the larger clausal structure, similar to the use of נְאֻם יְהוָה earlier in this pericope. Its movement mid-sentence differentiates and juxtaposes the speech of Edom from that of YHWH and further still, creates the type of A/B/B′/A′ pattern that dominates this first pericope.

Edom: A We are shattered,
B so let us rebuild the ruins;
YHWH: B′ they may build
A′ but I will destroy.

In 2:2, a similar, albeit slightly more complex, structure appears. There a conditional sentence with the messenger formula separates the protasis from the apodosis as well.

The structure of YHWH's response in v. 4e reveals the continued use of contrast: הֵמָּה יִבְנוּ וַאֲנִי אֶהֱרוֹס ("they may build, but I will destroy"). Because a subject pronoun is not necessary with a finite verb, its use marks pragmatic information. The personal pronoun "they," (הֵמָּה) is topic-fronted in the first half of YHWH's response, even as "I" (אֲנִי) is topic-fronted in the second, with the intent of juxtaposing the actions of each, i.e., "*they* may build, but *I* will destroy." Verse 4e extinguishes any thought that perhaps the earlier demise of Edom would be short-lived, and by extension, so too the covenant promises of YHWH with Israel. More importantly, YHWH's actions against Edom, now and in the future, signal that the nation is now explicitly cursed.[29] Although this may sound odd to the modern ear, such an affirmation was intended as a response to Israel's initial question, "In what way have you chosen us?" Even as Edom's demise is a sign that God has not chosen them, so too Israel's continued existence confirms YHWH's continued covenantal faithfulness with Israel.

As part of the futility curse, YHWH announces Edom's new identity; they will be called a "a wicked territory" and "the people with whom YHWH is angry (זעם) forever." Their wickedness refers to the actions against Jerusalem and those in Yehud during the exile (cf. Obadiah). The verb זעם, meaning "to curse, anger, or scold," appears repeatedly in the Old Testament, and while it can be directed against the nations (e.g., Isa 26:20: 66:14), the term is used primarily in reference to Israel. Of the thirty-four appearances of the root (including both the verb and noun forms) in the Old Testament, four times the term appears in conjunction with a temporal marker of some sort (Isa 10:25; 26:20; Zech 1:12; Mal 1:4). The first three texts refer to Israel and suggest that the curse will come to an end for God's people, but in Mal 1:4, the language of curse is applied to Edom with the temporal marker עַד־עוֹלָם, "forever." Thus, in response to the initial question by those in Yehud, "In what way have you chosen us?," YHWH explains that a nation "not chosen" (e.g., Edom) will remain under a curse forever, while also implicitly suggesting that Yehud remains in existence bcause they have indeed been chosen by YHWH.

4. Resulting Confession of Israel (1:5a–c)

Verse 4 focused on the Edomites, including their new identity as a territory of wickedness and a cursed people. Beginning in verse 5, however, attention returns to those in Yehud. The fronting

29. Petersen, *Zechariah 9–14 and Malachi*, 172.

of וְעֵינֵיכֶם ("[and] your eyes") and וְאַתֶּם ("and you") signals the shift in subject matter, differentiating the fate of those in Yehud from those referenced earlier in Edom.[30]

Those who have witnessed the demise of Edom will declare "Great is YHWH beyond the borders of Israel." To declare YHWH "great" however is to do far more than make a subjective assessment about the nature of God (i.e., remarkable, noteworthy). In the ancient Near East, the label "great" was applied to deities in combination with their role as divine kings. Examples of this abound in ancient texts, stela, and iconography. In ancient Mesopotamia, for example, the prologue to the Lipit-Ishtar law code begins "Anu, the great, the father of the gods."[31] In Egypt, the god Resheph is declared to be "the great god, lord forever, ruler of eternity and lifetime" on a stela found at Deir el-Medina.[32] And the Cyrus Cylinder, so named for the Persian king, refers to Marduk explicitly as the "king of the gods" and "the great lord."[33] A similar connection between the label "great" and divine kingship as it was applied to YHWH also appears in the Psalter (e.g., 95:3).

The association of the phrase "Great is YHWH" with kingship informs the latter half of this verse, and in particular, the debated meaning of the particle מֵעַל. Verhoef and Hill, among others, render the particle as "above" or "over."[34] Understood as such, those in Yehud are confessing YHWH as the one who stands over Israel as its protective suzerain, as its protective covenant partner. In addition to acknowledging the covenant relationship, the particle, in some sense, creates a spatial metaphor (i.e., YHWH stands protectively *over* Israel). Verhoef contends that "the greatness of YHWH is not so much seen in his judgment of Edom, but rather in the manifestation of his love for Israel."[35] Yet Verhoef's understanding fails to appreciate the (universal) royal claims inherent in the confession that YHWH is king, and moreover, his interpretation seems to ignore the fact that the bulk of the first pericope indeed has Edom as its focus. It is YHWH's dealings *with* Edom that functions as an object lesson *to* Yehud concerning YHWH's faithfulness.

Rather than rendering the preposition מֵעַל as "over," other scholars have understood the particle to have a comparative sense, "more than," and hence have rendered the particle as "beyond," i.e., "YHWH is great beyond the borders of Israel."[36] This rendering fits better contextually in the first pericope. That is, because YHWH's rule extends beyond the borders of Israel, the Divine King can govern the affairs of Edom while also ensuring the viability of Yehud. Moreover, the claim that YHWH

30. Weyde rightly notes that the phrase וְעֵינֵיכֶם תִּרְאֶינָה, "but your eyes shall see," is likely a modified recognition formula, a formula used elsewhere to refer to the reaction of an individual or group to YHWH's acts in history (*Prophecy and Teaching*, 105). Although the recognition formula typically employs the verb יָדַע, "to know," there are instances in which the verb רָאָה, "to see," appears, most notably in Ezek 35, a text that references Edom (cf. Ezek 21:4; 39:21).

31. *ANET*, 159.

32. Maciej M. Münnich, *The God Resheph in the Ancient Near East*, Orientalische Religionen in der Antike 11 (Tübingen: Mohr Siebeck, 2013), 83–84.

33. Amélie Kuhrt, "The Cyrus Cylinder," in *The Persian Period: A Corpus of Sources from the Achaemenid Period*, ed. Amélie Kuhrt (London: Routledge, 2007), 71.

34. Verhoef, *The Books of Haggai and Malachi*, 206; Hill, *Malachi*, 161,

35. Verhoef, *The Books of Haggai and Malachi*, 206.

36. Weyde, *Prophecy and Teaching*, 107; Smith, *Micah–Malachi*, 306; Glazier-McDonald, *Malachi*, 31; Petersen, *Zechariah 9–14 and Malachi*, 167.

is "great beyond the borders of Israel" also informs the affirmation made in the second disputation (1:11–14). And finally, beyond the book of Malachi itself, this claim concerning YHWH's universal rule accords well with the other post-exilic references to YHWH as the Divine King.[37]

Canonical and Theological Significance

Unmet Expectations and Divine Faithfulness

The utter devastation associated with the Babylonian exile was countered by the wondrous oracles of salvation delivered in Isa 40–55. Beyond simply announcing a return from exile (Isa 40), the prophet announced a restoration of Jerusalem and the temple using metaphorically rich imagery. In 54:11–13, the prophet declared

> Afflicted city, lashed by storms and not comforted,
> I will rebuild you with stones of turquoise,
> your foundations with lapis lazuli.
> I will make your battlements of rubies,
> your gates of sparkling jewels,
> and your walls of precious stones.
> All your children will be taught by [YHWH],
> and great will be their peace. (NIV)

The community in exile began its return from Babylon in 538 BCE under the rule of Cyrus, yet upon arriving in Jerusalem, there were no stones of turquoise to be found, no foundations of lapis lazuli. They returned to the same scene that some of them had left some fifty years before. And for some time, life in the small community called Yehud remained unchanged. The visions mentioned in Isaiah likely threatened to become nothing more than a memory, while the more pressing realities of drought, famine, and external threats began to dominate their existence.

Although Cyrus had permitted the rebuilding of regional temples, the Jerusalem temple remained in ruins (Hag 1:2–4). In 522 BCE, a new king rose up over Persia, King Darius I, who ruled 522–486 BCE, and as part of his imperial strategy, he ordered the completion of the temple (Ezra 6:6–12).[38] Given these imperial demands,

37. Konrad Schmid, "Himmelsgott, Weltgott, und Schöpfer: 'Gott' und der 'Himmel' in der Literatur der Zeit des Zweiten Tempels," in *Der Himmel*, ed. Martin Ebner and Irmtraud Fischer, *JBT* 20 (Neukirchen-Vluyn: Neukirchener, 2005), 111–48; W. Dennis Tucker Jr., "The God of Heaven and the Theology of Zion in Book 5 of the Psalter" in *The Psalter as Witness: Poetry, Theology and Genre. The Baylor University-University of Bonn Symposium on the Book of Psalms*, ed. W. Dennis Tucker Jr. and W. H. Bellinger (Waco, TX: Baylor University, 2017), 87–99.

38. Following Cyrus, his son Cambyses ruled 529–522 BCE, with his chief contribution being his Egyptian Campaign and the southern expansion of the Persian empire. For an overview,

at least in part, Haggai and Zechariah called for the rebuilding of the temple in 520 BCE. The people responded with unusual compliance and haste to the prophetic word. In addition to the call for a restored temple, Haggai delivered an oracle from YHWH Sabaoth to Zerubbabel declaring:

> "I am about to shake the heavens and the earth, and to overthrow the throne of kingdoms; I am about to destroy the strength of the kingdoms of the nations and overthrow the chariots and their riders; and the horses and their riders shall fall, everyone by the sword of a comrade. On that day," says YHWH of hosts, "I will take you O Zerubbabel my servant, son of Shealtiel," says YHWH, "and make you a signet ring." (2:21–23, author's translation)

Just as the oracles from Isa 40–55 did not fully materialize as expected, the oracles in Haggai and Zechariah also seemed to have languished. The disappointment and anguish of an unrealized future caused the people of Judah to consider the unthinkable: Was God still faithful to his people? In the eyes of those in Yehud, the circumstances of the day yielded little assurance of God's active intervention in the lives of his community, much less faithfulness to his covenantal commitments. The objection posed by the community in Mal 1:2 reflects the durative nature of this existential and theological crisis. Despite YHWH's claim to have chosen Israel, the community counters "In what way have you chosen us?" Both YHWH's claims and the community's objection signal that this opening disputation is thoroughly *theo*logical; it is about God. Here, and in the remainder of the book, readers are left to explore the identity and faithfulness of YHWH.

Mason has suggested that Mal 1:2–5 was intended as "nationalistic assurance of God's electing love" of Israel over that of Edom.[39] Such an assessment seems somewhat jaded and certainly too provincial. Hill has provided a necessary corrective to Mason's earlier claim, suggesting that the issue is not that of nationalism at all. To the contrary, those in Yehud needed "a remedy for doubt and despair that was not contingent upon the state of Israel's current or future sociopolitical circumstances."[40] What the community needed to know was that God still says "yes" to his people even when circumstances challenged such thinking, even when expectations did not unfurl as anticipated. To their questions about this God and this God's faithfulness, YHWH simply declares, "I have chosen Jacob."

see Briant, *From Cyrus to Alexander*, 49–61. For a brief sketch of Achaemenid history and its implications for the community in Yehud, see Kenneth G. Hoglund, *Achaemenid Imperial Administration in Syria-Palestine and the Missions of Ezra and Nehemiah* (Atlanta: Scholars Press, 1992), 1–36.

39. Rex Mason, *Preaching the Tradition: Homily and Hermeneutics after the Exile* (Cambridge: Cambridge University Press, 1990), 239.

40. Hill, *Malachi*, 164.

Edom's Destruction and Israel's Restoration

Although the opening line of the first disputation refers to YHWH's love of Israel, the figure of Esau/Edom plays a central role in this pericope, with particular focus on that nation's downfall (vv. 3–4). This apparent focus on Edom in the opening disputation may lead some readers to think that the pericope reflects a form of *Schadenfreude*, a German word that means "pleasure or joy derived from the misfortune of others." To adopt such an interpretation, however, would be a misguided reading of the text altogether. Israel's disdain for Edom, particularly as expressed in exilic and post-exilic prophecy, is rooted in events associated with the Babylonian destruction of Jerusalem.[41] Edom's failure to demonstrate kinship loyalty is articulated most clearly in Obadiah:

> Because of the violence against your brother Jacob,
> you will be covered with shame;
> you will be destroyed forever.
> On the day you stood aloof
> while strangers carried off his wealth
> and foreigners entered his gates
> and cast lost for Jerusalem,
> you were like one of them.
> You should not gloat over your brother
> in the day of his misfortune,
> nor rejoice over the people of Judah
> in the day of their destruction,
> nor boast so much
> in the day of their trouble. (vv. 10–12 NIV)[42]

Following the condemnation of Edom, the book of Obadiah concludes with the promise that Zion will be restored (vv.19–21). The twin themes of condemnation and restoration are rhetorically significant in that book. The structure of Obadiah implies that the downfall of Edom is understood as a precursor to the reestablishment

41. Prior to the destruction of the temple and the environs in 586 BCE, the relationship between Judah and Edom generally mirrored the relations Judah had with surrounding people groups. See Jacob M. Myers, "Edom and Judah in the Sixth-Fifth Centuries B.C.," 377. See more recently, Elie Assis, "Why Edom? On the Hostility Towards Jacob's Brother in Prophetic Sources," *VT* 56 (2006): 1–20. Although Assis follows Myers and others in their assessment of the pre-exilic relationship between Judah and Edom, Assis contends that the source of the hostility extended well beyond the Edomite participation in the destruction of the temple and was based primarily upon the Edomite incursions into southern Judah (44).

42. On the book of Obadiah, more generally, see Daniel I. Block, *Obadiah*, 2nd ed., ZECOT (Grand Rapids: Zondervan, 2017).

of Zion (vv. 19–21). In other prophetic literature (Isa 34–35; 63:1–6; Ezek 35–36), a similar pattern appears. The other prophets castigate Edom, declaring that her treachery will lead to her destruction. And like Obadiah, the oracles of judgment against Edom in these texts are coupled with promises of Israel's restoration. The argument in these prophetic texts moves from Edom's treachery to Edom's destruction, culminating in Israel's restoration. When read through the lens of the earlier prophetic texts, Malachi may have understood the fall of Edom as a sign that pointed to the coming restoration of Zion.[43]

Although Malachi draws language and imagery from other prophetic texts associated with the Edom tradition, the book of Malachi deviates in one significant way. In the opening disputation there is no mention of Edom's treachery, only her downfall. The sin of Edom is not the focus; it is the faithfulness of YHWH. There is no explanation provided for Edom's destruction other than YHWH's declaration that he has not chosen her (v. 3a). Like Edom, Israel was assailed by the Babylonian forces, but unlike Edom, Israel endured. The fall of Edom at the hands of Nabonidus is meant to stand in stark contrast to Israel's continued survival into the post-exilic period. How could this be? Malachi asserts that Israel's resilience is not attributable to her own power but to that of YHWH's faithfulness alone.

43. Hill, *Malachi*, 168; Verhoef, *The Book of Haggai and Malachi*, 202.

CHAPTER 3

Malachi 1:6–2:9

III. Dishonoring the Divine King

Main Idea of the Passage

The primary focus of this disputation speech is the honor and reverence due YHWH, but absent nonetheless in the cultic community in Yehud.

Literary Context

The opening disputation speech was a response to the people's allegation that YHWH had failed in his covenant faithfulness (v. 2d). To rebut this claim, the prophet provided ample evidence of YHWH's covenantal commitments. The second disputation shifts attention away from the certainty of YHWH's faithfulness and instead gives considerable attention to the priests' *lack* of faithfulness. Thus, the first two speeches juxtapose a faithful God with an unfaithful people. At the root of this unfaithfulness, however, is a distorted understanding of YHWH. If, as the community asserts in the first disputation, YHWH is no longer committed to his covenant people, then there is little reason to honor this god. The failures, both in practice (i.e., sacrifice) and instruction, reflect the eschewing of any sense of the fear of God.

Translation and Exegetical Outline

(See pages 51–54.)

Structure and Literary Form

As noted in the introduction, since Pfeiffer, scholarship has suggested that the book of Malachi is comprised of six disputation speeches.[1] The first speech (1:2–5)

1. In his treatment of Malachi, Verhoef breaks with Pfeiffer and divides this pericope into two separate units, thus raising the number of speeches to seven (*The Books of Haggai and Malachi*, 162). Michael Floyd (*Minor Prophets: Part 2*, 567–69) jettisons the divisions proposed by Pfeiffer altogether and suggests that following the introduction to the book (1:2–5), the book can be divided into two sections (1:6–2:16; 2:17–3:24[4:6]). Floyd suggests that, while 1:6–14 and 2:1–9 are "closely related," they focus on "somewhat different concerns" and deserve separate treatments.

Malachi 1:6–2:9

	Hebrew	English	Outline
			III. Dishonoring the Divine King (1:6–2:9)
			A. The Priests' Dishonoring of YHWH through Sacrifice (1:6a–10e)
6a	בֵּן יְכַבֵּד אָב	"'A son honors a father;	1. An Aphorism and an Accusation (1:6a–i)
6b	וְעֶבֶד אֲדֹנָיו	and a servant [honors] his master.'	
6c	↓ וְאִם־אָב אָנִי	↓ If I am a father,	
6d	אַיֵּה כְבוֹדִי	then where is the honor due me?	
6f	↓ וְאִם־אֲדוֹנִים אָנִי	↓ And if am a master,	
6g	אַיֵּה מוֹרָאִי	then where is the fear due me?"	
6h	אָמַר יְהוָה צְבָאוֹת לָכֶם הַכֹּהֲנִים	says YHWH Sabaoth to you, O priests	
6i	↑ בּוֹזֵי שְׁמִי	↑ who despise my name.	
6j	וַאֲמַרְתֶּם	"But you say,	2. Despising and Defiling YHWH (1:6j–8e)
6k	בַּמֶּה בָזִינוּ אֶת־שְׁמֶךָ	'How have we despised your name?'	
7a	מַגִּישִׁים עַל־מִזְבְּחִי לֶחֶם מְגֹאָל	By presenting defiled food upon my altar.	
7b	וַאֲמַרְתֶּם	But you say,	
7c	בַּמֶּה גֵאַלְנוּךָ	'How have we defiled you?'	
7d	בֶּאֱמָרְכֶם	When you say,	
7e	שֻׁלְחַן יְהוָה נִבְזֶה הוּא	'The table of YHWH, it is despised.'	
8a	וְכִי־תַגִּשׁוּן עִוֵּר	And when you present blind [animals]	
8b	↑ לִזְבֹּחַ	↑ in order to sacrifice,	
8c	אֵין רָע	[you say] 'There is no defect.'	
8d	וְכִי תַגִּישׁוּ פִּסֵּחַ וְחֹלֶה	And when you present lame and sick [animals],	
8e	אֵין רָע	[you say] 'There is no defect.'	
8f	הַקְרִיבֵהוּ נָא לְפֶחָתֶךָ	Offer that to your governor.	3. A Challenge to the Priests (1:8f–9e)
8g	הֲיִרְצְךָ	Will he accept you	
8h	אוֹ הֲיִשָּׂא פָנֶיךָ	or regard you?"	
8i	אָמַר יְהוָה צְבָאוֹת	says YHWH Sabaoth.	

Continued on next page.

Continued from previous page.

9a	וְעַתָּה חַלּוּ־נָא פְנֵי־אֵל	"So now, entreat the face of God	3. A Challenge to the Priests (1:8f–9e), *cont.*
9b	↑וִיחָנֵנוּ	↑so that he may be gracious to us.	
9c	מִיֶּדְכֶם הָיְתָה זֹּאת	This is from your hand.	
9d	הֲיִשָּׂא מִכֶּם פָּנִים	Will he regard you?"	
9e	אָמַר יְהוָה צְבָאוֹת	says YHWH Sabaoth.	
10a	מִי גַם־בָּכֶם וְיִסְגֹּר דְּלָתַיִם	"Who among you would shut the doors	4. A Declaration of Judgment (1:10a–e)
10b	↑וְלֹא־תָאִירוּ מִזְבְּחִי חִנָּם	↑and not light my altar in vain?	
10c	אֵין־לִי חֵפֶץ בָּכֶם	I take no delight in you,"	
10d	אָמַר יְהוָה צְבָאוֹת	says YHWH Sabaoth,	
10e	וּמִנְחָה לֹא־אֶרְצֶה מִיֶּדְכֶם	"and I will not accept offerings from your hands.	
			B. The Greatness of YHWH's Name (1:11a–14g)
11a	↓כִּי מִמִּזְרַח־שֶׁמֶשׁ וְעַד־מְבוֹאוֹ	↓From the rising of the sun until its setting,	1. A Statement Concerning the Name of YHWH (1:11 a–e)
11b	גָּדוֹל שְׁמִי בַּגּוֹיִם	great is my name among the nations.	
11c	וּבְכָל־מָקוֹם מֻקְטָר מֻגָּשׁ לִשְׁמִי וּמִנְחָה טְהוֹרָה	In every place, incense is being offered up to my name—a pure offering.	
11d	כִּי־גָדוֹל שְׁמִי בַּגּוֹיִם	Indeed, great is my name among the nations,"	
11e	אָמַר יְהוָה צְבָאוֹת	says YHWH Sabaoth.	
12a	וְאַתֶּם מְחַלְּלִים אוֹתוֹ בֶּאֱמָרְכֶם	"And you are polluting it when you say,	2. The Reiteration of Cultic Malpractice (1:12a–14d)
12b	שֻׁלְחַן אֲדֹנָי מְגֹאָל הוּא	'The table of the Lord, it is treated as defiled.	
12c	וְנִיבוֹ נִבְזֶה אָכְלוֹ	And its fruit—its food—is despised.'	
13a	וַאֲמַרְתֶּם	And you say,	
13b	הִנֵּה מַתְּלָאָה	'Behold what a hardship!'	
13c	וְהִפַּחְתֶּם אוֹתוֹ	Yet you ignite it,"	
13d	אָמַר יְהוָה צְבָאוֹת	says YHWH Sabaoth.	
13e	וַהֲבֵאתֶם גָּזוּל וְאֶת־הַפִּסֵּחַ וְאֶת־הַחוֹלֶה	"And you bring the stolen, the lame and the sick	
13f	וַהֲבֵאתֶם אֶת־הַמִּנְחָה	And you bring them as an offering.	
13g	הַאֶרְצֶה אוֹתָהּ מִיֶּדְכֶם	Shall I accept it from your hand?"	
13h	אָמַר יְהוָה	says YHWH.	
14a	וְאָרוּר נוֹכֵל	"Cursed is the deceiver	
14b	↑וְיֵשׁ בְּעֶדְרוֹ זָכָר	↑and there is a male in his flock.	
14c	וְנֹדֵר	He vows	
14d	↑וְזֹבֵחַ מָשְׁחָת לַאדֹנָי	↑yet sacrifices a blemished animal to the Lord.	

Verse	Hebrew	English	Outline
14e	כִּי מֶלֶךְ גָּדוֹל אָנִי	For I am the Great King,"	3. The Response of YHWH (1:14e–g)
14f	אָמַר יְהוָה צְבָאוֹת	says YHWH Sabaoth,	
14g	וּשְׁמִי נוֹרָא בַגּוֹיִם	"And my name is feared among the nations."	
			C. Priestly Instruction That Dishonors YHWH (2:1–9c)
2:1	וְעַתָּה אֲלֵיכֶם הַמִּצְוָה הַזֹּאת הַכֹּהֲנִים	"And now to you, O priests, this commandment:	1. The Challenge to the Priests (2:1–4d)
2a	אִם־לֹא תִשְׁמְעוּ	If you do not listen	
2b	וְאִם־לֹא תָשִׂימוּ עַל־לֵב	and take [it] to heart	
2c	↑ לָתֵת כָּבוֹד לִשְׁמִי	↑ to give honor to my name,"	
2d	אָמַר יְהוָה צְבָאוֹת ↓	says YHWH Sabaoth, ↓	
2e	וְשִׁלַּחְתִּי בָכֶם אֶת־הַמְּאֵרָה	"then I will send on you the curse.	
2f	וְאָרוֹתִי אֶת־בִּרְכוֹתֵיכֶם	and I will curse your blessings.	
2g	וְגַם אָרוֹתִיהָ	Indeed, I have already cursed it	
2h	↑ כִּי אֵינְכֶם שָׂמִים עַל־לֵב	↑ because you did not take it to heart.	
3a	הִנְנִי גֹעֵר לָכֶם אֶת־הַזֶּרַע	Behold, I am about to rebuke your offspring,	
3b	וְזֵרִיתִי פֶרֶשׁ עַל־פְּנֵיכֶם פֶּרֶשׁ חַגֵּיכֶם	and I will spread dung on your faces, the dung of your festivals,	
3c	וְנָשָׂא אֶתְכֶם אֵלָיו	and someone will carry you to it.	
4a	וִידַעְתֶּם	And then you will know	
4b	↑ כִּי שִׁלַּחְתִּי אֲלֵיכֶם אֵת הַמִּצְוָה הַזֹּאת	↑ that I sent this commandment to you	
4c	↑ לִהְיוֹת בְּרִיתִי אֶת־לֵוִי	↑ so that my covenant with Levi will continue,"	
4d	אָמַר יְהוָה צְבָאוֹת	says YHWH Sabaoth.	
5a	בְּרִיתִי הָיְתָה אִתּוֹ הַחַיִּים וְהַשָּׁלוֹם	"My covenant, one of life and peace, was with him.	2. The Ideal Priesthood (2:5a–7c)
5b	וָאֶתְּנֵם־לוֹ מוֹרָא	And I gave them to him, along with fear,	
5c	↑ וַיִּירָאֵנִי	↑ and he feared me.	
5d	וּמִפְּנֵי שְׁמִי נִחַת הוּא	Before my name, he was dismayed.	
6a	תּוֹרַת אֱמֶת הָיְתָה בְּפִיהוּ	True instruction was in his mouth	
6b	↑ וְעַוְלָה לֹא־נִמְצָא בִשְׂפָתָיו	↑ and deceit could not be found on his lips.	
6c	בְּשָׁלוֹם וּבְמִישׁוֹר הָלַךְ אִתִּי	In peace and in uprightness, he walked with me	
6d	↑ וְרַבִּים הֵשִׁיב מֵעָוֹן	↑ and he turned many from iniquity.	
7a	↓ כִּי־שִׂפְתֵי כֹהֵן יִשְׁמְרוּ־דַעַת	↓ Because the lips of the priest should preserve knowledge,	
7b	וְתוֹרָה יְבַקְשׁוּ מִפִּיהוּ	they should seek torah from his mouth	
7c	↑ כִּי מַלְאַךְ יְהוָה־צְבָאוֹת הוּא	↑ for he is the messenger of YHWH Sabaoth.	

Continued on next page.

Continued from previous page.

8a	וְאַתֶּם סַרְתֶּם מִן־הַדֶּרֶךְ	But you have turned aside from the way;	3. Concluding Accusation and Resulting Punishment (2:8a–9c)
8b	הִכְשַׁלְתֶּם רַבִּים בַּתּוֹרָה	You have caused many to stumble through your instruction.	
8c	שִׁחַתֶּם בְּרִית הַלֵּוִי	You have corrupted the covenant of Levi,"	
8d	אָמַר יְהוָה צְבָאוֹת	says YHWH Sabaoth.	
9a	וְגַם־אֲנִי נָתַתִּי אֶתְכֶם נִבְזִים וּשְׁפָלִים לְכָל־הָעָם ↑	"I, in turn, will make you despised and humiliated before all the people, ↑	
9b	כְּפִי אֲשֶׁר אֵינְכֶם שֹׁמְרִים אֶת־דְּרָכַי	in as much as you are not keeping my ways	
9c	וְנֹשְׂאִים פָּנִים בַּתּוֹרָה	and [you are not] properly regarding matters of torah."	

followed the generally expected format outlined in the introduction: statement—objection—response. The second disputation speech (1:6–2:9), however, is far more complex in its construction and does not move so neatly through the threefold format. This, the second disputation speech, is the longest pericope in the book (eighteen verses out of fifty-five total), but length alone is not the complicating factor. To be sure, this pericope contains statements (1:6a–g, 11; 2:5–7), objections (1:6j, 7b–e), and responses (1:14; 2:1–4, 8–9), but not necessarily in linear fashion.[2] The material in this pericope is more thematically arranged in order to construct a particular argument.[3]

Despite the length of this pericope and the wide-ranging nature of its content, the repetition of key terms unite this disputation speech. Words from the root ירא, "fear," for example, appear in each of the three subunits mentioned above (1:6, 14; 2:5). Other terms that have a similar "linking" function include: כָּבוֹד, "honor" (1:6; 2:2); ארר, "curse" (1:14; 2:2); and שֵׁם, "name" (1:11, 14; 2:2). The term בזה ("despise") appears in the opening and concluding verses of this speech (1:6; 2:9) creating something of an *inclusio* around the entire pericope. This construction reinforces the condemnation of the priests; the ones who despise YHWH's name have become despised themselves.

Explanation of the Text

A. The Priests' Dishonoring of YHWH through Sacrifice (1:6–10)

1. An Aphorism and an Accusation (1:6a–i)

The second disputation opens with an aphorism concerning honor, and in particular, the honor due a father and a master from a son and servant, respectively. In the Hebrew text, the verb in the second line is absent due to gapping.

בֵּן יְכַבֵּד אָב
A son honors a father

וְעֶבֶד אֲדֹנָיו
A servant [honors] his master.[4]

Although some have equated gapping with ellipsis, the two are not entirely identical.[5] Ellipsis refers to a sequence in which part of the linguistic structure

2. Gibson suggests a linear movement that more nearly follows the threefold form of a disputation speech: Declaration (Statement), 1:6a–h; Rebuttal (Objection), 1:6i–j; Refutation (Response): Sacrifices, 1:7–14; Refutation: Torah, 2:1–9 (*Covenant Continuity and Fidelity*, 81).

3. Adapted from Nogalski, *The Book of the Twelve: Micah-Malachi*, 1017.

4. In the first line of v. 6, the noun אָב, "father," occurs in the singular, while in the second line the noun is plural. This plural form אֲדוֹנִים is likely due to the repeated and regular use of the plural construct form אֲדֹנָי across an array of Old Testament literature in reference to YHWH (e.g., Gen 15:2; Josh 7:7; Ezek 17:9; Ps 130:2).

5. Hill, *Malachi*, 174.

has been omitted but "is recoverable from a scrutiny of context."[6] By contrast, gapping refers "to the absence of a *repeated* verb in clauses which have been *conjoined*."[7] In Mal 1:6, the two lines are conjoined by a *vav*, with the operative verb, כבד, absent in the second line. The absence of כבד, however, should not be construed as a reduction in its importance for the aphorism, but in fact, just the reverse, drawing even greater attention to the centrality of the concept for the aphorism, and by extension, the entire second disputation; from beginning to end, this disputation centers on YHWH as the one to whom honor is due. To assume this section is *only* about right sacrifice or *only* about correct instruction is to miss the fundamental assertion of this disputation: YHWH deserves honor in all aspects of life.

The origins of this aphorism, as with most aphorisms, remains murky at best. More often than not, aphorisms are best understood as common folk sayings, the kind of sayings, for example, found throughout the book of Proverbs. In his analysis of 1:6a–b, Weyde noted the similarities in structure between Mal 1:6a and two texts in Proverbs (see below).[8]

Weyde and Snyman have also suggested that the reference to a child honoring a parent is clearly an allusion to the Decalogue and the commandment to honor mothers and fathers (Exod 20:12; Deut 5:16).[9] Although others are willing to note a correlation between the Decalogue and Mal 1:6, most stop short of noting any explicit relationship.[10]

This connection of Mal 1:6 to Israel's wisdom and legal traditions leads Weyde to conclude that one need not associate the language of father/son and master/servant with covenant or treaty language, but instead simply to understand the proverb as a maxim that refers to a "relationship in everyday life."[11] While Weyde may be correct that the opening line of the aphorism (בֵּן יְכַבֵּד אָב וְעֶבֶד אֲדֹנָיו) is likely a proverbial saying from "everyday life," more must be said. The question is not simply *from whence* Malachi gets this saying but, more importantly (and reflective of the larger scribal culture), *how* does Malachi make use of the saying? Within the larger Old Testament, the father-son relationship repeatedly reflects covenantal connotations.[12] (On the parent-child metaphor in the Old Testament as a reflection of divine-human

Prov 10:1	Prov 15:20	Mal 1:6a
בֵּן חָכָם יְשַׂמַּח־אָב	בֵּן חָכָם יְשַׂמַּח־אָב	בֵּן יְכַבֵּד אָב
A wise son makes glad a father.	A wise son makes glad a father.	A son honors a father.

6. The following example reflects this sequence: A: *Where are you going?* B: *To town.* The phrase omitted in line B ("I am going") is omitted but recoverable nonetheless from context. David Crystal, *A Dictionary of Linguistics and Phonetics*, 6th ed. (Oxford: Blackwell, 2008), 166.

7. Italics added. Crystal, *Dictionary of Linguistics and Phonetics*, 205.

8. Weyde, *Prophecy and Teaching*, 114–16.

9. Weyde, *Prophecy and Teaching*, 114. Snyman suggests that the use of כבד "creates an undeniable link with the Decalogue" and suggests further that it links the text with the Sinai tradition more generally (*Malachi*, 58).

10. E.g., Jacobs, *The Books of Haggai and Malachi*, 182–83; Petersen, *Zechariah 9–14 and Malachi*, 177; Verhoef, *The Books of Haggai and Malachi*, 211.

11. Weyde, *Prophecy and Teaching*, 116. Cf. Hill, *Malachi*, 174.

12. See Christopher J. H. Wright, "אָב," *NIDOTTE* 1:22. For an extended treatment, see F. Charles Fensham, "Father and Son as Terminology for Treaty and Covenant," in *Near Eastern Studies in Honor of William Foxwell Albright*, ed. Hans Goedicke (Baltimore: Johns Hopkins Press, 1971), 121–35. See also the earlier work of Dennis J. McCarthy, "Notes on the Love of God in Deuteronomy and the Father-Son Relationship Between Yahweh and Israel," *CBQ* 27 (1965): 144–47.

relationship, cf. Exod 4:22–23; Deut 1:31; 8:5; 14:1; Hos 11:1; Isa 1:2–3; 43:6; 63:16.)[13] Thus, with this aphorism, Malachi has appropriated the proverb from "everyday life" in a manner consistent with other uses in the Old Testament in an effort to draw attention to the covenant relationship that appears strained. In short, the covenant concepts on display in the first pericope (i.e., "love," "hate") are continued in the second through the use of these metaphors.[14]

The content of the initial aphorism is then reconfigured to construct the first accusation in this disputation. The accusation is presented in the form of two rhetorical questions with the protasis of each containing a verbless clause, i.e., literally, "If a father [am] I . . . If a master [am] I." Typically the word order of a verbless clause is subject-[null verb]-complement.[15] In Mal 1:6, however, the complements are fronted for focus, suggesting that YHWH indeed occupies these metaphorical roles and is thus justified in expecting a proper response from his covenant people. The apodosis of the question actually includes an embedded question beginning with אַיֵּה, "where:" "Where is the honor due me (כְבוֹדִי) . . . Where is the fear due me (מוֹרָאִי)?" When used in a rhetorical question, the interrogative אַיֵּה presupposes a negative response. Thus, the line of questioning is not meant to be understood literally, but instead is making a claim, i.e., "Where is the honor due me?" "Nowhere." Or to be more succinct, the question is meant to imply that no one is honoring YHWH. This is the problem under review in the second disputation.

What precisely then is the content of the accusation? It is the failure of the priests to "honor" and "fear" Yahweh. At its most basic level, the verb כבד in the *qal* means "to be heavy or weighty," but in the *piel* (as in 1:6a), it refers to ascribing honor to something (i.e., to acknowledge something or someone as important, weighty). The noun form in 1:6d reflects a similar meaning here ("the honor due me"). The other term in v. 6, "fear due me" (מוֹרָאִי), is often translated as "respect" (e.g., NIV; NRSV), but this rendering likely fails to capture the nuance.[16] Elsewhere in the Old Testament, the term מוֹרָאִי typically refers to a "palpable fear before Yahweh," even at times referring to the terror or dread that Yahweh can invoke.[17] This sense of palpable fear is rooted in the language of covenant obligation. To be in a covenant relationship with *this* God demands exclusive loyalty and fear (Deut 6:13).[18] Thus, the issue at hand in this second disputation is not simply that of "dishonoring" or "disrespecting" God; it is more fundamental than that. The actions of the priests, which are rehearsed in the remainder of the disputation, suggest that the priests have failed to acknowledge (i.e., "honor") their covenant partner, and worse yet, they have failed to understand the very identity of their covenant partner, the one who should be rightly feared and obeyed.

13. For the master-servant relationship as a metaphor for the divine-human, relationship, see Ex 3:12; 9:1; Lev 25:55; 1 Sam 3:9; Zeph 3:9; Ps 123:2.

14. Jonathan Gibson, *Covenant Continuity and Fidelity*, 83.

15. For a brief explanation, see Robert D. Holmstedt, John A. Cook, and Phillip S. Marshall, *Qoheleth: A Handbook on the Hebrew Text*, BHHB (Waco, TX: Baylor University Press, 2017), 9–12.

16. Contra Kessler, *Maleachi*, 137.

17. Fuhs, perhaps in overstating the matter, suggests that the term מוֹרָא might be best understood as "terror instilled by God" (H. F. Fuhs, "יָרֵא *yārē*," *TDOT* 6:290–315, 303). Cf. Deut 11:25; 26:8; Isa 8:12, 13; Jer 32:21; Ps 9:21[20]; 76:12; Job 33:16. Cf. Jacobs, *The Books of Haggai and Malachi*, 185–86.

18. Even as "love" and "hate" in the first disputation had covenantal connotations, so too "fear" (ירא). Moshe Weinfeld notes that the language of "fear" was part of the "diplomatic vocabulary of the Near East" and was employed in treaty language to suggest "exclusive allegiance" (*Deuteronomy and the Deuteronomic School* (Oxford: Oxford University Press, 1972), 83–84. See also Gibson, *Covenant Continuity, and Fidelity*, 84.

The expanded messenger formula in 1:6h–i ("says YHWH Sabaoth to you, O priests who despise my name") plays a critical role in this disputation. As with the other messenger formulas in Malachi, this attribution affirms that the declaration in 1:6 was not simply the musings of a faithful prophet or a disgruntled citizen, but instead it was meant to be received as a word from Israel's God, the very God who has not received the honor or fear due him. Beyond this, however, the expanded messenger formula explicitly identifies the audience with the vocative "O priests." This reference to the priests at the start of the disputation prepares the way for the rather lengthy discussion that remains in this disputation related to cultic matters proper (1:7–14) and torah instruction (2:1–9).[19] The priests are further identified by the subsequent participial clause; they are the ones "[who are] despising my [YHWH's] name."[20] The verb בזה, "to despise," can refer more generally to a dismissive attitude, but it can also carry with it covenantal overtones.[21] In the book of Ezekiel the term appears five times (16:59; 17:16, 18, 19; 22:8) and in the first four occurrences, despising refers to a breach in covenant. For example, Ezekiel announces in 16:59 (author's translation), "Thus says the Adonai YHWH: I will deal with you as you have done, you who have despised [בזה] the oath, breaking the covenant." In the final occurrence (22:8), YHWH declares, "You have despised [בזה] my holy things and profaned my Sabbaths" (NRSVUE). The use of the term in Ezekiel, particularly as it relates to covenantal claims, provides a helpful analog to Malachi and the argument being constructed in the second disputation, as will be suggested below.

2. Despising and Defiling YHWH (1:6j–8e)

Following the aphorism and the opening accusation, per the disputation format, the priests respond with a question, "How have we despised your name?" In what follows (vv. 7–14), the prophet appears to be invoking the cultic language from the book of Leviticus in an effort to identify the failures of the priests. In verse 7a, the priests are chastised for "presenting [נגשׁ] defiled food upon my altar." The *hiphil* form of נגשׁ, "to present," appears in Lev 2:8 and 8:14, and there clearly suggests cultic activity, i.e., "presenting" an offering. The former text (Lev 2:8) is instructive for reading the remainder of this disputation in Malachi. The relevant portion of that verse (Lev 2:8b NET) reads "Present [קרב] it to the priest and he will bring [נגשׁ] it to the altar." Weyde notes a distinction between the two verbs and their complements. Although both verbs have clear cultic connotations, נגשׁ refers only to items brought to the altar whereas קרב refers to items brought to human beings, i.e., the priests.[22] This Levitical distinction remains operative in the book of Malachi. See Mal 1:7a (author's translation, "presenting upon my altar;" מַגִּישִׁים עַל־מִזְבְּחִי) over

19. Although the first disputation fails to identify the audience explicitly, the use of the plural throughout (e.g., "I have chosen you") implies that the people of Yehud are in view.

20. As Holmstedt has suggested, the vast majority of participles are the complement of a null verb inside a relative clause structure (Robert D. Holmstedt, *Biblical Hebrew Syntax: A Linguistic Introduction*, [Grand Rapids: Baker Academic, forthcoming]). Understood this way, 1:6h–i should be rendered, "O priests, the ones [who] [are] despising my name."

21. While the covenantal overtones are likely at the forefront of the text, the mention of the Jacob/Esau narrative in the first disputation calls to mind another story of the brothers in the second disputation. The use of בזה may be an allusion to the tradition that Esau "despised" (בזה) his birthright and sold it to Jacob. Perhaps, as Hill suggests, the priests of Yehud are in danger of despising their "birthright" and are in danger of forfeiting the position of prestige (*Malachi*, 176). Petersen (*Zechariah 9–14 and Malachi*, 178) suggests, alternatively, that to despise the name of Yahweh involves "improper ritual practice at the place where Yahweh has caused his name to dwell."

22. Weyde, *Prophecy and Teaching*, 118–19.

against Mal 1:8f (author's translation, "Offer that to your governor" הַקְרִיבֵהוּ נָא לְפֶחָתֶךָ) as evidence of this distinction.

The problem identified in Mal 1:7a echoes the concerns found in Leviticus, particularly as it pertains to matters of sacrifice and offerings. Malachi alleges that the priests are presenting "defiled food" (לֶחֶם מְגֹאָל) upon the altar, with "food" (לֶחֶם) understood more generally as any form of sacrifice.[23] The word "defiled" is a *pual* participle from גאל II, here functioning attributively and meaning "to desecrate or defile" something. But to declare the "food" as "defiled" means far more than simply that the food *itself* is defiled or unclean. That which is defiled also has a polluting effect, making that which it contacts also defiled.[24] Herein lies the logic (and the disconnect) of the initial exchange between the priests and the prophet.

Priests: "How have we despised your name?" (1:6k)
Prophet: "By presenting defiled food upon my altar." (1:7a)
Priests: "How have we defiled you?" (1:7c)

The act of despising Yahweh's name (1:6k) is clarified in 1:7a; presenting defiled food upon the altar is in fact analogous to despising YHWH's name (on the "name," see Canonical and Theological Significance). The response of the priests in 1:7c ("How have we defiled you?"), however, reveals that they do not see any such connection between what occurs on the altar and their esteem of YHWH.[25] Yet this is precisely the point being argued. The effect of presenting defiled food (1:7a) is to defile YHWH (1:7c).[26]

In response to the question, "How have we defiled you?," the prophet provides three case examples from the speech and action of the priests. In the first instance, defilement results from the priests' declaration concerning the table of YHWH (1:7e). Form critically, "it is despised" is best understood as a priestly declaratory formula.[27] In a cultic context, the formula expresses a decision about a situation or offering, usually as it pertains to cultic purity or impurity.[28] Frequently English translations simply reduce this line to "YHWH's table is contemptible/despised" (NIV, HCSB, JPS).[29] Yet closer attention to the Hebrew construction proves instructive for

23. Cf. Lev 22:25.

24. For a helpful discussion on holiness and sacrifice, see Gordon J. Wenham, *The Book of Leviticus*, NICOT (Grand Rapids: Eerdmans, 1979), 18–29.

25. The LXX translates 1:7c as ἠλισγήσαμεν αὐτούς, "we have defiled *it*." The replacing of the second-person pronoun with a third-person pronoun makes the antecedent to be the altar. Among English translations, the NRSV follows the LXX. In their attempts at clarity both the LXX and NRSV miss the critical role that metonymy plays in the prophetic argument (on metonymy, see n26).

26. Jacobs labels the relationship between "you" and "your name" and that of "my altar" and even "the table of YHWH" (1:7e) as an example of synecdoche (*The Books of Haggai and Malachi*, 190). Although the terms are quite similar in meaning, metonymy might be the preferred linguistic term for the language employed here. With synecdoche, the attribution substitutes "a part for the whole" (i.e., "all hands on deck" with "hands" referring to the hands of the crew as a substitute for "crew"). Metonymy, however, reflects a close association between the items compared but differs from synecdoche in that one is not part of the other. Thus, "my altar" is not part of Yahweh, so to speak, but the prophet makes clear there is an exceedingly close association between the two.

27. Weyde, *Prophecy and Teaching*, 125–26.

28. Not surprising, the declaration formula (with various pronouncements, e.g., most holy [קֹדֶשׁ קָדָשִׁים], unclean [שֶׁקֶץ], pure [טָהוֹר]) is found throughout the book of Leviticus (e.g., Lev 6:10, 11[17, 18]; 11:4, 10; 13:13, 15; 14:13; 15:2). But it is also found elsewhere in the Old Testament (e.g., Exod 30:10; Num 19:15; Deut 14:10; Hag 2:14; Ezek 18:9).

29. The NRSVUE renders the clause modally, i.e., "the Lord's table *may* be despised."

understanding the force of the statement. In linguistic terms, the line is an example of "left-edge dislocation." In such instances a noun or noun phrase appears "just outside and in front of the following clause and is resumed within that clause by a coreferential constituent" (here, "it", הוּא).[30] In Hebrew, left-edge constituents (e.g., "table of the YHWH") never introduce *new* topics, but instead activate a *known* entity. In other words, שֻׁלְחַן יְהוָה is not a new topic but instead returns to or reactivates the language of the "altar" mentioned in 1:7a—an altar that is defiled and defiling.

The left-edge dislocation also creates a construction in which the following clause makes a propositional statement about the noun or noun phrase (i.e., "table of the YHWH").[31] Linguistically, the statement that follows, נִבְזֶה הוּא, has a marked word order. The expected word order of a participle clause is subject + participle, but in this instance the participle has been fronted.[32] Fronting often signals that an entity or an aspect of the entity is the *focus* of the utterance. In this instance, the left-edge constituent introduces the topic of the utterance, and the subsequent marked word order in the participle clause makes a claim about it—"It is despised."

Left edge constituent	Fronted clause
נִבְזֶה הוּא	שֻׁלְחַן יְהוָה
lit., "The table of the YHWH, despised is it."	

Because נִבְזֶה is a *niphal* participle, it raises the question, "Who is doing the despising?" Most English translations (and many commentators) argue that this statement reflects the sentiments of the priests, i.e., "the priests despise the table of Yahweh" or they hold the table in contempt.[33] Understood this way, the argument runs, the declaration is meant to reflect the dismissive attitude of the priests to all things cultic. But as Nathan Hays has convincingly argued, the use of the *niphal* here closely matches that found in Lev 22.[34] In that chapter, cultic items that are accepted or rejected by YHWH are identified. Perhaps the clearest example is found in Lev 22:27:

> יֵרָצֶה לְקָרְבַּן אִשֶּׁה לַיהוָה
> "It shall be accepted as an offering of fire by YHWH" (author's translation)

In this verse, the *niphal* form of רצה appears and the agent of the action is clearly identified, "by YHWH." Similar examples of this construction appear elsewhere in Leviticus as well.[35] Taken as an analog, Mal 1:7 might best be understood as "The table of YHWH, it is despised [by YHWH]." Thus, the quotation by the priests in 1:7e reflects the priests' complaints "about *Yahweh's* seemingly unfair rejection of the altar and the offerings on it."[36] With the appearance of such a claim, a connection between the first disputation and the second becomes quite clear. In the first disputation,

30. The idea of "left edge" does not imply its location in the Hebrew utterance but is simply a linguistic label applied to this phenomenon. In English, the label more nearly applies to its location, i.e., the front of the sentence ("left edge"); see Robert D. Holmstedt, "Critical at the Margins: Edge Constituents in Biblical Hebrew," *KUSATU* 17 (2014): 119.

31. Holmstedt, "Critical at the Margins," 128.

32. *BHRG* §46.2.1.

33. Cf. Verhoef, *The Books of Haggai and Malachi*, 216; Snyman, *Malachi*, 62. The NET renders the phrase as "'How have we offended you?' By treating the table of the Lord as if it is of no importance."

34. Nathan Hays, "Malachi as a Response to its Interlocutors" (Ph.D. Dissertation, Baylor University, 2017), 136–37.

35. Within Lev 22 alone see 22:20b; 22:21b, 23b, 25a, 27. Beyond that see also Lev 1:4b; 7:18a; and 19:7b.

36. Hays, "Malachi as a Response to its Interlocutors," 146.

the people clamored that Yahweh no longer loves (אהב) them based upon their current plight in the land. In the second disputation, the priests surmise that YHWH's apparent absence is due to his rejection of cultic worship. In both instances, those in Yehud want to place the blame squarely on YHWH and his failure to remain steadfast in his covenantal faithfulness.

The second and third examples highlighted by Malachi involve the presentation of animals for sacrifice. Malachi chastises the priests for the types of animals they are presenting to YHWH, and further still, for their assessment of such offerings. Leviticus 22:18–25 and Deut 15:19–23 make abundantly clear that an animal with any blemish is not an acceptable sacrifice to YHWH. Both legal texts stipulate what constitutes a "defect" (מוּם). Although allusions to Lev 22 appear earlier in this disputation, here the prophet appears to echo the list of defects in Deut 15:21 (author's translation):

> But if it has any defect—lameness [פִּסֵּחַ], blindness [עִוֵּר], or serious defect—you shall not sacrifice [זבח] it to YHWH your God.

Malachi 1:8a mentions blind animals and 1:8d mentions lame animals, and the reference to these two classifications within the context of sacrifice (זבח) appears in 1:8b. In the Deuteronomy text, lameness and blindness appear as part of a list, but in Malachi, they are separated and placed in two parallel statements. Further still, the second statement is expanded: "When you present lame [פִּסֵּחַ] and sick [חֹלֶה] [animals]." Interestingly, neither Lev 22 nor Deut 15 utilize the Hebrew word חֹלֶה, "sick." The addition of this "new" category may have been included as a nod to the list of additional defects provided elsewhere in the book of Leviticus.[37]

The first clause in 1:8a, d (i.e., "And when you present . . .") is a temporal clause followed by a verbless clause (אֵין רָע), which functions as the main clause in each sentence. Understanding the structure of these statements seems straightforward; how to render the phrase אֵין רָע has proven more problematic. The most common rendering, as reflected in a number of English translations (e.g., NIV, NRSV, NASB, HCSB, NET), is to understand the phrase as a rhetorical question. Understood this way, 1:8a–c reads, "And when you present blind [animals] for sacrifice, is that not evil (or wrong)?" The challenge with this reading, however, is that there is no interrogative particle associated with אֵין רָע. One could assume that the interrogative is simply inferred but, given that the book of Malachi contains twenty-five questions, *each* marked by an interrogative, the notion of an "inferred" or "implied" question seems, well, questionable. Even within this disputation, marked questions appear in 1:6c–d, f–g, 6k, 7c, 8g–h, 9d, and 10a–b. Thus, the absence of any form of interrogative particle, particularly given the prominence of such particles in the remainder of the book, suggests that this may in fact be a statement. If it is a statement, then who is saying it and to whom? In 1:7c, the priests asked how they have defiled YHWH; verse 7d is YHWH's response back to the priests, "When you say . . ." What follows then are three statements separated by two simple *vav* conjunctions (vv. 7e–8e).

37. The appropriation of earlier traditions likely reflects the scribal nature of the book of Malachi. Weyde, *Prophecy and Teaching*, 133.

Statement 1: "The table of YHWH, it is despised [by YHWH]."
Statement 2: When you present blind animals for sacrifice, [you say], "there is no defect [אֵין רָע]."
Statement 3: When you present lame and sick [animals], [you say], "there is no defect [אֵין רָע]."

Understood this way, statements 2 and 3, those typically worded as questions, are actually quotations of the priests to the people. Leviticus 27:11–12 notes that one of the roles of the priests is to assess the animals brought for an offering to determine whether they are good or whether they have a "defect" (רָע).[38] When blind and lame animals are brought forward, those animals should be pronounced as רָע, as having a defect. Instead, Malachi reports that when these kinds of animals are brought forward, the priests declare, "there is no defect" (אֵין רָע).[39] Thus the problem is actually twofold. The priests are accepting and offering defective sacrifices and further, they are providing faulty instruction in the torah. These two violations signal the focus of the remainder of the disputation. In 1:9–14, the prophet gives attention to the nature of the sacrifices offered (and its implications for worship). Beginning with 2:1, the prophet turns attention to the priests' failure to provide "true instruction" (2:6).

3. A Challenge to the Priests (1:8f–9e)

Following the citation of priestly quotes in 1:7e–8e, YHWH issues a challenge to the priests, daring the priests to take such imperfect sacrifices to the governor. As noted in the previous section, קרב ("to bring near" in the *hiphil*) refers to the process of bringing items to human beings (whereas נגשׁ refers only to items brought to the altar). The suggestion to bring food to the governor is a plausible notion. In fact, Neh 5:14, 18 refer to the governor's food allowance. Although the command in 1:8f is rooted in apparent practice, the imperative actually functions sarcastically here.[40] This air of sarcasm continues in 1:8g–h with the use of two "yes-no," or "polar questions," both functioning rhetorically.[41] The verb רצה, often translated as "to be pleased with," is understood in the sense of being accepted or received favorably. This notion plays into the second question, "Will he regard you" (הֲיִשָּׂא פָנֶיךָ, woodenly, "lift your face")? As Hill has suggested, when this phrase appears in the context of entreating a dignitary, "this phrase has a more technical meaning like 'grant a favor.'"[42] With this in mind, then, the full force of the question becomes apparent: Would anyone dare bring imperfect sacrifices to a dignitary or person in power and actually expect them to grant that person a favor or response to a petition. The answer should be "no," and yet, this is precisely the circumstance the priests have created; they are bringing forward imperfect sacrifices to YHWH and expecting in return a favorable response.

The point is explicitly reinforced in the invitation that follows in 1:9. The verse begins with וְעַתָּה, "So now." This conjunctive adverb functions as a discourse marker in biblical Hebrew. After an exposition of a situation, the discourse marker וְעַתָּה "is used to point to the implications of X for

38. Snyman hypothesizes that perhaps inferior sacrifices were offered due to the socio-economic conditions that plagued the community in Yehud, thus likely prompting concessions by the priests (*Malachi*, 62).

39. Cf. Verhoef, *The Books of Haggai and Malachi*, 217–18.

40. Although the dominant use of the imperative is to issue direct commands, Waltke and O'Connor note other regular uses of the form, including sarcasm (*IBHS* §34.4). Cf. Amos 4:4.

41. *BHRG* §42.2; *IBHS* §40.3.

42. Hill, *Malachi*, 81.

the here and now of a speaker or addressee."[43] Just as the priests were invited to seek the favor of the governor, they are now invited to "entreat the face of God." But that invitation is informed by what has been said in verses 7–8. The collocation חִלָּה + פְּנֵי־, "entreat the face of," appears thirteen times in the Old Testament in reference to seeking God's favor, frequently with the desired goal of YHWH responding to a petition.[44] That desired goal appears in the subsequent clause in Mal 1:9b, וִיחָנֵנוּ, "so that he may be gracious to us."[45] The first-person plural suffix "us" on the verb חנן has long puzzled interpreters.[46] Why would Malachi include himself in this request? Likely the prophet expresses what he wishes for the priests and for all of God's people—for God to be gracious (חנן). Although the prophet speaks against the priests throughout the book, he still understands himself as part of the people. While such a request may reflect a genuine desire, the exhortation to the priests is tinged with sarcasm: "Go ahead, entreat the face of God so that he may be gracious to us." That indeed may be what everyone wants, but such a request remains futile.[47] The two subsequent lines bear this conclusion out.

In line 1:9c (מִיֶּדְכֶם הָיְתָה זֹּאת, literally, "from your hand is this"), the prepositional phrase has been fronted in this clause to identify the persons whose actions have made such a request futile. The comment here is not intended to be explanatory but accusatory. Snyman's rendering of this clause captures well that sense "This is your fault."[48] Gibson understands lines 9c–d as one complex sentence, "With such a thing from your hand, will he show favor to any of you?"[49] It is conceivable to understand the מִן, "from," as denoting the ground or reason for an event or state of affairs.[50] Regardless of which way one renders the first clause, the point remains: the answer to the question in 9d is secured by the claims in 9c.

In verse 9d, the prophet invokes the same collocation used in 8h, נשׂא+ פְּנֵי, "to lift the face of." And similar to its usage in 8h, the more technical meaning of "to grant a favor" is in view. Will God grant the petitions of the priests who are entreating God on behalf of the people to pour out his graciousness? The answer to the question is simply "no." And the fault rests not with God, but with the priests (v. 9c).

4. A Declaration of Judgment (1:10a–e)

Malachi's question in 9d is followed by a subsequent question in 10a–b. In 9d, the prophet ponders rhetorically whether Yahweh will show favor to the priests. The implied response is in the negative. As further evidence of that claim, the prophet considers a second rhetorical question in 10a–b, likewise with an implied negative response. The structure of the latter verse and the relationship between the various clauses has generated considerable discussion.[51] Grammatically verse 10a contains

43. *BHRG* §40.39. For a similar interpretation of וְעַתָּה, see *IBHS* §39.3.4f. Contra Snyman who contends that the discourse marker serves as an indication "of a turning point in the argumentation by the prophet" (*Malachi*, 65).

44. Ex 32:11; 1 Sam 13:12; 1 Kgs 13:6 (2x); 2 Kgs 13:4; 2 Chr 33:12; Jer 26:19; Zech 7:2; 8:21, 22; Mal 1:9; Dan 9:13; Ps 119:58. Hill, *Malachi*, 181–82; Verhoef, *The Books of Haggai and Malachi*, 219–20.

45. An imperative followed by a jussive is meant to express purpose, i.e., "so that."

46. For discussion on the various options, see Weyde, *Prophecy and Teaching*, 136–38.

47. Rather than understanding the initial request to entreat God in 1:9a–b as sarcastic or ironic, Paul Redditt (*Haggai, Zechariah, Malachi*, NCBC [Grand Rapids: Eerdmans Publishing, 1995], 165) and S. D. Snyman (*Malachi*, 66–67) understand it as a genuine hope of the prophet.

48. *Malachi*, 65, 67.

49. Gibson, *Covenant Continuity and Fidelity*, 75.

50. *BHRG* §39.14.4b.

51. Hill, for example, contends that וְיִסְגֹּר דְּלָתַיִם is epexegetical, but such an analysis offers little explanatory power for understanding the relationship to the prior phrase (*Malachi*, 184).

an example of "marked" focus fronting. Fronting involves the movement of a constituent (e.g., the subject) from the end or middle of a construction to the clause initial position. Here, however, the fronted constituent is "marked" because it appears "outside the boundary of the clause," i.e., prior to the *vav*.[52] Thus, in this instance, the phrase "who even among you" (מִי גַם־בָּכֶם) actually functions as the subject of the verb "close" (סגר), and consequently, the subject of the entire clause.[53]

Complement/Object	Verb	Marked Fronted Subject
דְּלָתַיִם	וְיִסְגֹּר	מִי גַם־בָּכֶם

The imperfect (*yiqtol*) form of the verb יִסְגֹּר has a modal (*irrealis*) sense and should be understood as "might" or "would," as would the subsequent verb תָּאִירוּ, "to light" (with fire). Thus, 10a–b should be rendered as "Who among you would shut the doors and not light my altar in vain?"[54] The question is directed at the priests, asking which of them would close the doors of the temple and not light the altar.[55] Only those who have recognized the failures of current cultic practices would be inclined to do so. That which is implied by the rhetorical question, i.e., that none of the priests would be inclined to close the doors, is because none of the priests apparently recognize the failures of the system as practiced. Their actions, consequently, prove to be "vain" (חִנָּם). In this way, the question itself has become condemnatory.

The condemnatory language becomes all the more acute in 10c and 10e. YHWH declares that he takes no delight (חֵפֶץ) in the priests, he despises them, and will not accept (רצה) offerings from them.[56] The problem rests with the priests themselves (v. 10c); the blemished offerings are only a manifestation of that problem (v. 10e).[57]

B. The Greatness of YHWH's Name (1:11–14)

As noted above, the second disputation began with an aphorism, followed by an accusation, culminating in an exchange between YHWH and the priests. Verses 11–14 appear, in large part, to replicate that pattern (see below).

v. 6a–b	aphorism/statement	v. 11
v. 6c–h	accusation	v. 12
vv. 7–10	exchange between YHWH and priests	vv. 13–14

52. Van der Merwe, Naudé, and Kroeze consider this to be an example of left-dislocation similar to what was observed in 1:7e, yet with the main (matrix) clause lacking a resumptive pronoun typically observed in such dislocated constructions, 10a is better understood as an example of marked focus fronting (*BHRG* §48.1.3).

53. The use of גַּם actually makes the prepositional phrase emphatic "*Who* among *you* . . ." or perhaps "*Who* even among *you* . . ." (Glazier-McDonald, *Malachi*, 54–55). Or worded differently, "Is there *anyone* among *you* (i.e., the priests)" that would close the door. The implication is that the entire priesthood has become corrupt.

54. Typically, the second clause, וְלֹא־תָאִירוּ מִזְבְּחִי חִנָּם, is understood as a purpose clause, "so that you do not light my altar in vain." More likely the *vav* simply joins two irrealis or modal clauses as suggested in the translation above.

55. The use of דְּלָתַיִם in v. 10 is "multivalent," as Jacobs has suggested, and could refer to the temple courtyard, the doors to the inner sanctuary, or more generally to the large temple doors (*The Books of Haggai and Malachi*, 197). Precision on the matter, however, is not necessary; the implication in that the cultic practices of the priests are no longer acceptable.

56. On the connection between not taking delight in a person and despising (בזה), see Jer 22:28. The priests despise the table of YHWH, and by extension, YHWH. The reverse is true concerning YHWH's regard of the priests.

57. Hill argues similarly, i.e., that the priests are rejected because of the offerings they bring: "Yahweh takes no pleasure [חפץ] in the Levitical priests because he cannot accept [רצה] the offerings they present to him" (*Malachi*, 185).

1. A Statement Concerning the Name of YHWH (1:11)

Even though the name of YHWH received attention earlier in the disputation (vv. 6h, 6j, 7a), the prophet references it here as a means of contrast with the previous verse. In verse 10, YHWH calls for the closing down of the temple and the ceasing of cultic activity. Such an action, however, is not a reflection upon God, but of the community's failure to recognize the honor due this God.

Malachi shifts quickly in verse 11 to note that while those in Jerusalem have "despised [YHWH's] name" (v. 6i), the same cannot be said elsewhere. YHWH declares, "Great is my name among the nations" and equally striking, that incense is being offered up "to my name." The final prepositional phrase in the clause, בַּגּוֹיִם, "among the nations," has engendered considerable discussion as to its meaning. The views proposed can be grouped into one of four categories. Some have suggested that the reference is to the worship carried out by the foreign nations. Reflecting the reading that dominated the turn of the twentieth century, S. R. Driver explained that sacrifices offered to the gods of other people, "if offered honestly and earnestly is accepted by God [YHWH] as if it is offered to himself."[58] Driver's thesis, and others who followed a similar course of interpretation, rooted their conclusions primarily in the tenets of natural theology. While perhaps attractive to some, this view must ultimately be abandoned on the grounds that it "is foreign to the real universalistic concept of the relationship between YHWH and the people of the earth."[59] Nowhere else in the Old Testament is "pagan" religion, or the cultic practices of other religions, considered acceptable to YHWH. In fact, the contrary is true time and again.

Some have suggested that the references to the "nations" (גּוֹיִם) points to foreigners who have converted to YHWH worship. Such a proposition, however, remains problematic on several grounds. Admittedly, there are texts in the Old Testament that refer to foreigners who have apparently converted, but in Mal 1:11, such specificity is altogether lacking, making such a hypothesis speculative at best. Further, as Snyman has noted, it remains questionable whether there were large numbers of gentiles converting to Yahwism in this period of Yehud's history. He rightly cautions, "One must keep in mind that Judah was a minor part of the Persian Empire, so there would have been little reason for people to convert to the God of a subjected nation."[60] Taken together, this reading also must be rejected.

A third option for understanding verse 11, reflected in several English translations (NIV, ESV, NET, HCSB), is to interpret this verse as having an eschatological thrust ("my name *will be great* among the nations"). The implication being that while YHWH's name is despised *now*, there will be a day when all nations will acknowledge YHWH. Those who have argued for such a reading observe that the phrase "from the rising of the sun until its setting" in verse 11a is frequently found in texts that point to a demonstration of YHWH's power on the world stage (Pss 50:1; 113:3; Isa 45:6;). Interpreters have also suggested that "the note of universality" in this verse (i.e., בַּגּוֹיִם, "among the nations") is part of the "essential content of prophetic eschatology."[61]

58. S. R. Driver, "Sermon III," in *Christianity and Other Religions: Three Short Sermons*, ed. S. R. Driver and W. Sanday (London: Longman, Green and Company, 1908), 31–46, esp. 45. A subset of this theory is that because both Israel and Persia referred to their deities as "the God of Heaven," both religions were monotheistic, hence making all worship in the Persian period worship of "the one true God." Such a claim, however, grossly misunderstands the complex nature of Persian religion as well as the rhetorical force of the prophetic speech itself.

59. Verhoef, *The Books of Haggai and Malachi*, 228.

60. Snyman, *Malachi*, 71.

61. Glazier-McDonald, *Malachi*, 60.

Neither observation is incorrect as it pertains to *the larger prophetic corpus*; indeed, both phrases *can* have a future orientation. The question that remains, however, is whether the use of these themes *here* necessarily requires the same temporal understanding (i.e., future). Clendenen admits that the "future setting" of v. 11 is "indicated more by the situation than by the grammar."[62] He suggests that since "Gentile nations in general were not recognizing YHWH's greatness and worshiping him" at that time, this verse must refer to a future time.[63] Yet, as will be suggested below, the situation *and* the grammar actually argue against a "future" setting.

This leads to a fourth option and the one adopted in this commentary: the verse points to Jewish worship in the diaspora. Grammatically, the structure of the verse can be understood as follows:

11a–b	prepositional phrase + verbless clause
11c	prepositional phrase + verbless clause
11d	כִּי + verbless clause

The parallel prepositional phrases have a locative sense, followed by two verbless clauses that reference proper acknowledgement of YHWH.

Location	Worship
From the rising of the sun to its setting,	great [is] my name among the nations.
And in every place,	incense [is] being offered up to my name—a pure offering.[64]

The phrase "from the rising of the sun to its setting" is a merismus meant to indicate metaphorically the spatial area in view, i.e., "everywhere," and this locative sense is reiterated in the subsequent line, "and in every place" (וּבְכָל־מָקוֹם). The second half of each line follows with a claim that in those places, "in every place," YHWH is properly recognized. But it is not the "nations" (גּוֹיִם) themselves who make this confession, as suggested by others above, but instead it is "*among* the nations" that this confession is made. The final line in v. 11 (v. 11d) reiterates the claim offered explicitly in the first line (v. 11a–b) and implicitly in the second (v. 11c): "Indeed, great is my name among the nations."[65] Those who are "among the nations" and who are offering up "pure offerings" would be the Jewish community in the diaspora not the pagan nations offering up sacrifices to their own deities.[66]

The comparison is not between Israel and the nations, nor the inclusion of the nations in the future (eschatological), the comparison is between improper worship taking place *in Jerusalem* over against the proper worship taking place *beyond* Jerusalem. The temple is in Jerusalem, as are the cultic officials and priests, and yet worship that honors God is absent and only to be found in the diaspora community. The point is that *even* if the priests in Jerusalem no longer take YHWH seriously, others will. The honor due God will come, even if from another quarter of the Jewish community.

62. Clendenen, "Malachi," 276–77.

63. Clendenen, "Malachi," 277.

64. Of the two lines, the second is the more challenging grammatically. Frequently interpreters take the second *hophal* participle (מֻגָּשׁ, "being offered up) as the operative verb in the clause. More recent study on participles has suggested that they are "best understood as adjectives that encode an activity or event rather than a quality. Thus, when participles are used 'verbally,' they are actually complements of a verbless clause [as in Mal 1:11]. The core semantics of the Hebrew participle is progressive aspect" which was used for habitual statements rather than the *yiqtol* (Holmstedt, Cook, and Marshall, *Qoheleth*, 54). For a more granular analysis of the issue, see John Cook, "The Hebrew Participle and Stative in Typological Perspective," *JNSL* 34 (2008): 1–19, see esp. 13–16.

65. The opening כִּי should be understood as emphatic, "indeed."

66. For a similar reading, see Snyman, *Malachi*, 74–76. In

2. The Reiteration of Cultic Malpractice (1:12–14)

Following the surprisingly positive assessment of worship in the diaspora, Malachi returns to the deficiencies of those in Jerusalem. This comparison is highlighted by the structure of the verse. The *vav* is disjunctive with the pronoun "you" being "focus fronted." Focus fronting compares one member of a set with another. Here the people of God are the "set." Verse 11 refers to the people of God in the diaspora while וְאַתֶּם, "but you," indicates that a different member of the set is now being considered—those in Jerusalem. Whereas those among the nations are making YHWH's name great, those in Jerusalem are polluting it.[67] The question is, how are they polluting the name of YHWH when those among the nations are so ably "making it great"?

Similar to line 7e, line 12b is an example of "left-edge dislocation." The initial constituent, שֻׁלְחַן יְהוָה, is not a new topic but returns to a previous topic. The two lines are identical in structure, with the principal difference being the participle. In verse 7, the participle is a *niphal*, whereas in verse 12b, a *pual* from גאל, "to defile."

Left-Edge Constituent	Fronted Clause
v. 7e	נִבְזֶה הוּא
"The table of YHWH, it is despised [by YHWH]."	
v. 12b	מְגֹאָל הוּא
"The table the Lord, it is treated as defiled [by YHWH]."	

In v. 12c, the prophet goes even further and notes that the priests declare that not only is the altar despised, but so is the very food offered on it. As suggested above in the comments on v. 7, it is unlikely that the priests would declare the table of YHWH and the offerings as defiled; that would seem counterintuitive and counterproductive for those whose livelihood is the cultic activity in Jerusalem. More likely, the priests are complaining about YHWH's apparent rejection of the altar and the offerings on it, based upon the current condition of the community, i.e., their perceived lack of blessing.[68]

YHWH then cites another saying of the priests in v. 13b, "Behold, what a hardship [מַתְּלָאָה]!" Although some label "Behold" (הִנֵּה) as a presentative, it is better understood as an expressive that functions as a discourse marker.[69] As an expressive, however, הִנֵּה introduces positive or negative feelings about a state of affairs; clearly the latter is in view here. The priests bemoan that the current circumstance has become a תְּלָאָה, a hardship to them.[70] Some have translated the noun as "nuisance" or "weariness," yet both renderings fail to capture the full sense of the word.[71] The noun תְּלָאָה appears four other times in the Old Testament and in each instance it alludes to the difficult circumstances suffered by the people (Exod 18:8; Num 20:14; Lam 3:5; Neh 9:32). Exodus 18:8 recounts the hardships faced as the nation departed Egypt while Num 20:14 recounts the hardships experienced while in

his assessment of v. 11, Snyman explains that "Yahweh's name is great *among* the nations; the point these verses wish to make is not that Yahweh's name is made great *by* the nations. The interpretation from a historical perspective favoured here is that the reference to offerings brought 'in every place' 'to my name,' is best understood when it is taken as referring to the Jews in the diaspora. They knew Yahweh by name and it is a known fact that Jews worshipped Yahweh outside the boundaries of Judah" (46). See also, Weyde, *Prophecy and Teaching*, 148–49; Nogalski, *Book of the Twelve: Micah–Malachi*, 102–23.

67. The pronominal suffix on אוֹתוֹ is anaphoric referring back to the YHWH's name.

68. Hays, "Malachi as a Response to its Interlocutors," 146.

69. Contra Hill, *Malachi*, 191, who labels it as a presentative. See *BHRG* § 40.22.4.4. When functioning as a presentative, הִנֵּה typically "presents" an entity to an addressee (cf. Gen 12:19).

70. This construction is the interrogative particle מָה, "what," plus the noun תְּלָאָה.

71. Petersen, *Zechariah 9–14 and Malachi*, 184–85; Verhoef, *The Books of Haggai and Malachi*, 232–33.

Egypt. Lamentations 3:5 equates the suffering of the community at the hands of the Babylonians as תְּלָאָה and Neh 9:32 traces more generally the hardship faced by Israel, beginning with the Assyrians. In these four texts, תְּלָאָה never carries the sense of "weariness" or "nuisance;" the word has a much weightier connotation. The priests are complaining that the table is burdensome to the people, perhaps even oppressive.[72]

YHWH charges in verse 13c that the priests still light the altar fires ("yet you ignite it"). The verb נפח means "to blow, breathe," which prompts the majority of English translations to render the verb as "sniff, snort," or even "turn your nose up" (NET). Yet there are instances in which the verb refers to blowing in order to set something ablaze (cf. Ezek 22:20; Job 20:26). Given the cultic context of Malachi, and the references to sacrifice, the latter rendering seems more likely.[73] Here, YHWH juxtaposes their claim (v. 13b) with their action (v. 13c). In other words, the charge levied against the priests is *not* that they complain about cultic activity only to turn their noses up to it, but more ominously, they complain about the oppressive nature of cultic activity only to continue to practice it. Understood this way, the priests conduct worship even though they are no longer convinced of its efficacy, a far more damning indictment.

The fact that the priests are keeping the altar lit despite their confessions in vv. 12c and 13b hints at the discrepancy between the priests' attitudes and their behaviors; their subsequent actions in vv. 13e–14d not only confirm that discrepancy, but they also scandalize it. The very ones who charge that YHWH now treats the altar table as defiled bring forward the very things that indeed make it defiled. In vv. 13e–14d the priests are chastised for the sacrifices they keep bringing to the altar. This list of unacceptable sacrifices somewhat mirrors the list in v. 10, except that a reference to that which is stolen (גָּזוּל) has been added. Admittedly, there is no law that explicitly forbids a stolen animal from being offered as a sacrifice, thus raising the question as to its inclusion here.[74] Weyde has argued that Malachi is likely drawing from Lev 5:20–26[6:1–6] and 19:13.[75] Because both texts prohibit stealing of any kind from one's neighbor, it only stands to reason that stolen animals would be disqualified as acceptable offerings. The legal traditions have been carefully applied to the cultic setting to arrive at a logical conclusion. The scribal tendencies in Malachi, already evident in the book, appear once more here.

The rhetorical question that follows, "Shall I accept it from you hand?" echoes the question raised in 1:8. In that verse, the prophet invites the priests to take their blind, lame, and sick animals to the governor to see whether such insufficient offerings would be accepted. The statement assumes that the governor would not receive what is from their hand (v. 9c). The rhetorical self-referential question in v. 13 anticipates the very same conclusion. If such offerings are unfit for a human ruler, then how much more so for the Divine King.

72. Jacobs, *The Books of Haggai and Malachi*, 204.

73. Weyde, *Prophecy and Teaching*, 152–53; Petersen, *Zechariah 9–14 and Malachi*, 201; Jacobs, *The Books of Haggai and Malachi*, 185.

74. The root גזל can mean "to tear off," leading some interpreters to conclude that the reference is not to stolen animals, but to mutilated animals, those that might have been attacked by a predator. Because Leviticus explicitly prohibits humans eating mutilated animals (17:15; 22:8), the argument runs, then it would seem inconceivable that these animals would be accepted as an offering to God. See Snyman, *Malachi*, 78; Glazier-McDonald, *Malachi*, 63; Smith, *Micah–Malachi*, 316.

75. Weyde, *Prophecy and Teaching*, 153.

Verse 14 extends the critique beyond that of just the priests, those mentioned initially in v. 6h, to include more broadly anyone in the community. The critique comes in the form of a curse formula based upon the corrupt actions of both the priests and the people. Lest one assume that the offering of animals that were blind and stolen, lame, and sick, were simply a result of the challenging socio-economic conditions of the day, the prophet declares otherwise and suggests that such a person is accursed.

Typical curse formulas include אָרוּר ("cursed") followed by a participle that identifies the offending action as well as the recipient of said action.[76] For example, Deut 27:24 declares, "Cursed is the one who kills his neighbor in secret" (author's translation), אָרוּר מַכֵּה רֵעֵהוּ בַּסָּתֶר (*qal* passive participle + participle + complement of the second participle + adjunct). Were Malachi to offer a similar curse formula, the expected form would read, "Cursed is the one who vows a male animal but sacrifices to YHWH what is blemished." In Mal 1:14, however, the curse formula differs in form. The participle of נכל ("deceiver") immediately follows אָרוּר, with the participle (נוֹכֵל) having a "characterizing function," in that it characterizes the person who does the following actions.[77] Put differently, the reason people are offering "blemished" animals is that they assume they can deceive God, and the reason they believe they can deceive God is because they assume God is not readily present or fully attentive to the worship of his people.

3. The Response of YHWH (1:14e–g)

The curse levied against the one who attempts to deceive YHWH (v. 14a–d) is justified by the claims articulated in v. 14e and g. Such deception is an affront because YHWH is the "great king" (מֶלֶךְ גָּדוֹל). The confession in v. 14e includes the verbless clause: מֶלֶךְ גָּדוֹל אָנִי (lit., "a great king am I"). The typical word order for such clauses is subject-[null verb]-complement, but in this instance the word order is inverted with the complement appearing first, thus making מֶלֶךְ גָּדוֹל an example of focus fronting. The point of this construction becomes evident when considered in light of the larger religious context.[78] In the ancient Near East, the label "great" was often applied to deities in combination with their role as kings. Examples of this abound in ancient texts, stela, and iconography. More specifically within the Persian period, such evidence is found in the Cyrus Cylinder, so named for the Persian king. In that text, Marduk is extolled as the "king of the gods" and "the great lord."[79] And later under Darius I, Ahuramazda is praised as the "great god" in connection with his role as the divine king.[80] Other inscriptions from the Achaemenid period reflect similar adulations for Ahuramazda. Understanding this background is necessary to understand the rhetorical move being made in v. 14. The cultic activity of the priests and the larger community suggests that they are not operating with the presupposition that YHWH is the great king. Consequently, YHWH reasserts his position as the "great king" (as evident by focus fronting,)

76. The curse formula utilizing the *qal* passive participle of ארר appears with considerable regularity, occurring thirty-eight times in the Old Testament, but strikingly only here in the Book of the Twelve.

77. Weyde, *Prophecy and Teaching*, 156.

78. On the use of this language as a means of resistance to the larger Persian ideology, see Innocent Himbaza, "« YHWH Seba'ot devient le grand roi ». Une interprétation de Ml 1,6–14 à la lumière du contexte perse," *VT* 62 (2012): 357–68.

79. "The Cyrus Cylinder," in *The Persian Period: A Corpus of Sources from the Achaemenid Period*, ed. Amélie Kuhrt (London: Routledge, 2007), 71.

80. "DNa §1–2," Kuhrt, *The Persian Period*, 502.

and even more, that his rule extends "among the nations."[81]

Despite the seemingly innocuous affirmation in v. 14 ("I am the Great King)," this affirmation serves as a biting rebuke to what has preceded it. Whether the priests honor YHWH, or give him the fear that is due him, what remains true is that this God is the great king. Whether one doubts the real presence of God amid acts of worship, this much is true: Yahweh, the God of Israel, remains king overall.

C. Priestly Instruction That Dishonors YHWH (2:1–9)

The next section of the disputation shifts the focus away from cultic impropriety specifically, to the failure of the priesthood in matters of instruction.

1. The Challenge to the Priests (2:1–4)

The opening verse signals a shift in the argument with the presence of וְעַתָּה, which functions here as a discourse marker. Frequently, after the exposition of a situation, וְעַתָּה is employed "to point to the implications of [that situation] for the here and now of the speaker."[82] The cultic failures of the priests rehearsed in 1:6–14 lead now to this challenge to the priests.[83] These are not two separate critiques of the priesthood, but in fact they are intimately connected.

The opening verse in this section contains a fronted prepositional phrase following the initial discourse marker, "And now *to you*, O priests, this commandment." This fronted prepositional phrase as well as the location of the vocative prove critical to the development of the argument. Whereas 1:14 seemed to have the entire community in view, as noted above, the focus narrows once more in 2:1 to that of the priests. In prose, the vocative ("O priests") typically occurs either in a clause initial or clause final position. When in the clause-final position, as in 2:1, vocatives typically appear between clauses that are syntactically related.[84] The priests referred to in verse 1 function as the antecedent to the second-person-plural pronouns that appear throughout the remainder of the pericope, i.e., the priests are mentioned explicitly in v. 1 with the vocative and remain in view throughout the second half of the disputation.

The prophet mentions "this commandment" in vv. 1 and 4. Upon first glance, the precise referent remains ambiguous. What exactly is *this* command? Is it referring to the curse that follows in vv. 2–3 or is something greater in view? Rather than understanding "this commandment [הַמִּצְוָה הַזֹּאת]" in v. 1 as simply having an introductory function to what follows, this phrase likely refers more broadly to the expectations associated with their priestly roles, and in particular, their responsibility to provide instruction to the people.[85] The association of "this commandment" with the

81. Focus fronting "distinguishes between the information assumed by speakers and that which is at the centre (or 'focus') of their communicative interest; *'focus' in this sense is opposed to presupposition.*" Crystal, *A Dictionary of Linguistics and Phonetics*, 192–93; italics added.

82. *BHRG* §40.39.

83. Although the subject matter of the discourse "shifts," vv. 1–2 function as a "hinge" to the entire pericope. The language employed in these verses recalls the language operative in the introduction to the entire disputation (v. 6). In 1:6 and 2:1, הַכֹּהֲנִים ("the priests") are addressed (vocative). In v. 2:2, the issue of honor (כָּבוֹד) reappears as well (cf. 1:6). Beyond these, there are other verbal connectors between the 1:6 and 2:2 as well: "name" (שֵׁם); "YHWH of hosts" (יְהוָה צְבָאוֹת).

84. On the clausal positioning of vocatives, see Cynthia Miller-Naudé, "Vocative Syntax in Biblical Hebrew Prose and Poetry," *JSS* 55 (2010), 347–64, esp. 355–56.

85. Petersen (*Zechariah 9–14 and Malachi*, 186–87) and

covenant with Levi in Mal 2:4 further confirms this reading. Deuteronomy 33:8–11 explains the responsibilities of Levi. Most significant for understanding the second disputation in Malachi is Deut 33:10 (author's translation): "They teach Jacob your ordinances and Israel your law; they place incense before you, and whole burnt offerings on your altar." Yet as the prophetic discourse in Malachi has already suggested, the very things they are called to do, i.e., to provide instruction and lead in acceptable sacrifice, are missing altogether in their service. The connection to what follows cannot be overlooked as Weyde has noted. He contends that the reference to "this commandment" actually looks backward and forward: "If the priests do not listen to the commandments given earlier (i.e., those in the legal traditions), YHWH will send a new command against them, that is, a word of punishment."[86] Thus, as it relates to understanding "this commandment" perhaps the option is not either/or, but both/and.

Because of the failure of the priests to live up to the covenantal expectations, YHWH issues an admonition in the form of a conditional clause using אִם־לֹא followed by a *yiqtol* (imperfect), understood here in a modal sense: "If the priests do not do X, then Y will follow."[87] The priests are instructed to listen or obey and to "take [it] to heart" (v. 2b) or "place [it] upon the heart." Although English speakers tend to equate the "heart" with emotion, the concept of the heart refers more nearly to the seat of knowledge and decision-making within the human. Understood this way, the instruction is not for the priests to listen and then place it upon the heart, in the sense of meditating or reflecting upon the covenant expectations, but instead they are to obey the covenant expectations and in so doing, alter the way they are living. The intended result of their reoriented lives appears in the purpose clause in v. 2c ("[in order] to give honor to my name"). Earlier in this disputation, the priests are chastised for despising (בזה) and polluting (חלל) the name of YHWH (1:6k, 12a), even though YHWH's name is declared great among the nations (1:11d) and feared (1:14g), but here the priests are called to reverse course and ensure that the name of YHWH receives the honor due it.[88]

If, however, the priests fail to give honor to YHWH's name, then YHWH will send "the curse." Because the noun הַמְּאֵרָה ("the curse") includes the definite article, the threat is not simply a curse in the general sense, but more likely a specific curse or curses, i.e., the type of covenant curses found in Deut 28. In further support of this claim, the collocation שׁלח ("to send") followed by הַמְּאֵרָה ("the curse") is only found in Deut 28:20. There the text reads, "YHWH will send [שׁלח] on you the curse [הַמְּאֵרָה], confusing you and rebuking you in all that you undertake, until you are destroyed and quickly perish because of your evil deeds, in which you have forsaken me" (author's translation). This understanding of הַמְּאֵרָה ("the curse") may also shed light on verse 2f and YHWH's promise to "curse your blessings." Due to the priests' failure to "take to heart" the covenantal expectations, YHWH will curse the material blessings of the priests.

Hill (*Malachi*, 197) both note that "this commandment" is best understood as a Deuteronomic term; cf. Verhoef, *The Books of Haggai and Malachi*, 237.

86. Weyde, *Prophecy and Teaching*, 171.

87. Contra Jacobs, *The Books of Haggai and Malachi*, 211, who understands the *yiqtol* to have a "future orientation."

88. The reference to honor in 2:2c recalls the opening aphorism in this disputation.

Verse 3 provides two examples of the curse that will befall them as a result of their disobedience.[89] In v. 3a, YHWH announces his intent to rebuke the offspring of the priests.[90] Interpreters have frequently emended this text based on the LXX: ἰδοὺ ἐγὼ ἀφορίζω ὑμῖν τὸν ὦμον, "I am going to take away/remove your shoulder." The LXX understands the MT "to rebuke" (גער) as "to remove" (גרע), an example of metathesis involving the *resh* and the *ayin*. Although the *BHS* suggests reading "to cut off" (גדע) instead of "to remove" (גרע), the BHQ opts for reading the MT. In addition to the verb itself, a second difference occurs in the latter half of the line (i.e., the complement). The LXX renders MT "seed" (זֶרַע) as "arm" (זְרוֹעַ). Based on the LXX translation, the assumption is that as part of the curse the priests will no longer be fit to carry out their priestly duties because their arm will be cut off or removed. Petersen follows the LXX in the first instance but then retains the MT in the second, preferring to translate the line as "I am removing your progeny."[91]

As noted above, however, Mal 2 appears to allude to Deut 28 and this is no less true with Mal 2:3a. Deuteronomy 28:20 reads, "YHWH will send [שלח] on you the curse [הַמְּאֵרָה], confusing you and rebuking [גער] you." The presence of "to rebuke" (גער) in Deut 28:20 confirms the MT reading in Mal 2:3a. Near the end of the pericope in Deut (28:46), the curse is said to be directed against "you and your seed [זֶרַע]." The language of "seed" in Mal 2:3a echoes that in Deut 28, providing additional justification for retaining the MT over the LXX.

Beyond text critical issues, Deut 28:20 is instructive for understanding what is being conveyed in Mal 2:3a. One could read Mal 2:2e, "I will send on you the curse" and 2:3a "Behold I am about to rebuke your offspring" as two separate acts but, as reflected above in Deut 28:20, being rebuked (גער) is not different from the curse (הַמְּאֵרָה). In fact, גער is the operative sense of the curse, i.e., being rebuked is the curse in action.[92]

In the second part of the curse, YHWH announces that he will spread the dung, or offal, from the festivals upon the faces of the priests. The word "spread" (זרה) is used thirty-nine times in the Old Testament with more than one third occurring in Ezekiel. In those instances, the term refers to God scattering the people in judgment. Although in Malachi the act of scattering or spreading has a different connotation, the underlying theme of judgment remains in view. The word "dung" (פֶּרֶשׁ) is relatively rare, occurring only in the priestly traditions.[93] The skin, flesh, and entrails of the sacrificial animals, i.e., the dung, were to be burned outside the cultic area. In the appositional phrase, "the dung of your festivals" (פֶּרֶשׁ חַגֵּיכֶם), the noun חַג specifies that this refers to the animals sacrificed at the festivals.[94] The communal events intended for celebration will become the sources of public shame for the priests. Having "dung" spread upon the faces of the priests threatened to contaminate

89. When referring to future situations, the grammatical construction הִנְנִי followed by a participle typically conveys a sense of immanence, "I am about to . . ." On the so-called *futurum instans* participle, see *IBHS* §37.6f.

90. Those retaining the MT include the following: Jacobs, *The Books of Haggai and Malachi*, 209–10; Weyde, *Prophecy and Teaching*, 159; Verhoef, *The Books of Haggai and Malachi*, 236; Hill, *Malachi*, 171, 200.

91. See Petersen, *Zechariah 9–14 and Malachi*, 176.

92. See Weyde, *Prophecy and Teaching*, 162–64.

93. Exod 29:14; Lev 4:11; 8:17; 16:27; Num 19:5.

94. The phrase פֶּרֶשׁ חַגֵּיכֶם, "the dung of your festivals," is an example of extraposed apposition, i.e., the appositional phrase appears separate from the anchor (the initial use of פֶּרֶשׁ). On apposition more generally, see Robert D. Holmstedt and Andrew R. Jones, "Apposition in Biblical Hebrew: Structure and Function," *KUSATU* 22 (2017): 21–51.

them, i.e., to make them unclean, as well as to humiliate them. But as Hill has correctly observed, "the portent of smearing dung upon the priests' faces is merely a symbolic action representing spiritual deficiencies that already disqualify them from priestly service."[95] The outward act of judgment presupposes the priests' inward disposition.

Because dung is not found in the cultic area, YHWH announces that "someone will carry [the priests] to it." The abrupt change from first person in previous lines to third person in v. 3c likely explains the emendation of the text by the LXX and Syriac, "I will lift . . . ," suggesting that YHWH will take the priests to the dung hill. This harmonizes the lines but problematizes the text in other ways. Both the NEB and the NRSV adopt this emendation.[96] Although the emendation makes for a smoother reading, the MT should be retained. The point is clear: someone within the community will carry the priests outside the cultic area to the place where dung and excrement are properly disposed. The priests do not belong in the sphere of the holy but instead, to the sphere of the defiled and defiling.

Verse 4 concludes this section with a rationale for the action described in vv. 1–3. The explanation is expressed by way of a "recognition formula ("to know that," ידע כִּי). Elsewhere in the Old Testament, the recognition formula appears after an account of divine action.[97] YHWH declares that he sent "this commandment," לִהְיוֹת בְּרִיתִי אֶת־לֵוִי ("so that my covenant with Levi will continue"). The *qal* infinitive construct (לִהְיוֹת) introduces a purpose clause that offers the rationale for YHWH's actions. While the actions proposed in verses 2–3 serve to threaten the role of the current priests, they also serve to reinforce YHWH's commitment to the covenant with Levi (on the nature of this covenant, see 2:5–7 below).

2. The Ideal Priesthood (2:5–7)

The reference to the "covenant with Levi" in v. 4 concludes the previous subunit while also introducing the focal point for vv. 5–7.[98] This reference to a "covenant with Levi," however, raises questions given that there is no specific account of such a covenant in the Old Testament. That said, the mention of Levi in Mal 2:4, and the subsequent description of his priestly activity, appears to echo earlier biblical traditions, in particular Num 25:10–13 and Deut 33:8–11. Numbers 25:10–13 recounts the zeal of Phineas in response to the idolatry and intermarriage of Israel in the wilderness.[99] Because of his devotion, Phineas, a grandson of Aaron, is granted a "covenant of permanent priesthood" (v. 13, NET), a covenant described as a one of peace (שָׁלוֹם) in 25:12 (cf. Mal 2:5a).[100] In Deut 33, Levi is praised for having been faithful to the covenant (v. 9; Mal 2:5).[101] In addition, and as noted earlier, the descendants of Levi are described as teachers of the torah: "They teach Jacob your ordinances,

95. Hill, *Malachi*, 201.

96. Petersen cites "incorrect word division" and proposes, "you shall be carried away from me" (*Zechariah 9–14 and Malachi*, 176).

97. Weyde, *Prophecy and Teaching*, 175.

98. On the notion of the "ideal priest" in this passage, see Lear, *Scribal Composition*, 126–34.

99. O'Brien notes that these two themes, idolatry and intermarriage, are central to the message of Malachi, and may explain the reference to this tradition (*Priest and Levite in Malachi*, 105).

100. The mention of "offspring" or "seed" in Num 25:13 and Mal 2:3 provide another example of the possible influence of Num 25 on Mal 2. Whereas the "seed" of Phinehas will be rewarded for their fervent devotion, the "seed" of the priests in Mal 2 will be rebuked.

101. Joseph Blenkinsopp argues similarly for the significance of Deut 33:8–11 for understanding this text (*A History of Prophecy in Israel: Revised and Enlarged* [Louisville: Westminster John Knox, 1996], 212).

and Israel your law" (v. 10a NRSVUE; Mal 2:6–7). Beyond their instructional duties, they are assigned cultic roles, including the handling of the Urim and Thummin as well as placing incense and whole burnt offerings on the altar (v. 10b). Thus, rather than an allusion to a specific text or episode in Israel's history, the reference to the covenant with Levi should be understood as a "composite picture," as a "distinctive portrait of the ideal priest."[102] In contradistinction to the priests in Malachi's audience, the ideal priest is to be lauded for fierce devotion in the face of competing claims (e.g., idolatry and intermarriage) and for faithfulness in matters of torah instruction and sacrifice.[103]

Although the current priesthood lacked a proper sense of fear (1:6g–i), Levi did not; he feared YHWH and stood in awe before his name. In addition to this proper posture of fear adopted by the ideal priest, Malachi notes two other features of Levi that are germane to the critique on the current priesthood: his instruction and his action. According to 2:6a, the instruction provided by Levi was אֱמֶת. This feminine noun is generally taken to mean "trustworthiness, faithfulness," thus producing the translation, "true instruction." The phrase תּוֹרַת אֱמֶת only occurs here in the Old Testament, but it does appear in the plural in Neh 9:13, referring specifically to the giving of the law at Mt. Sinai. Thus, the phrase תּוֹרַת אֱמֶת means more than Levi simply taught error free, but instead implies that Levi's instructions were rooted in the laws of YHWH.

Verse 6b makes a similar claim but in the negative, "Deceit (עַוְלָה) could not be found on his lips," once more affirming the "true instruction" of Levi. Although עַוְלָה often refers to iniquity or wickedness, particularly as it refers to some actions, the term also appears in contexts related to speech. In those contexts, עַוְלָה is often paralleled with רְמִיָּה, meaning "deceit" (cf. Job 13:7; 27:4). The failure of the current priesthood to provide this kind of instruction is rehearsed later in v. 8.

In addition to providing true instruction, Levi embodied covenantal faithfulness. Malachi explains that Levi "walked" (הלך) with God "in peace and in uprightness" (v. 6c). The verb הלך signals a "life lived in obedience . . . , that is, with reference to covenant standards."[104] The character of Levi's "walk" is clarified further by the two fronted prepositional phrases. To declare that Levi walked "in peace" (בְּשָׁלוֹם) is to suggest that Levi walked in right relationship with YHWH. Malachi announces that he also walked "in uprightness." The noun מִישׁוֹר literally means "a plain" or "level ground" (Deut 3:10), but here the metaphorical use of the term seems in view, i.e., "uprightness," in the sense of moral integrity.[105] The fronting of the two prepositional phrases ("in peace and in uprightness") qualifies what it means to truly "walk with God," and in so doing, it accentuates what is sorely lacking among the current priesthood.

Because Levi feared YHWH (v. 5c), provided true instruction, and modeled a life consistent with the covenant, "he turned many from iniquity." The complement "many" (רַבִּים) is focus fronted in an effort to contrast the positive impact of the ideal priest on the "many" and the negative impact of the current priesthood upon the "many," as described in v. 8b. In v. 6d, due to the instruction of Levi, many turned from iniquity; in v. 8b, due to

102. O'Brien, *Priest and Levite*, 106.

103. As an example of the priests providing faithful interpretation on the torah for the post-exilic community, see Hag 2:10–14.

104. Eugene H. Merrill, "הלך," *NIDOTTE* 1:1033. Although the collocation הלך את, "to walk with" God occurs infrequently in the Old Testament, only in Mal 2:6 and Gen 5:22, 24; 6:9 does it refer specifically to a human's relationship with God (Weyde, *Prophecy and Teaching*, 191).

105. Snyman, *Malachi*, 89.

the instruction of the current priesthood, many stumbled in the torah.

Verses 5–6 revisit claims about the ideal priest in Israel's past. This retrospective is confirmed by the presence of *qatal* and *wayyiqtol* verb forms in these two verses; clearly the past is in view. In verse 7, however, these verb forms give way to *yiqtols* in 7a–b and a verbless clause in 7c. The *yiqtol* verbs are best understood here in a modal sense, i.e., "should": the lips of the priest "*should* preserve knowledge;" many "*should* seek torah from his lips." Thus, the shift in verb forms reflects the flow of the argumentation. The prophet began with a retrospective glance in verses 5–6, and in so doing, rooted the ideal expectations of priestly service in the past. What appears in v. 7, however, is more akin to a maxim.[106] Thus, whereas vv. 5–6 point to the past, v. 7 functions as a maxim meant to describe the ideal priest in any age.[107] The purpose of the maxim is twofold. It reinforces Levi as the ideal priest (vv. 5–6), as one who embodies the maxim, but it provides an ominous foreshadowing of the accusatory comments made in the final two verses of the disputation (vv. 8–9); the current priests fall woefully short of the ideal articulated in the maxim.

The opening clause of the maxim (v. 7) begins with the particle כִּי. Interpreters have rendered the כִּי clause in one of three ways: as a conjunction "for," which assumes the clause functions as a subordinate clause;[108] as a causal adverb used emphatically ("indeed, surely");[109] or as a causal adverb with a logical force, "because."[110] The last option ("because") seems preferable here. The particle כִּי can introduce a causal clause that precedes the main or matrix clause. The reason the causal clause comes first "is that the speaker wishes to remove any doubt about the grounds of the situation."[111] Thus the flow of the argument in the first two lines of v. 7 is as follows:

Matrix clause (v. 7b):	"They should seek torah from his mouth"
Causal clause (v. 7a):	"because the lips of the priest should preserve knowledge."

The community *should* feel confident in turning to the priests for instruction in the torah because the priests should be the ones preserving this knowledge. What precisely is this "knowledge?" Given that the word דַּעַת ("knowledge") in v. 7a stands parallel to תּוֹרָה in v. 7b, there can be little doubt that Malachi has in view instruction in God's law.[112] The only other occurrence of דַּעַת ("knowledge") in the Book of the Twelve occurs in Hos 4:6, and in that context דַּעַת ("knowledge") also stands in parallel to תּוֹרָה ("torah"). There the priests are chided for ignoring the torah and rejecting God's דַּעַת.

The final כִּי in v. 7 introduces a motivation clause. The people should seek instruction from the

106. Weyde, *Prophecy and Teaching*, 195. See also, Hill, *Malachi*, 211. Earlier in 1:6, the prophet references an apparent aphorism in that section of the argumentation and here, as the argument is drawing to a close, the prophet relies upon another saying.

107. Snyman argues that vv. 6a–7c form an "interesting concentric structure" (*Malachi*, 91), but upon closer examination the "concentric" nature of his proposal seems to break down. What can be said, however, is that the retrospective view of Levi and the maxim are bound together by the shared vocabulary (torah, mouth, lips).

108. Cf. NRSV.

109. A number of commentators opt for this rendering. See Verhoef, *The Books of Haggai and Malachi*, 249–50; Hill, *Malachi*, 171; Snyman, *Malachi*, 91; Petersen, *Zechariah 9–14 and Malachi*, 175.

110. Smith, *Micah-Malachi*, 309; Jacobs, *The Books of Haggai and Malachi*, 223.

111. *BHRG* §40.28.1.

112. Weyde, *Prophecy and Teaching*, 197.

priest "for he is the messenger of YHWH Sabaoth." This collocation ("messenger of YHWH") appears frequently in the Old Testament, referring almost exclusively to prophets or a "supernatural being" (cf. Gen 16:7; 22:11; Exod 3:2; Num 22:22).[113] The unusual application of this title to a priest, however, has generated a number of explanatory comments. Glazier-McDonald, among others, has suggested that this reflects a significant shift in post-exilic Yehud with "a diminution of the prophetic role in society . . . their authority was superseded by that of the priests."[114] Verhoef rejected this argument and averred that Malachi was referring to the role of the priest in the "classical period" and that such a reference in no way signaled the "demise" of the prophetic office.[115] Rather than understanding one office (priest) as replacing the other (prophet), as suggested by Glazier-McDonald, or that such a title only referred to a previous iteration of the priesthood (Verhoef), it is more likely that the application of this title to a priest signals that "the boundaries between teaching priest and prophet sage were fading in the Persian period."[116] The use of this title in Mal 2:7 confirms the teaching role of the priests in the post-exilic period, but even more, confirms what is the sole source of their knowledge, YHWH.[117] Within the context of the argument, the latter point is obviously the most critical. The last clause in the maxim, then, provides the motivation for the claim in the matrix clause. Thus, the flow of the argument in the maxim is as follows:

People should seek torah from the priests because they are to be the purveyors of such knowledge, and such knowledge is "true instruction" (v. 6a) because YHWH is the source of that knowledge.

3. Concluding Accusation and Resulting Punishment (2:8–9)

The accusations levied against the priests in verse 8 highlight the disparity between the current priesthood and that of the ideal priesthood as embodied in Levi. The topic-fronting of the personal pronoun וְאַתֶּם confirms the intended comparison between the two, "but you." The prophet makes three charges against the priests, but as will be suggested below, these are not three separate charges, but in fact are closely linked due to the lack of a conjunction (asyndeton) in v. 8b–c.

In 2:6c, Levi is said to have walked with God "in peace and uprightness," but the current generation of priests have "have turned aside [סוּר] from the way" (v. 8a). This latter phrase appears repeatedly in the Deuteronomistic literature (Deut 9:12, 16; 11:28; 31:29; Judg 2:17) in reference to turning away from YHWH and the commands of YHWH.

Matrix clause (v. 7b):	"They should seek torah from his mouth"
Causal clause (v. 7a):	"because the lips of the priest should preserve knowledge"
Motivation clause (v. 7c):	"for he is the messenger of YHWH Sabaoth."

113. The only reference to a priest as the "messenger of YHWH" is found in Eccl 5:6[5].

114. Glazier-McDonald, *Malachi*, 72. For a similar assessment, see J. M. P. Smith, "Malachi," in Hinckley G. Mitchell, John Merlin Powis Smith, and Julius A. Brewer, *Critical and Exegetical Commentary on Haggai, Zechariah, Malachi and Jonah*, ICC (Edinburgh: T&T Clark, 1912), 40. See also Robert P. Carroll, *When Prophecy Failed* (New York: Seabury, 1979), 204–5.

115. Verhoef, *The Books of Haggai and Malachi*, 250.

116. Eric M. Meyers, "Priestly Language in the Book of Malachi," *HAR* 10 (1986), 231.

117. Nogalski, *Book of the Twelve: Micah–Malachi*, 1027.

In the book of Malachi, this notion of "turning aside" is reflected in the priests' cultic activity, activity that confirms their disregard for YHWH and YHWH's torah. The verb (סוּר) also appears in the story of the golden calf (Exod 32) where סוּר, "to turn aside," appears alongside the verb שׁחת, "to corrupt" (32:7–8). Led by Aaron and the priests, the people are said to have acted corruptly and "turned aside quickly from the way."[118] If an allusion to the golden calf incident is intended, then the improper instructions on offerings by the current generation of priests are more than simply malpractice or poor teaching, they are comparable with that of apostasy in Israel's past.[119]

In v. 6d, Levi is said to have "turned many from iniquity," but the current generation of priests has "caused many to stumble [כשׁל]" (v. 8b). The verb "stumble" (כשׁל) often functions metaphorically to suggest a life that is not aligned with God. Beyond the meaning of the verb itself, two issues demand further consideration. The first concerns how to translate the collocation כשׁל ("stumble") + ב, and the second, the precise meaning of תּוֹרָה ("torah"). The preposition ב functions instrumentally here, i.e, "by." While the word תּוֹרָה ("torah") can refer to the stipulations of the law or even the law itself, here it is better understood as "instruction," i.e., the instruction of the priests. This seems consistent with its usage in vv. 5–6. Understood this away, Malachi chastises the priests: "you have caused many to stumble through your instruction."[120] Thus in verse 8a the priests are condemned for turning aside from YHWH and *his* instruction which in so doing has caused many people to stumble because of *their* instruction.

In the final accusation (v. 8c), Malachi charges the priests with having "corrupted" the covenant with Levi. Elsewhere in the Old Testament, the verb שׁחת refers to things that are so "spoiled" or "ruined" that they have rendered themselves useless.[121] For example in the book of Jeremiah, both the loin cloth (13:7) and the clay pot (18:4) are described as שׁחת because they are ruined, they are useless. A similar use of the root appears in Mal 1:14. The prophet labels an animal שׁחת because it is blemished; it is "ruined" and useless for the purpose originally set forth.[122] Here in Mal 2:8c, the prophet declares that the covenant with Levi has been corrupted and ruined, the covenant has been "rendered inoperative by being broken."[123] In short, by corrupting the covenant with Levi, the priests have made themselves useless.

As suggested above, the three accusations in verse 8 are logically connected. The relationship between the first accusation and that of the second and third accusations is reflected in the asyndetic construction (the absence of a *vav*) in v. 8b–c. Because Hebrew tends generally toward constructions with a *vav*, its absence here is notable. Frequently asyndetic clauses function explicatively, i.e., they develop what was mentioned in the previous clause.[124] This seems to be the case in v. 8 as well. Thus, because the priests have "turned aside from the way" (v. 8a), they have caused many to stumble (v. 8b) and they have corrupted the covenant with Levi (v. 8c). Their initial act of disobedience and

118. Weyde, *Prophecy and Teaching*, 201–3; Snyman, *Malachi*, 92; Jacobs, *The Books of Haggai and Malachi*, 228.

119. Weyde, *Prophecy and Teaching*, 203.

120. Verhoef, *The Books of Haggai and Malachi*, 236; Weyde, *Prophecy and Teaching*, 204; Glazier-McDonald, *Malachi*, 45. Cf. NAB, NIV, NRSV. This rendering supplies, or assumes, a second person plural suffix on תּוֹרָה, i.e., "your torah," despite its absence in the Hebrew text. The LXX, however, renders the phrase "you have caused many to become weak in law" (ἐν νόμῳ), understanding תּוֹרָה as a reference to the law of Yahweh not the instruction of the priests.

121. Cornelis Van Dam, "שׁחת," in *NIDOTTE* 4:92–93.

122. Cf. Mal 3:11.

123. Clendenen, "Malachi," 317.

124. JM §177a.

apostasy threatened the entire community and the identity of the priesthood itself.

Verse 9 concludes the disputation with an announcement of judgment. Although the opening focus particle גַּם is often translated with an "additive force," i.e., "And so . . . (NRSV, NIV, NASB), the usage demands closer scrutiny. Often the particle is used in judgment speeches to signal the introduction of a reciprocal action (i.e., what *x* does is a corresponding reaction to what *y* did).[125] For example, in Jer 13:25–26, YHWH charges the people with having forgotten YHWH and having started to listen to lies, and then he declares, וְגַם־אֲנִי חָשַׂפְתִּי שׁוּלַיִךְ עַל־פָּנָיִךְ ("and I, *in turn*, will lift up your skirts over your face"). Similarly, the announcement of judgment in Mal 2:9 is a "corresponding reaction" to the actions of the priests outlined in v. 8. This sense of contrast is reinforced through the use of personal pronouns. Paralleling the topic-fronting of the second-person pronoun in v. 8, אֲנִי is fronted in v. 9, serving to highlight the contrast between the actions of the priests and subsequent action of YHWH (i.e., "*you* [the priests] have turned aside from the way . . . so *I* will make you despised").

In v. 9a, the prophet announces the judgment that is to befall the priests and in so doing, returns to the language of honor and shame found in the opening lines of this disputation. The opening aphorism with its subsequent questioning in 1:6a–g refers to the honor due YHWH and its glaring absence in the current cultic climate. Instead of honoring YHWH, the priests are labeled as those who despise (בזה) the name of YHWH (1:6h). The same root appears in 1:7 and 12. Because the priests have despised YHWH's name and have corrupted the covenant of Levi, YHWH declares in 2:9 that he will make *them* despised and humiliated "before all the הָעָם ('the people')." But who in fact are the הָעָם? Following the LXX and Vulgate, Snyman emends the word to make it plural, "before all the peoples."[126] Rendered this way, the "peoples" are understood to be the nations. Thus, even as YHWH's name will be made great beyond the borders of Israel (1:11, 14) so too will be the humiliation of the priests.

While such a proposal is appealing, ultimately it must be rejected and replaced with a more contextually relevant reading. According to the maxim in 2:7, the community in Yehud should seek instruction from the lips of the priests because they are the messengers of YHWH Sabaoth (v. 7b–c). That view implies a certain social standing within the community. That social standing, however, will be reversed when punishment is meted out, according to v. 9. Rather than being sought out, the priests will be despised; rather than being lifted up as messengers of YHWH, they will be brought low (שְׁפָלִים), "humiliated."

The rationale for this change in status is explained in v. 9b–c. The opening conjunction in v. 9b, כְּפִי אֲשֶׁר, "in as much" or "because of," is only used here in the MT. Gesenius lists it among "special conjunctions often used in combination to introduce causal clauses."[127] In v. 8a, the prophet condemned the priests for having "turned aside from the way," i.e., from YHWH and his ways. That indictment now serves as a justification in v. 9b for the change in social status of the priests; those who deviate from the ways of YHWH open themselves up to the punishment of YHWH.

The priests' change in status is explained further in v. 9c. The precise meaning of the clause is dic-

125. *BHRG* §40.20.2b.

126. Snyman, *Malachi*, 93. The critical apparatus in *BHQ* assesses the variant readings of הָעָם to be in error.

127. GKC §158a.

tated by two issues. The first concerns the negative particle plus the pronominal suffix ("you are not," אֵינְכֶם) which appears in v. 9b. Some interpreters contend that the particle אֵין, "there is not," governs only the clause in v. 9b. While plausible, it seems best to understand אֵינְכֶם as governing both clauses. Its absence in v. 9c can be attributed to gapping:

> in as much as you are not keeping my ways
> and [you are not] properly regarding matters
> of torah.[128]

The second issue to be considered in this verse concerns the meaning of the phrase וְנֹשְׂאִים פָּנִים. The collocation literally means "to lift the face," and frequently it appears in judicial texts with the connotation of showing partiality (e.g., Lev 19:15; Deut 10:18). Those interpreters who argue that אֵינְכֶם ("you are not") does not govern the clause in v. 9c suggest that the priests are being condemned for malpractice of some sort and translate the clause in a manner similar to that of Petersen: the priests are "showing partiality in matters related to the Torah."[129] Yet if this is a correct rendering of the phrase, it would mean that in the final verse of the disputation, where one might expect some type of summative statement, the prophet is introducing an entirely new idea (i.e., the unjust treatment of some within the community). In this, the longest disputation in the book of Malachi, however, the matter of partiality has not been raised.

Other translations have been proposed. Paul Redditt argues that the literal translation of v. 9b–c is "you are neither following my ways nor lifting up faces by the law."[130] The problem, according to Redditt, is that rather than showing kindness or "favor" (i.e., "lifting up faces"), the priests were not being gracious to worshipers, perhaps even demeaning them. Hill offers a similar reading of the text.[131] Unfortunately, such a proposal is subject to the same criticism as above; it introduces a new idea in the final line of the disputation.

As noted above, the phrase וְנֹשְׂאִים פָּנִים can mean "to show favor" or "have regard for." Even the more negative association, "showing partiality," implies that one object is given favor over another, or that one object is regarded higher than another object. Earlier in the disputation, this same phrase appears when the prophet invites the priests to present the imperfect offerings to the governor. Malachi inquires in 1:8, הֲיִשָּׂא פָנֶיךָ, "Will he regard you?" A verse later in 1:9 the prophet suggests bringing the same offerings to YHWH and he asks once more, הֲיִשָּׂא מִכֶּם פָּנִים, "Will he regard you?" In both instances the question is whether the governor or YHWH will regard (or even consider) those bringing such defective sacrifices. Applying the same meaning to 2:9, the issue is not about showing partiality but instead, about properly regarding or giving proper consideration to the torah. Thus, the priests will be despised and humiliated because they are not keeping the ways of YHWH (v. 9b) and they are not showing proper regard for matters related to the torah (v. 9c). As Snyman surmises, these two lines function as "an apt review of the many statements made about the priests and their way of thinking about and their handling of the Torah of Yahweh."[132] From the beginning to the end of the second disputation, the priests are chastised for their failure to follow the ways of YHWH properly.

128. Hill, *Malachi*, 217–18, actually suggests that both כְּפִי אֲשֶׁר and אֵינְכֶם are gapped in v. 9c.

129. Petersen, *Zechariah 9–14 and Malachi*, 175, 192–93; Weyde, *Prophecy and Teaching*, 208–9; Verhoef, *The Books of Haggai and Malachi*, 253. Cf. NRSV, HCSB, NIV.

130. Redditt, *Haggai, Zechariah, Malachi*, 169.

131. Hill, *Malachi*, 217–18.

132. Snyman, *Malachi*, 94.

Canonical and Theological Significance

The Name of God

As noted earlier, this disputation is the longest of the six and arguably the most complex thematically and structurally. In many ways the claims constructed in this section of Malachi are predicated upon a proper recognition of the "name" of YHWH. The Hebrew word שֵׁם ("name") appears ten times in the book of Malachi with eight of those appearances in this disputation alone.

Although "name" is frequently associated with character or reputation (i.e., a person's name), its usage in Malachi aligns more closely to that found in the book of Deuteronomy.[133] In that book, by way of circumlocution, Jerusalem is referred to as "the place which YHWH your God will chose to make his *name* dwell" (e.g., 12:11; 14:23, 24; 16:2, 6). In the history of scholarship, the prevailing understanding has been that the "name theology" in the book of Deuteronomy represented a significant development in Israel's theological claims about YHWH. According to this view, the reference to the name of YHWH was an attempt to address questions of God's transcendence and immanence. Lest one assume that God was located only and fully within the temple, this name theology sought to recast an understanding of YHWH's presence. The reference to "the place which YHWH your God will chose to make his name dwell" was meant to suggest that while God was not located in the earthly sphere, his name most assuredly was.[134]

More recent studies have contested the earlier proposals, particularly as it pertains to how the book of Deuteronomy construes the presence of God.[135] In his thorough analysis, Ian Wilson considered the occurrences of "before YHWH" (לִפְנֵי יְהוָה) in Deut 12–26 and observed that in each instance a locative sense was implied, that is, the use of "before YHWH" referred "to the localized presence of [God] at the 'chosen place.'"[136] In other words, to be "before YHWH" meant being in the presence of God. This understanding of the phrase "before YHWH" (לִפְנֵי יְהוָה) proves important for understanding the phrase "the place which YHWH your God will chose to make his name dwell" and, in particular, what is meant by "name." Deuteronomy 16:11 reads,

133. On the meaning of the term more generally in the Old Testament, see Allen P. Ross, "שֵׁם," in *NIDOTTE* 4:148–50.

134. See Gerhard von Rad, *Deuteronomium-Studien*, FRLANT 58 (Gottingen: Vandenhoeck & Ruprecht, 1947), 25–30; Moshe Weinfeld, *Deuteronomy and the Deuteronomic School* (Oxford: Clarendon Press, 1972); T. N. D. Mettinger, *The Dethronement of Sabaoth: Studies in the Shem and Kabod Theologies*, ConBOT 18 (Lund: CWK Gleerup, 1982).

135. Most notably, Ian Wilson, *Out of the Midst of Fire: Divine Presence in Deuteronomy*, SBLDS 151 (Atlanta: Scholars Press, 1995) and Sandra L. Richter, *The Deuteronomistic History and the Name Theology: lešakkēn šemô šām in the Bible and the Ancient Near East*, BZAW 318 (Berlin: de Gruyter, 2002). See also, Michael Hundley, "To Be or Not to Be: A Reexamination of Name Language in Deuteronomy and the Deuteronomistic History," *VT* 59 (2009): 533–55.

136. Wilson, *Out of the Midst of Fire*, 204.

> Rejoice before YHWH your God—you and your sons and your daughters, your male and female slaves, the Levites resident in your towns, as well as the strangers, the orphans, and the widows who are among you,—at the place which YHWH your God will choose to make his name dwell. (author's translation)

Thus, to be in the place where YHWH's name dwells is to stand "before YHWH," it is to be in God's presence.[137] This understanding is reflected most clearly in the exchange between the priests and YHWH in 1:6j–7c:

> Priests: "How have we despised your name?"
> YHWH: "By presenting defiled food upon my altar."
> Priests: "How have we defiled you?

By despising God's name and bringing defiled food to the altar, the priests have brought that which is defiled into God's presence.

In light of this understanding, the violations reported in this disputation are particularly egregious. They are egregious in that the problem is not simply that "they failed to follow directions," but instead that they failed to recognize in whose presence they were. Such action surely leads to the conclusion that they had no fear of God, the very indictment mentioned in 1:6f–g. There is no need for fear; there is no need for proper reverence when one believes that the Other is not really present. Malachi chastises the priests because they have in fact worshipped *as though* God is not fully and faithfully present with his people. What seems entirely unimaginable has in fact become their operating presupposition.

The Scandal of Unfaithful Instruction

The second half of the disputation focuses on the priests' failure to take seriously their responsibility to provide faithful instruction. YHWH lifts up Levi as the ideal priest in 2:6 (NRSVUE): "True instruction was in his mouth, and no wrong was found on his lips. He walked with me in integrity and uprightness, and he turned many from iniquity." According to the maxim in v. 7, priests are meant to "preserve knowledge" for those seeking instruction. Yet the actions of the present generation of priests fall woefully short of such expectations.

The root cause for the priests' pedagogical failure in the book of Malachi is simple: they themselves have turned aside from the "way"; they have turned aside

137. This is not to suggest, however, that God is "confined" to one place, but instead that the "name" functions as "a metonym of sorts that captures some of the divine essence yet does not encapsulate the whole" (Hundley, "To Be or Not to Be," 554).

from YHWH and his commands. Similar concerns regarding faithful instruction are expressed in the first book in the Book of the Twelve. Following a stinging rebuke of Israel for their waywardness in Hos 4:1–4, the prophet then turns to the priest. YHWH declares, "my contention is with you, O priest" (v. 4c), and chief among the charges is that the priests have forgotten the law and worse yet, forsaken Yahweh (vv. 6, 10).

While the priests' apparent abnegation of God (both in Hosea and Malachi) is troubling enough, it is the consequences of such actions that garner the particular attention of these two prophets. In both instances, the instruction of the priests proved scandalous because it in fact proved disastrous for the larger community. Hosea suggests that the priests' failure has led to the demise of the people because of their "lack of knowledge" (v. 6a). Similarly, Malachi reports that such poor instruction has caused many to stumble in the law (v. 8). In both books, the inherent connection between faithful instruction and communal covenant faithfulness is quite evident. As Hill explains, "Right behavior on the part of the people of Israel in covenant relationship with Yahweh was dependent upon sound priestly instruction."[138] Thus, while the priests remain the focal point of Malachi's trenchant rebuke in 1:6–2:9, the implications for the larger community remain squarely in view (1:10; 2:8b).

138. Hill, *Malachi*, 221.

CHAPTER 4

Malachi 2:10–16

IV. An Unfaithful Community

Main Idea of the Passage

Marriage serves as the arena in which the community's covenant faithfulness to God and their covenant faithfulness to one another is measured fully.

Literary Context

In the first disputation (1:2–5), the people questioned the covenant faithfulness of YHWH, a claim that was roundly rebutted by YHWH. In the second disputation (1:6–2:9), attention turned to the priests and their lack of faithfulness, as evident in their cultic malpractice and their misguided instruction in matters of the torah. In this disputation, the focus extends to the entire community. Even as the priests had engaged in acts of faithlessness, so too had the entire community. The two practices highlighted in this section include (1) the intermarriage between Jewish men who worshipped YHWH and the "daughters of foreign gods," and (2) the practice of Jewish men divorcing the "wives of their youth." At a purely sociological level, both actions pose a threat to the structure of the covenant community, but for the prophet, such actions also reveal a far deeper flaw in the people's faithfulness to YHWH.

Translation and Exegetical Outline

(See pages 85–86.)

Structure and Literary Form

As suggested in the introduction, the book of Malachi contains six disputations of varying length and complexity. This, the third disputation, differs from the first two both in voice and in structure.[1] In the opening lines of the first two disputations, YHWH makes a claim, which is then subsequently challenged by the audience. In this disputation, however, there is a noticeable shift to first-person-plural language, i.e., "Do *we* not have one father ? Did not one God create *us*?" (cf. 2:10a, b). With this shift in voice, obviously YHWH is no longer the one uttering the claim, but is in fact the object of the claim. This pattern continues in much of the remainder of the disputation.

1. Floyd divides this pericope into two sections 2:10–12 and 2:13–16, and includes them within a much larger collection, 1:6–2:16. Further, as noted in the introduction, Floyd rejects the notion of a disputation genre in the book of Malachi altogether. Instead, he labels 2:10–12 as a "prophecy of punishment," which includes an accusation (vv. 10–11) followed by an announcement of punishment (v. 12), and 2:13–16 as a "prophetic call to repentance" (*The Minor Prophets: Part 2*, 605, 609).

Malachi 2:10–16

			IV. An Unfaithful Community (2:10–16)
			A. Marriage to the Daughters of Foreign Gods (2:10a–12b)
10a	הֲלוֹא אָב אֶחָד לְכֻלָּנוּ	Do we not have one father?	1. YHWH's Rhetorical Questions (2:10 a–d)
10b	הֲלוֹא אֵל אֶחָד בְּרָאָנוּ	Did not one God create us?	
10c	מַדּוּעַ נִבְגַּד אִישׁ בְּאָחִיו	Why then does each act faithlessly against his brother,	
10d	↑ לְחַלֵּל בְּרִית אֲבֹתֵינוּ	↑ thereby profaning the covenant of our ancestors?	
11a	בָּגְדָה יְהוּדָה	Judah has acted faithlessly;	2. The Evidence of Faithlessness (2: 11a–e)
11b	↑ וְתוֹעֵבָה נֶעֶשְׂתָה בְיִשְׂרָאֵל וּבִירוּשָׁלָ͏ִם	↑ that is, an abomination has been committed in Israel and in Jerusalem,	
11c	כִּי חִלֵּל יְהוּדָה קֹדֶשׁ יְהוָה	because Judah has profaned the holy [people] of YHWH,	
11d	↑ אֲשֶׁר אָהֵב	↑ whom he loves,	
11e	וּבָעַל בַּת־אֵל נֵכָר	and married the daughter of a foreign god.	
12a	יַכְרֵת יְהוָה לָאִישׁ אֲשֶׁר יַעֲשֶׂנָּה עֵר וְעֹנֶה מֵאָהֳלֵי יַעֲקֹב	May YHWH cut off from the man who does it offspring from the tents of Jacob,	3. YHWH's Curse against the Offspring (2:12a–b)
12b	וּמַגִּישׁ מִנְחָה לַיהוָה צְבָאוֹת	although he brings an offering to YHWH Sabaoth.	
			B. Faithlessness to the Wives of Their Youth (2:13a–16f)
13a	וְזֹאת שֵׁנִית תַּעֲשׂוּ	And another thing you do:	1. Observation of Communal Lament (2:13a–d)
13b	כַּסּוֹת דִּמְעָה אֶת־מִזְבַּח יְהוָה בְּכִי וַאֲנָקָה	[You] cover the altar of YHWH with tears, weeping and wailing,	
13c	↑ מֵאֵין עוֹד פְּנוֹת אֶל־הַמִּנְחָה	↑ because he no longer regards the offering	
13d	↑ וְלָקַחַת רָצוֹן מִיֶּדְכֶם	↑ or accepts it favorably from you.	

Continued on next page.

Continued from previous page.

14a	וַאֲמַרְתֶּם עַל־מָה	But you say, "Why?"	2. The Community's Objection (2:14a)
14b	עַל כִּי־יְהוָה הֵעִיד בֵּינְךָ וּבֵין אֵשֶׁת נְעוּרֶיךָ	Because YHWH was a witness between you and the wife of your youth	3. The Prophet's Response concerning the Community (2:14b–16f)
14c	↑ אֲשֶׁר אַתָּה בָּגַדְתָּה בָּהּ	↑ with whom you dealt treacherously.	
14d	וְהִיא חֲבֶרְתְּךָ וְאֵשֶׁת בְּרִיתֶךָ	She is your companion and the wife of your covenant.	
15a	וְלֹא־אֶחָד עָשָׂה	No one does [it]	
15b	וּשְׁאָר רוּחַ לוֹ	and has a remnant of the spirit in him.	
15c	וּמָה הָאֶחָד מְבַקֵּשׁ זֶרַע אֱלֹהִים	What is that one seeking? Godly offspring.	
15d	וְנִשְׁמַרְתֶּם בְּרוּחֲכֶם	So guard your spirit	
15e	וּבְאֵשֶׁת נְעוּרֶיךָ אַל־יִבְגֹּד	and do not act treacherously against the wife of your youth.	
16a	כִּי־שָׂנֵא שַׁלַּח |	| "If a man hates [and] divorces [his wife],"	
16b	אָמַר יְהוָה אֱלֹהֵי יִשְׂרָאֵל ↓	says YHWH, the God of Israel, ↓	
16c	וְכִסָּה חָמָס עַל־לְבוּשׁוֹ	"then he covers his garment in violence,"	
16d	אָמַר יְהוָה צְבָאוֹת	says YHWH Sabaoth.	
16e	וְנִשְׁמַרְתֶּם בְּרוּחֲכֶם	So guard your spirits	
16f	וְלֹא תִבְגֹּדוּ	and do not act treacherously.	

In vv. 10–15, YHWH is referenced in the third person at least once in each verse, with only v. 16 suggesting a speech of YHWH. Therefore, unlike the first two disputations, the third disputation appears to be spoken by the prophet to the larger community.

The disputation includes two statements, or claims, before the community actually responds. Generally speaking, the disputation divides into two sections. The first, vv. 10–12, addresses questions associated with marriage to "the daughter of a foreign god" (v. 11) and the second, vv. 13–16, chastises the males in Yehud for their treatment of their wives. The basic elements of a disputation found in the previous pericopes in Malachi are present in this disputation as well, albeit, in a slightly modified structure. The first statement includes two rhetorical questions meant to establish the presupposed unity of the covenant community, followed by a third question that undercuts the initial claim, or more specifically, that cast doubts on the reality of such unity within the covenantal community. That which follows in 2:11 particularizes the affront committed by the people, which then leads to an announcement of judgment in 2:12. The prophet then issues a second "statement" which is then followed by a short objection by the people in 2:14a. In the remainder of the pericope, the prophet provides a response.

Even as the larger marital themes (i.e., intermarriage and divorce) provide coherence and continuity to this disputation so too does the repetition of selected terms, in particular בגד, "break faith, faithless" (2:10, 11, 14, 15, 16) and אֶחָד, "one" (2:10 [2x], 15 [2x]).[2] These two terms "envelop the pericope and highlight the central theme of loyalty" as expressed in relation to the covenant of the fathers and in the marriage covenant.[3]

Explanation of the Text

A. Marriage to the Daughters of Foreign Gods (2:10–12)

In the first section of this disputation, the prophet chastises the community for actions that clearly profane the covenant of the ancestors. Moreover, this action, i.e., marrying daughters of foreign gods, also defiles the people of YHWH.

1. The Prophet's Rhetorical Questions (2:10)

The interrogatives in the opening lines of this disputation appear to stand in marked contrast to the declarative statements that open the other disputations.[4] Here, the first two questions are introduced by the interrogative particle הֲלוֹא ("Is not . . . ?") with a third question introduced by מַדּוּעַ, "Why?" Frequently הֲלוֹא introduces

2. The repetition of other terms also contributes to the larger sense of coherence: רוּחַ, "spirit" (2:15 [2x], 16); אִשָּׁה "wife" (2:14 [2x], 15); כסה "to cover" (2:13, 16); בְּרִית "covenant" (2:10, 14); חלל "to profane" (2:10, 11); מִנְחָה "offering" (2:12, 13); שׁמר "to guard" (2:15, 16).

3. Gibson, *Covenant Continuity and Fidelity*, 122.

4. Hill suggests that the changes "in the form and style of this disputation call attention to the central theme of Malachi's message, loyalty to God and to one another" (*Malachi*, 224).

a rhetorical question that is meant to make an assertion or a claim, and clearly the two parallel questions in v. 10a–b serve that function.[5] The nature of those claims is spelled out below. The third question, introduced by מַדּוּעַ, "why," suggests the "thesis" of the entire disputation.[6] If the claims in vv. 10a and 10b are true, as the rhetorical form of the questions is meant to suggest, then why are the people demonstrating such faithlessness (בגד) to one another (v. 10c)? What follows in vv. 11–12 and 13–16 is the evidence necessary to support the implied charge in v. 10c, i.e., that the people are indeed faithless to one another.[7]

The first rhetorical question (v. 10a) refers to "one father," thus prompting a question concerning the identity of the father.[8] Baldwin proposed that the prophet may have in view one of the patriarchs, perhaps Abraham or Jacob, given the reference to Jacob in the first disputation (1:2).[9] While Baldwin is correct in that a patriarch is mentioned in an earlier disputation, when weighed carefully the evidence suggests the reference is to YHWH. Interpreters often point to the use of the father-child metaphor earlier in book (1:6) with clear reference to YHWH as אָב, "father," but that alone is not sufficient grounds for an interpretive decision. Although the references to YHWH as father are relatively few (e.g., Exod 4:22, 23; Deut 32:6, 18; Isa 63:16; 64:8; Jer 2:27; 3:4), three instances are particularly instructive. In Deut 32:6, YHWH is referred to as both father and creator: "Is he not your father, who created you, who made you and established you?" (ESV). The subsequent verses in Deut 32 recount how YHWH formed the Israelites into a people and gave them an inheritance. The same sentiment is expressed in Jer 2:27. The prophet chastises the people because "they say to wood, 'You are my father,' and to stone, 'You gave me birth'" (NIV). The implied critique is that the people have assigned to idols the accolades that belong to YHWH. The one who brought Israel into being is YHWH and YHWH alone. The close association between "father" and "creator" appears once more in Isa 64:8 with אָב, "father," bringing his people into being much as a potter does with clay.

Although the verb ברא, "to create," may appear to allude to Gen 1, Snyman is correct in his assessment that "the statement is not about God as Creator in the sense that he created the universe . . . , but rather God as the one who founded Israel, the one they owe their existence to."[10] Consequently if the community in Yehud shares this common heritage, i.e., they are a people brought into existence by YHWH, then their faithlessness (בגד) toward one another appears all the more egregious, hence the question in Mal 2:10c–d, "Why then does each

5. הֲלוֹא introduces a polar or "yes-no" question. When used rhetorically, the assertion is meant to reverse the polarity of the question, i.e., "Do we not all have one Father?" makes the claim "We all have one father" (*BHRG* §42.2.1c).

6. Clendenen, "Malachi," 322.

7. Snyman contends that "not one of these three questions is really answered in the rest of the pericope, but it serves as a way of bringing another matter in Judean society under prophetic scrutiny" (*Malachi*, 102). Rhetorically speaking, none of these questions is intended to be answered explicitly; their purpose is to introduce the inconsistency between the community's confession and their action. In this way, these opening questions are intended as prefatory to the charges levied in the remainder of the disputation.

8. The LXX actually reverses the order of the questions in v. 10a–b: "Did not one God create us? Is there not one father of us all?" Gibson surmises that the reversal signals that the LXX understands "father" as a reference to the patriarchs (*Covenant Continuity and Fidelity*, 117). While possible, an argument could also be mounted that the lines were reversed in an effort to resolve any potential ambiguity. The reference to YHWH in v. 10a informs the reading of "father" in v. 10b.

9. Baldwin, *Haggai, Zechariah and Malachi*, 237. Baldwin also contends that the reference to the "covenant of our fathers" in v. 10c provides additional support for the claim that "one father" could well be one of the patriarchs.

10. Snyman, *Malachi*, 103. Similarly, Hill, *Malachi*, 224; Glazier-McDonald, *Malachi*, 83.

act faithlessly against his brother, thereby profaning the covenant of our ancestors?"

The repetition of the verb בגד throughout this disputation (vv. 10, 11, 14, 15, 16) binds the two sub-collections together (vv. 10–12, 13–16), but even more, it highlights the loss in communal fidelity. Although the verb can be translated as "treacherous" elsewhere, here the emphasis is placed squarely on the breach in the community's covenantal commitment to one another.[11] This breach in commitment leads to the "profaning [of] the covenant of our ancestors."[12] As Kessler has rightly noted, חלל ("to profane") is rarely used in reference to the abrogation of the covenant or covenant demands.[13] Yet, by employing such terminology, the prophet contends that even as the actions of the priests in 1:12 profaned (חלל) the table of YHWH so too have the people engaged in similar acts of profanation.[14] In this instance, the faithless actions of the people have profaned the "covenant of our ancestors." In attempting to identify which covenant is in view, Baldwin, Lear and Glazier-McDonald point to the Abrahamic covenant.[15] Others, however, argue that the Sinaitic covenant stands in the background, particularly given the considerable influence of Deuteronomy upon the book. Petersen notes that the Sinaitic covenant is frequently described as "a covenant made with your fathers" (Deut 4:30–31; cf. 29:24–25; Jer 34:13–14).[16] In those instances, the emphasis is on the communal implications of the covenant, i.e., an emphasis on communal identity and communal solidarity (cf. Deut 29:25). In the book of Malachi, the faithless actions of the community (בגד), as recounted in this disputation, reveal a mindset that runs counter to such commitments.

2. The Evidence of Faithlessness (2:11)

The opening clause of v. 11 confirms the charges levied by the question in verse 10c: "Judah has acted faithlessly (בגד)."[17] Some translations, and a number of commentators, render the *vav* in the subsequent clause as though it were a simple coordinating conjunction, "and an abomination has

11. The phrase אִישׁ בְּאָחִיו ("each . . . against his brother") suggests reciprocity and highlights the community's betrayal of their shared identity. The ב is best understood here as adversarial. Cf. *BHRG* §39.9.b.iii. A similar "reciprocal phrase" is used in Jer 34:15 in describing communal fidelity.

12. לְחַלֵּל is best understood as introducing a result clause; the infinitive clause communicates the consequence of the verb in the matrix clause (*IBHS* §36.2.3d), i.e., the faithless behavior of the community leads to the profaning of the covenant with the ancestors.

13. Kessler, *Maleachi*, 193. The terms חלל and בְּרִית occur together only in Isa 56:6; Ezek 44:7; Mal 2:10; Pss 55:21[20]; 89:35[34], 40[39], with the collocation בְּרִית + חלל occurring outside of Mal 2 only in Pss 55:21[20] and 89:35[34].

14. Lear argues that the prophet may have drawn from Ezek 44:7 based on the amount of shared vocabulary between this disputation and Ezek 44:7–8 (*Scribal Composition*, 32). More likely is Weyde's assessment that Mal 2:10 "gives an example of a confluence of terms and phrases in prophetic and cultic traditions" (*Prophecy and Teaching*, 224).

15. Baldwin, *Haggai, Zechariah and Malachi*, 237; Lear, *Scribal Composition*, 33–34; Glazier-McDonald, *Malachi*, 88. Jacobs presents both the Abrahamic and Sinaitic covenants as possible options but fails to suggest whether one or the other is in view, or both (*The Books of Haggai and Malachi*, 241).

16. Petersen, *Zechariah 9–14 and Malachi*, 197. See also 1 Kgs 8:21; 2 Kgs 17:15.

17. The MT reads בָּגְדָה יְהוּדָה, a *qal* perfect 3fs verb followed by the subject, apparently understood as feminine noun given the form of the verb. In v. 11c, however, יְהוּדָה appears once more, but given the verb form there, יְהוּדָה is understood as masculine. To remedy this apparent inconsistency, both Petersen (*Zechariah 9–14 and Malachi*, 194) and *BHS* propose emending the text to בָּגַד. *BHQ*, however, removes any proposed emendation, suggesting that the MT can be understood as it stands. When understood as feminine in v. 11a, יְהוּדָה likely refers to the Persian province of Yehud as whole. When יְהוּדָה appears as masculine in v. 11c, the actual individuals within the province are in view (Verhoef, *The Books of Haggai and Malachi*, 267–68; A. S. van der Woude, "Malachi's Struggle for a Pure Community: Reflections on Malachi 2:10–16," in *Tradition and Re-Interpretation in Jewish and early Christian Literature: Essays in Honor of Jürgen C. H. Lebram*, eds. J. W. van Henten, et. al., StPB 36 [Leiden: Brill, 1986], 67; Clendenen,

been done."[18] Clearly the structure is not meant to imply that Judah has committed two violations, i.e., acting faithlessly *and* committing an abomination, rather, the second clause is meant to explain the first clause more fully.[19] Thus, the faithless action of Judah is more specifically identified as an "abomination" (תּוֹעֵבָה). The clausal structure itself in v. 11b points in this direction as well. וְתוֹעֵבָה נֶעֶשְׂתָה בְיִשְׂרָאֵל וּבִירוּשָׁלָם ("an abomination has been committed in Israel and Jerusalem") is an example of topic fronting; the fronting of תּוֹעֵבָה signals the "aboutness" of the subsequent clauses, reframing the notion of faithless action. Both the violation (v. 11e) and the punishment to be meted out (v. 12) are meant to be understood in light of the larger category of תּוֹעֵבָה, an "abomination."

"Abomination" (תּוֹעֵבָה) covers a wide range of social and cultic activities that represent a violation of covenant expectations. Leviticus 18, perhaps most famously, outlines a rather lengthy list of such behaviors. In the book of Deuteronomy, however, the term is most often associated with idolatry and the worship of other gods (cf. 13:13–15; 17:3–4).[20] Most instructive for understanding Mal 2:11 is found in Deut 7. The chapter opens with reference to the nations and people groups surrounding them, the "seven nations larger and stronger than you" (7:1 NIV). The power dynamic reflected in Deut 7 (i.e., the attraction of associating with those stronger surrounding nations) may also explain the prophet's allusion to this tradition in his own day.[21] In vv. 3–4, the people are prohibited from intermarrying with the nations, and the explanation provided for this command is that those from other nations "will turn your children away from following [YHWH] to serve other gods" (NIV).[22] At the end of the chapter such behavior is labeled as a תּוֹעֵבָה ("abomination"; Deut 7:25–26). This understanding of תּוֹעֵבָה informs what follows in the remainder of Mal 2:11.

The subsequent כִּי clause in v. 11c is causal in that it provides a "motivated accusation against Judah."[23] The precise nature of the accusation, however, is complicated by the structure of the clause and the language employed. As noted above, Judah appears as the subject of a feminine verb in v. 11a whereas here in v. 11c the verb is masculine. In the prior usage, the noun functioned collectively (i.e., Judah as the province), but in v. 11c, the noun refers to individuals within Judah. According to the prophet, the actions of individuals within Judah are said to have profaned (חלל) the קֹדֶשׁ יְהוָה.

"Malachi," 331; Kessler, *Maleachi*, 195). Snyman follows this line of argumentation but also ponders whether the feminine and masculine forms functioned as a subtle reminder of the primary issue here, marriage (*Malachi*, 104).

18. Cf. NRSV, NET. See also Snyman, *Malachi*, 104; Jacobs, *The Books of Haggai and Malachi*, 236; Kessler, *Maleachi*, 183; Glazier-McDonald, *Malachi: The Divine Messenger*, 82.

19. The so-called epexegetical or explicative *vav*. See *BHRG* §40.23.4.2 (10).

20. The term "abomination" (תּוֹעֵבָה) occurs seventeen times in the book of Deuteronomy, only behind Ezekiel (43x) and Proverbs (22x). The connection between the worship of other gods and the defilement of God's sanctuary identified in Mal 2:11 appears readily evident in the book of Ezekiel as well (Ezek 8).

21. As van der Woude explains, "the background of our pericope should be sought in the social and economic situation prevailing in Judah during Malachi's lifetime. By marrying foreign women, Judeans tried to share the privileges of their alien overlords" ("Malachi's Struggle," 66). See also the comments by Gordon P. Hugenberger, *Marriage as a Covenant: Biblical Law and Ethics as Developed from Malachi*, VTSup 52 (Leiden: Brill, 1994). Hugenberger contends that since "wealth and status were primarily in non-Israelites hands, the temptation for the returned exiles to secure these through intermarriage must have been significant" (103–4).

22. The subsequent verses in Deut 7 repeatedly employ the root אהב, "to love," the same language employed in the opening line of the first disputation "'I have loved (אהב) you,' says YHWH" (Mal 1:2). This relationship between Malachi's use of key theological terms at the heart of Deuteronomy's torah rhetoric deserves more attention: love, hate, fear, abomination, etc.

23. Weyde, *Prophecy and Teaching*, 227.

Scholars remain divided on the meaning of the latter phrase, קֹדֶשׁ יְהוָה. A number of scholars and translations understand this as a reference to the temple of YHWH.[24] Without question, there are a number of texts where קֹדֶשׁ refers to the temple (Exod 36:1, 3; Lev 4:6) and things associated with the temple. Likely following this line of reasoning, the LXX renders the noun as plural, ἅγια, "the holy things." A second option, based on the notion that the activity of the priests in the second disputation clearly takes place in association with the temple, holds that the violations implied here seem more broadly construed.[25] Understanding this view, Hill and Jacobs render the phrase literally, "the holiness of YHWH," suggesting that what has been profaned is the character of God.[26] This suggestion, however, is complicated by the relative clause that follows, "whom he loves," particularly given the previous use of אהב in 1:2.

The third option, and the one adopted here, is that the phrase קֹדֶשׁ יְהוָה refers specifically to the covenant community.[27] As suggested above, the prophet's comments referring to intermarriage in v. 11b point to Deut 7. In Deut 7:6, the community is referred to as a "holy people belonging to YHWH your God" (עַם קָדוֹשׁ אַתָּה לַיהוָה אֱלֹהֶיךָ). And further still, the "holy people" are said to be a people "loved" (אהב) by YHWH (7:8).[28] Both themes echo in Mal 2. As Weyde explains, the comments in Mal 2:11 "allow us to draw the conclusion that by intermarriage the holiness of the elected people, whom YHWH loves, will be profaned."[29] Further, throughout Deut 7, the emphasis is on YHWH's covenantal commitment to his people and his expectation of a reciprocating commitment (7:11). If the people remain faithful to God by not intermarrying, YHWH will love (אהב) them and bless them (7:13). Malachi, however, points to the failure of his community to abide by those expectations.

The rhetorical question first asked in Mal 2:10c appears to confirm the suggestion that קֹדֶשׁ יְהוָה refers to the community. There the prophet queries, "Why then does each act faithlessly against his brother?" Clearly the actions of some in the community have had a deleterious effect upon the larger community. Moreover, such actions are said to profane (חלל) "the covenant of our ancestors" (see above). Thus, what is profaned in v. 10c is not the sanctuary of YHWH or the character of YHWH, but the very thing that binds them together as God's beloved community. In v. 11c–d, the prophet returns to this theme and admonishes those in Yehud for profaning this holy community, which is loved by YHWH.

The final line in v. 11 makes clear the act that has profaned the community of YHWH: those in

24. Cf. Glazier-McDonald, *Malachi: The Divine Messenger*, 90; Gibson, *Covenant Continuity and Fidelity*, 116; see also NIV, NASB, NRSV, NET. Snyman proposes that perhaps both the temple *and* the covenant community are intended by קֹדֶשׁ יְהוָה (*Malachi*, 105–6).

25. In Ezra 9:1–2 (NIV), the "people of Israel, including the priests and Levites," are condemned for committing an "abomination," i.e., marrying the daughters from the surrounding nations.

26. Hill, *Malachi*, 230–31; Jacobs, *The Books of Haggai and Malachi*, 243.

27. See also Kessler, *Malaechi*, 194–95; Arndt Meinhold, "Dialogische Strukturen in den Streitreden des Buches Maleachi," *ZAW* 102 (1990): 207; van der Woude, "Malachi's Struggle," 68–69; Weyde, *Prophecy and Teaching*, 233–34; Verhoef, *The Books of Haggai and Malachi*, 183, 268. Verhoef argues that while the phrase קֹדֶשׁ יְהוָה quite often refers to the temple, here the context demands a different rendering.

28. This combination of themes (i.e., intermarriage with the nations, the community as the holy people, and abomination) also appears later in Ezra 9–10. The community is labeled as "holy" in 9:2 (זֶרַע הַקֹּדֶשׁ) and the act of intermarriage is labeled as an abomination repeatedly (9:1, 11, 14).

29. Weyde, *Prophecy and Teaching*, 233. Contra Hill, who understands the subject of the relative clause to be Judah, thus making Judah the subject matter of each clause in v. 11c–e (*Malachi*, 231).

Judah have "married the daughter of a foreign god." The question that remains is whether such a charge is to be understood figuratively or literally. Petersen argues for a cultic interpretation that adopts a figurative understanding of marriage.[30] In arriving at this conclusion, he revocalizes v. 11d and proposes that the relative pronoun אֲשֶׁר, "which," be rendered אֲשֵׁרָה, "Asherah."[31] Petersen argues that the mention of this female goddess also informs the reading of v. 11e: "and he married the daughter of a foreign god." Based on his reconstruction, Judah functions as the subject (i.e., husband) with the object being Asherah (i.e., wife). Thus, what is in view is not actual exogamous marriage between those in Yehud and non-Jewish spouses, but cultic idolatry writ large. Although the cultic figure Asherah is mentioned regularly in the Old Testament (40x), the metaphorical relationship configured here by Petersen is not. Elsewhere in the Old Testament, the deity always functions as the husband with Israel as the spouse (Isa 54:5; Hos 2:16–25[14–23]) and not the reverse (as proposed by Petersen). Given the typical construction of the metaphor elsewhere in the Old Testament, the figurative reading must be abandoned in favor of a more literal reading.

The prophet chastises those within the community for having "married the daughter of a foreign god" (וּבָעַל בַּת־אֵל נֵכָר). The verb בעל means "to rule over" or "to marry," with the latter meaning operative here in a literal sense.[32] Had the prophet's primary complaint simply been the status of the woman as a foreigner, he could have employed a label similar to 1 Kgs 11:1, נָשִׁים נָכְרִיּוֹת, "foreign women," but he did not. The extended label, "daughter of a foreign god" is intentional in that it extends the familial metaphor that was operative in the opening lines of this disputation. Verse 10 declares that Yehud owed its very existence to YHWH, their father and creator; in short, they are the children of YHWH. It was that designation that distinguished them from those who understood themselves as children of another god. Similar examples are found elsewhere in the Old Testament. People are referred to as the sons and daughters of Chemosh (Num 21:29) as well as that of YHWH (Deut 32:19), both illustrative of a similar familial metaphor at work. Thus, for the prophet, the primary issue is not simply that of exogamous marriage, i.e., that the woman was outside the Yehudite community, but rather that there was a potential religious threat posed by exogamous marriages.[33]

3. YHWH's Curse against the Offspring (2:12)

The purpose of v. 12 is readily apparent: to level a curse against the violators mentioned in v. 11. The meaning of that curse, however, is less clear, and consequently has engendered considerable discussion. Two issues dominate the conversation surrounding v. 12a–b: the syntax of the verse itself, and the meaning and function of עֵר וְעֹנֶה. The curse begins with a jussive, יַכְרֵת, "May [YHWH] cut off." The question concerns who or what is the object of the verb, or more precisely, who exactly is cut off. The LXX and the Vulgate appear to understand the

30. See also Martin A. Shields, "Syncretism and Divorce in Malachi 2,10–16," *ZAW* 111 (1999): 68–86. Shields contends that only vv. 11–12 should be understood figuratively; the remainder of the disputation should be understood literally.

31. Petersen contends that the final ה was likely lost due to haplography (*Zechariah 9–14 and Malachi*, 194). There are no textual witnesses that support this emendation, but the LXX does render the text ἐπετήδευσεν εἰς θεοὺς ἀλλοτρίους, "and he pursued foreign gods."

32. Given the concern that exogamous marriage could lead to idolatry, the use of the verb בעל was likely meant also as a subtle reference to the Canaanite god Baal. Cf. Snyman, *Malachi*, 107; Hill, *Malachi*, 232.

33. Markus Zehnder, "A Fresh Look at Malachi II 13–16," *VT* 53 (2003): 227; Snyman, *Malachi*, 107.

lamed as marking the object (לְאִישׁ), "May YHWH cut off the person."[34] A number of recent commentators have adopted a similar reading as well.[35]

Rather than understanding אִישׁ, "person," as the object of the verb, others have suggested that לְאִישׁ functions differently, with the *lamed* marking the indirect object (i.e., the so-called *dativus commodi*).[36] There is textual warrant for this reading. Gibson analyzed the biblical passages that contained a formula similar to that found in verse 12: כרת ("to cut off") + ל PP + two coordinated participles/nouns, especially those that display some form of alliteration or assonance.[37] He observed several texts within the Deuteronomistic History and the prophetic corpus that followed this pattern: 1 Kgs 14:10; 21:21; 2 Kgs 9:8; Isa 14:22; Jer 44:7; Jer 47:4. In each instance, the *lamed* marks the indirect object of the verb, and similar to Mal 2:12, that person is considered an evildoer or violator. Thus, the translation is better rendered as "May YHWH cut off from the man who does it [יַעֲשֶׂנָּה]." [38]

In the texts identified by Gibson, the object of the verb כרת ("cut off") is always a word pair (i.e., coordinated participles or nouns). Given that Mal 2:12 appears to follow the same formula, the phrase עֵר וְעֹנֶה is best understood as the object of the verb כרת.[39] This then leads to the vexing question concerning the exact meaning of that phrase.[40] What exactly did YHWH "cut off?" Each word is a participle, with the first from the root עור, "awake," and the second, arguably from ענה, "to answer." Thus literally, the phrase refers to those who are "awaking and answering," but that seems to make little sense contextually. As a result, some have opted to emend עֵר to עֵד, "witness," thus the NRSV, "any to witness or to answer." Hill follows similarly and suggests that the terms likely have "legal connotations, perhaps related to the juridical procedure requiring two witnesses (a 'witness' and an 'answerer' [i.e., corroborating witness])."[41] Although the logic of this modest emendation of the MT seems reasonable, Anthony Gelston is correct that "the difficulties of this phrase [עֵר וְעֹנֶה] are exegetical rather than textual."[42] The more difficult reading is found in the MT and should be retained, with the changes in the LXX and Vulgate understood as attempts to resolve a challenging text.

If the phrase עֵר וְעֹנֶה should be retained, how should it be understood? The fact that these two terms appear together only here in the Old

34. LXX, ἐξολεθρεύσει κύριος τὸν ἄνθρωπον; Vulgate, *disperdat Dominus virum*. Both texts read: "The Lord will utterly destroy the person."

35. Aaron Schart, *Maleachi*, IEKAT (Stuttgart: Kohlhammer, 2020), 85; Jacobs, *The Books of Haggai and Malachi*, 236; Snyman, *Malachi*, 107. See also Glazier-McDonald, *Malachi*, 82; Verhoef, *The Books of Haggai and Malachi*, 270; Petersen, *Zechariah 9–14 and Malachi*, 194.

36. In this instance, the *lamed* "marks the person for or against whom an action is directed" (*IBHS* §11.2.10d). Cf. Weyde, *Prophecy and Teaching*, 236–40; O'Brien, *Priest and Levite*, 71.

37. Jonathan M. Gibson, "Cutting off 'Kith and Kin,' 'Er and Onan'?: Interpreting an Obscure Phrase in Malachi 2:12." *JBL* 133 (2014): 519–37.

38. The third feminine singular suffix ("it") on יַעֲשֶׂנָּה refers to the feminine noun "abomination" (תּוֹעֵבָה) in v. 11, and confirms the violation committed by the subject of the verb. עשׂה is the operative verb in both clauses, providing further correlation between v. 11b and the relative clause in v. 12b.

39. Some have understood the word pair as standing in apposition to אִישׁ. E.g., "May Yahweh cut off the man who does it—witness or respondent—from the tents of Jacob" (Jacobs, *The Books of Haggai and Malachi*, 236), among others (Snyman, *Malachi*, 107).

40. In his analysis of this text, Gibson reviews the wide array of proposals in the history of scholarship, "Cutting off 'Kith and Kin,' 'Er and Onan'?," 519–26. He identifies no less than ten different categories of interpretation for this phrase.

41. See *Malachi*, 234–35. See also Martin A. Shields, "Syncretism and Divorce in Malachi 2:10–16," 73–75. Similarly, in 4QXII[a], עֵד appears rather than עֵר. See Russell Fuller, "Text-critical Problems in Malachi 2:10–16," *JBL* 110 (1991): 47–57.

42. Anthony Gelston, *The Twelve Minor Prophets*, *BHQ* 13 (Stuttgart: Deutsche Bibelgesellschaft, 2010), 150.

Testament makes their interpretation even more challenging. The parallel texts identified by Gibson in the Deuteronomistic history and the prophetic corpus once again may prove instructive. He observed that the word pair in these texts shared a number of common features. In nearly every instance, the word pair exhibits alliteration and/or assonance. The presence of this feature may suggest that this phrase may be intended as an idiom of some kind.[43] In Mal 2:12, both terms begin with *ayin* which then raises the question as to the idiom intended and indeed a number of proposals have sought to provide some type of idiomatic rendering. This leads to the second observation by Gibson. He argues that these word pairs frequently denote the offspring of the evildoer.[44] Thus rather than rendering עֵר וְעֹנֶה literally (i.e., "awaking and answering"), the phrase is best understood as an enigmatic idiom referring to offspring. According to the curse, the offspring of the male Yehudite and the "daughter of a foreign god" is "cut off" from the tents of Jacob.[45] The offspring of that union which defiles the people of God (v. 11) stands in stark contrast to the desire for "godly offspring" mentioned later in v. 15.

The final clause in v. 12 begins with a *vav* which is best understood as contrastive (e.g., "although"). The curse formula calls for the offspring of the Yehudite man to be cut off even though the man brings offerings to YHWH of hosts. The efficacy of offerings in 2:12 recalls similar issues raised in 1:10, 13 as it related to the priests. Given the marital actions of the Yehudite man, his offerings are in vain.[46] The apparent assumption was that "proper" offerings would override improper alliances, an assumption that the prophet roundly rejected.

B. Faithlessness to the Wives of Their Youth (2:13–16)

The second subsection begins with a statement, cast in the form of an observation and followed by a brief query by the community (2:14a). Although concerns are introduced in v. 14c, the particularities of the violation are not fully explained until v. 16.

1. Observation of Communal Lament (2:13)

Verse 13 begins the second major section in this disputation with attention turning to a second (שֵׁנִית) thing, or "another thing," that the community does. The issue raised in v. 13 serves as a statement, or better yet, an indictment of the community's inability to grasp the gravity of their current behavior. The prophet charges them with "covering the altar of YHWH with tears, weeping and wailing." Interpretations of that charge have generally fallen into one of three categories. Some have connected the actions in v. 13 with the mourning rituals associated with foreign cultic practices.[47] Presumably the marrying of the "daughters of foreign gods," whether that is understood literally or figuratively, would have introduced syncretism into the cultic life of Yehud (cf. Deut 7:1–6). Just as crying out to YHWH and weeping was part of Israel's cultic

43. Gibson, "Cutting off 'Kith and Kin,' 'Er and Onan'?," 530.

44. Gibson, "Cutting off 'Kith and Kin,' 'Er and Onan'?," 532. He also observes that in the larger context of each passage, the offspring are to be utterly wiped out as a result of YHWH's punishment.

45. Jacob Milgrom argues that the use of כרת in Mal 2:12 refers to the "extirpation of the offender's entire line" (*Leviticus 1–16*, AYBC 3 [New Haven: Yale University Press, 1998], 459). For an extended treatment of the verb כרת, see pages 457–60.

46. Weyde, *Prophecy and Teaching*, 249.

47. Petersen, *Zechariah 9–14 and Malachi*, 201–3; Glazier-McDonald, *Malachi*, 82; F. F. Hvidberg, *Weeping and Laughing in the Old Testament* (Leiden: Brill, 1962), 120–23.

life, so too were such rituals associated with other ancient Near Eastern religions. Even within the Old Testament, weeping before foreign gods is reported. For example, in Ezek 8, the women gathered at the north gate of the temple in order to weep for the god Tammuz. Although the act of weeping before gods occurs elsewhere in the Old Testament, that does not appear to be in view here. The use of the word שֵׁנִית introduce a new topic in the disputation rather than extending the one raised in vv. 10–12.

Others point to the matter of divorce raised later in this section. They suggest that perhaps those weeping were the Israelite wives who had been sent away, or divorced, by their husbands.[48] Zehnder acknowledges that women could not literally approach the altar of YHWH, a fact that seems to rule this option out entirely, but as he explains, the covering of the altar by the women's tears is a "figurative expression" rooted in mourning, but a mourning that seeks the presence of God.[49] While that explanation seems plausible, an additional problem that confronts this position is that these women are not named in this verse nor is there a feminine pronoun that might refer to them in this verse. Zehnder finds the resolution to this problem with the infinitive כסה, "to cover." The *piel* form can have a causative sense, "causing to cover," which stands in contrast to the previous verb, תַּעֲשׂוּ, "you do," second masculine plural form. Zehnder suggests that תַּעֲשׂוּ, "you do," is addressed to the men mentioned earlier in the disputation (v. 11), hence the 2mp form, while the *piel* infinitive refers to those who were "caused to cover" the altar with tears, i.e., the women. Given the repeated references to the "wife," אִשָּׁה, in the subsequent verses, such an oblique reference here seems unlikely. In addition, Zehnder's argument suggests that the use of the *piel* stem had semantic implications, but that seems questionable upon closer analysis. The verb כסה, "to cover," occurs 153 times in the Old Testament with 132 occurrences in the *piel* stem. Thus, the use of the *piel* stem in v. 13 is simply the expected form of the verb and is not meant to stand in contrast to the use of the *qal* in תַּעֲשׂוּ, as Zehnder suggests.

The third option is to take מֵאֵין in v. 13c as introducing a causal clause, i.e., "because." The people are covering YHWH's altar with tears *because* YHWH does not turn to their offering. As Verhoef suggests, the weeping and tears "had a least a partial basis in the people's concrete experience."[50] If indeed the community was enduring hardship (e.g., 3:10–12), then perhaps they assume either that God has abandoned them (the theme of the first disputation) or that God is readily absent (a theme in the second disputation). The problem, however, is not with God, but with the community. The community failed to grasp the connection between covenant faithfulness *with one another* and covenant faithfulness *with God*. The benefit of the latter will not be enjoyed at the expense of the former; one cannot presume covenant faithfulness with God while ignoring the demands of covenant faithfulness to others.[51] Verse 13 reports that the community weeps and mourns, a genuine sign of lament and distress in the Psalms, but such actions must be measured against the lack of covenant faithfulness that is reported in vv. 14–16. The community pleads with YHWH to accept their offerings, while remaining entirely oblivious to

48. Most recently, Lear, *Scribal Composition*, 46–52; see also Markus Zehnder, "A Fresh Look at Malachi II 13–16," *VT* 53 (2003): 224–59.

49. Zehnder, "A Fresh Look at Malachi II 13–16," 234.

50. Verhoef, *The Books of Haggai and Malachi*, 273.

51. Cf. 1 John 4:21. Strikingly, the "love"/"hate" language of 1 John echoes that of Malachi.

their own violations. Therein lies the prophetic critique.

2. The Community's Objection (2:14a)

The community responds, עַל־מָה, literally "concerning what?" or idiomatically, "why?" or "on what basis?" Why has YHWH not looked favorably upon that which has been offered up? The previous objections, as well as those that follow, are couched in full sentences, but here the objection is greatly reduced. Kessler suggests that this "speechlessness" is an "expression of a state in which communication between God and the people is almost completely interrupted."[52] At minimum, the brevity of the community's objection to the prophetic critique underscores their failure to grasp the issue at hand, i.e., their faithlessness (בגד). Although one example of בגד was mentioned in vv. 10–12, the prophet turns to another example in vv. 14–16 to reinforce the critique.

3. The Prophet's Response concerning the Community (2:14b–16)

The opening words of the prophetic response, עַל כִּי, introduce a causal clause with the divine name fronted.[53] If the people surmised that the rejection of their offerings was because YHWH had abandoned them or was not readily present, as suggested by their actions in v. 13, then they would only be partially correct.[54] YHWH indeed rejected their offerings, but not due to his absence. Instead, the rejection of their offerings is predicated upon YHWH's very presence as witness (עוד) to their marriages with the wives of their youth (אֵשֶׁת נְעוּרֶיךָ).[55] By focus-fronting the name "YHWH," the prophet announces that beyond any others who might have been present for the ratification of the marriage covenant, to be sure, YHWH was there as witness. It is because YHWH was a witness in the past that he can now serve as the prosecutor and judge in the present.[56]

The initial reference to the Yehudite wife occurs in v. 14b, the "wife of your youth" (אֵשֶׁת נְעוּרֶיךָ). The phrase alludes to the social convention that Jewish men and women would marry at a relatively young age, yet it is not meant to highlight their "youthful vigor," as Glazier-McDonald has suggested, but instead, it points to the legally binding covenant between husband and wife.[57] Further, the language of "youth" suggests that this was the first wife of the man. From his youth, he was bound to this woman in covenant commitment. This unique phrase occurs only here in Mal 2 and Prov 5:18. In the book of Proverbs, the male student is extolled to "rejoice

52. Kessler, *Maleachi*, 202.

53. On עַל כִּי, see *IBHS* §38.4a. The typical word order of a Hebrew clause is S-V, but certain grammatical words which appear at the beginning of the clause and suggest subordination actually trigger constituent movement, thus the expected order in a subordinate clause would be V-S. In this case, the subject YHWH has been moved to the front of the clause for focus. On the S-V word order, see Robert Holmstedt, "Word Order and Information Structure in Ruth and Jonah: A Generative-Typological Approach," *JSS* 54 (2009): 111–39. See also the brief discussion in Holmstedt, Cook, and Marshall, *Qoheleth*, 9–13.

54. Note that second person singular pronouns dominate in v. 14: אַתָּה, ךָ-. While the larger community is always in view, the prophet is particularly concerned with the faithlessness exhibited by individual males against their spouses.

55. On the range of meaning for עוד, see Robert B. Chisholm, "עוד," in *NIDOTTE* 3:334–40. The role of YHWH as legal witness in a marriage scene recalls Gen 31:31–50. In that context, Laban issues the following stipulation for Jacob: "If you ill-treat my daughters, or if you take wives in addition to my daughters, though no one else is with us, remember that God is (עֵד) witness between you and me" (v. 50). The marriage scene in Gen 31 is devoid of any form of religious ceremony; it is a legal and civil act that required a witness. Lear suggests that the prohibition against taking other wives in Gen 31:50 is further evidence that this text stood in the background of the prophet's critique (*Scribal Composition*, 52–55).

56. Kessler, *Maleachi*, 204. Snyman follows similarly, attributing to YHWH the role of judge (*Malachi*, 112).

57. Glazier-McDonald, *Malachi: The Divine Messenger*, 100.

in the wife of your youth" (אֵשֶׁת נְעוּרֶיךָ) and warned against pursuing other women "lest strangers feast on your wealth, and your toil make rich the house of another" (v. 10). In both texts, fidelity to the first wife is celebrated.[58]

The noun phrase "the wife of your youth" functions as the antecedent of the relative clause that begins "whom you have dealt treacherously with her" (אֲשֶׁר אַתָּה בָּגַדְתָּה בָּהּ).[59] Given that Hebrew is a pro-drop language (i.e., the pronoun can be dropped), the presence of אַתָּה, "you," in the relative clause is worth noting. As a focus-fronted constituent, it identifies one constituent over against others. Verse 14b declares that YHWH was a witness between "you [2ms] and the wife of your youth," but the structure of v. 14c clearly identifies "you" (אַתָּה), the husband, as the violator. The egregious nature of the husband's action (בגד) is reinforced with the two subsequent references to the wife, "companion" and "wife of your covenant." The word חֲבֶרֶת, "companion," comes from the root חבר, which can refer to the physical joining together of items such as the curtains in the tabernacle (Exod 26:6–11), or more figuratively, it can refer to military and political alliances (Gen 14:3). It is the latter, more figurative sense that is in view here.[60] In some ways, the use of the term actually accentuates the position of the first wife within the relationship, communicating her status in this partnership.[61] Kessler contends that the focus is on "marital solidarity," something that has been undermined by the faithless and treacherous action of the husband.[62]

The third phrase employed in reference to the woman is the "wife of your covenant" (אֵשֶׁת בְּרִיתֶךָ). The phrase could simply refer to the legal contract between a man and a woman. To that end, Verhoef renders the phrase as "your covenant wife" or "your legal wife."[63] This seems to accord well with the previous reference to the woman as a חֲבֶרֶת, "companion." Others have noted that within this disputation the word בְּרִית appeared earlier in v. 10c, the "covenant of our ancestors" (בְּרִית אֲבֹתֵינוּ). As noted above, the Sinaitic covenant frequently referenced "a covenant made with your fathers" (Deut 4:30–31; 29:24–25; Jer 34:13–14), and in those texts, the emphasis was placed on a shared communal identity. Based on this observation, van der Woude suggests that the term implies that the woman belongs "to the same national-religious community as that of her husband."[64] Carrying this interpretation one

58. Lear suggests that the prophet has appropriated Prov 5 in Mal 2. While the reference to the "wife of your youth" (אֵשֶׁת נְעוּרֶיךָ) certainly appears in both texts, the contextual differences between the texts merit some caution in adopting Lear's proposal (*Scribal Composition*, 56). Similarly, see Schart, *Maleachi*, 90.

59. In the relative clause, אֲשֶׁר אַתָּה בָּגַדְתָּה בָּהּ, the prepositional phrase בָּהּ is not pleonastic as some might suggest, but instead a feature of resumption. Bivalent and trivalent verbs require complements of one sort or another, with many requiring some type of noun phrase. Some verbs, however, require prepositional phrase complements, as in this instance in which the verb בגד requires a prepositional phrase (ב) as its complement. "When the (pronominal) complement of the PP [prepositional phrase] complement happens to be co-referential with the relative head . . . the result is overt relative resumption." To leave aside the resumptive prepositional phrase complement (even if it appears redundant) would be to make the phrase ungrammatical. See Robert Holmstedt, *The Relative Clause in Biblical Hebrew* (Eisenbrauns: Winona Lake, 2016), 178–79. On resumption within the relative clause more generally, see 169–86.

60. The LXX translates חֲבֶרֶת as κοινωνός, "partner, companion."

61. Snyman, *Malachi*, 113. Zehnder suggests that the term "connotes the lasting character of the relationship on the one hand and the equality of the spouse who is seen as a real partner of her husband and not a subordinated possession" of his ("A Fresh Look at Mal II, 13–16," 236).

62. Kessler, *Maleachi*, 205.

63. Verhoef, *The Books of Haggai and Malachi*, 274. Others who adopt the second view include, van der Woude, "Malachi's Struggle," 68.

64. Van der Woude, "Malachi's Struggle," 68. Van der Woude also rules out any suggestion that the phrase refers to literal marriage, but that view has been rightly rejected.

step further, Kessler suggests that the reference is meant to stand in contrast to the "daughter of a foreign god."[65] The ambiguous phrase likely invokes both meanings. The references to offspring in vv. 12 and 15, as well as the mention of divorce in v. 16, suggest that literal marriage is clearly in view. That said, however, the mention of YHWH as a witness to the marriage (v. 14) suggests that the legal act of marriage was carried out within a particular religious community, one which is in covenant with YHWH. Together these three phrases, "wife of your youth," "companion," and "wife of your covenant" suggest an unbreakable bond, which then makes the treacherous or faithless actions of the male (בגד) all the more nefarious.

Due to its unusual, if not seemingly impossible syntax, v. 15 is the *crux interpretum* of this disputation. The questions posed by the structure of the MT are considerable, and they largely center around the meaning of the first clause, and in particular, the word אֶחָד, "one." Is אֶחָד the subject or complement of the verb עשׂה ("to do, make"), and to whom or to what does it refer? God? Abraham? Marital unity? Or perhaps the unfaithful person? Should that clause be read as an interrogative clause even though there are no interrogative particles present? What does the second clause mean and what is its relation to the first clause? How does אֶחָד in the first clause relate to הָאֶחָד in the third clause? Questions such as these reflect the challenges inherent in this verse. Most scholars contend that the MT is corrupt and they offer a number of emendations in an attempt to create a more sensical text. The interpretations of v. 15 generally fall into one of two approaches. The first approach understands v. 15 as an allusion to Gen 2:23–25 and the introduction of marriage.[66] Interpreters note the appearance of אֶחָד in Gen 2:24, "and they shall become one flesh" and suggest that אֶחָד in Mal 2:15 carries a similar connotation. Those opting for this reading contend that אֶחָד functions as the complement to the verb with YHWH understood as the implied subject (e.g., "Did [YHWH] not make [them] one?"). Further, in the subsequent clause, scholars adopting this approach often emend the noun שְׁאָר, "remnant," to שְׁאֵר, "flesh," and then shift the *vav* so that it functions as a coordinating conjunction, *שְׁאֵר וְרוּחַ, "flesh and spirit," ("Has not [YHWH] made [them] one? In flesh and spirit they are his").[67] There is no textual warrant to support this emendation, however.

Although this reading has been widely adopted, it does not come without its difficulties. First, the word for "flesh" in Gen 2 is not שְׁאֵר but בָּשָׂר, and the verbs employed to describe the creative act are יצר and בנה rather than עשׂה; the only true common lexeme between v. 15 and Gen 2:23–25 is אֶחָד.[68] Second, this interpretive approach also tends to render the first clause as an interrogative clause: "Has not YHWH made them one?" This decision is predicated on the fact that the word order may be suggestive of an interrogative and that the subsequent clause does in fact begin with an interrogative (מָה). As noted in the discussion

65. Kessler, *Maleachi*, 205. Jacobs seems to hint at a similar reading (*The Books of Haggai and Malachi*, 257–58). She suggests that the mention of covenant "may be used to refer to the covenant between Yahweh and the community."

66. See the extensive argument of Gordon P. Hugenberger, *Marriage as Covenant*, 124–51.

67. Clendenen, "Malachi," 342. Cf. ESV, CEV. The NIV also renders the verse in light of Gen 2, but understands אֶחָד not as a reference to marriage but to YHWH: "Has not the one God made you? You belong to him in body and spirit."

68. Martin A. Shields, "Syncretism and Divorce in Malachi 2,10–16," *ZAW* 111 (2010): 79–80. Gibson acknowledges as much but then contends that Gen 1:26–27 should be examined as well in relation to Mal 2:15. For Gibson, the use of עשׂה in Gen 1:26 may provide another shared lexeme between Gen 1–2 and Mal 2:15 (*Covenant Continuity and Fidelity*, 137).

related to 1:8 (another text often assumed to be an interrogative clause), however, the book of Malachi contains twenty-five questions, *each* marked by an interrogative. Because the first three clauses in this disputation begin with interrogatives (הֲלוֹא 2x; מַדּוּעַ) as does the subsequent clause (v. 15c) and, given the prophet's propensity for using interrogatives when a question is intended, it seems unlikely that an implied question is in view here.

A second interpretive approach involves understanding אֶחָד as the subject of the verb עשׂה, rather than the object. Instead of reading v. 15a as a question alluding to Gen 2, the clause may be understood as a critique against those divorcing their wives and intermarrying.[69] In this rendering, the object of עשׂה is null: "And no one does [it]," with the antecedent of the null object being the faithless (בגד) treatment of one's wife mentioned in v. 14c (which presumably would also include the taking of foreign wives [vv. 10–12]). Hugenberger challenges this reading and argues that typically "no one" is construed as לֹא followed by אִישׁ elsewhere in the Old Testament.[70] It may be possible, however, that the prophet intentionally opted for אֶחָד rather than אִישׁ in order to draw a contrast; the focus fronting of אֶחָד in v. 15a appears to point in that direction.[71] The typical order in a negated clause is particle of negation + verb + subject, but understood as proposed here, the subject (אֶחָד) has been focus-fronted.[72] Whereas the אֶחָד ("one") God and אֶחָד ("one") father in v. 10 are the source of the community's *unity*, the אֶחָד ("one [person]") in v. 15 is that which threatens the *dissolution* of the community. The one who deals treacherously with the wife of his youth acts in a manner that stands in contradistinction to God and God's design for his people.[73] The rendering of אֶחָד ("one") in this manner may also aid in addressing another issue in v. 15e (see below).

If v. 15a is read as a critique, then there is no need to emend וּשְׁאָר רוּחַ לוֹ as proposed by those who read this in light of Gen 2. Verse 15a–b can be rendered simply as "And no one does [it] and has a remnant of the spirit in him" (lit., "belonging to him"). The word "spirit" (רוּחַ) has been interpreted in various ways, but it seems best to understand it as human will, mind, or even character.[74] In Ezra 1:5, God is said to have stirred up the רוּחַ of the people, which led to the rebuilding of the temple. A similar usage of רוּחַ appears in Jer 51:11. Snyman's paraphrase of v. 15a–b conveys well this sense of רוּחַ: "No one in his right mind would do such a thing."[75]

The subsequent interrogative clause in verse 15c asks "What is הָאֶחָד (that one) seeking? Godly

69. Kessler has suggested that "even with the cryptic language in v. 15, text changes are not needed. The individual words are quite understandable; it is their connection that creates difficulties" (*Maleachi*, 185). Schart, *Maleachi*, 86, argues similarly.

70. Hugenberger, *Marriage as Covenant*, 130–31.

71. More than a century ago in his explanation of אֶחָד ("one"), J. M. P. Smith noted "it is an usual position for the subject of a verbal sentence, unless it is intended to be emphatic" ("Malachi," ICC, 54).

72. On word order, more generally, see Holmstedt, "Word Order and Information Structure," 111–39. See also the brief discussion in Holmstedt, Cook, and Marshall, *Qoheleth*, 9–13, esp. 10–11.

73. Cf. Deut 24:1–5. The text in Deuteronomy addresses the misbehavior of the husband toward the first wife in a divorce case. That kind of abuse is labeled as תּוֹעֵבָה, an "abomination" before God, and threatens to bring guilt upon the entire land. For an extended analysis, see Daniel I. Block, *Deuteronomy*, NIVAC (Grand Rapids, Zondervan), 556–60.

74. Hans Walter Wolff, *Anthropology of the Old Testament* (Philadelphia: Fortress, 1974), 37–39. Others have offered a similar rendering of the term. Verhoef suggests "intelligence" or "sound judgment" (*The Books of Haggai and Malachi*, 277); Zehnder renders רוּחַ as "organ of reason" or "understanding" in this context ("A Fresh Look at Malachi II, 13–16," 242); Shields opts for "moral character" ("Syncretism and Divorce in Malachi 2,10–16," 80–81).

75. Snyman, *Malachi*, 116. For a similar reading, see Daniel I. Block, "The View from the Top: The Holy Spirit in the Prophets," in *Presence, Power, and Promise: The Role of the Spirit of God in the Old Testament*, ed. David G. Firth and Paul D. Wegner (Downers Grove, IL: IVP Academic, 2011), 178n16.

offspring."[76] In v. 15a, אֶחָד ("one") functioned as the subject of the verb and was in reference to those who were dealing treacherously with their wives. In v. 15c, אֶחָד appears once more, but with a definite article attached. Some have understood this as a reference to Abraham.[77] The NET, for example, renders the clause as "What did our ancestor do when seeking a child from God?" Others have argued that הָאֶחָד refers to YHWH, "What does the One (YHWH) seek? Godly offspring." The appearance of אֶחָד here is often connected to its use in 2:10 to refer to God.[78]

Alternatively, the presence of the definite article could simply be understood as anaphoric. In such instances, the definite article appears "when a person or thing already spoken of is mentioned again and is consequently more definite to the mind of the reader."[79] Thus, "that one" (הָאֶחָד) in v. 15c points back to "one" (אֶחָד) in v. 15a.[80] As a result, the line could be rendered "What is that one seeking? Godly offspring?" The reference to godly offspring, however, is not a statement about ethnicity, as though rejecting the wife of one's youth for a foreign daughter is simply a matter related to ethnic purity.[81] Rather the pressing issue concerns fidelity to YHWH and "producing children who are faithful to YHWH."[82] A central question throughout the book of Malachi is that of faithfulness and that is the operative issue here. Being faithless against the wife of your youth by intermarrying the daughters of foreign gods creates a context whereby fidelity to YHWH is jeopardized. Thus, the question in verse 15c may in fact be understood as ironic or sarcastic.[83] If a man were *really* seeking godly offspring, he would not follow this course of action (see below).

Despite its difficulty, the argument in verse 15 remains coherent and logical: the actions condemned (v. 15a–b) and the actions encouraged (v. 15d–e) reinforce the covenantal commitment to the wife of one's youth, and by extension, it reinforces a commitment to the community in Yehud (v. 15c).

Verse 16, the final verse in this disputation, provides a concluding statement concerning the faithless treatment exacted by some husbands against the wives of their youth. The verse begins with the particle כִּי followed by two verbs: שׂנא, "to hate/reject," and שׁלח, "to send out," i.e., divorce.

v. 15a–b	"No one does [it] and has a remnant of spirit in him" (been treacherous to one's wife and married daughters of foreign gods).
v. 15c	"What is that one seeking? Godly offspring" (as though one could actually produce godly offspring from such treacherous behavior).
v. 15d–e	"So guard your spirit and do not act treacherously against the wife of your youth."

76. The Masoretic accent above הָאֶחָ֔ד (*zaqeph qaton*) suggests rendering the clause: "What is the one (purpose of marriage)? Seeking godly offspring." The reading proposed here reads against the accent and understands the question to be וּמָה הָאֶחָד מְבַקֵּשׁ, "what is that one seeking?"

77. See Verhoef's discussion (*The Books of Haggai and Malachi*, 277). This suggestion remains untenable for the reasons outlined by Gibson, *Covenant Continuity and Fidelity*, 127–28.

78. Cf. NIV, HCSB; see also Jacobs, *The Books of Haggai and Malachi*, 259; Smith, *Micah–Malachi*, 319.

79. GKC §126.2(*a*). Joüon and Muraoka suggest that when used anaphorically, the definite article is "equivalent to a weak demonstrative" (JM §137f.I.).

80. Gibson also understands the definite article as anaphoric, pointing back to the use of אֶחָד in verse 15a, but for Gibson, both uses of אֶחָד are understood as a reference to marital oneness (*Covenant Continuity and Fidelity*, 135–36).

81. Contra Graham S. Odgen and Robert R. Deutsch, *Joel and Malachi*, ITC (Grand Rapids: Eerdmans, 1987), 96–97.

82. Jacobs, *The Books of Haggai and Malachi*, 260.

83. Snyman, *Malachi*, 116; Stefas Schreiner, "Mischehen—Ehebruch—Ehescheidung," *ZAW* 91 (1979), 217.

There are a number of terms that refer to divorce in the Old Testament (גרשׁ—Lev 21:7; 22:13; כְּרִיתוּת—Deut 24:1, 3) and שׁלח clearly fits within that larger semantic domain. In Deut 24:1 for example, the man sends out (שׁלח) or expels his wife from his household and in the process issues her a certificate of divorce (e.g., Deut 24:1).[84] A similar scenario is described two verses later in Deut 24:3, and in that verse שׁלח, "to send out," is found alongside שׂנא, "to hate," the two terms used here in verse 16.[85]

A quick scan of commentaries and translations will reveal a variety of renderings. Some understand the כִּי particle as a causal conjunction, "for" or "because," but they differ in how they construe the subject of the clause. The traditional rendering, "'For I hate divorce,' declares YHWH God of Israel," requires some form of emendation to the text. To arrive at this emendation, proponents of this view note the form of the verb. These verbs, שָׂנֵא שַׁלַּח, can be parsed as a *qal* perfect 3ms verb + a *piel* infinitive, and when read literally, can be rendered, "'For he hates divorcing,' declares YHWH God of Israel." Yet, this seems to make little sense, as argued by the proponents of this view, given that YHWH is clearly speaking. As a result, interpreters have emended the verb שׂנא to reflect first person. Smith emended שׂנא to read שׂנאתי, *qal* perfect 1cs, "I hate."[86] Others such as Verhoef repoint שָׂנֵא to a participle (שֹׂנֵא) and suggest that the first-person-singular pronoun "I" is supplied by context.[87] Several English translations follow this line of argument, including NASB and NET. The challenge posed by rendering Mal 2:16a as a seemingly sweeping rejection of divorce is that it strikes a discordant note with other Old Testament texts that refer to divorce, in particular Deut 24:1–4 and Ezra 10, not to mention Jesus's comments on divorce in Matt 19.

Other attempts to render this verse point back to הָאֶחָד ("the one") in v. 15 and suggest that the term proves decisive for a correct reading. Hill and Jacobs, for example, both understand הָאֶחָד ("the one") in v. 15 to be a reference to God.[88] Rather than emending שָׂנֵא, they leave the third-person form intact and understand the antecedent for the null subject to be הָאֶחָד, i.e., YHWH. As a result, they propose rendering the verse along the lines of "'For he ["the One"] hates divorce,' says YHWH God of Israel." Although the use of third person in DD in this manner seems awkward, it is possible (cf. 1:9). The challenge with this position, however, is the rather abrupt change in subject between the first and second clauses, between the subjects of שָׂנֵא (YHWH) and וְכִסָּה (the husband).

Instead of interpreting the כִּי particle as introducing a causal clause, other readings have understood the particle as a conditional, "if."[89] This is the preferred reading here both for linguistic and

84. Cf. Isa 50:1; Jer 3:8.

85. Although the verb שׂנא, "to hate," appears in Deut 23:3 alongside שׁלח, "to send out," the meaning and force of the verb is contingent in part on how various interpreters have sought to translate the initial clause.

86. Smith, *Micah—Malachi*, 320. The critical apparatus in *BHS* suggests a similar emendation.

87. Verhoef, *The Books of Haggai and Malachi*, 278. Rather than repointing שָׂנֵא, Wilhelm Rudolph understands the verb as an alternate form of a participle ("Zu Mal 2,10–16," *ZAW* 93 [1981]: 85–90). Elsewhere in the Old Testament, however, the only participle form of שׂנא attested is שֹׂנֵא, thus calling into question the suggestion of Rudolph. On rendering this clause as an absolute prohibition, see the extended assessment by Hugenberger, *Marriage as a Covenant*, 62–66. Although rendered differently, Petersen's translation suggests a strong condemnation of divorce, similar to the view of Smith and Verhoef. Petersen reads the two verbs as part of a verbless (i.e., null copula) clause: "'Divorce is hateful!' says YHWH God of Israel." He understands the particle כִּי as an asseverative which he attempts to capture with the exclamation point (*Zechariah 9—14 and Malachi*, 194).

88. Hill, *Malachi*, 250; Jacobs, *The Books of Haggai and Malachi*, 252–53.

89. The ancient textual witnesses (LXX, Vulgate, and Targums) all rendered the כִּי particle as a conditional. In two

contextual reasons. When כִּי functions as a causal conjunction, the main clause (i.e., matrix clause) usually precedes the כִּי causal clause.[90] For example, Lev 19:2 reads "You shall be holy *because* [כִּי] I, YHWH your God, am holy." When כִּי functions as a conditional, however, it introduces the protasis, followed by the apodosis in an independent clause, e.g., "If X then Y." Verse 16 follows the latter pattern. So, if Mal 2:16 is understood as a conditional statement, who or what is the subject? Given the content of the disputation and its focus on the treacherous and faithless action of some divorcing husbands, it seems reasonable to understand the null subject as the divorcing man, "If one hates [and] divorces [his wife] . . ."

References to "hating" and "divorcing" are best understood in light of the larger ancient Near Eastern context. In his analysis of Akkadian parallels, Raymond Westbrook observed that "hate" is not simply a cipher for divorce, but instead a reference to the husband's aversion to his wife.[91] According to Westbrook, "The verb ['to hate'] invariably appears in combination with a verb of action, providing the motivation for that action. The motivation appears to turn what might otherwise be an innocent act into a guilty one . . . 'hate' is used to show that the action arose from a subjective motive"[92] According to Deut 24:1, a man may divorce his wife for עֶרְוַת דָּבָר, an "indecent matter," but the action of the first wife seems nowhere in view in Mal 2:16; the focus seems to be on the husband's motivation alone. The first verb שׂנא, "to hate," in שָׂנֵא שַׁלַּח refers to the man's "subjective motive," i.e, he does not have justifiable grounds for a divorce, while the second verb, שַׁלַּח, "to send away," refers more specifically to the act of divorcing.[93]

This reading has several advantages.[94] First, rather than emending the first clause so that the text reads first person, as though God were the subject ("I hate divorce"), the text can stand as presently configured. Second, this reading removes the potential awkwardness posed by a shift in subjects from the protasis to the apodosis. Rather than "Because I hate divorce . . . then he covers," the translation would read, "If a man hates [and] divorces . . . then he covers." Third, and perhaps more significant, when the verb שׂנא appears together with שׁלח in other biblical texts, the subject of שׂנא is typically one of the marriage partners (cf. Gen 29:31; Deut 21:15–17; 22:13, 16; 24:3; Prov 30:23 and Isa 60:15).

The impact of the husband's action appears in the apodosis, וְכִסָּה חָמָס עַל־לְבוּשׁוֹ, "then he covers his garment in violence." The preposition

Greek texts (LXX[L,W]), the translation actually appears to call for divorce: "If you hate, divorce!" The Vulgate and Targums follow similarly. In 4QXII[a], the text reads כי אם שנתה שלח, "If you hate her, divorce [her]." See the larger discussion of 4QXII[a] in Russell Fuller, "Text-Critical Problems in Malachi 2:10–16," *JBL* 10 (1991): 47–57. Clendenen is no doubt correct in his assessment that the readings provided in these ancient witnesses reflect an attempt at "harmonizing the verse with current practice and with accepted interpretation of Deut 24:1–4" (Taylor and Clendenen, *Haggai, Malachi*, 363–64).

90. There are of course instances in which a casual clause appears first (e.g., Exod 1:21), but in many of those instances, one must consider whether the causal clause has been fronted for pragmatic reasons.

91. Raymond Westbrook, "The Prohibition on Restoration of Marriage in Deuteronomy 24:1–4," in *Studies in the Bible*, ed. Sara Japhet, Scripta Hierosolymitana 31 (Jerusalem: Magnes, 1986), 387–405.

92. Westbrook, "The Prohibition on Restoration of Marriage," 401–2.

93. The two verbs appearing together in an asyndectic construction has parallels with Neo-Assyrian marriage contracts (Westbrook, "The Prohibition on Restoration of Marriage," 403). The second verb שׁלח could be repointed as a *piel* perfect, thus reinforcing the parallel form of the asyndectic construction or, as Hugenberger has suggested, שַׁלַּח as it presently stands can be construed as a variant form of the infinitive absolute, which can function as a perfect (*Marriage as Covenant*, 72–73). See also *IBHS* §35.5.2.

94. See Hugenberger, *Marriage as Covenant*, 70.

עַל frequently follows the verb כסה and identifies the object covered (e.g., Lev 4:8; Ezek 31:15; Hab 2:14; Job 21:26), and in this instance, the noun חָמָס, "violence," signals that with which the object is covered.[95] A number of suggestions have been offered as to the meaning of לְבוּשׁ, "garment," but, generally speaking, they can be reduced to two.[96] לְבוּשׁ has been understood as a metonym for the marriage covenant generally or for the wife more specifically. The reference to "garment," in particular, recalls betrothal scenes elsewhere in the Old Testament (Deut 22:20; Ezek 16:8; Ruth 3:9). The NIV understands the metonynmic use of garment in this way, rendering the second half of the verse as: "[the man] . . . does violence to the one he should protect." The reference to a person's clothing or garment can also refer to the person or even the person's inner character.[97] Thus, for a man to divorce his wife out of "hatred" (שׂנא) marks his character publicly; he is a man of violence.[98] Elsewhere in the Old Testament, acts of violence are associated with wickedness, greed and oppression (e.g., Ezek 7:11; 45:9; Hab 1:2; Zeph 1:9), and thus those who commit such acts are subject to YHWH's scorn.[99]

Canonical and Theological Significance

God as Father

The opening lines of this disputation invoked the image of God as father. For most contemporary readers of the Bible, this metaphorical imagery seems routine and hardly surprising. Yet as noted above, the use of father imagery in association with YHWH is relatively rare in the Old Testament.[100] The same cannot be said among other ancient Near Eastern religions, however. In Sumero-Akkadian literature, Anu, the god of heaven, and Enlil, god of the earth, are often referenced as "father," and in the Ugaritic texts, the same title is applied to El. He is recognized as the father and creator both of humans and the gods within the Canaanite pantheon. While the Old Testament does share a number of common religious concepts with its broader ancient Near Eastern context, the attribution of YHWH as father remains relatively muted.[101]

95. For a nearly identical structure, see Ezek 24:7. The Hebrew reads לְכַסּוֹת עָלָיו עָפָר, "to cover him [with] dust." The object of כסה is marked by עַל, with עָפָר ("dust") signaling that which will cover the object.

96. Verhoef suggests that covering one's garment with violence refers to actual cultic activity. "In their eagerness to serve the Lord, they brought 'thousands of rams' (Mic 6:7), they splashed the blood of the sacrificial animals on their garments, and in the process committed violence to these animals" (*The Book of Haggai and Malachi*, 280). Verhoef argues this reflects the "aggravated circumstance of sinning combined with religious activity," a pervasive issue in the book of Malachi. Although Verhoef is correct on the latter point, his reference to actual cultic activity in v. 16 seems pressed.

97. Cf. Zech 3:3-5 where the adjective לָבֻשׁ appears. See also Ps 73:6. Although the specific term לְבוּשׁ is not used specifically, the psalmist does refer to violence covering a person like a garment.

98. Gibson, *Covenant Continuity and Fidelity*, 150.

99. Cf. Ps 11:5.

100. Cf. Exod 4:22, 23; Deut 32:6, 18; Isa 63:16; 64:8; Jer 2:27; 3:4.

101. Reinhard Feldmeier and Hermann Spieckermann postulate that "the firm integration of the father metaphor in

While the metaphor is indeed muted, it is not altogether absent, as evident in the pre-exilic royal theology. YHWH's relationship with the Davidic dynasty is often cast in "father-son" imagery.[102] The foremost example of this can be found in 2 Sam 7, where a number of key themes associated with royal theology are unpacked. In a vision to Nathan, YHWH refers to the Davidic dynasty and declares, "I will be a father to him and he shall be a son to me" (v. 14). As part of this "father-son" relationship, YHWH promises "to establish the throne of [David's] kingdom forever." This connection between YHWH and the king clearly signaled the special status of the king, but even more, it conveyed a certain sense of stability and wellbeing for the entire land.

With the demise of the monarchy (and the destruction of Jerusalem) at the hands of the Babylonians, the father-son imagery that had served Israel's royal theology so well had become somewhat vacuous. One might imagine that after such a traumatic event, older metaphors would give way to new metaphors. With the king in exile and the father-son metaphor somewhat in tatters, it would seem unlikely that the community would still employ the metaphor of God as father, yet that is exactly what occurs in selected texts. The post-exilic community appropriated the metaphor of God as father in new ways. Rather than reserving the "father" metaphor for royal imagery alone, the metaphor invoked earlier traditions that cast the community of Israel as the "children" of YHWH (cf. Deut 14:1). Other post-exilic texts reflect the renewed understanding about the community. Twice in Isa 63:16, the community declares YHWH as their father, as their "redeemer." But the most striking confession, especially in light of Mal 2:10, occurs in the following chapter of Isaiah. In Isa 64:7[8], the people confess "O YHWH, you are our Father; we are the clay and you are the potter; we are all the work of your hand" (author's translation). The two passages together assert that as "father," YHWH is the one who redeems, sustains, and creates his people anew. In the New Testament, Paul seems to echo such thoughts in Rom 8. There Paul celebrates that through a "spirit of adoption," those in the community together can cry out, "Abba, Father" (v. 15). Further, Paul asserts, the community may be best understood as the "children of God," and as such, "heirs of God."[103]

the mythical worlds of divine genealogies with their rich concretions in theogony, theomachy and cosmogony had a limiting effect on the Old Testament adaptation of the name Father" (*God of the Living: A Biblical Theology* [Waco, TX: Baylor University Press, 2011), 55. On the broader ancient Near Eastern worldview and its impact on the Old Testament, see John H. Walton, *Ancient Near Eastern Thought and the Old Testament: Introducing the Conceptual World of the Bible*, 2nd ed. (Grand Rapids: Baker Academic, 2018).

102. The royal theology in Egypt employs a similar metaphorical relationship between the deity and the pharaoh, with a significant difference being the divine status accorded the pharaoh. Feldmeier and Spieckermann suggest that the "stability and welfare of the land were linked inseparably to this close 'father-son' liaison" (*God of the Living*, 55). See also Jan Assmann, "Das Bild des Vaters im Alten Ägypten," in *Das Vaterbild in Mythos und Geschichte* (Stuttgart: Kohlhammer, 1976), 12–49.

103. Similar language of God as father and adoption can be found in Gal 4:4–7. On the father-child metaphor and its perceived implications, see also 1 John 3:1–2.

That which belongs to the father will come to the "children." In a somewhat similar vein, the opening verses of 1 Peter reference God as father, and then declare that "he has given us a new birth into a living hope" (1:3). The images of the father as one who redeems, sustains, and recreates reverberate once more.

When Malachi declares that YHWH is the community's father and creator (2:10), a similar confession is being expressed. Similar to the community's confession in Isa 63–64 and similar to later confessions by the early Christian community, Malachi employs the metaphor "father" to acknowledge who and what binds them together; they are the family of God, created and sustained by the one who offers hope. The post-exilic community and the early Christian community alike could no longer rely on the power dynamics inherent in the "father-son" metaphor employed by pre-exilic royal theology. These later communities had no power whatsoever, particularly in the face of the massive Persian and Roman empires. Yet what bound them together was a common belief that God remained fully present and fully faithful to the "family" that he had created. Although those later communities had no empire of which to speak (as did David), they had something much greater, a kinship founded by and rooted in YHWH. This is what makes the community's acts of abomination (marrying foreigners) and faithlessness (divorcing the wives of their youth) in Malachi so egregious. These actions are not simply another example of communal waywardness; they are an affront to that which the potter has formed.

Marriage to Those outside the Community

As mentioned in the introduction, the social and political shift in Yehud likely placed significant economic strain upon the post-exilic community. Hill is no doubt correct in his assessment that the "social ills confronted by Malachi were not so much the by-product of baalism, as sheer pragmatism . . . in response to the depressed local economy."[104] Natural disasters (Hag 1:6), oppressive taxation (Neh 5:15), and economic and political corruption (Neh 5:7–8, 15) only exacerbated this bleak situation. As a remedy, it appears that families in Yehud intermarried with those outside of Yehud, likely for economic and political reasons, a move that is thoroughly rejected by Malachi based on theological grounds.

If Mal 2:10–12 is understood as a literal (and not figurative) reference to marriage, as suggested in the previous section, then the question could be raised, "Is Malachi simply xenophobic?" Does his rejection of those "outside the community" suggest an aversion to "foreigners?" These questions start from the wrong presupposition. The prohibition against exogamous marriages in Malachi is not rooted in

104. Hill, *Malachi*, 75.

xenophobia, but instead in covenant expectations.[105] The people are warned in Deut 7 that when they enter the land, "do not intermarry with [those in the land], giving your daughters to their sons or taking their daughters for your sons, for that would turn your children away from following me, to serve other gods" (7:3–4, NRSVUE). A similar concern is expressed in Exod 34:11–16 as well. The justification for the condemnation in both the Exodus and Deuteronomy texts is that the initial action (intermarriage) would lead to a subsequent action (worshiping other gods), and it is that latter action that proves most distressing.[106] The act of intermarriage is condemned, not because of xenophobic tendencies, but because of what it might portend for the individual and for the community. Worshiping other gods would be an act of covenant faith*less*ness by the people, and further, a slow dissolution of the community and its identity.[107]

Divorce and the Book of Malachi

Rather than a universal prohibition on divorce, v. 16 must be read in light of its larger literary and historical context. The entirety of this disputation is focused on that which unites the people of God ("one father," "one God") and the actions taken by the community which threaten to subvert that unity. Through their marriage to the "daughters of foreign gods" and through the divorcing of the wives of their youth, rather than preserving their future, the community in Yehud actually threatened it. These actions, rather than establishing their corporate identity, placed it in jeopardy, and concomitantly, imperiled their covenant relationship with YHWH.

The second half of this disputation began in v. 13 with people weeping at the altar due to YHWH's apparent rejection of their offerings. The final verse makes explicit what is inferred in v. 13. As suggested above, the problem was not with God, but with the community. The community expected the full benefits of a covenant with YHWH without adhering to the requisite demands. Even though the community pled with YHWH to accept their offerings, their "garments [covered] in violence"

105. On intermarriage more generally, see Christian Frevel, "Introduction: The Discourse on Intermarriage in the Hebrew Bible," in *Mixed Marriages: Intermarriage and Group Identity in the Second Temple Period*, ed. C. Frevel, LHBOTS 547 (London: T&T Clark, 2011), 1–14.

106. A similar concern related to intermarriage is expressed in Ezra 9–10 and Neh 13:1–3. Similar to the point made above related to Malachi's concern, Mark A. Throntveit writes, "It is not their racial or national ties that are at issue but the religious practices that the foreign wives brought to their marriages and the effects those practices would surely have had upon family and community structures" (*Ezra-Nehemiah*, Interpretation [Louisville: John Knox, 1992], 57).

107. Those who use Mal 2:10–12 to justify condemnation of interracial marriage, however, have grossly misunderstood and misapplied the text. Regrettably, miscengenation laws (the prohibition of interracial marriage) in the United States remained on the books in most states until *Loving v. Virginia* (1967) and frequently support of such laws was rooted in a superficial appeal to Scripture. While such laws were struck down by *Loving v. Virginia*, the underlying sentiment remains in some quarters as does a continued misuse of Scripture to this end.

(v. 16) made that impossible.[108] The divorcing of the wives of their youth suggests that the community operated with the assumption that faithfulness is contingent, and that when necessity demands, faithfulness is even optional. But Malachi chastises that understanding of faithfulness because of the harm that it does to the community and also because of the underlying thesis that it represents. Covenant faithfulness to the wife of one's youth and to God, their "one father," is not optional or contingent. The community failed to grasp the connection between covenant faithfulness with one another and covenant faithfulness with God, between ethical behavior and cultic practice.[109] Thus even as Malachi chastised the priests for behavior and instruction that runs counter to the torah, so too does Malachi chastise the people for their behavior and their flagrant disregard for covenant demands.

If contemporary readings of this text focus attention solely on the issue of divorce, particularly as construed in a modern context, then they will miss Malachi's much deeper concern.[110] Divorcing the "wife of their youth" is not the issue; it is the symptom. With this act, the husbands practiced a form of infidelity to their community and, worse yet, infidelity to the God who served as a witness to that marriage (v. 14). Whether this decision was made out of pragmatic concern or selfish desire, the prophet seems uninterested. The message is clear, however: what YHWH longs for is a community absent of such faithless action (בגד), fully committed to one another, and unflinching in their devotedness to their God.

108. On the social justice implications, see Corinna Körting, "Marriage and Divorce as a Matter of Social Justice in Mal 2:10–16," *Canon and Culture* 10 (2016): 205–25.

109. Snyman, *Malachi*, 118.

110. This is not to suggest that Mal 2:10–16 cannot theologically inform our contemporary models of marriage. As Nogalski suggests, "It is not clear that the church's ability to perpetuate the sacred nature of a marital promise has kept pace with the broader culture's message that marital fidelity represents a quaint, archaic expectation of a bygone age. Marital infidelity is not a new problem, as shown by Malachi and other biblical stories, but the erosion of a sense of sacred promise threatens to exacerbate the problem in our day beyond measure" (Nogalski, *The Book of the Twelve: Micah–Malachi*, 1040–41).

CHAPTER 5

Malachi 2:17–3:5

V. The Coming of the God of Justice

Main Idea of the Passage

In response to the community's allegation that YHWH has been derelict in his role as Divine Judge, the prophet announces the coming of a messenger who will prepare the way for the coming of YHWH.

Literary Context

As suggested in the introduction, the book of Malachi contains six disputations and this, the fourth disputation, stands at a critical juncture in the linear orientation of the book (see the introduction to the book of Malachi). The first three disputations appear to confront the theological, cultic, and communal issues that plagued the current generation. The prophet chided the community and called for changed behavior and thought. In the fourth disputation, the prophet responds to the current claims of the community (2:17) by pointing to the coming day of YHWH. In doing so, the fourth disputation signals an eschatological shift in the book. The resolution of the issues raised in this disputation has been pushed out to a future event.

Translation and Exegetical Outline

(See pages 110–11.)

Structure and Literary Form

The fourth disputation follows the expected form of statement—objection—response with the primary theme developed in the response. The disputation opens with a declaration concerning the "words" of the community that have proven wearisome to YHWH (2:17a). The community challenges the initial claim in the subsequent line (2:17c). The remainder of the disputation includes a complex response to the community's challenge in 2:17d–3:5. As evidence of the wearisome words of the community, two quotes are referenced (2:17d–h). Whether these are actual quotes from the community or representative of the *Zeitgeist* of that period is inconsequential. At their core, they challenge the integrity of YHWH. The remainder of the disputation seeks to dismantle the presuppositions embedded within the two communal quotes (2:17c–h).

Malachi 2:17–3:5

			V. The Coming of the God of Justice (2:17–3:5)
17a	הוֹגַעְתֶּם יְהוָה בְּדִבְרֵיכֶם	"You have wearied YHWH with your words.	A. The Initial Statement (2:17a)
17b	וַאֲמַרְתֶּם	But you say,	B. The Objection by the Community (2:17b–c)
17c	בַּמָּה הוֹגָעְנוּ	'How have we wearied [him]?'	
			C. The Response (2:17d–3:5d)
17d	בֶּאֱמָרְכֶם	When you say,	1. A Reference to Wearisome Words (2:17d–h)
17e	כָּל־עֹשֵׂה רָע טוֹב בְּעֵינֵי יְהוָה	'All who do evil are good in the eyes of YHWH	
17f	וּבָהֶם הוּא חָפֵץ	and in them he delights.'	
17g	אוֹ	Or [when you say],	
17h	אַיֵּה אֱלֹהֵי הַמִּשְׁפָּט	'Where is the God of justice?'	
3:1a	הִנְנִי שֹׁלֵחַ מַלְאָכִי	Behold, I am about to send my messenger	2. The Arrival of a Messenger (3:1a–b)
1b	וּפִנָּה־דֶרֶךְ לְפָנָי	and he will prepare a way before me.	
1c	וּפִתְאֹם יָבוֹא אֶל־הֵיכָלוֹ הָאָדוֹן	And suddenly, he will come into his temple, the Lord	3. The Arrival of YHWH (3:1c–g)
1d	↑ אֲשֶׁר־אַתֶּם מְבַקְשִׁים	↑ whom you are seeking	
1e	וּמַלְאַךְ הַבְּרִית אֲשֶׁר־אַתֶּם חֲפֵצִים	and the messenger of the covenant, for whom you long,	
1f	הִנֵּה־בָא	behold he is coming,"	
1g	אָמַר יְהוָה צְבָאוֹת	says YHWH Sabaoth.	

	Hebrew	English	Section
2a	וּמִי מְכַלְכֵּל אֶת־יוֹם בּוֹאוֹ	"Who will be able to endure the day of his coming?	4. YHWH's Action: Purification (3:2a–4)
2b	וּמִי הָעֹמֵד בְּהֵרָאוֹתוֹ	And who will be able to stand	
2c	↑ בְּהֵרָאוֹתוֹ	↑ when he appears	
2d	↑ כִּי־הוּא כְּאֵשׁ מְצָרֵף וּכְבֹרִית מְכַבְּסִים	↑ because he is like a refiner's fire and a launder's soap	
3a	וְיָשַׁב	And he will act as one	
3b	↑ מְצָרֵף וּמְטַהֵר כֶּסֶף	↑ who refines and purifies silver.	
3c	וְטִהַר אֶת־בְּנֵי־לֵוִי	And he will purify the sons of Levi	
3d	↑ וְזִקַּק אֹתָם כַּזָּהָב וְכַכָּסֶף	↑ and refine them like gold and silver	
3e	↑ וְהָיוּ לַיהוָה	↑ so that they might be	
3f	↑ מַגִּישֵׁי מִנְחָה בִּצְדָקָה	↑ the ones who present proper offerings to YHWH.	
4	וְעָרְבָה לַיהוָה מִנְחַת יְהוּדָה וִירוּשָׁלָ͏ִם כִּימֵי עוֹלָם וּכְשָׁנִים קַדְמֹנִיּוֹת	The offering of Judah and Jerusalem will be pleasing to YHWH as in the days of old and the former years.	
5a	וְקָרַבְתִּי אֲלֵיכֶם לַמִּשְׁפָּט	And then I will draw near to you for judgment	5. YHWH's Action: Judgment (3:5a–d)
5b	וְהָיִיתִי עֵד מְמַהֵר בַּמְכַשְּׁפִים וּבַמְנָאֲפִים וּבַנִּשְׁבָּעִים לַשָּׁקֶר וּבְעֹשְׁקֵי שְׂכַר שָׂכִיר אַלְמָנָה וְיָתוֹם וּמַטֵּי גֵר וְלֹא יְרֵאוּנִי אָמַר יְהוָה צְבָאוֹת	and I will be a swift witness against sorcerers, against adulterers, against those who swear falsely and those who oppress hired workers, [and those who oppress] the widow, the orphan and those who turn aside the sojourner—	
5c	וְלֹא יְרֵאוּנִי	they did not show me fear,"	
5d	אָמַר יְהוָה צְבָאוֹת	says YHWH Sabaoth.	

Several elements within the disputation suggest the overall unity of the pericope.[1] For example, the objections raised by the community and subsequent responses form something of an A-B-B′-A′ pattern within the disputation.

A Objection: YHWH delights in those who do evil (2:17d–f)
  B Objection: YHWH, the God of justice, is absent (2:17g–h)
  B′ Response: YHWH is coming (3:1c–2c)
A′ Response: YHWH will judge the evildoers (3:5)

Further, as with the other disputations, the repetition of vocabulary contributes to the thematic unity of the whole. For example, the vocabulary employed in the two questions posed by the community appears again as part of the response (cf. "delight," [חפץ] 2:17f and 3:1e; "justice" [מִשְׁפָּט] 2:17h and 3:5a). Perhaps more significantly is the threefold repetition of the verb "to come" (בוא) at the very center of the disputation (3:1c, f; 3:2a). The question of God's absence at the beginning of this section and the implications of his arrival in the latter section frame the repeated confession that YHWH is coming.

Explanation of the Text

A. Initial Statement (2:17a)

The opening line in the fourth disputation lays out the charge against the community; they have wearied YHWH with their words. The verb יגע, "to weary," appears in the perfect. Quite often in DD, a perfect verb points back to a prior event that nonetheless still has relevance for the moment in which the "speech act" takes place.[2] In such instances the verb is better rendered in English as a present perfect, "have wearied" (cf. NET, NRSV). Understood this way, the verb suggests that the community has repeatedly and continually wearied YHWH with their words, and that such actions continue to have a bearing on the community. The announcement of YHWH's coming in judgment mentioned later in the disputation is not in response to a flippant comment or a passing thought, but rather to persistent and inveterate speech that reflects a particular way of assessing YHWH's perceived inaction.

The *hiphil* form of the verb יגע, "to weary," occurs only two times in the Old Testament with YHWH as the one who is wearied (Isa 43:24; Mal 2:17a). In Isa 43, YHWH contends that the people have wearied him with their iniquities, whereas in Mal 2, it is "with their words" (בְּדִבְרֵיכֶם). Glazier-McDonald

1. Scholars have posited a number of theories regarding the literary growth of this disputation, particularly given the shift from first person to third person language in 3:1c–4 and the relative difficulty in assigning an identity to the various figures mentioned in 3:1a–g. See, for example, Petersen, *Zechariah 9–14 and Malachi*, 211; Weyde, *Prophecy and Teaching*, 130–32. See also the diachronic analysis by Schart (*Maleachi*, 105–6). Although these arguments merit serious consideration, the interpretive approach in this commentary remains focused on the final form of the biblical text.

2. *BHRG* §19.2.1.2.

translates "words" as "prattle" and suggests that it refers to "foolish, idle talk, childish babble."[3] Such a translation, however, fails to capture the weightiness of the charge in Mal 2. If it is iniquities that weary YHWH in Isa 43:24, then surely it must be more than "idle talk" in Mal 2:17a that has had the same impact. These "words" refer to a fundamental rejection of YHWH's identity. The seriousness of "their words," and their challenge to the identity of YHWH, are confirmed in the two subsequent quotes.

B. The Objection by the Community (2:17b–c)

Similar to other disputations, the objection by the community invokes the language found in the initial charge in 2:17a (יגע, "to weary"). Although most English translations (e.g., NIV, NRSV, NASB, NET) provide the complement to the verb, i.e., "How have we wearied *him*," the complement is actually absent in the MT. Rather than emending the text, as suggested by *BHS* and many commentators, the construction can be better explained as simply having a null complement.[4]

C. The Response (2:17d–3:5)

1. A Reference to Wearisome Words (2:17d–h)

In response to the community's objection, the prophet references two sayings which are meant to represent the problematic outlook espoused by the community. While each comment or claim has a separate point or focus, together they challenge YHWH's integrity, particularly as it relates to his covenantal obligations to his people. In the first instance, the people allege that "All who do evil are good in the eyes of YHWH and in them he delights" (v. 17e–f). This claim picks up two key themes from the book of Deuteronomy and reworks them in light of current experience. Repeatedly the book of Deuteronomy affirms that those who "do evil in the eyes of YHWH" will provoke him to anger (כעס, *hiphil*).[5] By contrast, for "those who do right [טוֹב] in the eyes of YHWH," it will go well (יטב) with them.[6] Both sayings reflect a certain assurance that is rooted in retributive theology, i.e., disobedience results in negative consequences, obedience in blessings. Experience should bear both claims out, yet for this community, the first claim in particular can no longer be validated.

3. Glazier-McDonald, *Malachi*, 127. Hill suggests similarly that the issue is likely "insincere prayer and mechanical worship," but again, this must be rejected in light of the comparison with Isa 43 and based on the content of the fourth disputation (Hill, *Malachi*, 261).

4. A null construction means that the constituent is often omitted when clear inferences can be drawn from the larger context, as seems to be the case here. *BHS* proposes הוֹגַעְנֻהוּ given that a number of LXX manuscripts include a third masculine plural pronoun (as does the Syriac and Vulgate). The addition of the pronoun makes explicit what is inferred by the null complement. *BHQ* retains the MT. Cf. Petersen, *Zechariah 9–14 and Malachi*, 206–7.

5. E.g., Deut 4:25; 9:18; 17:2; 31:29. Repeatedly in the book of Deuteronomy as well as the Deuteronomistic History, the definite article is attached to the noun (הָרַע). In the majority of those cases, the collocation "to do *the* evil" refers explicitly to abandoning YHWH for other gods, as when the nation "did *the evil* [הָרַע]" and worshipped the golden calf (Deut 9:18). Cf. Deut 17:2; Judg 2:11; 3:7; 10:6; 1 Kgs 11:6. In rehearsing the failures of kings from both the Northern and Southern Kingdoms, the Deuteronomistic historian frequently invoked this phrase in condemnation for idolatrous actions (e.g., 2 Kgs 14:24; 15:18). Other instances within these books, however, simply refer to evil or wicked actions, as when Nathan chastises David for his murder of Uriah (2 Sam 12:9). Cf. 1 Sam 15:19. The list of covenant violations in v. 5 suggest that Malachi has the latter usage in mind. These violations confirm the community's disregard for YHWH. A similar usage appears in Qoh 4:17[5:1]. Cf. Neh 9:28.

6. E.g., Deut 6:18; 12:25; 13:19[18] (SP; MT does not have טוֹב). Frequently, "upright" (יָשָׁר) is included in parallel with "good" or "right" (טוֹב) to stress the nature of the behavior under review (cf. 6:18).

As a result, the community reworks the first premise borrowing from the language of the second in an effort to articulate what is apparent: "All who do evil are *good* [טוֹב] in the eyes of God." In addition, and perhaps even more shocking, is the last clause of this sentence: "in them he delights" (v. 17f). Although the book of Deuteronomy claims those who do evil provoke YHWH to anger, experience seems to suggest that those who do evil in fact are the recipients of YHWH's delight. The prepositional phrase "in them" (בָּהֶם) has been focus-fronted in an effort to highlight this unsettling claim, "in them he delights."

The primary issue centers on God's alleged approbation of the evildoers as "good"; there is no mention of the faithful enduring unjust treatment, however. The issue is not the wicked prospering *and* the righteous suffering, but rather, as Jacobs suggests, the disconcerting claim that YHWH evaluates good *and* evil as good.[7] The apparent failure of YHWH to distinguish between the two suggests that God has abandoned his role as faithful judge.

The disjunction אוֹ ("or") introduces the second objection in v. 17g, but its use here should not be understood as providing an alternative to the first objection, i.e., the community said this *or* that. Instead, the second objection is better understood as a consequence of the first.[8] In the first objection the community concluded that based on their experience and the apparent success of the evildoers, the world was not operating in a way consistent with covenantal expectations. In short, the evildoers seemed to live without any repercussions for their actions. Although Scripture repeatedly confesses that YHWH is a God of justice (e.g., Deut 1:17; Jer 9:23[24]; Pss 37:28; 99:4), what the community observed seemed inconsistent with that confession and worse yet, appeared to signal God's absence. As result, in Mal 2:17h the people cry out "Where is the God of justice [הַמִּשְׁפָּט]?"[9] Because the interrogative "where" (אַיֵּה) is often used to introduce laments (Isa 63:11, 15; Joel 2:17), the question here should be taken seriously; the community utters a lament over the perceived remoteness of God in the wake of the prosperity of the evildoers.[10] Thus, the question in v. 17 does not want "to know *whether* God is 'the God of justice.' It wants to know *where* this god is. The community has seen nothing of him. For them, he is a God who does nothing, neither good nor bad, and, if God does nothing, then it is as though there is no God at all."[11] The remainder of the disputation functions as a response to the claims of the community. Any perceived absence of God will be fully remedied by the coming of YHWH.

7. Jacobs, *The Books of Haggai and Malachi*, 267. This charge against YHWH is made even more explicitly in Zeph 1:12.

8. Kessler, *Maleachi*, 227.

9. Hill renders the construct phrase in 2:17h, "the God of the judgment." Although the closest analog appears in Isa 30:18, the noun מִשְׁפָּט ("judgment/justice") lacks the definite article in that text. In Mal 2:17, however, the noun does include the definite article (הַמִּשְׁפָּט), which leads Hill to conclude that "Malachi has in mind 'the judgment' of the eschaton—the Day of Yahweh" (*Malachi*, 264). Clearly the reference to YHWH coming in 3:1 invokes Day of YHWH imagery, and such imagery is made even more explicit in 3:19[4:1], "Behold, the day is coming," yet this language does not necessarily determine the interpretation in 2:17h. As suggested above, the two questions are sequential. In the first, the community notes the apparent inconsistency observed while in the second they lament the apparent absence of the God of justice. What the community desires is for God to enact justice. The subsequent references to the Day of YHWH affirm that while justice may appear absent, it is coming nonetheless.

10. Weyde, *Prophecy and Teaching*, 281–83. Within the psalms of lament, the nations or enemy frequently taunt the psalmist with a similar question "Where [אַיֵּה] is your God?" Cf. Pss 42:3, 10; 79:10; 115:2. Similar to the situation in Mal 2, the apparent inactivity of God is perceived as the absence of God.

11. Kessler, *Maleachi*, 227.

2. The Arrival of a Messenger (3:1a–b)

The interpretive challenge in v. 1 centers on the identities of those mentioned. Four figures are readily identifiable in the text: the speaker ("I"), "my messenger" (מַלְאָכִי), the "Lord" (הָאָדוֹן), and "the messenger of the covenant" (מַלְאַךְ הַבְּרִית). The first figure, the speaker, is clearly YHWH Sabaoth (3:1g); the identification of the remaining three, however, has proven more challenging and consequently has resulted in a number of proposals.[12] Rather than presenting the varying proposals (and their plausibility) at the outset of this section, discussion related to the identity of each will be considered within the context of the verse itself.

In 3:1a, YHWH announces, "Behold I am about to send my messenger." The collocation הִנֵּה ("behold") followed by a participle frequently signals immediacy, often with foreboding overtones;[13] its usage here is understandable. In 2:17, the community laments the apparent absence of the God of justice; the announcement in 3:1a, in response, signals that such action is on the horizon. The questions that remain, however, center on the identity of the one being sent and the precise role of the messenger. Some interpreters have suggested that "my messenger" is best understood as a "heavenly forerunner" that will precede the coming of YHWH in 3:1c.[14] The prevailing interpretation, however, is that the reference in 3:1a is to a human agent. In the post-exilic period, the label "messenger" (מַלְאָךְ) was applied to humans, even to prophets (cf. 2 Chr 36:15). As a result, some interpreters have suggested that the messenger is an unnamed prophet or perhaps even Malachi.[15] Snyman suggests that the label in 3:1a is a reference to the prophet himself, given the use of "Malachi" both here and in the superscription (1:1).[16] While intriguing, Snyman's suggestion must be abandoned. As noted above, the collocation הִנֵּה plus a participle has a future connotation. Thus, rather than aligning the *current* work of the prophet with the work of the *coming* messenger, it seems preferable to understand the prophet's role as announcing the human messenger who has yet to come.[17] In the book of Malachi, the human messenger is sent to prepare the people for the coming of YHWH.

The verb פנה, often translated as "prepare," appears in the *piel* and is better understood as "clear away" or "to remove," as in to remove an object. The meaning is reflected in Isa 57:14: "Build it! Build it! Clear a way! Remove all the obstacles out of the way of my people!" (NET). For a similar usage, see Isa 62:10.[18] In both instances, the announcement concerns clearing a way, i.e., a road, for God's people to return home to Jerusalem (cf. Isa 35:8). In Isa 40:3, the same collocation פנה + דֶּרֶךְ

12. For a thorough review of the various proposals, see Weyde, *Prophecy and Teaching*, 284–95.

13. *IBHS* §40.2.1b.

14. Hill, for example, argues that "my messenger" in Mal 3:1a is a reference to the "Angel of Yahweh" commissioned as Israel's forerunner in the covenant ratification ceremony at Mt. Sinai (*Malachi*, 288). See also the reading proposed by Wilhelm Rudolph, *Haggai, Sacharja 1–8, Sacharja 9–14, Maleachi*, 278–79. Hill, *Malachi*, 288, argues that Mal 3:1 points to three different divine beings: "my angel," "the Lord," and "the angel of the covenant." On the identity of the latter, see below.

15. On the argument for an unnamed prophet yet to arrive, see Bruce Malchow, "The Messenger of the Covenant in Mal 3:1," *JBL* 103 (1984): 252–55.

16. Snyman, *Malachi*, 130–31. He argues that the "messenger of Yahweh is not a heavenly being or an angel but the prophet himself. Malachi, the prophet, is the one performing the duties of preparing the way through his prophecies."

17. Within the larger context of the book, this seems to be implied. The reference to Elijah as one sent by YHWH "before the coming great and awesome day of YHWH" (3:23[4:5]) confirms that: (1) this messenger has yet to arrive and (2) the messenger will be human. On the role of Elijah in the book of Malachi, see the comments on 3:23[4:5].

18. For similar, but more mundane, uses of the *piel* stem of פנה, cf. Gen 24:31; Lev 14:36. See also Ps 80:10[9].

("clear a way"), appears, but this time in reference to YHWH.[19] The imagery in Isa 40:3 (and Mal 3) invokes the ancient Near Eastern practice of creating a processional road for the entrance of a king (or god) into a city. Although this was utilized in Babylon to great effect, it was not limited to the Babylonian empire alone.[20] "The primary function of the highways was to allow the great processions to display the power and majesty of the gods."[21] Malachi announces that a messenger is coming to prepare a way for YHWH's appearance among his people. Obviously "preparing a way" is best understood figuratively here, to mean "readying the people to receive Yahweh."[22] Although the language and imagery between the Isaiah and Malachi texts are similar, there is one critical difference. In Isa 40, the processing king (YHWH) comes to deliver his people; in Malachi, the king comes in judgment.[23]

3. The Arrival of YHWH (3:1c–g)

The final three lines function as a response to the haunting question posed by the community in 2:17, "Where is the God of justice?" The opening word in line 1c signals a shift in the argument from 3:1a–b with its focus on the "messenger" (מַלְאָךְ) to 3:1c–g with its focus on the arrival of the "Lord" (הָאָדוֹן) and the "messenger of the covenant" (מַלְאַךְ הַבְּרִית). The conjunction plus adverb (וּפִתְאֹם) can be translated as "suddenly," but in the sense of "surprisingly." Even as the messenger (מַלְאָךְ) will be sent by YHWH to prepare the way (1a–b), so too will the "Lord" (הָאָדוֹן) and the "messenger of the covenant" (מַלְאַךְ הַבְּרִית) come suddenly, without notice, into the temple. Equally important for understanding this text is the foreboding and ominous sense that the adverb פִּתְאֹם, "suddenly," conveys as evident by its use in other prophetic texts. Elsewhere YHWH's judgment is said to come upon the people of God "suddenly" (e.g., Isa 47:11; Jer 4:20; 6:26; 15:8; 18:22).

As suggested above, questions concerning the precise identities of the latter two figures have generated a number of proposals, particularly as it relates to the "messenger of the covenant." The identity of "the Lord" (הָאָדוֹן) in 3:1c can be none other than YHWH, Israel's covenant God. Several factors confirm this. In 1:6, the noun "lord," אָדוֹן, is mentioned and YHWH uses the label self-referentially in that same verse. Here, however, the definite article is attached to the noun, "*the* Lord," but this somewhat unusual construction actually confirms the identity of the figure. The noun + definite article, "*the* Lord" (הָאָדוֹן), only appears in nine other texts in the Old Testament and in each instance the word appears alongside the divine name, יְהוָה.[24] Although the divine name does not appear adjacent

19. Kessler suggests that the references to "weariness" in Mal 2:17 and the language of "preparing the way" in 3:1 likely signals that the prophet leaned heavily upon the language and imagery of Second Isaiah (*Maleachi*, 228–29). Even as the prophet in Second Isaiah addressed the "despair" of the people as the exile came to a close, Malachi addresses a similar despair experienced by those living in Yehud and Jerusalem under Persian rule. In both instances, the prophets pointed to the coming irruption of God into the world.

20. The complex road system that developed across the vast Persian empire during this time would have made such imagery even more vivid. On the Persian network of roads, see Briant, *From Cyrus to Alexander*, 357–77.

21. Glazier-McDonald, *Malachi*, 137.

22. Jacobs, *The Books of Haggai and Malachi*, 272. Hill labeled the obstacles as "self-interest, spiritual lethargy and evil behavior," the very issues addressed in the preceding disputations (*Malachi*, 266–67). Clendenen suggests more generally that preparing the way involves "clearing away the obstacles of unbelief" ("Malachi," 386). Kaiser is even more specific in his analysis with the suggestion that this involved a "removal of all spiritual, moral and ethical impediments" prior to the coming of YHWH ("The Promise of the Arrival of Elijah in Malachi and the Gospels," *GTJ* 3 [1982], 225).

23. Snyman, *Malachi*, 131.

24. Exod 23:17; 34:23; Deut 10:17; Isa 1:24; 3:1; 10:16, 33; 19:4; Ps 136:1 with 3.

to הָאָדוֹן here, as in the other texts, clearly YHWH remains in view based on the prepositional phrase utilized in line 1c. The prophet announces that "the Lord" (הָאָדוֹן) will come "into his temple" (cf. Zech 6:12–13). Who else could this be but YHWH? If הָאָדוֹן is in fact YHWH, as suggested here, then what is the purpose of this designation within this disputation? To declare YHWH as "the Lord" is to "emphasize Yahweh's role as sovereign over all the world."[25] The one who is coming is indeed the one with the authority to judge.

The coming of the "messenger of the covenant" (מַלְאַךְ הַבְּרִית) is mentioned in 3:1e. Identifying this figure has been particularly challenging, given that this is the only instance of the phrase in the Old Testament; no one else, human or divine, receives such a label. Some have argued that the "messenger of the covenant" in 3:1e is the same as the messenger in 3:1a, and further, that both are human figures.[26] Although the word "messenger" (מַלְאַךְ) is used in both instances, they appear to have different functions. Most interpreters associate the "messenger of the covenant" (מַלְאַךְ הַבְּרִית) with "the Lord" (הָאָדוֹן) in line 1c, and they arrive at this conclusion based upon the parallelism of the two lines:

A He will come into his temple,
  B the Lord whom you are seeking.
  B′ And the messenger of the covenant, for whom you long,
A′ behold [he] is coming.

Together they form an A-B-B′-A′ pattern with the two figures at the center and with both announced as "coming" (בוא). While such a highly structured arrangement does not necessarily confirm that the two figures are identical, it does suggest that there is an inherent connection in one way or another.

Hill mentions yet another analysis that would link "the Lord" (הָאָדוֹן) with the "messenger of the covenant" (מַלְאַךְ הַבְּרִית) and thereby establish their sameness. He offers the possibility that the *vav* conjunction on וּמַלְאַךְ הַבְּרִית could be understood epexegetically in that the second line restates the first line: "He will come into his temple, the Lord whom you are seeking, that is, the messenger of the covenant, for whom you long, behold [he] is coming."[27]

Beyond the assessments mentioned above, there is yet another approach to 3:1e that might aid in determining the relationship between "the Lord" and the "messenger of the covenant." The reference in 3:1f could be analyzed as an example of left-edge dislocation.[28] Typically the interjection הִנֵּה introduces a core clause, e.g., "Behold [he] is coming" (line 1f). The noun phrase "the messenger of the covenant for whom you long," however, stands outside the core clause; it is on the "left edge," so to speak: "And the messenger of the covenant for whom you long, behold [he] is coming." In these types of constructions "left-dislocated constituents are never new to the discourse," that is, they are not introducing something new.[29] Consequently,

25. Hill, *Malachi*, 268.
26. Cf. Petersen, *Zechariah 9–14 and Malachi*, 211–12.
27. Hill, *Malachi*, 269. Jacobs appears to follow Hill's suggestion of an epexegetical *vav* (*The Books of Haggai and Malachi*, 275). Even though Hill mentions this possible reading, he abandons it in favor of reading the *vav* as a simple conjunction, "and," due to his understanding that the messenger of the covenant is likely a "third eschatological figure" (Hill, *Malachi*, 289).
28. Robert Holmstedt, "Critical at the Margins: Edge Constituents in Biblical Hebrew," *KUSATU* 17 (2014): 115–32.
29. Ibid., 127. Holmstedt explains that left-dislocated constituents require some type of resumptive pronoun in the core clause. In this instance, however, the pronoun has dropped out to due to ellipsis.

the "messenger of the covenant" refers either to the messenger (3:1a) or to "the Lord" (3:1c). While both figures are mentioned in this discourse, the same verb (בוא) only appears with the latter. The messenger is "sent," but the Lord, הָאָדוֹן, is coming (בוא), even as the messenger of the covenant is coming (בוא). The one who is coming is the "one you are seeking" (3:1d) and the "one for whom you long" (3:1e). Both relative clauses serve to connect this announcement back to the initial query by the community in 2:17h, "Where is the God of justice?"

If both titles reference YHWH, then why did the prophet bother to utilize both? It is likely that together they serve as a response to the challenges in 2:17. As noted above, the reference to YHWH as "the Lord" confirms YHWH's role as sovereign over the world and the one with the authority to judge, likely a response to the challenge in 2:17h. The label "messenger of the covenant" responds to the challenge in 2:17e–f ("All who do evil are good in the eyes of YHWH and in them he delights"). Based on their observations, the community complains that YHWH has seemingly abandoned the tenets of the covenant, or worse yet, subverted them. The prophet declares just the opposite; the one who is coming is the messenger of the covenant, "the one who enforces the covenant."[30]

4. YHWH's Action: Purification (3:2–4)

The significance of YHWH's arrival is highlighted in the opening lines of this subsection with two rhetorical questions, followed by a subordinate clause that provides the necessary rationale for the claims made in the questions.[31] The two rhetorical questions stand in parallel construction (מִי + participle), and together reinforce the magnitude of what is to come. The prophet inquires, "Who will be able to endure [מְכַלְכֵּל] the day of his coming?" The verb כול in the *pilpel* form often refers to providing something for sustenance, such as food or water (e.g., Gen 45:11; 50:21; 2 Sam 19:33), but it can also have the sense of containing something (e.g., 2 Chr 2:5[6]). Here, however, as in Prov 18:14, the verb means "to endure" or "withstand," as in withstanding the "day of his coming." A nearly identical question appears in Joel 2:11, with both the interrogative מִי ("who") and the verb כול ("endure," in the *hiphil*) employed within a larger pericope focused on the Day of YHWH.[32] The second question begins with the same interrogative (מִי), followed by the verb עמד, "to stand," but to stand in the sense of survive. Elsewhere in the Old Testament, the verb עמד can be associated with God's judgment (1 Sam 6:20; Jer 49:19; 50:44; Ezek 22:14; Nah 1:6), and in each instance, the conclusion remains the same: the wicked will not survive the judgment of YHWH.[33]

The "day of his coming," mentioned in 3:2a, invokes day-of-YHWH language (see Canonical and Theological Significance, pp. 128–29). Elsewhere in the prophetic corpus the verb בּוֹא frequently appears alongside יוֹם, "day," in reference to the Day of YHWH (e.g., Isa 13:6; cf. Zeph 2:2; Zech 14:1). Later in Malachi, both terms appear yet again in 3:19[4:1] (2x), and in 3:23[4:5], בּוֹא appears alongside the expanded phrase, יוֹם יְהוָה, "the Day of

30. Jacobs, *The Books of Haggai and Malachi*, 275.

31. *BHRG* §40.29.2.

32. The precise direction of influence remains a matter of some debate. See the assessment of the issues in Gibson, *Covenant Continuity and Fidelity*, 177–81, and Weyde, *Prophecy and Teaching*, 292–95. Unlike Gibson and Weyde, who understand the priority to lie with Joel, Nogalski argues for the reverse (*The Book of the Twelve: Micah-Malachi*, 1049–50.

33. Glazier-McDonald is correct in her assessment, contra Verhoef (*The Books of Haggai and Malachi*, 290), that the answer to the questions cannot be "no one," given that in subsequent verses in this chapter those who fear YHWH indeed survive (cf. 3:19–20[4:1–2]). Consequently, Glazier-McDonald proposes that the answer to the two rhetorical questions is "Certainly not the wicked!" (*Malachi: The Divine Messenger*, 145).

YHWH." The repeated use of language focused on the Day of YHWH throughout ch. 3 confirms the eschatological shift in the book as mentioned above (see Literary Context, p. 108).

The subordinate clause that appears in 3:2d provides the rationale for the claims made in the two rhetorical questions: no one will endure the day of YHWH's coming "*because he is like a refiner's fire and lye soap*."[34] Although the first simile clearly invokes images associated with metallurgy, the mention of fire (אֵשׁ) likely functions as a double entendre of sorts. Fire is frequently associated with theophanic experiences in the Old Testament (e.g., Exod 19:18; 24:17; Deut 4:11, 12); the presence of fire signals the very presence of the Divine. Equally significant for the text at hand is the association of fire with the divine judgment that will be meted out on the Day of YHWH (e.g., Isa 66:15–17; Joel 1:19–20). Although YHWH can be depicted as a destructive, all-consuming fire (Deut 4:24; Zeph 1:18), here the reference to YHWH as a refiner's fire redirects the image from that of destruction to that of purification.[35] Even as the dross is removed in smelting so that what remains is made pure, so too will YHWH come near to remove the evildoers and refine the community.[36]

The question concerning the second simile in 3:2d is whether the mention of "launder's soap" is a continuation of the smelting imagery or a new simile altogether. The word "soap" (בֹּרִית) refers to an alkaline salt that comes from the soap plant (*Mesembryanthemum crystallinum*). Glazier-McDonald, following earlier interpreters, argues that the soap simile actually extends the metallurgy reference. Because silver "is mined in an impure form, an agent is required to help reduce the ore to metallic purity, to help separate the dross from the metal."[37] בֹּרִית would easily serve as a helpful reagent that would aid the refinement process. This argument offers an explanation for the seemingly unexpected mention of "launder's soap" in a section focused on metallurgy; YHWH is depicted as the refiner's fire and the agent used to bring about "metallic purity."

Ultimately, however, this proposal must be abandoned on a number of grounds. First, the noun בֹּרִית appears in only one other biblical text, Jer 2:22, and there the reference is to the community's futile attempt to wash away the stain of iniquity. Given there is no metallurgic reference within that chapter in Jeremiah, the noun can only be understood in reference to washing and cleansing. Second, the use of בֹּרִית in Mal 3:2d was likely an intentional wordplay on בְּרִית, "covenant." Such wordplay should not be understood as literary ornamentation, however, but as "a rhetorically serious device of some performative power."[38] Similar to other prophetic books (Jer 1:11–13; Amos 8:1–2), wordplay shaped and informed the rhetorical point being made. Here the failure of the people to keep the covenant (בְּרִית) necessitates YHWH's role as בֹּרִית. Third, Malachi refers to YHWH as "launder's soap," בֹּרִית מְכַבְּסִים. The word for launderer is a *piel* participle from the root כבס, "to wash."[39] The *piel* form of the verb כבס appears a total of forty-four times, and in thirty-nine occurrences the complement to the verb is

34. Hill argues that the personal pronoun הוא is in an "emphatic position" (*Malachi*, 273). The standard word order for a verbless clause, however, is subject-[null copula/verb]-predicate; here the pronoun simply occupies the expected location within the structure of the clause.

35. On the use of smelting imagery in the Old Testament, see Isa 1:25; 48:10; Jer 6:29; Zech 13:9.

36. Verhoef, *The Books of Haggai and Malachi*, 290.

37. Glazier-McDonald, *Malachi: The Divine Messenger*, 147.

38. Scott Noegel, "'Word Play' in Qoheleth," *JHS* 7 (2007): 3.

39. The only other instances of the participial form of כבס occur in 2 Kgs 18:17; Isa 7:3; 36:2. In all three instances, the collocation שְׂדֵה כוֹבֵס, "field of the washer" appears, an apparent reference to where people washed and dried clothes (cf. NET).

either "garments" or "clothes." כבס does not appear elsewhere in conjunction with metallurgy. Fourthly, and perhaps somewhat more speculatively, Nogalski rejects Glazier-McDonald's proposal suggesting that such knowledge is too specialized and likely would have been unavailable to a larger audience.[40] The simplest and preferred understanding of the second simile is that of washing or cleansing. The presence of the image should not be construed as an interruption of a longer argument based on metallurgy in this section, but a second simile meant to reinforce the central claim. The acts of refining and of washing are meant to remove impurities from an object, and that is precisely what is needed for the community in Yehud.

Although the metallurgy imagery continues in v. 3, there is a shift. In v. 2, the prophet compared YHWH to the actual agents of purification and cleansing, i.e., fire (אֵשׁ) and soap (בֹּרִית). In v. 3, however, YHWH is no longer depicted as the active agent in the process of refinement and cleansing, but instead, as the one who brings both to fruition. The prophet declares that YHWH will ישׁב, "sit or dwell," as a refiner and purifier. Verhoef proffers an explanation for this image by suggesting that silversmiths and goldsmiths of that day "sat bending forward over their small melting furnaces to ascertain from the color of the metal whether it was pure."[41] While such an explanation is possible, there seems to be more at stake with this image. Snyman and Weyde are correct to note that the verb ישׁב frequently occurs in texts associated with judging (cf. Joel 4:12).[42] The image of YHWH sitting is not that of a smelter, but more significantly, that of the Divine Judge, an image readily associated with Day of YHWH language. This judicial image is the operative image in these verses and serves rhetorically to connect these verses (vv. 3–4) with the larger disputation. In the opening verse, the people complained about YHWH's failure to judge correctly (2:17e–f), and worse yet, his apparent abdication of his role as judge (2:17h). The prophet declares in 3:1f that YHWH is indeed coming and asks who could stand (before the judge) on "the day of his coming" (3:2a–b). The imagery in 3:3 graphically depicts YHWH as the one who sits as judge over the sons of Levi, and in that role, he will "act as one who refines and purifies silver." Rather than meting out total destruction, however, YHWH brings cleansing and purification.

Verse 3:3a–b refers to YHWH as "one who refines" (צרף) and "purifies" (טהר). Both roots are suggestive. In exilic texts, the participle of צרף can refer to those who craft idols (Isa 40:19; 41:7; 46:6; Jer 10:9, 14; 51:17), and when used in reference to the work of God, the refining is associated with destruction and adversity (Isa 48:10). In post-exilic texts, however, the emphasis shifts to that of purification (Zech 13:9; Mal 3:2, 3).[43] Paired with צרף is the verb טהר, "to purify, cleanse." Of the ninety-four occurrences of the verb, however, none is in reference to smelting or metallurgy; they pertain to matters of cultic purity.[44] Not surprisingly, well over half (fifty-three) of the occurrences are

40. Nogalski, *The Book of the Twelve: Micah-Malachi*, 1051.

41. Verhoef, *The Books of Haggai and Malachi*, 290.

42. Snyman, *Malachi*, 136; Weyde, *Prophecy and Teaching*, 299.

43. Eric M. Meyers and Carol L. Meyers, *Zechariah 9–14: A New Translation with Introduction and Commentary*. AYBC 25C (New Haven: Yale University Press, 1998), 394–95.

44. Glazier-McDonald seemingly connects the root to metallurgy by noting the considerable use of the adjectival form (טָהוֹר) in association with gold, particularly in Exod 25–39 (*Malachi: The Divine Messenger*, 149–50). In these instances, however, the point is not the smelting process, or metallurgy more generally, but an assessment of the noun in question; the gold is pure, i.e., clean. Similarly, the adjective refers to "pure" (טָהוֹר) incense (Exod 30:35; 37:29). More often, it refers to the state of a person, place, or thing as "clean" (טָהוֹר) versus "unclean" (טָמֵא).

in the books of Leviticus and Numbers, followed by Ezekiel (twelve). By pairing טהר, "to purify, cleanse," with צרף, "to refine," the prophet points to the cultic context that is in view in this section of the disputation. The addition of a third term, זקק, "to refine, purify" (v. 3c), extends the metallurgy references from the first term (צרף), while accentuating the notion of purification associated with the second (טהר).[45] In v. 3a–d, the object of this refining and cleansing is not the nation as a whole, but instead the sons of Levi, the priests (v. 3c).[46] In 1:6–2:9, the failures of the priests were rehearsed, including their corruption of the covenant of Levi (2:8). With the coming of YHWH, the priests will not be destroyed because of their failures, but instead refined and purified for service.

The first of two results from the purification of the priests is mentioned in v. 3e–f. Because of YHWH's work of purification, the priests will be capable of bringing forward proper offerings: "so that they might be the ones who present proper offerings to YHWH." Much of v. 3e–f recalls a similar phrase in 2:12: וּמַגִּישׁ מִנְחָה לַיהוָה צְבָאוֹת, "although he brings an offering to YHWH Sabaoth."[47] In v. 3, however, two changes have been introduced: the prepositional phrase לַיהוָה, "to YHWH" has been focus-fronted and the prepositional phrase בִּצְדָקָה, literally "in righteousness," has been added as an adjunct. By focus-fronting לַיהוָה, the prophet addresses both the shortcomings of the priests (1:6–2:9) and the complaints of the community (2:17). In the second disputation, the priests failed to honor and fear YHWH (1:6) as evident by the deficient sacrifices and their failure to adjudicate them properly (1:8). Such action by the priests showed disregard for YHWH, leading YHWH to declare that he would no longer accept sacrifices from them (1:10). By fronting לַיהוָה, "to YHWH," the prophet declares that those who have been refined and purified by YHWH will, once again, bring offerings to YHWH, i.e., YHWH will accept their sacrifices. In so doing, the priests will find themselves in the presence of the God assumed absent by the larger community (2:17). The prepositional phrase בִּצְדָקָה, "in righteousness," has been added to suggest that the priests will now bring sacrifices in accordance with the demands of the torah. The actions of the purified priests will stand

45. Of the seven occurrences of the verb זקק in the Old Testament, five refer specifically to metals; in addition to Mal 3:3, see 1 Chr 28:18; 29:4; Job 28:1; Ps 12:7[6].

46. On the use of priests and Levites interchangeably to refer to the priesthood more generally in the post-exilic period, see O'Brien, *Priest and Levite*, 24–25.

47. The verb נגשׁ is typically trivalent, meaning that the verb often requires two complements. Although the forms in 2:12 and in 3:3d are participles, the valency of the verb remains. In 2:12, the noun מִנְחָה, "offering," and the prepositional phrase לַיהוָה, "to YHWH," function as complements to נגשׁ, with the former identifying the object brought near and the latter the recipient of the object. In 3:3e-f, the same phrase appears: וְהָיוּ לַיהוָה מַגִּישֵׁי מִנְחָה בִּצְדָקָה. Both Glazier-McDonald and Hill, followed by Jacobs, note that the collocation היה + ל can function as an idiom showing ownership (i.e., "they will belong to X"); see Glazier-McDonald, *Malachi*, 153; Hill, *Malachi*, 277; and Jacobs, *The Books of Haggai and Malachi*, 280. If the first two words in 3:3e are understood this way, then the line would be rendered, "Then those who bring an offering in righteousness will *belong to YHWH*." The MT accent mark (*zaqeph*) which appears above לַיהוָה in 3:3e suggests this reading. The LXX, however, renders the verse καὶ ἔσονται τῷ κυρίῳ προσάγοντες θυσίαν ἐν δικαιοσθύνῃ ("and they shall be bringing an offering to the Lord in justice"). Here the prepositional phrase לַיהוָה is translated with the dative τῷ κυρίῳ with the apparent assumption that the prepositional phrase is a complement to προσάγω, "to bring," a reading that would align with the proposed reading of the Hebrew text here. On the idea of verbal valency, see the brief explanation in Holmstedt, Cook, and Marshall, *Qoheleth*, 6–8. For an extended treatment, see John A. Cook, "Verbal Valency: The Intersection of Syntax and Semantics," in *Contemporary Examinations of Classical Languages (Hebrew, Aramaic, Syriac, and Greek): Valency, Lexicography, Grammar, and Manuscripts*, ed. Timothy Martin Lewis, Alison G. Salvesen, Beryl Turner Perspectives in Linguistics and Ancient Languages 8 (Piscataway, NJ: Gorgias, 2016), 53–86.

in stark contrast to the cultic activity mentioned previously (cf. 1:6–14).

Verse 4 suggests that YHWH's coming will impact those beyond the priesthood; it will extend to those in Judah and Jerusalem, i.e., the entire province.[48] The offerings of the community will be pleasing (ערב) to YHWH. The verb ערב, "to be pleasing," appears only eight times in the OT, and while it can refer to a positive emotional response to something such as sleep (Prov 3:24) or an achieved desire (Prov 13:19), the closest analog to its usage in Mal 3 appears in Jer 6:20. There YHWH declares that the gifts brought forward (frankincense, sugar cane, offerings, and sacrifices) are not pleasing (ערב) or acceptable (רָצוֹן) to YHWH. In that context, the problem is not that these offerings do not elicit a positive emotional response for YHWH, but instead, that these offerings do not meet the expectations of YHWH, and thus are found to be wholly unacceptable. Based on the term's usage in Jer 6:20 (and Hos 9:4), Holladay contends that both terms ("pleasing," ערב; "acceptable," רָצוֹן) were likely "technical terms from the cult and may have been the term used by the priests in pronouncing the sacrifice worthy."[49] Holladay's suggestion appears confirmed in the book of Malachi. Although ערב, "pleasing," is not used elsewhere in Malachi, the verb "to accept" (רצה) appears in 1:8, 10, 13, and in each instance, the context is in reference to whether one party (i.e., God; the governor) would find acceptable the gifts and sacrifices from the other party.[50] In those contexts, and in Mal 3:4 where ערב is used, the issue is not whether the gifts and offerings elicit a "positive emotional response," but whether they sufficiently meet the criteria to be accepted.

The prophet declares that with the coming of YHWH and the subsequent purification of the priests, the life of the entire community will be changed. The refined and purified priests, "the ones who will present proper offerings to YHWH," will now lead the larger community in Yehud to bring sacrifices to YHWH that will be deemed acceptable. This time of purified priests and pleasing gifts is compared to "the days of old and the former years." The collocation עוֹלָם + יוֹם + כּ ("as day[s] of old") refers to an earlier time, i.e., a bygone era.[51] Although some interpreters have attempted to associate a particular period in Israel's history as the "days of old," more likely, this is an idealized reference that serves a rhetorical purpose. The other uses of this collocation (Isa 63:9, 11; Amos 9:11; Mic 5:1[2]; 7:14) occur in a context pointing to restoration. Perhaps the force of this phrase rests not as much with the precise identity of a period in the past as much as with the hope for what is yet to come.

5. YHWH's Action: Judgment (3:5)

Lest one think the book of Malachi is concerned about cultic and ritual matters for their sake alone,

48. The combination (in various phrases) יְהוּדָה וִירוּשָׁלָםִ, "Judah and Jerusalem," refers to the region by name, followed by the capital. The combination appears regularly in post-exilic literature. Cf. Ezra 4:6; 5:1; 7:14; 10:7; 2 Chr 32:12; 34:3. On Yehud as a province during the Persian Empire, see the overview in Erhard S. Gerstenberger, *Israel in the Persian Period: The Fifth and Fourth Centuries BCE*, Biblical Encyclopedia, trans. Siegfried S. Schatzmann (Atlanta: SBL Press, 2011), 1–32.

49. William L. Holladay, *Jeremiah I: A Commentary on the Book of Jeremiah*, Hermeneia (Philadelphia: Fortress, 1986), 223. HALOT lists five different roots associated with ערב. For a general overview of the issues involved, see J. A. Emerton, C.E.B. Cranfield, and G.N, Staton, *Hosea*, ICC (Edinburgh: T & T Clark, 1997), 343-44. See also the brief discussion in Eric J. Tully, *Hosea: A Handbook on the Hebrew Text*, Baylor Handbook on the Hebrew Bible (Waco, TX: Baylor University Press, 2018), 211.

50. Snyman, *Malachi*, 138; Taylor and Clendenen, *Haggai, Malachi*, 390–91; Weyde, *Prophecy and Teaching*, 300–301.

51. Cf. Isa 63:9, 11; Amos 9:11; Mic 5:1[2]; 7:14. Hill, *Malachi*, 279.

the announcement in v. 5 proves otherwise. In addition to the refinement of the priesthood and its implications for the cultic life of the community (vv. 2–4), YHWH's coming has other implications for the community as well. Even as YHWH has purified and refined the priesthood, so too will YHWH refine the entire community.

Whereas 3:1c–4 appeared in third person, the text returns to first-person language in 3:5 with YHWH declaring "I will draw near [קרב] to you for judgment [מִשְׁפָּט]." This announcement on the lips of YHWH functions as an unequivocal response to the rhetorical question posed in 2:17h, "Where is the God of justice?" The collocation קרב + אֶל, "to come near to X," is used elsewhere in reference to those coming against a foe in battle (e.g., Josh 8:5; Judg 20:24); such imagery remains highly suggestive here. While other texts speak of drawing near to YHWH for judgment (e.g., Isa 41:1, 5; 57:3), such imagery is reversed in Malachi. The God of justice (מִשְׁפָּט) will draw near to them. The noun מִשְׁפָּט, "justice," which appeared earlier in 2:17h, invokes judicial imagery, i.e., judgment. In both 2:17 and 3:5a, the noun includes the definite article, further confirming this implied judicial context.[52] In 2:17h, the community is longing for the God that will exact judgment, and in 3:5a, YHWH declares that indeed he is coming for just such a task. The God, once presumed absent, will be fully present as both Divine King and Divine Warrior to exact judgment.[53] The coming day of YHWH will be a day of confrontation and reckoning for the "evildoers" (2:17d; כָּל־עֹשֵׂה רָע) *within* the community.

The judicial imagery continues in 3:5b with YHWH's declaration that he will be a "swift witness" (עֵד מְמַהֵר) against a rather lengthy list of evildoers, a role similar to that mentioned in Mic 1:2. The participle מְמַהֵר, "swift," comes from the root מהר, which often functions adverbially when paired with another verb (e.g., סָרוּ מַהֵר, "to turn aside quickly" [Exod 32:8]). That said, the term does not always refer simply to the haste with which something is done. In other cognate languages, the verb refers to being skilled or trained, thus allowing one to carry out a task with both speed and accuracy.[54] The adjectival form of מהר in the Old Testament typically connotes a similar meaning. Ezra, for example, is described as a סֹפֵר מָהִיר, a "skilled scribe." Similar usage is found in Ps 45:1[2] and Prov 22:29. In Mal 3:5b, the participle functions attributively, thus likely incorporating this latter sense to some degree. Thus, to translate עֵד מְמַהֵר as "swift witness" is not incorrect, but it does need further explication. In 2:17e–h, the people accuse YHWH of subverting or mismanaging covenantal expectations. In response, YHWH declares in 3:5 that when he comes near, he will exact judgment posthaste but with skilled precision. The entire community will not fall under judgment (cf. 3:16–17), but neither will the perpetrators of evil and injustice escape

52. The noun plus definite article (הַמִּשְׁפָּט) appears thirty-four times in the Old Testament, often as a synonym for the statutes and commandments (e.g., Exod 21:1; Lev 26:46; Deut 4:1). This form is relatively rare in the prophetic literature, occurring only five times but, when it does appear, the idea of judgment is in view (e.g., Ezek 21:32[27]; Hos 5:1). In Isa 28:6, for example, the noun מִשְׁפָּט, "justice," appears twice, first without the definite article and then again with the definite article attached: "and [he will give] a spirit of justice [מִשְׁפָּט] to the one who sits in judgment [הַמִּשְׁפָּט]."

53. Within Israel's tradition, the role of YHWH as the divine warrior was central to YHWH's exercise of his kingship. See Ben C. Ollenburger, *Zion the City of the Great King: A Theological Symbol of the Jerusalem Cult*, JSOTSup 41 (Sheffield: Sheffield Academic, 1987), 100–140. On the use of divine warrior and divine kingship imagery as part of the Day of YHWH motif here, see Glazier-McDonald, *Malachi: The Divine Messenger*, 155–58. On the divine warrior imagery and its connection with the Day of YHWH, see Tremper Longman III and Daniel G. Reid, *God Is a Warrior*, Studies in Old Testament Biblical Theology (Grand Rapids: Eerdmans, 1995), 61–71.

54. Anthony Tomasino, "מהר," *NIDOTTE* 2:857–59. See also Hill, *Malachi*, 280–81.

the consequences of their violations. God's exacting judgment will prevail.

A rather lengthy list of "evildoers" appears in v. 5. In addition to being violations of the covenant with YHWH, these actions threatened to subvert the community's identity and stability at a time when both were quite tenuous. YHWH calls out the "sorcerers" (כשף) first. Although this root appears infrequently in the Old Testament, there are ample references to sorcery and witchcraft. Most notably, perhaps, is the encounter between Saul and the woman at Endor (who is called בַּעֲלַת אוֹב, NIV "medium," literally, "mistress of a ghost/necromancy") in 1 Sam 28 (cf. with the root כשף Isa 47:9–12; Mic 5:11[12]). The most expansive prohibition appears in Deut 18:9–11 where sorcery (כשף) is listed alongside divination, casting of spells, contacting the dead, and child sacrifice, "abominable practices" of the nations in the land (18:9). To practice such things is to align, both in behavior and commitment, with that of the nations. Consequently, anyone who dares to practice such abominations will be driven out from among the faithful (18:12); they are no longer considered part of the community. Similarly, for Malachi, those who engage in the abominable practices of the nations have forfeited the right to remain a part of the community and should stand under judgment. Given the communal focus in this verse, some interpreters have posited that the issue at hand is the use of sorcery to threaten or even harm others. While a number of the violations listed in v. 5 do address social abuses (e.g., adultery, false witness, oppression), the first and last violations address fidelity to YHWH. The list begins with a reference to those who practice sorcery and concludes with a reference to those who do not fear YHWH. The former suggests an accommodation to the ways of the nations, the latter, a rejection of who this God is, the one worthy of honor and fear.[55]

The prohibition against adultery (נאף) appears in the Decalogue (Exod 20:14; Deut 5:18) and, similar to sorcery, may be punishable by death (Lev. 20:10; Deut 22:22). Casuistic laws provide greater clarity as to what constitutes adultery in ancient Israel. It can refer to sexual relations between a man and a betrothed girl (Deut 22:23–27) or relations between a man and a married woman (Lev 20:10). These acts were "detrimental on both sociological and theological grounds."[56] The previous disputation (Mal 2:10–16) outlined the theological grounds for faithfulness in marriage; it was rooted in a covenant to which God was a witness. To commit adultery would be to show flagrant disregard to what God has witnessed, blessed, and ordained (Gen 2:24). Sociologically, adultery is a transgression against the other; it is a violation of the covenant between a neighbor and his wife or his betrothed. Understood this way, the act of adultery could be construed as a "breach in communal solidarity."[57] At its core, adultery threatened to dismantle the fundamental structure within Israelite culture, the family.[58] The fact that adultery is frequently paired with murder elsewhere suggests the perceived seriousness of

55. Clendenen suggests that what may be in view here is the use of sorcery to threaten or harm others ("Malachi," 393). Redditt argues similarly, explaining that this reference "has to do with influencing people or events for personal gain or that of their clients" (*Haggai, Zechariah, Malachi*, 177). Snyman, by contrast, suggests that the primary issue in view here concerns the worship of other gods (and their religious practices) as it "jeopardizes the exclusive worship of YHWH alone" (*Malachi*, 139).

56. Gary H. Hall, "נאף," in *NIDOTTE* 3:3. On the treatment of adultery in the Old Testament and the larger ancient Near Eastern context, see Bruce Wells, "Sex Crimes in the Laws of the Hebrew Bible," *Near Eastern Archaeology* 78 (2015): 294–300.

57. Glazier-McDonald, *Malachi*, 161.

58. On sexual violence in the ancient world, see Sandra J. Richter, "Rape in Israel's World . . . and Ours: A Study of Deuteronomy 22:23–29," *JETS* 64 (2021): 59–76.

this infraction as it relates to communal life (Ezek 16:38; 23:37; Job 24:14–15).

Those who swear falsely, literally, "those who swear to a lie" (שָׁקֶר), are also listed among the evildoers. The Decalogue includes a prohibition against such action (Exod 20:16; Deut 5:20) and its prohibition is referenced in other legal texts as well (Lev 5:22, 24[6:3, 5]; 19:12). See also its condemnation in the prophetic corpus (Jer 5:2; 7:9; Zech 5:4). In both the Decalogue and the related texts, the issue of perjury and "swearing falsely" reveals the problematic nature of such behavior for the community.

The other actions listed reveal a similar disregard for the community, particularly those most vulnerable. To "oppress hired workers" (lit., "oppress the hired worker of wages") refers to the withholding of payment at the end of the day and is likely drawn from the prohibitions in Deut 15:18 and 24:14.[59] Widows (אַלְמָנָה) and orphans (יָתוֹם) are mentioned next; they represent the most vulnerable in the population. Without a husband or father, they were at grave risk economically, legally, and socially. The absence of the participle עֹשְׁקֵי, "those who oppress," in reference to the widows and orphans is an example of gapping and might best be rendered as "against those who oppress the hired workers, [against those who oppress] widows, [against those who oppress] orphans." Typically, the paired terms appear with the mention of "orphan" first, followed by "widow"; this is particularly true in the book of Deuteronomy and in a number of prophetic texts (e.g., Deut 10:18; 14:29; 16:11, 14; 26:12; Isa 9:16[17]; Jer 7:6; 22:3; Ezek 22:7). In Exod 22:21, however, the word order reflected in Mal 3:5 appears ("widows" then "orphans"), with the community being warned not to "afflict" (ענה) them. Malachi's verbiage has its closest parallel to Zech 7:10, where the verb עשק, "oppress," is used in association with both the widow (אַלְמָנָה) and orphan (יָתוֹם), in that order, as well as the sojourner (גֵּר). Hill suggests that perhaps Malachi's appropriation of Zechariah's language (and word order) signals that the community in Yehud had failed to heed the previous prophet's admonition a number of years before.[60] This would imply that such social abuses had been longstanding within the postexilic community.

The verb "to turn aside" (נטה) often takes the noun "justice" (מִשְׁפָּט) as a complement and, in such instances, the phrase refers to depriving a person of just treatment (Exod 23:6; Deut 16:19; 24:17; Prov 17:23; 18:5). Here the one deprived of justice is the sojourner (גֵּר).[61] On the legal requirement to provide justice to a sojourner, cf. Deut 24:17. According to Deut 27:19, if one chooses otherwise, then "Cursed is the one who turns aside [נטה] justice [מִשְׁפָּט] for the (גֵּר)." Even as the widows and orphans were considered a part of the community, as well as part of the *responsibility* of the community, so too were the sojourners (Deut 24:19). YHWH declares his love for the גֵּר in Deut 10:18, promising to clothe and feed them. He then assigns that responsibility to the entire community in the next verse, explaining that they should care for the sojourner in their midst because they were once sojourners in Egypt.

59. The LXX renders "oppress" (עשק) as ἀποστερέω, "to defraud," likely an attempt to draw greater attention to the economic implications associated with abusing day laborers. In reference to the abuse of the orphans, the translators sought a more graphic depiction. Although the verb in the MT is gapped (see above), the LXX supplies the verb κονδυλίζω, "to strike with the fist." On violence committed against orphans, cf. Job 22:9.

60. Hill, *Malachi*, 283.

61. For an overview of the concept of the sojourner, see Robin J. Dewitt Knauth, "Alien, Resident," in *The Dictionary of the Old Testament: Pentateuch*, ed. T. Desmond Alexander and David W. Baker (Downers Grove, IL: InterVarsity, 2002), 26–37.

Even though the previous disputation wrestled with issues concerning marriage to a foreign woman, the content of that disputation does not conflict with the condemnation expressed here, particularly as it relates to the גֵּר, "sojourner." In Mal 2:10–16, the community is chided for having been treacherous (בגד) with one other; they have profaned the covenant that unites them by aligning themselves with those outside their community. Their actions threaten to dismantle the community itself (2:15–16). In this disputation (3:5), however, those who may possibly be non-Israelite (גֵּר) are understood as part of the community and protected by the laws that govern the community. The "other" is not a threat, nor the source of conflict. The threat comes from within. Those who will come under judgment in that "day" are the ones who repeatedly threaten to dismantle the community through their unjust actions toward those in their own community, particularly the most vulnerable among them.

The disputation concludes with the line, "they did not show me fear." Although a *vav* joins this clause with the preceding list of evildoers, its function is best understood as epexegetical, i.e., it introduces a clause that is meant "to clarify or specify the sense of the preceding clause."[62] The root issue for all of those who practice sorcery, engage in adultery, and participate in the unjust treatment of others is fear, or rather, the lack thereof. The reference to "fear" in this context recalls the frequent use of this term throughout the book of Deuteronomy where the community is instructed repeatedly to fear YHWH. In Deut 6:2, the people are told to fear YHWH "by keeping [לִשְׁמֹר] all of his statutes and commandments."[63] While fearing YHWH and keeping his ways are not synonymous, they are intimately connected. Those who rightly fear God keep his ways; those who brush aside his statutes give evidence of an unenviable fearlessness that will garner the judgment of God. Malachi closes out the fourth disputation with a brief two-word clause that is meant to sum up the problem with the evildoers, וְלֹא יְרֵאוּנִי, "they do not fear me."

Canonical and Theological Significance

Wrestling with Theodicy

As Israel's time in exile was drawing to a close, prophecies from Isa 40–55 spoke of redemption and a glorious return to their homeland. These oracles of salvation envisioned this return as a second exodus (Isa 43), as a recreation of their identity as the people of God (Isa 48). The anticipated joys of resettlement were quickly dashed by the realities that beset them in Yehud. Famine, drought (Hag 1), and crop failure (Mal 3:11) plagued the community. Circumstances proved so challenging that the people were weeping at the altar (Mal 2:13). The overthrowing of the nations and the promise of Zerubbabel as the signet ring of YHWH did not materialize as expected

62. *IBHS* §39.2.4.

63. On the gerundive use of the infinitive, cf. *IBHS* §36.2.3e; JM §124o.

(Hag 2:20–23), or at least, such promises were understood as long delayed. Any hope they had of political independence and the restoration of a national identity quickly disappeared under the expansive rule of the Persian Empire.

Any community experiencing these kinds of challenges could easily fall into despair. In the first disputation (Mal 1:2–5), for example, the community queried over whether God still "loved" them, whether God was still faithful in his covenant with them. No doubt what prompted that line of investigation was their current circumstances, particularly the issues mentioned above. In the fourth disputation, another issue proves more challenging and vexing, and similar to the first disputation, it is brought on due to the current circumstances within the community. The apparent unchecked success and prosperity of the "evildoers" led them to question YHWH's justice (2:17). The issue at hand was not simply that people participated in activity that was contrary to the torah or that such activity proved counterproductive to the survival of the community, but that God seemed unmoved by their behavior. Why would YHWH allow such behavior to continue unabated?

The problem of theodicy is obviously not unique to Malachi in the Old Testament, but perhaps its closest analog can be found in the book of Habakkuk. In the opening verses (1:2–4), the prophet laments the injustice and violence that seems rampant and unchecked in pre-exilic Judah. While most prophets in ancient Israel called the community back to covenant faithfulness, Habakkuk appears to be "calling God to account when [God's] actions did not seem to correspond to those demanded by the covenant."[64] Similar to the issues in Mal 2:17, Habakkuk is concerned over the apparent silence of the Divine in the face of such gross injustice, including the flagrant disregard of torah demands by those within the community (Hab 1:4).[65] While the issue of theodicy may appear similar in the two books, the response of those raising the question are quite different. In Habakkuk, following his articulation of the problem in chapter 1, the prophet announces in chapter 2 that he will station himself on the rampart and "keep watch to see what [YHWH] will say to me" concerning his complaint (2:1 NRSVUE). Although current circumstances are troubling, the prophet's hope remains in the coming of God and his capacity to bring resolution. A similar move is made in the psalms of lament. Repeatedly the psalmists ask "how long" (13:2[1]; 74:10–11), or they raise concerns about God's apparent hiddenness (10:1; 42:10[9]), but time and again, they confess that they will wait on God.[66]

The "wearisome words" offered by the community in Malachi stand in contrast to the expression of faith articulated by Habakkuk and the psalmists when they

64. David W. Baker, *Nahum, Habakkuk, and Zephaniah*, TOTC (Downers Grove, IL: InterVarsity, 2009), 41.

65. Phillip Whitehead, "Habakkuk and the Problem of Suffering: Theodicy Deferred," *JTI* 10 (2016): 265–81.

66. Hill suggests that the statement and question posed by the community has the "formal semblance" of honest doubt as reflected in the psalms, but it appears to lack the "personal conviction and spiritual character evidenced in psalms of 'desperate trust' in Yahweh" (Hill, *Malachi*, 286).

encountered similar questions of theodicy. Had those within Malachi's community only asked the second question, "Where is the God of justice?," then their voice would have joined a chorus of others who have asked about the hiddenness of God. It is the first statement posed by the community, however, that signals their divergence from traditional, more orthodox, responses. In their accusation that God counts the evildoers as "good," and more problematic still, that God "delights" in evildoers, the community in Yehud has sought to redefine the character of God based upon *their own experience.*[67] From their angle of vision, if the wicked appear to prosper and if God has not responded in judgment, then there can only be one conclusion: God must have changed the rules. It is this faulty assessment by the community that wearied God (2:17a) and necessitated a prophetic response in 3:1–5. To wrestle with God, to plumb the depths of theodicy, invites us to explore the mystery of God and God's ways in the world, but such explorations are not an invitation to redescribe the very character of God.

The Coming of God

In response to the community's misguided assessment of YHWH's character, the prophet announces the coming of a messenger to prepare the way, followed by the coming of YHWH for the refinement of the priests and the judgment of the evildoers. This reference to the coming of YHWH in 3:1c–2a invokes the full range of imagery associated with the day of YHWH. Embedded within this larger concept (i.e., the day of YHWH) are two themes that are particularly germane to the complaint levied by the community against YHWH. Central to the Day of YHWH is the concept of judgment. Although most in Israel assumed this judgment would be directed at nations, the prophets frequently subverted this claim, preferring instead to speak of the judgment that will come against Israel and Judah "in that day" (cf. Amos 5:18–20; 8:9–14; Zeph 1:7–18). YHWH comes not only as Divine Judge of Israel and Judah, but more ominously, as Divine Warrior. In most prophetic discourses, when the day of YHWH is directed against Israel and Judah, the prediction of that which is to come is devastating. In Amos 5:19–20, that day is described as darkness and gloom; it will be "as if someone fled from a lion and was met by a bear" (NRSVUE). There will be no escaping the punishment meted out by the Divine Warrior Judge. Elsewhere the day of YHWH is described as a day of ruin and devastation in which the whole earth will be consumed (Zeph 1:15, 18). The prophets are clear; the Day of YHWH will be proof that this God has not abdicated his role as just judge regardless of what those in Malachi's community might allege.

67. Verhoef labels their response a "blasphemous reproach" of YHWH (*The Books of Haggai and Malachi*, 286).

In the book of Malachi, the imagery has morphed from that of darkness and gloom to that of refinement and purification. On the day of his coming, YHWH will set things right so that offerings may once again be brought before him, so that the divine-human relationship which had been askew may be renewed once more. Central to this renewal, however, is the judgment of those who have chosen not to fear YHWH (3:5). This nuance is important. YHWH has not given up on his community, as evident in his willingness to refine the priesthood, but nor has YHWH given a pass to covenant infidelity by his people. The former is sustained by his steadfast love while the latter is evident by his commitment to justice.

The two claims contained in the "wearisome words" (cf. 2:17a) of the community are that YHWH has failed in adjudicating any violations in the law and, worse yet, YHWH has abandoned his role as the divine judge. The announcement of YHWH's coming stands as a sharp rebuke against such short-sighted theological reflection.

The Coming of the Messenger and the Coming of God

On the implications of this section in Malachi for the early Christian community, see the comments associated with the mention of Elijah in 3:23[4:5].

CHAPTER 6

Malachi 3:6–12

VI. The Call to Return to YHWH

Main Idea of the Passage

Although this disputation deals with tithing, the principal theme is that of repentance, of turning back to God. Malachi understood the community's neglect of the tithe as a communal failure, one rooted in covenantal disobedience.

Literary Context

As suggested in the introduction and in the treatment of Mal 2:17–3:5, the book shifts its orientation in the second half to a decidedly more eschatological frame of reference, with eschatological understood here simply as a focus on the future work of God. The interpretation of 3:6–12 is informed by the disputations that appear both before and after it.[1] The fourth (2:17–3:5) and sixth (3:13–21[4:3]) disputations share a number of key thematic links. References to inaccurate beliefs held about YHWH's justice appear in both disputations (cf. 2:17; 3:15). In addition, the coming day of YHWH plays a central role in both (cf. 3:2; 3:19[4:1]), as does the judgment of the evildoers and the wicked (3:5; 3:19[4:1]). Rather than isolating 3:6–12 as a separate disputation, this text should be understood as operating in concert with the two

1. The appearance of the parashah setumah ("closed paragraph," marked with ס) in the MT following 2:16 and 3:12 denotes that the Masoretes understood 2:17–3:12 as a smaller literary unit which has led to some variation in division between the two disputations. The majority of scholars, however, follow the traditional division of 2:17–3:5 and 3:6–12 as proposed here. Cf. Glazier-McDonald, *Malachi*; Verhoef, *The Books of Haggai and Malachi*; Petersen, *Zechariah 9–14 and Malachi*; Hill, *Malachi*; Scalise, "Malachi." By contrast, Weyde divides the two disputations following v. 6 (*Prophecy and Teaching*, 325–26). Snyman, *Malachi*, 144–46, understands the break to come after 3:7a (i.e., 2:17–3:7a; 3:7b–12) and Jacobs simply adopts 2:17–3:12 as one literary unit (*The Books of Haggai and Malachi*, 264). The NRSVUE concludes the first disputation just after v. 7, but that division seems improbable considering that such a break would leave a question by the community (i.e., "How shall we return?") as the concluding element in the disputation.

surrounding texts. As suggested above, repentance is at the center of this disputation, yet rather than understanding this disputation as an invitation to tithing, it is better understood as an invitation to divine blessing. The fourth and sixth disputation make clear that the future does not bode well for the evildoers and the wicked but for the truly repentant—for those who turn back to God (fifth disputation)—divine blessings will be poured out upon the entirety of the community.

I. Superscription (1:1)
II. YHWH's Relentless Love (1:2–5)
III. Dishonoring the Divine King (1:6–2:9)
IV. An Unfaithful Community (2:10–16)
V. The Coming of the God of Justice (2:17–3:5)
➡ **VI. The Call to Return to YHWH (3:6–12)**
A. The Initial Statement (3:6a–7e)
1. YHWH's Fidelity and the Community's Waywardness (3:6a–7b)
2. An Invitation to Return to YHWH (3:7c–e)
B. The First Objection by the Community (3:7f–g)
C. The First Response by YHWH (3:8a–b)
D. The Second Objection by the Community (3:8c–d)
E. The Second Response by YHWH (3:8e–12c)
1. YHWH's Assessment of the Current Situation (3:8e–9b)
2. An Invitation to Test YHWH (3:10a–d)
3. Promises to the Community (3:10e–12c)
VII. The Hope of Those Who Fear God (3:13–21[4:3])
VIII. An Exhortation and a Looming Curse (3:22–24[4:4–6])

Translation and Exegetical Outline

(See pages 132–33.)

Structure and Literary Form

The structure of this disputation is considerably more complex than the opening disputation (1:2–5), although it does contain the basic elements of a disputation identified in the introduction. The pericope opens with an extended statement by YHWH that culminates in an invitation for the people to return to YHWH (v. 7c–e).

Malachi 3:6–12

6a	↓כִּי אֲנִי יְהוָה לֹא שָׁנִיתִי	↓"Because I, YHWH, have not changed,
6b	וְאַתֶּם בְּנֵי יַעֲקֹב לֹא כְלִיתֶם	you, O sons of Jacob, have not come to an end.
7a	לְמִימֵי אֲבֹתֵיכֶם סַרְתֶּם מֵחֻקַּי	From the days of your ancestors, you have turned aside from my statutes
7b	וְלֹא שְׁמַרְתֶּם	and you have not kept [them].
7c	שׁוּבוּ אֵלַי	Return to me
7d	↑וְאָשׁוּבָה אֲלֵיכֶם	↑so that I may return to you,"
7e	אָמַר יְהוָה צְבָאוֹת	says YHWH Sabaoth.
7f	וַאֲמַרְתֶּם	"But you say,
7g	בַּמֶּה נָשׁוּב	'In what sense should we return?'
8a	הֲיִקְבַּע אָדָם אֱלֹהִים	Can a person rob God,
8b	↑כִּי אַתֶּם קֹבְעִים אֹתִי	↑yet you are robbing me.
8c	וַאֲמַרְתֶּם	But you say,
8d	בַּמֶּה קְבַעֲנוּךָ	'In what sense are we robbing you?'
8e	הַמַּעֲשֵׂר וְהַתְּרוּמָה	Tithes and offerings.
9a	בַּמְּאֵרָה אַתֶּם נֵאָרִים	With the curse, you are being cursed
9b	↑וְאֹתִי אַתֶּם קֹבְעִים הַגּוֹי כֻּלּוֹ	↑and you are robbing me, the entire nation.
10a	הָבִיאוּ אֶת־כָּל־הַמַּעֲשֵׂר אֶל־בֵּית הָאוֹצָר	Bring the full tithe into the storehouse
10b	↑וִיהִי טֶרֶף בְּבֵיתִי	↑so that there will be food in my house.
10c	וּבְחָנוּנִי נָא בָּזֹאת	And test me in this, I pray.
10d	אָמַר יְהוָה צְבָאוֹת	says YHWH Sabaoth.

VI. The Call to Return to YHWH (3:6–12)

- A. The Initial Statement (3:6a–7e)
  - 1. YHWH's Fidelity and the Community's Waywardness (3:6a–7b)
  - 2. An Invitation to Return to YHWH (3:7c–e)
- B. The First Objection by the Community (3:7f–g)
- C. The First Response by YHWH (3:8a–b)
- D. The Second Objection by the Community (3:8c–d)
- E. The Second Response by YHWH (3:8e–12c)
  - 1. YHWH's Assessment of the Current Situation (3:8e–9b)
  - 2. An Invitation to Test YHWH (3:10a–d)

10e	אִם־לֹא אֶפְתַּח לָכֶם אֵת אֲרֻבּוֹת הַשָּׁמַיִם	"Surely I will open for you the windows of heaven	3. Promises to the Community (3:10e–12c)
10f	וַהֲרִיקֹתִי לָכֶם בְּרָכָה עַד־בְּלִי־דָי	and pour out for you blessings until there is no more need.	
11a	וְגָעַרְתִּי לָכֶם בָּאֹכֵל	Then I will rebuke for you the devourer	
11b	↑ וְלֹא־יַשְׁחִת לָכֶם אֶת־פְּרִי הָאֲדָמָה	↑ so that it will no longer destroy the fruit of the ground that belongs to you.	
11c	וְלֹא־תְשַׁכֵּל לָכֶם הַגֶּפֶן בַּשָּׂדֶה	The vine in the field will no longer drop its fruit prematurely,"	
11d	אָמַר יְהוָה צְבָאוֹת	says YHWH Sabaoth.	
12a	וְאִשְּׁרוּ אֶתְכֶם כָּל־הַגּוֹיִם	"And all nations shall call you blessed	
12b	↑ כִּי־תִהְיוּ אַתֶּם אֶרֶץ חֵפֶץ	↑ because you will be a land of delight,"	
12c	אָמַר יְהוָה צְבָאוֹת	says YHWH Sabaoth.	

In response, the community issues its first objection in verse 7g, inquiring about the nature of their violation. A brief response by YHWH follows in verse 8a–b, which then leads to a second objection in v. 8d, "In what sense are we robbing you?" The remainder of the disputation includes a tripartite response by YHWH. In vv. 8e–9b, YHWH answers the question posed by the community but embedded within his response is an assessment of the current situation, i.e., they are under a curse (vv. 8e–9b). In v. 10a–d, YHWH issues an invitation for the community to "test" him. The response by YHWH concludes with a series of promises to be realized by those who turn to him and test him in these matters.

Although the pericope is quite complex, a number of features point to its unity, chief among which is the notion of reversal that pervades the disputation.[2] A disobedient people (v. 7a–b) are invited to return to YHWH (v. 7c–d). Those accused of robbing God of the tithe (v. 8) are encouraged to bring in the tithe (v. 10). Those presently under a curse receive a promise of a blessing; they shall become a land of delight (v. 12).

The theme of reversal is furthered by the two imperatives in vv. 7c and 10a ("return," שׁוּב; "bring," הָבִיאוּ). Both imperatives call for a change in the community. Together they establish the hortatory nature of the entire disputation. Similar to the third disputation which called the community to faithfulness to one another, the fifth disputation calls the community to faithfulness to YHWH.[3]

Explanation of the Text

A. The Initial Statement (3:6a–7e)

Like each of the four preceding disputations, the fifth one opens with an initial statement. In the first two disputations, YHWH uttered the initial statement while in the third and fourth disputation that role is carried out presumably by the prophet. This disputation returns to the earlier format with YHWH leveling the initial claim. The opening remark actually begins with a claim (vv. 6a–7b) and concludes with an invitation (v. 7c–e).

1. YHWH's Fidelity and the Community's Waywardness (3:6a–7b)

The opening line in this disputation points back to the community's complaint in 2:17. The community was said to have wearied YHWH with their words, but as noted earlier in the commentary, it was the *content* of those words that proved wearisome. In declaring that "all who do evil are good in the eyes of YHWH and in them he delights," the community reconfigured their assumptions regarding YHWH's covenantal commitments based

2. Jonathan Gibson, *Covenant Continuity and Fidelity*, 185.

3. The second person plural forms that dominate this disputation signal that the entire community is in view.

upon their own observations. More to the point, the community alleged a reversal in that commitment. In the opening line of this disputation, YHWH challenges such an assumption by declaring that he has not changed. This declaration, however, should not be construed as a metaphysical claim concerning the immutability of YHWH, but instead, as an affirmation of YHWH's firm resolve to his covenantal commitments to Israel.[4]

The opening clause begins with the particle כִּי and, not surprisingly, given the elasticity of meaning associated with this particle, it has been translated in various ways. Some have understood the particle emphatically and rendered it "indeed," or "surely," but typically, when the particle has this type of function, it usually appears in solemn oaths or in the apodosis of conditional clauses.[5] Weyde understands the particle as introducing a causal clause (i.e., "for," "because"), which leads him to connect v. 6a with what precedes it in v. 5 ("YHWH will judge for he has not changed").[6] If the disputation begins in v. 6, as proposed here, then neither option seems plausible. Here the particle כִּי may be best understood as introducing a subordinate causal clause prior to the matrix (main) clause. In such occurrences, the causal clause appears first because "the speaker/narrator wishes to remove any doubt about the grounds of a situation."[7] Understood this way, the causal clause in v. 6a explains "the grounds of the situation" in 6b. There is only one reason why the sons of Jacob have not come to an end. It is *not* because of their own might or even their own perseverance, it is "because [כִּי] I, YHWH, have not changed [שׁנה]."

The verb שׁנה can mean "to change" (e.g., Job 14:20) or "to repeat" (e.g., Prov 17:9) but, in the two instances beyond Mal 3:6 where YHWH functions as the subject of the verb (Pss 77:11[10] [see NRSV against NIV, ESV]; 89:35[34]), the reference alludes to change but in the more narrow sense of covenant breaking.[8] Here the complement to the verb שׁנה, "to change," has likely elided but, nonetheless, can easily be recovered from the context, "Because I, YHWH, have not changed [in my covenantal commitment to Israel], you, O sons of Jacob, have not come to an end [כלה]." Although the verb כלה can carry positive connotations (e.g., Exod 39:32; Ruth 2:23), the term typically has a negative meaning associated with it. The term generally refers to something coming to an end, and in certain instances, the term can even convey something much more graphic. For example, Isa 1:28 explains that "the rebellious and the sinners will be shattered and those who forsake YHWH will be destroyed [כלה]."[9]

The parallel construction of the two lines (Mal 3:6a–b), and the use of fronting in particular,

4. Contra Clendenen who offers a lengthy analysis of this verse in light of the doctrine of divine immutability ("Malachi," 404–8).

5. Sometimes labeled the asseverative function. Cf. JM §164.b; *BHRG* §40.29.2(4). Cf. Isa 7:9.

6. Weyde, *Prophecy and Teaching*, 318.

7. *BHRG* §40.29.1(3).

8. Verhoef, *The Books of Haggai and Malachi*, 299; Hill, *Malachi*, 295; Weyde, *Teaching and Prophecy*, 316–17. Ryan Stokes suggests emending the שׁ (*shin*) on שָׁנִיתִי to שׂ (*sin*) and understanding the root to be שׂנא, "to hate," rather than שׁנה, "to change." Stokes's argument rests largely on three major points. First, he contends that the use of the *qal* form of שׁנה elsewhere in the Old Testament does not comport with the notion of "change." Second, because verbs III-א and III-ה can can appear identical in the first-person singular form, his proposed emendation is at least morphologically possible. Third, given the use of שׂנא ("to hate") in the opening disputation, Stokes argues that its use here would provide a logical connection between the texts ("I, YHWH, Have Not '*Changed*'? Reconsidering the Translation of Malachi 3:6; Lamentations 4:1; and Proverbs 24:21–22," *CBQ* 70 [2008]: 264–76). Stokes's proposal, however, fails to find any textual support in the traditions. For example, the LXX reads ἠλλοίωμαι from ἀλλοιόω, "to cause to be different, to change."

9. On reading כלה as "destroyed," see Verhoef, *The Book of Haggai and Malachi*, 300; Hill, *Malachi*, 297.

highlights the connection between the lines. The clauses in v. 6a and 6b include a subject pronoun ("I," אֲנִי; "you," אַתֶּם), yet, because subject pronouns are not necessary with finite verbs, their appearance typically marks pragmatic information. Here the pronouns are topic-fronted in order to highlight the comparison between the two parties. The actions of the one (YHWH) have implications for the other (sons of Jacob). It is because "*I* have not changed" that "*you*, sons of Jacob, have not come to an end." Thus, in many ways, the affirmation in the fifth disputation reinforces the claim made in the first disputation (1:2–5), i.e., evidence of YHWH's loyalty to those in Yehud could be found in the destruction of Edom and the continued survival of those in Yehud.

Following YHWH's affirmation of his constancy toward the sons of Jacob, YHWH acknowledges that such constancy has not been reciprocated (v. 7a–b). To highlight the durative nature of Israel's waywardness, the prepositional phrase לְמִימֵי אֲבֹתֵיכֶם, "from the days of your ancestors," has been fronted.[10] Although the previous disputation reported a number of covenant violations practiced by the current generation (3:5), the claim here is meant to suggest that such waywardness is not restricted to this generation alone; it extends across the entirety of the community's existence, i.e., from the days of your ancestors."

The community is chastised because they have "turned aside" from YHWH's statutes. Although the verb סוּר can simply mean to turn or turn aside, as in Moses "turned aside" (סוּר) to see the burning bush (Exod 3:3), in the book of Deuteronomy the collocation סוּר ("turn aside") + מִן ("from") + noun appears repeatedly, often in reference to willful disobedience. For example, the phrase, "Do not turn aside [סוּר] from [מִן] the way [הַדֶּרֶךְ] which I am commanding you" appears repeatedly in the book (cf. 9:12, 16; 11:28; 17:11; 31:29) and highlights the waywardness of Israel. In two other instances, the formula appears but with other nouns utilized: הַמִּצְוָה "the commandment(s)" (17:20); הַדְּבָרִים, "the words" (28:14). In Mal 3:7, yet another term is employed in this formula: חֻקִּים, "statutes." The noun חֹק, along with the other terms employed in Deuteronomy, appear to function synonymously with תּוֹרָה, "torah." Even as the priests "turned aside from the way [הַדֶּרֶךְ]" in Mal 2:8, so too has the entire community turned aside from YHWH's חֻקִּים, "statutes," and failed to keep them.[11]

2. An Invitation to Return to YHWH (3:7c–e)

Following the opening declaration in this disputation, YHWH issues an invitation to return to him. Despite the community's waywardness and their history of covenant failures, rather than rejecting them, YHWH invites them to return. The verb שׁוּב, "to turn back, to return," appears repeatedly across the prophetic corpus and embodies the prophetic notion of repentance (see Canonical and Theological Significance).[12] Even as the people have "turned aside" (סוּר) from the statutes of YHWH, they are invited to "turn back" (שׁוּב) to the one who seeks to restore his people fully (Deut 30:1–10). The invitation itself is constructed of

10. The prepositional phrase includes the preposition לְ, lit., "to," plus מִן, "from," followed by the construct plural form of יוֹם, "day." In an effort to capture the sense conveyed in this construction, some have opted to render the phrase, "Ever since the days of . . ." (NIV, Verhoef, *The Books of Haggai and Malachi*, 300) or "Since the days of . . ." (HCSB; Clendenen, "Malachi," 410).

11. In the latter phrase, וְלֹא שְׁמַרְתֶּם, the verbal complement is null (i.e., absent), but can be inferred from the previous clause. In Deuteronomy, the noun חֻקִּים, "statutes," frequently appears together with the verb "to keep" שָׁמַר (e.g., Deut 4:40; 5:1; 7:11; 28:45), but here the complement (i.e., "statutes") is absent due to ellipsis.

12. Cf. Isa 31:6; 44:22; 55:7; Jer 3:22; 4:1; 8:4–5; Ezek 3:17–21; 14:7; Hos 12:6; Joel 2:12–14. The only prophetic book not to include the verb is Haggai.

two clauses. Verse 7c begins with an imperative followed by a second clause (7d) that begins with a cohortative. In such constructions (i.e., imperative → cohortative) the second clause is better understood as a purpose clause, "Return to me *so that* I may return to you."[13] If those in Yehud would turn back to YHWH, then they would enjoy the benefits of the covenant relationship with their God.

B. The First Objection by the Community (3:7f–g)

Similar to the previous disputations, the opening statement is met with a question. As noted in the treatment of the first disputation (1:2–5), the purported questions of the people and priests throughout the book of Malachi reflect the *Zeitgeist* of Yehud during this time. The interrogative בַּמֶּה (preposition + inanimate pronoun) can be rendered literally "in what."[14] Although the English is awkward, the question in v. 7g might be rendered, "In what sense should we return?" This question should not be understood as a sincere request for information on behalf of the community but, quite the contrary, as a challenge to YHWH's invitation to return. The underlying assumption is clear: the people believe they have no need to "return" or "turn back" (שׁוּב) because they have done nothing wrong.[15]

If one were to interpret the question in v. 7g as a sincere question by the community, then the subsequent response by YHWH appears as something of a *non sequitur*. Their sincere question would have been met with a sharp rebuke. If, however, the question posed is intended to insinuate that the community believes itself innocent of any wrongdoing, then what follows is logically consistent. The community declares their presumed innocence in v. 7g; YHWH announces their covenant violation in v. 8a–b, e (i.e., failing in their tithes and offerings).

C. The First Response by YHWH (3:8a–b)

In responding to the community's claim of innocence, YHWH does not move immediately to the charge, but instead answers the community's question with another question: "Can a person rob God?" Here the interrogative *he* introduces a rhetorical question with an assumed negative response. The verb "rob" (קבע) appears only in Mal 3:8–9 and Prov 22:23, and strikingly only here is God the complement of the verb.[16] The rhetorical questions operate at a very general level. To reinforce this, the noun אָדָם, "man," is employed to refer to an "unspecified, representative person" (i.e., can "any person" rob אֱלֹהִים, God?).[17] By invoking אֱלֹהִים rather than the divine name, יְהוָה, the prophet accentuates "Yahweh's sovereignty as Israel's creator and suzerain and Israel's dependence and subservience to God as creature and vassal."[18] Thus, the question on its face seems absurd and leaves little doubt that a response in the negative is the only viable option,

13. *BHRG* §21.5.1.

14. Cf. *IBHS* §18.3.d. Glazier-McDonald captures the sense of the full question well in her translation: "In respect of what shall we return?" (*Malachi*, 173).

15. The NLT captures this sense nicely: "How can we return when we have never gone astray."

16. Given the use of πτερνίζω, "to deceive" throughout vv. 8–9, the LXX appears to have understood the underlying Hebrew text to be עָקַב, "to deceive," perhaps a wordplay on the name Jacob (יַעֲקֹב) mentioned in the opening verse of this disputation. The Greek witnesses (Aquila, Symmachus, and Theodotion), however, render the verb ἀποστερέω, "to rob," with the Vulgate and Syriac rendering similarly. Hill suggests this divergence may reflect two textual traditions at work among the ancient versions (*Malachi*, 303). The MT clearly reflects the more challenging reading (*lectio difficilior*) and should be retained (as reflected in most English translations).

17. *BHRG* §36.5.3.

18. Hill, *Malachi*, 304.

i.e., "no person can rob God." Shockingly, however, YHWH asserts that indeed this is true of those in Yehud, "yet you are robbing me" (3:8b). Hill and Jacobs, among others, understand the particle כִּי to be emphatic, thus rendering the clause as "Indeed, you are robbing me."[19] While possible, others argue that a rhetorical question that anticipates a negative answer (as here in 3:8) is typically followed by a כִּי clause, and in such constructions, the כִּי has an adversative force ("yet, but").[20] Applied here, the claim in verse 8b ("yet you are robbing me") undercuts the presumed answer to the rhetorical question in verse 8a, thus highlighting the audacity of the community's action: the community is doing the very thing that seems unimaginable. They are robbing God.

D. The Second Objection by the Community (3:8c–d)

In response to the charge levied by YHWH, the community asks, "In what sense are we robbing you?" The same interrogative employed in v. 7g introduces the second objection: בַּמָּה (preposition + inanimate pronoun; lit., "in what"). Even as the first objection in verse 7g sounded a note of incredulity, so too with the second objection. The community is not inquiring into how they have robbed God, but instead, challenging the charge itself. In some ways, their question echoes the presumed response to the rhetorical question in v. 8a. "Can a person rob God?" Of course not. And if it is impossible to rob God, the argument runs, then how can YHWH make such a claim.

E. The Second Response by YHWH (3:8e–12c)

YHWH's response to the community's objection is multifaceted, focusing on the present (vv. 8e–9b) while pointing to a future that is contingent upon the people's response to YHWH's demand (v. 10c).

1. YHWH's Assessment of the Current Situation (3:8e–9b)

YHWH's response to the community's query in v. 8d is curt and to the point: "tithes and offerings," הַמַּעֲשֵׂר וְהַתְּרוּמָה.[21] The mention of robbing YHWH and, in particular, the reference to tithes and offerings appears at first glance to have shifted the focus of the disputation away from YHWH's initial invitation to return to him (v. 7c–e), yet such is not the case. The community's failure to give their tithes and offerings is evidence that, like their ancestors, the current community continues to turn aside from the statutes of YHWH (v. 7a).

The act of giving a tithe (הַמַּעֲשֵׂר) as a means of supporting both the cultic and political activity of a community was widespread in the ancient Near East.[22] Even though the practice was not uniquely Israelite, the Old Testament community framed it in light of its covenant with YHWH.

19. Jacobs, *The Books of Haggai and Malachi*, 286; Hill, *Malachi*, 304.

20. Weyde, *Prophecy and Teaching*, 330; A. Schoors, "The Particle כִּי," in *Remembering All the Way. A Collection of Old Testament Studies Published on the Occasion of the Fortieth Anniversary of the Oudtestamentlich Werkgezelschap in Nederland*, ed. A. S. Woude, OTS 21, (Leiden: Brill, 1981), 240–76. For similar constructions, cf. 1 Sam 17:25; Jer 18:20. There are other instances in which כִּי does follow the interrogative but, unlike the construction in Mal 3:8, כִּי introduces an object or complement clause, particularly when it follows certain verbs (e.g., ידע). Cf. Jer 40:14.

21. The first part of YHWH's response in verse 8e is absent due to gapping: "In what way are we robbing you? [You are robbing me of] tithes and offerings."

22. See the overview in Richard E. Averbeck, "הַמַּעֲשֵׂר," in *NIDOTTE* 2:1035–55.

The particulars associated with tithing in the Old Testament are spelled out in Lev 27:30–33, Num 18:21–32, and in selected texts in Deuteronomy (12:6–18; 14:22–29; 26:1–15). Because the development of the tithe in ancient Israel remains a complex topic in scholarship, a full review of the scholarship and prevailing theories is beyond the scope of this study. Despite its complexity, however, some general observations can be made based on the pentateuchal texts mentioned above, particularly as it relates to the reference of "tithes and offerings," הַמַּעֲשֵׂר וְהַתְּרוּמָה, in Mal 3:8e.

In Israel, tithing was closely connected with the idea of land. Deuteronomy 12 explains that

> When you cross over the Jordan and live in the land that YHWH your God is allotting to you . . . then you shall bring everything that I command to the place that YHWH your God will choose as a dwelling for his name: your burnt offerings and your sacrifices, your tithes [מַעְשְׂרֹתֵיכֶם] and the offering of your hands [וּתְרֻמַת יֶדְכֶם], and all your choice gifts that you vow to YHWH. (vv. 10–11, author's translation)

A similar connection between the giving of the land and the giving of the tithe is rehearsed in Deut 26:1–2. This rationale reflects the idea that although the people have received the land as an inheritance from YHWH, ownership still resides with YHWH alone; the people are only "sojourners and tenants" on the land (Lev 25:23). Consequently, they are to "set apart a tithe" of their yield to give to the true owner. This includes grain, wine, oil, and the firstlings of their herds and flock (Deut 14:23). When these items are brought forward, they are meant to be eaten together in community (Deut 14:26).

In several texts, special attention is drawn to the connection between the Levites and the offering of the tithe by the rest of the community. Deuteronomy 14:27 stipulates that "as for the Levite resident in your towns, do not neglect them because they have no allotment or inheritance with you" (cf. Deut 12:19). Because the Levites were granted no land, they were dependent upon the community for support. This connection between the giving of the tithe and the role of the Levites is made clearer still in Num 18. In reference to the Levites, YHWH declares, "But among the Israelites, [the Levites] shall have no allotment, because I have given to the Levites as their portion the tithe of the Israelites, which they set apart as an offering to [YHWH]" (18:23b–24, NRSVUE). Even as a tithe is required of the larger community, so too is one required of the Levites. Numbers 18:26 explains that the Levites are to offer up an "offering [תְּרוּמָה] from [the tithe] to YHWH, a tithe of a tithe [מַעֲשֵׂר מִן־הַמַּעֲשֵׂר]."[23]

The failure of the community to give tithes and offerings leads to YHWH's assessment of the community and their present circumstances in the subsequent verse. In Mal 3:9a, the community is told that they are "being cursed [נֵאָרִים] with the curse [בַּמְּאֵרָה]." In the Hebrew, the prepositional phrase is focus-fronted (בַּמְּאֵרָה אַתֶּם נֵאָרִים). This focus-fronting contrasts the current experience of the community (i.e., under a curse) against the potential future that is held out for them in vv. 10e–12c (i.e., blessing). The noun מְאֵרָה, "curse," is relatively rare in the Old Testament, occurring

23. On the "offering," תְּרוּמָה, see Jacob Milgrom, *Leviticus 1–16*, 473–78; Richard E. Averbeck, "תְּרוּמָה," *NIDOTTE* 4:335–38.

earlier in Mal 2:2, in Deut 28:20, and twice in the book of Proverbs (3:33; 28:27). In the three texts beyond Malachi, the only other location where both the verb ארר, "to curse," and the noun מְאֵרָה, "curse," appears in the same context is Deut 28:15–20.[24] There the community is cursed for their failure to maintain the covenantal commitments. Their fields will be cursed (v. 16) as will their food supply (v. 17a) and the fruit of the ground (v. 18). The agricultural hardships currently experienced by the community in Yehud (as suggested in Mal 3:10e–11c) were interpreted in light of the promises in Deut 28. Thus, the declaration that the community is under the curse in Mal 3:9 is a sweeping indictment of the community for their failure to maintain the stipulations of the covenant as seen most immediately by their withholding of tithes and offerings.

Verse 9b repeats the charge made in verse 8b. In the earlier instance, the word order remains unmarked, אַתֶּם קֹבְעִים אֹתִי, "you are robbing me," but in v. 9b the complement ("me," אֹתִי) has been focus-fronted. Thus, the line reads literally "and me, you are robbing, the entire nation." Whereas v. 9a announces that the people are now under the curse for covenant failure, v. 9b reiterates who is the offended party. The focus-fronted constituent ("me," אֹתִי) signals that the withholding of tithes and offerings is not a violation against the larger community or the priests, or even the temple itself, but instead a violation against YHWH alone.

The phrase "you . . . the entire nation" is a complex structure involving apposition. Although two constituents in apposition typically stand adjacent to one other, there are instances where the second noun (the appositive) is extraposed, and thus appears at or near the end of the sentence.[25] This phenomenon is on display in 3:9b. The anchor pronoun, אַתֶּם, "you," appears earlier in the clause with the appositive, הַגּוֹי, "the nation," appearing later. This extraposition allows for additional clarification of אַתֶּם, "you," while not disrupting the logical processing of the charge being levied (i.e., "me, you are robbing"). An additional example of apposition occurs with כֻּלּוֹ, "all of it." The phrase stands in apposition to הַגּוֹי, "the nation," thus, "the entire nation."[26] Interpreters have noted that because הַגּוֹיִם is used elsewhere in Malachi (1:11, 14; 3:12) in reference to foreign nations, perhaps the use of הַגּוֹי in 3:9b is meant to be pejorative.[27] In the Old Testament, Israel is often labeled as a גּוֹי when they have been unfaithful to YHWH, likely buttressing the claim of other interpreters. In 3:9, however, this type of subtle critique does not appear at work. In the three other occurrences of גּוֹי in Malachi, the term appears value neutral; it is

24. On the connection between Deut 28 and Mal 3:9–11, see Jonathan Gibson, *Covenant Continuity and Fidelity*, 190–93. Nogalski, by contrast, suggests that Malachi 3:10–11 is informed by the locust imagery in Joel 1 ("Intertextuality and the Twelve," in *Forming Prophetic Literature: Essays on Isaiah and the Twelve in Honor of James D. W. Watts*, ed. James W. Watts and Paul R. House; JSOTSup 235, [Sheffield: Sheffield Academic, 1996], 102–24). Although the reference to locusts (i.e., the "devourer") in Mal 3:11 makes Nogalski's suggestion intriguing, the dominate imagery appears to be that of blessing and cursing, and thus appears to point to Deut 28.

25. On apposition more generally, see Holmstedt and Jones, "Apposition in Biblical Hebrew: Structure and Function," 21–51. On extraposed apposition more specifically, see 42–47.

26. Similar use of the adjectival phrase כֻּלּוֹ appears in 2 Sam 8:9 and Isa 9:8. The appositive כֻּלּוֹ represents what Holmstedt and Jones classify as "weak" apposition. Generally speaking, in strict apposition the anchor and the appositive are from the same syntactic category, but "there are rare cases . . . where the [noun-phrase] anchor is modified by an adjective appositive that is clearly not in a typical adjectival phrase" ("Apposition in Biblical Hebrew," 26).

27. Cf. Deut 32:28; Isa 1:44; 10:6; Jer 5:9, 29; 7:28; 9:8; 12:12; 33:34; Ezek 2:3. Note that the Northern Kingdom is chastised for behavior that reflected that of the nations (2 Kgs 17:8, 11, 15; Ezek 20:32). Verhoef, *The Books of Haggai and Malachi*, 306; Glazier-McDonald, *Malachi*, 192; Hill, *Malachi*, 308.

simply in reference to other political structures. Jacobs argues for a similar reading in her assessment. She contends that the use of גּוֹי for those in Yehud "is not an indication of its apostasy, but a label for identifying the geographical, political, and social entity."[28] The point of the extraposed appositional phrase הַגּוֹי כֻּלּוֹ, "the entire nation," is not to condemn those in Yehud as though they resembled a "pagan nation" but, more to the point, to declare that the *entire* nation is responsible for the act of robbing YHWH and, consequently, are under a curse. In Mal 2:2, YHWH declared that the priests were under a מְאֵרָה, "curse," and indeed were being cursed (ארר) due to their covenantal failures. Here in Mal 3:9, the scope of that assessment has widened. The entire nation is now complicit in their unfaithfulness to the covenant.

2. An Invitation to Test YHWH (3:10a–d)

In light of the community's present circumstance, YHWH issues a two-part invitation to his people with the promise that blessings will follow should they heed YHWH. He instructs them first to "bring the full tithe [כָּל־הַמַּעֲשֵׂר] into the storehouse" (v. 10a). The mention of a "full tithe" occurs four times elsewhere in the Old Testament: once in Leviticus (27:30), once in Numbers (18:21), and twice in Deuteronomy (14:28; 26:12). The verbal parallels between Mal 3 and the texts in Deuteronomy, however, suggest that the latter appears to inform the prophet's rhetoric. In addition to the appearance of "full tithe" (כָּל־הַמַּעֲשֵׂר) in all three texts (Mal 3:10; Deut 14:28; 26:12), each text suggests that the bringing of the full tithe will result in blessings (ברך; Mal 3:10f; Deut 14:29; 26:15). Beyond those parallels, Mal 3:11 also mentions the land (אֲדָמָה) as a principle beneficiary of YHWH's blessing, a theme rehearsed as well in Deut 26:15.[29]

The purpose of the full tithe is spelled out explicitly in Deut 14:29 and 26:12 and provides yet another link to Mal 3. According to Deut 14 and 26, the full tithe is to be collected so that the Levites (who have no land allotment), the sojourners, the orphans, and the widows may come and eat. In the previous disputation (Mal 3:5), YHWH rebuked the community for their failure to care for the sojourners, orphans, and widows; the call for a full tithe here appears to redress that situation. Further, the book of Nehemiah reports that offerings had not been provided to the Levites in exchange for their service (13:10). Although Nehemiah is reporting on a period subsequent to Malachi, it is not inconceivable to assume that this was an ongoing issue in Yehud.[30] If so, then once again, the call for a full tithe appears contextually appropriate. The tithe is in fact a statute (חֹק) of YHWH with a primary purpose of addressing the social concerns of the most vulnerable and dispossessed. Thus, as Snyman explains, bringing in the full tithe is a "a religious act" that no doubt had social consequences.[31]

The implications of the full tithe are spelled out further in Mal 3:10b. The clause begins with a jussive, וִיהִי, but in order to translate the clause properly it must be read in light of the previous clause. When a jussive follows an imperative (v. 10a), the jussive introduces a purpose clause, "so that." Thus, the community is invited to bring in the full tithe "so that there will be food in my house." The Hebrew word "food" (טֶרֶף) is not the expected term

28. Jacobs, *The Books of Haggai and Malachi*, 294.

29. Strikingly, the references to blessing (בָּרַךְ) and land (אֲדָמָה) are absent in Lev 27:30 and Num 18:21. Weyde, *Prophecy and Teaching*, 331–32.

30. Cf. Neh 10:35, 37–40; 13:10–12.

31. Snyman, *Malachi*, 152. Similarly, cf. Jacobs, *The Books of Haggai and Malachi*, 296.

(אֹכֶל). Although טֶרֶף appears twenty-one times in the Old Testament, in nearly every instance it is in reference to the prey of a wild animal, almost exclusively that of the lion.[32] In Ps 111:5 and Prov 31:15, however, the term appears to refer more generally to food. The term's use in Mal 3:10b clearly aligns with the latter two texts and is meant to highlight what has been absent in the temple, "food." The rationale for bringing the tithe is not so that the coffers of the temple will be flush, but so that there will be food sufficient for those mentioned above.

YHWH declares that the food is to be brought into the "storehouse" (בֵּית הָאוֹצָר), into "my house" (בֵּיתִי). The "storehouse" is in reference to the rooms that surrounded the sanctuary proper and that were meant to house goods. Some broadly label this complex "the temple treasury," but that unfortunately shades the meaning with financial and monetary overtones. The image is more along the lines of a warehouse; the "storehouse" (בֵּית הָאוֹצָר) is the place goods are kept until distribution (cf. Joel 1:17, אֹצָרוֹת). Regarding the second term בַּיִת, "house," in exilic and post-exilic literature, the word became the preferred term for temple.[33] For example, in Ezekiel's vision of the restored temple (Ezek 40–48), בַּיִת appears more than fifty times, and it is the preferred term in the book of Joel as well (1:9, 13, 16; 3:18).

The second part of the invitation proves the more arresting command, "Test [בחן] me in this." The invitation in Malachi may appear to stand in considerable tension with the absolute prohibition found in Deut 6:16: "Do not put [YHWH] your God to the test as you tested him at Massah" [NRSVUE]. In the latter text, however, a different verb is operative. The verb for testing in Deut 6:16 is נסה and even the place name itself, "Massah," appears to be a derivative of that root. Although English renders both בחן and נסה as "to test," there is a difference and that nuance is important.[34] When humans are the subject of נסה and YHWH is the complement, typically such "testing" is understood as a provocation, one born out of unbelief or rebellion.[35] For example, in recounting Israel's history, the psalmist declared, "Yet they tested [נסה] the Most High God and rebelled against him. They did not observe his decrees" (Ps 78:56 NRSVUE). Similar usage appears in Exod 17:2; Num 14:22 and Pss 95:9; 106:14. By contrast, in nearly every instance of בחן (the verb employed in Mal 3:10b), YHWH is the subject of the verb, with Israel or individuals serving as the complement, i.e., the ones being tested. Through this action, God tests his people in order to know their ways (Jer 6:27); he tests them in order to prove their identity (Ps 26:2). In Mal 3:10b, the roles are reversed, but the connotation remains consistent. YHWH implores those in Yehud to בחן him, to prove him; they are to test him in order to understand the faithfulness of his character.

YHWH implores the community to test him "in this" (בְּזֹאת). The prepositional phrase בְּזֹאת might simply be rendered as "by this means," with the understanding that the demonstrative pronoun is referring back (anaphorically) to the full tithe mentioned in v. 10a, or more generally, to the act of giving the tithe (i.e., "test me by means of the tithe").[36]

32. In Ezek 22:27, the reference is to that of a wolf (זְאֵב), but beyond that, the image is leonine.

33. This is not to suggest, however, that הֵיכָל fell into disuse during this time. Cf. Isa 44:28; 66:6; Jer 7:4; 24:1; Hag 2:15; Zech 6:12, 13, 14; 8:9; Mal 3:1.

34. Hill helpfully notes the distinction made between the two verbs in the LXX. The verb נסה is nearly always rendered as πειράζω, meaning "to tempt, test or try" whereas בחן is rendered with δοκιμάζω, "to examine, prove or test" (*Malachi*, 312).

35. Hill, *Malachi*, 312.

36. Clendenden, "Malachi," 423; Hill, *Malachi*, 311; Snyman, *Malachi*, 153.

Similar elliptical usage of the prepositional phrase can be found in Gen 42:15, 33; Exod 7:17; Ps 41:12[11].[37]

3. Promises to the Community (3:10e–12c)

YHWH invites the community to test him in this matter so that the community may enjoy the benefits associated with covenantal faithfulness. To test YHWH would mean living into the statutes of YHWH (i.e., tithing) and, if the community did that, then they could anticipate a reversal of their current plight. Using oath language, YHWH promises that if the community will test him in this matter, then he will open up the "windows of heaven" and pour out blessings.[38] The reference to the windows of heavens reflects the tripartite concept of the cosmos in the ancient Near East: the heavenly realm, the earthly realm, and the watery chaotic region below. Within the heavenly realm there were also waters, the so-called "waters above" mentioned in Gen 1:6–7. These waters were held at bay by the firmament and only when the windows of heaven were opened could such water come down in the form of rain.[39] References to the "windows of heaven" (אֲרֻבֹּת הַשָּׁמַיִם) in this regard appear explicitly in the flood narrative. In Gen 7:11, for example, the windows were opened so that rain might pour forth and then, in 8:2, they were closed once again, causing the rain to cease. While the texts in Genesis confirm the view of the cosmos that Israel shared with her ancient Near Eastern neighbors, there are additional texts that likely inform the rhetoric of Mal 3:10e–f. The book of Deuteronomy explains the outpouring of rain within the context of covenantal faithfulness. For those who turn away from YHWH and fail to keep his statutes, YHWH will "shut up the heavens [הַשָּׁמַיִם] so that there will be no rain" (Deut 11:17 NRSVUE). In Deut 28:12, the parallel to Mal 3:10 is even more explicit. YHWH will "open [פתח] . . . the heavens [הַשָּׁמַיִם]" not only to give rain, but also to bless the people. It is this latter promise that dominates the rhetoric in Mal 3:10. Although agricultural concerns were central to the community,

37. Alternatively, זֹאת ("this") may be functioning cataphorically, that is, pointing forward to the feminine noun בְּרָכָה, "blessing," in v. 10. As noted above, Deut 14:29 and 26:15 make the explicit connection between the "full tithe" and "blessing;" the former is the precursor to the latter. Here YHWH invites the people to test him "in this matter," to prove his character, to see if indeed he will follow through with a blessing as he has promised. Although this is syntactically possible, most interpreters understand the text in light of the explanation above.

38. On אִם־לֹא as a fragment of oath formula, cf. Weyde, *Prophecy and Teaching*, 333–34. Weyde picks up the earlier argument of Manfred R. Lehmann ("Biblical Oaths," *ZAW* 81 [1969]: 74–92). Van der Merwe, Naudé, and Kroeze also associate אִם־לֹא with oath language, what they term "incomplete conditional clauses" (*BHRG* §41.9). In such constructions, אִם־לֹא appears in the protasis while the apodosis is frequently implied (or null). For example, Judg 11:10 reads: יְהוָה יִהְיֶה שֹׁמֵעַ בֵּינוֹתֵינוּ אִם־לֹא כִדְבָרְךָ כֵּן נַעֲשֶׂה ("YHWH will be a witness [lit., one who hears] between us; if we do not act in accordance with your proposal, [may we be cursed])." Although לֹא, "no, not," is utilized in this oath formula, its use in אִם־לֹא is meant to generate a reversal of meaning, i.e., a positive oath. As an example, see Judg 11:10, "YHWH will be a witness between us; we swear to act in accordance." Petersen's translation attempts to capture this sense: "I swear that I shall surely open for you the windows of heaven" (*Zechariah 9–14 and Malachi*, 213). Although others such as Jacobs (*The Books of Haggai and Malachi*, 297), and Hill (*Malachi*, 313) opt to read Mal 3:10e–f as a complete conditional clause, the use of oath language here seems rhetorically important. In v. 10c YHWH invites the people to test him by bringing in the tithe. The partial oath in verse 10e, then, is meant to serve as further impetus for doing so: YHWH swears that if they will bring in the tithe, he will open the window. It is a guarantee of his faithfulness.

39. On the various constructions of the cosmos in the ancient Near East, see Othmar Keel, *The Symbolism of the Biblical World: Ancient Near Eastern Iconography and the Book of Psalms* (Winona Lake: Eisenbrauns, 1997), 26–47; John Walton, *Ancient Near Eastern Thought and the Old Testament: Introducing the Conceptual World of the Hebrew Bible* (Grand Rapids: Baker Academic, 2018), 131–72.

as suggested by Mal 3:11–12, the prophet omits any explicit reference to rain, preferring instead to speak only in terms of blessings (בְּרָכָה) being poured out.[40] This subtle shift from the explicit mention of "rain" to that of "blessing" in verse 10f addresses immediate concerns, but perhaps more so, charges the text with eschatological overtones.[41] On the latter point, see Canonical and Theological Significance, pp. 148–49.

YHWH announces that he will do this "for you." Throughout vv. 10e–11c, the prepositional phrase לָכֶם appears five times. This fivefold repetition of לָכֶם signals two things at the close of this disputation. First, it stands in response to YHWH's earlier invitation to "return to me so that I may return to you" (v. 7c–d). Everything mentioned in these verses will be evidence of YHWH's return to his people; they will be the work of God for the people of God. Second, the pronominal suffix is second masculine plural. The outpouring of blessings is "for all of you," for the entire community; there is no allowance for individual appropriation in these verses (on this frequent error in interpretation, see Canonical and Theological Significance, p. 147).

The reference to the outpouring of blessings in v. 10e is qualified by the last phrase עַד־בְּלִי־דָי, literally, "until [there is] no sufficiency." The last word in the phrase, דָי means "sufficiency" or "enough," but, as Clendenen notes, a literal reading here would make little sense, i.e., "Judah would receive divine blessings until they no longer had enough."[42] As a result, a number of English translations interpret the phrase to mean that there will no longer be enough space to hold all of the produce that results from YHWH's blessings (Cf. NASB, NET, NIV, NKJV), or more generally, that the result will be an abundance of blessings (HCSB, NAB, NRSV).[43] Alternatively, the phrase might be better rendered here, "until there is no more need"; that is, there is no more need because the people have "enough."[44] The latter interpretation fits within the broader context outlined here in Mal 3. The point of bringing in the tithe is "so that there will be food" in the temple (v. 10b). The implication is that there is not "enough." YHWH invites the people to test him in the matter of the tithe so that he might reverse the curse (v. 9a) and replace it with blessing, per Deut 28:12. By reversing the curse, the people move from scarcity to sufficiency; they will have enough. The emphasis is not on receiving an abundance, as is often assumed here, but on the removal of need through the outpouring of God's blessings. See Canonical and Theological Significance, p. 148.

In addition to the oath issued in verse 10e–f, YHWH also announces that he will rebuke (גער) the locusts (אֹכֵל). The typical word for locusts is אַרְבֶּה (cf. Joel 1:4 [2x]), but here the locusts are labeled as "the devourer."[45] The image is apt, given the destructive and decimating work of locusts, particularly in a largely agrarian society, but in this instance, the label is also evocative of a larger range of meaning. Deuteronomy 28:38 announces that as a result of covenant disobedience, the locusts

40. Although the verb ריק, "to pour out," appears regularly in reference to the unsheathing of a sword, i.e., "pour out the sword" (Exod 15:9; Lev 26:33; Ezek 5:2, 12; 12:14; 28:7), the meteorological use appears also in Eccl 11:3. Weyde proposes that the verb ריק may have been employed in Mal 3 and Eccl 11 due to its similarity with רָקִיעַ, "firmament," thus producing another verbal link to Gen 1–11 (*Prophecy and Teaching*, 336).

41. Cf. Hill, *Malachi*, 315; Verhoef, *The Book of Haggai and Malachi*, 308; Smith, *Micah-Malachi*, 334.

42. Clendenen, "Malachi," 425.

43. Cf. Jacobs, *The Book of Haggai and Malachi*, 298.

44. Glazier-McDonald, *Malachi: The Divine Messenger*, 173, 198; Weyde, *Prophecy and Teaching*, 337; Smith, *Micah-Malachi*, 331; Andrew E. Hill, "דַּי," in *NIDOTTE* 1:935–36; Taylor and Clendenen, *Haggai, Malachi*, 425.

45. Frequently the verb אכל ("to eat, consume") appears in tandem with אַרְבֶּה, cf. Exod 10:5; 12:15; Ps 105:34; Joel 1:4; 2:25.

will "devour" (אכל) that which is in their fields. Elsewhere in the Old Testament, the nations that have come against Israel, particularly in judgment, are said to "devour" or "consume" Israel (cf. Jer 8:16; 10:25). In addition, Malachi's use of אָכַל for locusts likely points back to Joel 2:5 where the locusts are described as a "consuming fire" that will come prior to the Day of YHWH unless the people return (שׁוּב) to YHWH.[46] The reference to the "devourer" is meant to signal not only the devastation currently faced by the community, but even more ominously, the coming day of YHWH (Mal 3:1–4). The presence of the locusts is evidence that "with the curse, [they] are being cursed" (v. 9a).[47] If, however, the people will return (שׁוּב) to YHWH (3:7c–d) by bringing in the tithe as a sign of covenant faithfulness (v. 10a), then YHWH will forestall the curses associated with covenant unfaithfulness and rebuke (גער) the devourer. Although rebuking is an act of speech, the Old Testament is replete with examples where YHWH's rebuke yields action (e.g., Nah 1:4). In Ps 9:6[5], YHWH is praised for having "rebuked the nations," and causing the wicked to perish. In Mal 3:11a–b, YHWH promises to do the same to the invading devourers.

As part of this outpouring of blessing, v. 11c mentions that the vine will no longer "cast its fruit" (שׁכל). In the *piel* stem, the verb frequently refers to miscarriage, both in the case of animals (Gen 31:38; Job 21:10) and humans (Exod 23:26; 2 Kgs 2:21; Hos 9:14). Although some interpreters suggest that the plants were barren or dropped their fruit due to the locust plague, it is more likely due to the drought-induced conditions experienced by the community (cf. v. 10e and the need to open the windows of heaven). Excessive drought leads plants to premature fruit abscission. Without sufficient water, plants "drop their fruit" as a means of survival.[48] In opening the windows of heaven, however, YHWH promises to restore the plants to their natural fecundity.

The final promise made to the community occurs in v. 12 where YHWH announces that all of the nations (כָּל־הַגּוֹיִם) shall call the community in Yehud "blessed." Although the noun אַשְׁרֵי appears frequently in the Old Testament (forty-four times), the verb אשׁר appears in only seven other texts beyond Mal 3:12, 15.[49] A number English translations render the verb, "count as happy," (NRSV, NET) or "fortunate" (HCSB), but rendering it "to count as blessed" is not only possible but preferred, given the argument in this disputation. The entire movement in vv. 6–12 is from curse to blessing via repentance (v. 7c). Deuteronomy 28:37 warns that if the nation fails in keeping the covenant, then they will become "an object of horror, a proverb, and a byword among all the peoples [כֹל הָעַמִּים]" (NRSVUE). But for a repentant Yehud, a quite different outcome awaits.[50] Once the blessings (בְּרָכָה) of YHWH are poured out (v. 10), the nations can do none other than count Yehud as blessed; they will no longer be a "byword among the peoples."

46. Verhoef, *The Books of Haggai and Malachi*, 308; Glazier-McDonald, *Malachi*, 198; Hill, *Malachi*, 317; Nogalski, *The Book of the Twelve: Micah–Malachi*, 1058–59.

47. In v. 11b, the "fruit of the ground" (פְּרִי הָאֲדָמָה) is mentioned and it too recalls Deut 28. Although the phrase is mentioned twice in reference to blessing (vv. 4, 11), the loss of the blessing is mentioned four additional times in reference to that which is cursed due to covenant unfaithfulness (vv. 18, 33, 42, 51).

48. S. Reichart, H. Piepho, A. Stinzi and A. Scheller, "Peptide signaling for drought-induced tomato flowerdrop," *Science* 27 (2020): 1482–85.

49. Malachi's usage is the only occurrence of the verb (אשׁר) in the entire prophetic corpus. Cf. Gen 30:13; Job 29:11; Pss 41:3[2]; 72:17; Prov 3:18; 31:28; Song 6:9.

50. The nation's declaration that Yehud is blessed stands in stark contrast to that of Edom. In the first disputation (1:2–5), others observed the destruction and devastation that had befallen Edom and declared them "a territory of wickedness." The reverse is true for Yehud.

The confession of the nations, in effect, will serve to confirm the fidelity of YHWH.

The particle כִּי introduces a causal clause in verse 12b which provides the rationale for the nation's assessment of Yehud as blessed: "Because you will be a land of delight [חֵפֶץ]." The NIV renders the clause as "for yours will be a delightful land." Similarly, the TEV translates it "for your land will be a good place to live in," and the NET offers "for you indeed will live in a delightful land," a translation similar to that of Verhoef.[51] Yet, the Hebrew is clear, "you," (אַתֶּם, i.e., the entire community] will be a land of delight." The language in v. 12 recalls Hos 2. In that text, the metaphors associated with the people and the land merge, thus making them functionally one.[52] Even as the land soaks up the rain poured down upon the earth and even as the people benefit from the fruit because the curse has been lifted, they will become both a people and a place of חֵפֶץ, "delight."

The mention of חֵפֶץ in this disputation recalls the use of the term earlier in the book. In Mal 1:10, YHWH declares that because of the faulty sacrifices brought forth by the people and accepted by priests, coupled with the apparent disregard for YHWH's name, he will no longer take delight in them. In 3:1, חֵפֶץ appears once more in reference to the messenger of the covenant (מַלְאַךְ הַבְּרִית), the one for whom they long (חפצים). Then in this disputation, for those who turn to YHWH, the one in whom they delight, he will turn them into a land of חֵפֶץ. As suggested above, the entire movement of vv. 6–12 is from curse to blessing via repentance; from rejection to delight.

Canonical and Theological Significance

Tithing as Repentance

This text, along with Mal 2:10–16, is likely among the most well-known in the book of Malachi due to its explicit reference to tithes and offerings in 3:8e, 10a. The reference to tithes and offerings is frequently invoked in conversations focused on a biblical theology of stewardship, often with attention falling primarily on v. 10a, "Bring the full tithe into the storehouse." This of course leads to subsequent questions, including "What is a tithe?" and even more pressing, "How much is a tithe?" Yet when rightly understood, Mal 3:6–12 is not designed to answer those questions. For Malachi, the question is not about amount; it is about purpose.

As Scalise has rightly noted, this is a disputation inside a disputation.[53] The dispute on tithing is embedded within the larger dispute concerning the question of returning to YHWH. The opening verses explain the community's unfaithfulness; they continue to turn aside (סוּר) from the ways of God even as their ancestors had (v. 7a). Because of their waywardness, YHWH invites the community to "return

51. Verhoef, *The Books of Haggai and Malachi*, 309.

52. Cf. James L. Mays, *Hosea*, OTL (Philadelphia: Westminster John Knox 1969), 35; Hans Walter Wolff, *Hosea*, Hermeneia (Philadelphia: Fortress, 1974), 34.

53. Pamela J. Scalise, "To Fear or Not to Fear: Questions of Reward and Punishment in Malachi 2:17–4:3," *RevExp* 84 (1987): 413.

[שׁוּב] to me so that I may return [שׁוּב] to you" (v. 7c). While the verb שׁוּב can mean "turn," "turn back," or "return" (e.g., Josh 4:18) or more figuratively in reference to turning *away* from YHWH (e.g., Jer 2:19), it appears frequently across the prophetic corpus in the sense of turning back to God. It is this image of "turning back" that is operative in this disputation.

How then can tithing be understood as an act of turning back to God? As mentioned in the introduction to the commentary, the socio-economic situation of those in Yehud was challenging at best. This context may explain in part the failure of the community to tithe. Even as the marrying of foreign wives in Mal 2:10–16 was likely economic in nature so too was the decision not to tithe. Both decisions reflect a deep-seated inability to trust in YHWH to secure the future of his people. To give the tithe and offering is to relinquish the false assumption that we can secure our own futures, and instead, to trust in the only one who can.

There is a second way in which tithing involves a sense of returning to God. In verse 3:7a, the people are chastised for having turned aside from the statutes (חֻקִּים). As noted earlier in Explanation of the Text, references to tithing appear repeatedly in the legal corpora of the Pentateuch. Some will acknowledge this but declare that because Christians are no longer under the law (Rom 6:14), this stipulation ceases to apply to them. Others will explain that because the concept of the tithe does in fact appear repeatedly in the Old Testament and further because the notion of giving is even referenced in the New Testament (2 Cor 9:6–10), there is a mandate to give. Both responses are somewhat reductionistic in thinking—and they will not likely inspire anyone to develop a more robust theology of stewardship.

At a fundamental level, tithing becomes a way of turning back to God because that is the life envisioned by God. It is a life rooted in trust, expressed in community, focused on the Other, and characterized by generosity. As mentioned above, tithing invites the giver to trust in God. Further, careful review of the stipulations in the Pentateuch suggests that tithing is rooted in the life of the community. Deuteronomy 14:22–29 explains that the tithe is meant to be eaten together in community and that it is to be used for those in need within the community. Paul expands this notion further when he asked the church at Corinth to give generously to those in Jerusalem so that "you may share abundantly in every good work" (2 Cor 9:8, NRSVUE). Understood this way, tithing becomes an elixir to the hyper-individualized life so often celebrated in Western culture because the act itself is a reminder that we belong to one another but, even more, it is a reminder that we have embraced the vision of a corporate life intended by God.

Finally, the act of tithing is in response to the One who invites us to return to him (Mal 3:7). Whatever lofty ambitions a person may have apart from the life envisioned by God, such ambitions will always prove vacuous. Augustine understood well this truth. He prayed, "you have made us for Yourself, and our hearts are restless until they rest in You" (*Confessions* 1.1).[54] While tithing is not the *only* way to rest our hearts in God, it is one way, one very tangible way, in which we respond to the invitation to turn back to God. In this way, tithing is a homecoming of sorts. We return to the One who made us and the One for whom we long.

Creation Turned Aright

The imagery in verses Mal 3:10c–11c no doubt refers to the literal need of the community in Yehud: the need for rain and the need to eliminate locusts. Post-exilic prophets like Joel and Haggai make this need abundantly clear (cf. Joel 1:7, 12; Hag 1:6, 10–11). Yet, Verhoef and Hill have noted that the language employed in these verses is highly evocative, with Verhoef even labeling it "eschatological."[55] Verhoef is correct if what is meant by "eschatological" is a future reversal of the curse under which the community presently lives. The fact that this disputation is located in the second half of the book confirms that a future orientation remains in view.[56]

While the language is indeed attempting to address the current agricultural crisis, much more is being said. Other prophets make considerable use of the fructification of the land and, in particular, that of the grapevine when referring to the restoration of Israel. For example, in Zech 8:12–13, YHWH speaks of a restored Zion and declares that "the vine shall yield its fruit, the ground its produce, and the skies shall give their dew" (NRSVUE).[57] Malachi is making a similar move here. The promised bounty in Mal 3:10c–11c echoes the language of earlier prophets who understood restoration in light of covenant blessings.[58] But, as Deut 30 explains, this kind of restoration, i.e., the reversal of the curse, only occurs when people return (שׁוּב) to YHWH (30:2) so that he might return (שׁוּב) to them and create a rightly ordered world (30:3).[59]

This image of reversal and creation turned aright provides rich fodder for reflection on the notion of tithing. The book of Malachi in total makes clear that the world of Yehud was askew: improper sacrifice, failure to honor covenants with one another, abuse of the most vulnerable, and an inability to trust in YHWH to secure

54. Augustine, *Confessions, Volume I: Books 1-8* (translated by Carolyn J.-B. Hammond; Loeb Classical Library 26; Cambridge, MA: Harvard University Press, 2014), 3.

55. Verhoef, *The Books of Haggai and Malachi*, 309; Hill, *Malachi*, 320–21.

56. By contrast, Hill suggests that the final three disputations oscillate in their focus between the future and present, with the fourth (2:17–3:5) and sixth disputations (3:13–21[4:3]) addressing that which is to come, while 3:6–12 has a more immediate focus on the present (*Malachi*, 321). Cf. Scalise, "To Fear or Not to Fear," 413. While clearly the present is in view, as suggested by Verhoef and argued here, a future orientation remains clearly operative in this disputation.

57. Frequently the fig tree is referenced alongside that of the vine and productive lands. Cf. Joel 2:22; Zech 3:10. Similar imagery appears as well in Hos 14:6–7.

58. Cf. Snyman, *Malachi*, 154; Jacobs, *The Books of Haggai and Malachi*, 298–300; Petersen, *Zechariah 9–14 and Malachi*, 218. See also Gibson's brief analysis on the connection between Deut 30:1–3, 9–10 (*Covenant Continuity and Fidelity*, 194–96).

59. Hill also contends that repentance and reversal play a central role in this disputation (*Malachi*, 325).

the future. Out of this morass, the prophet points the way forward, but it is not the way some presume. Those who read Mal 3:6–12 as something of a *quid pro quo*, as a transaction between two parties, strip the text of its theological heft and diminish its powerful construal. The declaration is far more than simply that of a people who give the tithe and in return enjoy agricultural success. *It is the promise of a community turned aright, a community rightly restored where fertile land and a blessed community reflect the life envisioned by God.* Perhaps that is the purpose of the tithe. Not that individuals would enjoy "a return on their investment" but that they might find themselves in a world turned aright, where they experience the gift of living in the midst of a blessed community reflecting the life envisioned by God.

Those reluctant to consider this text for fear that it may sound like the vacuous (and narcissistic) promises of prosperity gospel must resist those simplistic readings for a far more robust reflection on tithing. To be clear, this text is not a promise for individual prosperity; it is always about the community. The pronouns throughout are plural and that should inform our interpretation. In short, Mal 3:6–12 is about a faithful God who loves an unfaithful people, and yet so great is his love that he beckons them—all of them—to return home and to test him with the certainty that he alone can turn creation aright.

Rather than speaking of tithing as religious obligation, we would do well to speak of tithing as a two-fold response: it is in response to a world that has gone awry and to a God who can turn it aright. In tithing, we declare that our own brokenness, along with the brokenness of the world, does not have the last word; that word belongs to God alone. *In tithing, we are making a confession that the brokenness of the world will be slowly righted by the work of God amid the people of God.*

CHAPTER 7

Malachi 3:13–21[4:3]

VII. The Hope of Those Who Fear God

Main Idea of the Passage

The final disputation returns to the question of God's justice in the face of the apparent prosperity of the wicked. The prophet points to the future and declares that present experiences do not fully define reality. Anguished faith finds its hope in a renewed commitment to the God whose in-breaking will make all things right. [1]

Literary Context

The sixth disputation (3:13–21[4:3]) shares many thematic features with the two preceding disputations.[2] For example, in the fourth (2:17–3:5) and the sixth disputations, the people question YHWH's justice and, in particular, his seemingly positive assessment of those who carry out evil (2:17e). Not only does God appear to delight in them (2:17f), but they appear blessed by God (3:15a). In response to the theological and existential crisis expressed in both disputations, YHWH declares that there is a day coming (cf. 3:2; 3:19[4:1]) on which the evildoers and the wicked will be judged (3:5; 3:19[4:1]). The present experience will not continue unabated; a day is coming. This announcement is meant to refute the community's claim concerning YHWH's perceived vacillation on covenantal norms.

1. Glazier-McDonald, *Malachi*, 210–11, explains that the issue is not "exhausted piety, but as the symptom of an anguished faith as the pious question how it could be consonant with God's righteousness to compel the devout to endure sufferings they have not merited."

2. Because this series gives attention to the Hebrew text, the versification in this section will accord with that of the MT, followed by the English. On the shift in numeration, see Structure and Form below.

The verbal links between the fifth (3:6–12) and sixth disputations suggest important contrasts between the two disputations; these contrasts serve to accentuate the issues presented in the final disputation.[3] In the fifth disputation, the people were invited to "test" (בחן) YHWH in the matter of tithing so that they might experience the blessings of YHWH (3:10). Were they to do this, they would be counted as blessed (אשׁר) by the nations (3:12). The same two verbs, "test" (בחן) and "counted as blessed" (אשׁר), appear in the final disputation as well. Yet rather than referring to the community, the terms refer to the arrogant and the evil doers; *they* are the ones who are seemingly blessed by God. The cognitive dissonance created by this observation requires some kind of redressing and that is precisely the focus of the final disputation. God will redress the observed inconsistency by demonstrating that indeed he is a God of justice contrary to the earlier allegations of the community in 2:17.

I. Superscription (1:1)
II. YHWH's Relentless Love (1:2–5)
III. Dishonoring the Divine King (1:6–2:9)
IV. An Unfaithful Community (2:10–16)
V. The Coming of the God of Justice (2:17–3:5)
VI. The Call to Return to YHWH (3:6–12)
➡ **VII. The Hope of Those Who Fear God (3:13–21[4:3])**
- **A. YHWH's Initial Statement (3:13a–b)**
- **B. The Community's Objection (3:13c–d)**
- **C. YHWH' Initial Response (3:14–15)**
  - **1. The Futility of Serving God (3:14a–e)**
  - **2. The Apparent Approbation of the Arrogant (3:15a–d)**
- **D. A Narrative Report (3:16)**
  - **1. The Response of Some within the Community (3:16a)**
  - **2. The Divine Response to the Godfearers (3:16b–f)**
- **E. A Second Response: YHWH's Words of Assurance (3:17–21[4:3])**
  - **1. The Godfearers as a Special Possession (3:17a–e)**
  - **2. The Reversal of Communal Assumptions (3:18a–c)**
  - **3. The Coming Day of YHWH (3:19–21[4:1–3])**

VIII. An Exhortation and a Looming Curse (3:22–24[4:4–6])

3. For a similar assessment, cf. Jacobs, *The Books of Haggai and Malachi*, 303, and Scalise, "Malachi," 357. By contrast, Verhoef who contends that the connections between 3:6–12 and 3:13–21[4:3] are "formal and arbitrary" and that any perceived connection is "purely casual" (*The Books of Haggai and Malachi*, 313).

Translation and Exegetical Outline

(See pages 153–54.)

Structure and Literary Form

As suggested in the introduction, the primary elements of a disputation (i.e., statement— objection—response) occur with considerable variation across the book of Malachi and this is particularly true in the final disputation. This pericope opens with a general statement in v. 13a–b concerning the troubling words of the people, a theme that echoes the initial statement mentioned in 2:17. In return, the community offers an objection in the form of a question (3:13c–d). YHWH then responds with greater specificity by recounting the troubling comments of the community (vv. 14–15). As with similar reports elsewhere in Malachi, whether these are actual quotes from the community or representative of the *Zeitgeist* of that period is inconsequential; they are meant to reflect the community's sentiments regarding their own faithfulness (i.e., it is futile) as well as their sentiments regarding the unfaithfulness of the arrogant and wicked (i.e., it begets apparent prosperity). The response of YHWH is interrupted, however, by a narrative report in v. 16. The dialogical elements in vv. 13–15 are replaced with third person language in reference both to those who "fear YHWH" (v. 16a) and YHWH himself (v. 16b–d). This feature is unique to the final disputation; none of the other disputations in Malachi record the response of some or all of the community to the prophet's declarations.[4] (The precise identity of the "fearers of YHWH" and its implication for understanding the disputation will be explored below in Explanation of the Text.) What follows in 3:17–21[4:3] is another divine response, but here it is focused on the implications of what is yet to come, i.e., the day of YHWH. Included within this response is an oracle of judgment (3:19[4:1]) followed by a longer oracle of salvation (3:20–21[4:2–3]). While the initial exchange in vv. 13–15 appears to involve the entire community, the focus narrows considerably in the latter half of the disputation. The recipients of the "second response" from YHWH are those labeled as the Godfearers, "those who fear YHWH" (יִרְאֵי יְהוָה).

The composition of the disputation has been a matter of some debate in scholarship. Paul Redditt, among others, argues that the original disputation likely "broke off" in v. 15, with perhaps v. 18 being included in the original disputation. The insertion of an apparent narrative in v. 16 and the accompanying response in v. 17 are,

4. Scalise suggests that the narrative in v. 16 "provides a key to understanding the passage and the book as a whole" (Pamela J. Scalise, "Malachi 3:13–4:3—A Book of Remembrance for Godfearers," *RevExp* 95 (1998): 572.

Malachi 3:13–21[4:3]

			VII. The Hope of Those who Fear God (3:13–21[4:3])
13a	חָזְקוּ עָלַי דִּבְרֵיכֶם	"Your words have been strong against me,"	A. YHWH's Initial Statement (3:13a–b)
13b	אָמַר יְהוָה	says YHWH.	
13c	וַאֲמַרְתֶּם	"But you say,	B. The Community's Objection (3:13c–d)
13d	מַה־נִּדְבַּרְנוּ עָלֶיךָ	'What have we said among ourselves against you?'	
			C. YHWH's Initial Response (3:14a–15d)
14a	אֲמַרְתֶּם	You say,	1. The Futility of Serving God (3:14a–e)
14b	שָׁוְא עֲבֹד אֱלֹהִים	'To serve God is futile,	
14c	וּמַה־בֶּצַע	And what gain is there	
14d	כִּי שָׁמַרְנוּ מִשְׁמַרְתּוֹ	because we have kept his requirements	
14e	וְכִי הָלַכְנוּ קְדֹרַנִּית מִפְּנֵי יְהוָה צְבָאוֹת	and because we walk as mourners before YHWH Sabaoth?	
15a	וְעַתָּה אֲנַחְנוּ מְאַשְּׁרִים זֵדִים	Now we pronounce the arrogant blessed.	2. The Apparent Approbation of the Arrogant (3:15a–d)
15b	גַּם־נִבְנוּ עֹשֵׂי רִשְׁעָה	Not only have those who have done wickedness been built up	
15c	גַּם בָּחֲנוּ אֱלֹהִים	but they have tested God	
15d	וַיִּמָּלֵטוּ	and escaped.'"	
			D. A Narrative Report (3:16a–f)
16a	אָז נִדְבְּרוּ יִרְאֵי יְהוָה אִישׁ אֶת־רֵעֵהוּ	Then those who fear YHWH spoke among themselves, each with his neighbor.	1. The Response of Some within the Community (3:16a)
16b	וַיַּקְשֵׁב יְהוָה	YHWH listened attentively	2. The Divine Response to the Godfearers (3:16b–f)
16c	וַיִּשְׁמָע	and he heard.	
16d	וַיִּכָּתֵב סֵפֶר זִכָּרוֹן לְפָנָיו	And then a book of remembrance was written before him	
16e	לְיִרְאֵי יְהוָה	for those who fear YHWH	
16f	וּלְחֹשְׁבֵי שְׁמוֹ	and those who respect his name.	

Continued on next page.

Continued from previous page.

			E. A Second Response: YHWH's Words of Assurance (3:17a–21c[4:3c])
17a	וְהָיוּ לִי	"They will belong to me,"	1. The Godfearers as a Special Possession (3:17a–e)
17b	אָמַר יְהוָה צְבָאוֹת	says YHWH Sabaoth,	
17c	לַיּוֹם אֲשֶׁר אֲנִי עֹשֶׂה סְגֻלָּה	"on the day that I act, a special possession.	
17d	וְחָמַלְתִּי עֲלֵיהֶם	And I will have compassion upon them	
17e	כַּאֲשֶׁר יַחְמֹל אִישׁ עַל־בְּנוֹ הָעֹבֵד אֹתוֹ	as a man has compassion upon his son who serves him.	
18a	וְשַׁבְתֶּם וּרְאִיתֶם בֵּין צַדִּיק לְרָשָׁע	Then you will once more distinguish between the just and the wicked,	2. The Reversal of Communal Assumptions (3:18a–c)
18b	בֵּין עֹבֵד אֱלֹהִים	between those serving God	
18c	לַאֲשֶׁר לֹא עֲבָדוֹ	and those who do not serve him."	
			3. The Coming Day of YHWH (3:19a–21c[4:1a–3c])
19a[4:1a]	כִּי־הִנֵּה הַיּוֹם בָּא בֹּעֵר כַּתַּנּוּר	"For behold, the day is coming, burning like an oven.	
19b[4:1b]	וְהָיוּ כָל־זֵדִים וְכָל־עֹשֵׂה רִשְׁעָה קַשׁ	All the arrogant and all the workers of wickedness shall be stubble	
19c[4:1c]	וְלִהַט אֹתָם הַיּוֹם הַבָּא	and the coming day shall set them ablaze,"	
19d[4:1d]	אָמַר יְהוָה צְבָאוֹת	says YHWH Sabaoth,	
19e[4:1e]	אֲשֶׁר לֹא־יַעֲזֹב לָהֶם שֹׁרֶשׁ וְעָנָף	"which shall not leave them root or branch.	
20a[4:2a]	וְזָרְחָה לָכֶם יִרְאֵי שְׁמִי שֶׁמֶשׁ צְדָקָה	A sun of righteousness shall rise for you who fear my name,	
20b[4:2b]	וּמַרְפֵּא בִּכְנָפֶיהָ	and healing will be in its wings.	
20c[4:2c]	וִיצָאתֶם	You shall go out	
20d[4:2d]	וּפִשְׁתֶּם כְּעֶגְלֵי מַרְבֵּק	and you shall skip as calves from the stall.	
21a[4:3a]	וְעַסּוֹתֶם רְשָׁעִים	You shall trample the wicked ones	
21b[4:3b]	כִּי־יִהְיוּ אֵפֶר תַּחַת כַּפּוֹת רַגְלֵיכֶם בַּיּוֹם אֲשֶׁר אֲנִי עֹשֶׂה	because they shall be ashes under the soles of your feet on the day that I will act,"	
21c[4:3c]	אָמַר יְהוָה צְבָאוֹת	says YHWH Sabaoth.	

according to Reddit, attributable to the work of a redactor.[5] Although v. 16 appears to break the flow of the disputation speech proper (and is a unique feature of this disputation), the thematic and lexical connections throughout the entire disputation signal considerable coherence nonetheless.[6] The accusations levied in regard to serving God (v. 14) are answered in vv. 17–18. Questions surrounding the apparent flourishing of the proud and evil doers (v. 15) find their rejoinder in 3:19[4:1]. The arrogant (זֵדִים) and the evil doers (עֹשֵׂי רִשְׁעָה; v. 15a) who appear blessed will be reduced to stubble (3:19b[4:1]), while those who fear YHWH (v. 16a) will experience the healing benefits of the sun of righteousness (3:20–21[4:2–3]). This reversal is predicated upon the thrice mentioned concept of the coming "day" (יוֹם) when YHWH will act (3:17c; 3:19a, c[4:1a, c]; 3:21b[4:3b]).

A final note regarding the numeration of verses should be mentioned. In the Hebrew text (MT) of Malachi, there are only three chapters, yet the English translations uniformly end the third chapter at v. 18 and begin a new chapter at v. 19[4:1]. This division appears to date back to the LXX and the Vulgate. Hill suggests that the presence of the setumah (ס) in the MT may have prompted modern translators to retain the division.[7] Despite the division in the English translations, vv. 13–21 function as a unit and should be interpreted as such.

Explanation of the Text

A. YHWH's Initial Statement (3:13a–b)

In 2:17, the prophet warned the community that their words have wearied (יגע) YHWH. In this final disputation, the charge against the community intensifies both in delivery and in content. Rather than being an announcement from the prophet, as in 2:17, this charge comes in the form of direct speech from YHWH; the announcement of the affront comes from the one who has been aggrieved. YHWH's grievance is filed in 3:13a. Although numerous translations render the verse with "you" as the subject, i.e., "You have spoken harsh words against me" (NRSVUE), "your words" (דִּבְרֵיכֶם) actually functions as the subject of the clause.[8] It is the assertions ("your words") made by the community that prove prob-

5. Redditt, *Haggai, Zechariah, and Malachi*, 181. Cf. Jakob Wöhrle, *Der Abschluss des Zwölfprophetenbuches. Buchübergriefende Redaktionsprozesse in den späten Sammlungen*, BZAW 389 (Berlin: de Gruyter, 2008), 247–51.

6. For a cautionary word on reading considerable growth within the various disputation speeches, cf. Scalise, "Malachi," 321; Kessler, *Maleachi*, 59–60, 271–72.

7. Hill, *Malachi*, 327. The addition of the פ (petuhah) and the ס (setumah) by the Masoretes in late medieval manuscripts served to mark the sections and divisions within the text. Although the introduction of the actual letters was a Masoretic convention, it represented a much older tradition of text division as evident from the Judean Desert texts. See Emanuel Tov, *Textual Criticism of the Hebrew Bible*, 3rd ed. (Minneapolis: Fortress, 2012), 198–200. See also, Tov's more sweeping assessment, *Scribal Practices and Approaches Reflected in the Texts Found in the Judean Desert* (Leiden: Brill, 2004), esp. 137–63.

8. Cf. "You have spoken arrogantly against me" (NIV); "You have criticized me sharply" (NET). See also Verhoef, *The Books of Haggai and Malachi*, 312. The LXX shifts the verb to a second masculine plural with "your words" functioning as the complement to the verb (Ἐβαρύνατε ἐπ' ἐμὲ τοὺς λόγους ὑμῶν, "you have made your words heavy against me.")

lematic. Literally the Hebrew reads "your words have been חָזְקוּ עָלַי," with the latter phrase often rendered "harsh against me." The collocation חזק + אל/על appears a handful of times in the Old Testament with its closest parallel appearing in 2 Sam 24:4//1 Chr 21:4. As here in Mal 3:13a, the subject is also דָּבָר in that text: "the king's word prevailed against (+ חזק על) Joab and the commanders of the army" (2 Sam 24:4 NRSVUE). David's words overpowered those under his charge. In other instances, the collocation חזק + על refers to the context of war (2 Chr 8:3; 27:5; Dan 11:5) with a clear reference to the power of one group over another. Admittedly, when חזק appears apart from the preposition (על), the meaning may shift but, as Weyde suggests, the phrase חזק + על "has a distinct profile" in that it "refers to the power of one person over against another and seems to presuppose a state of tension or hostility."[9] The problem is not that the community has spoken unkindly, or even harshly of YHWH, as though YHWH could not take such rhetoric, but that through their words they have sought to assert their feigned power by redefining YHWH based upon their own experience.[10] It is this act of hubris that proves intolerable.

B. The Community's Objection (3:13c–d)

The community rebuts YHWH's initial allegation by asking "what have we said among ourselves against you?" The verb דבר, "to speak," appears in the *niphal* and here functions reflexively, i.e., "among ourselves," implying that conversation about God and the ways of God has taken place among those within the community.[11] This action stands in stark contrast to the model provided in the book of Psalms. In those texts, the psalmists frequently voice their complaints and concerns, but such language is always directed to YHWH in the form of prayer.[12] In Malachi, however, something different is implied. Drawing from Dahood's treatment of the reflexive use of דבר in the *niphal* (Ps 119:23), Hill posits that the *niphal* in Mal 3:13 is closer to the notion of "gossip" or "slander."[13] Thus, the complaints and concerns of the community are not prayers but forms of idle speculation. In their objection, the community readily admits that God has been the subject of their allegations and they challenge YHWH to prove that what they have said is incorrect or inconsistent with reality.

C. YHWH's Initial Response (3:14–15)

In the next two verses, YHWH responds to the community's objection by citing their comments. The initial comment, "to serve God is futile" (v. 14b), functions as the operative claim in v. 14. The subsequent statement (v. 14c–e) functions as evidence in support of the initial claim: the righteous receive no reward for faithfulness. Verse 15

9. Karl William Weyde, *Prophecy and Teaching*, 350.

10. Hill, *Malachi*, 329. Scalise captures the hostility intended in this assertion, "The Malachi audience has schemed to think and speak wrongly about and against God" ("Malachi 3:13–4:3," 575). Glazier-McDonald proposes rendering the clause as "your words have been too much for me" or "your words have become too much for me" (*Malachi*, 208). She suggests that the words that had been "tiresome" (2:17) have now become intolerable.

11. The *daghesh* in the *nun* (מַה־נִּדְבַּרְנוּ) is best understood as a conjunctive *daghesh*. See *BHRG* §8.2.3; GKC §20.f.

12. Scalise suggests that "the people's rigid words had not been spoken to God in prayer. They had been said to one another. God had been the subject of their talk, not their refuge in trouble" ("Mal 3:13–4:3," 573). On language of lament in the Psalter, cf. W. H. Bellinger, Jr., *Psalms as a Grammar for Faith: Prayer and Praise* (Waco: Baylor University Press, 2019), 23–50; Philip S. Johnston, "The Psalms and Distress," in *Interpreting the Psalms: Issues and Approaches*, ed. David Firth and Philip S. Johnston (Downers Grove: InterVarsity, 2005), 63–84.

13. Mitchell Dahood, *Psalms III: 101–150*, AYBC 17A (New York: Doubleday, 1970), 176; Hill, *Malachi*, 331. In Ps 119:23 the collocation is דבר with ב (*niphal* reflexive), whereas in Mal 3:13 the preposition is עַל. Given that both prepositions can function adversatively (*IBHS* §11.2.5d; 11.2.13f), the phrases are semantically equivalent.

begins with an operative claim as well (v. 15a), followed by a supporting statement (v. 15b–c): the arrogant and wicked enjoy apparent prosperity and success. These comments are framed within a larger worldview that distinguishes between the wicked and the righteous. Within this worldview, the righteous, those who are attentive to the ways of God, can anticipate blessing, while the wicked should receive their just reward at the hands of God. Yet this community argues that such a worldview stands in stark contrast to their reality and it is that contrast that produces their objection.[14]

1. The Futility of Serving God (3:14a–e)

As suggested above, the initial claim functions as the governing idea in v. 14. Serving God is labeled as "futile" (שָׁוְא). Although some English translations (e.g., NIV, NRSVUE, ESV, NASB) render the noun שָׁוְא as "vain," the somewhat imprecise nature of that word in contemporary English fails to capture the meaning of the Hebrew. The noun, which occurs fifty-three times in the Old Testament, carries the sense of "worthless," but often in the sense of "ineffectiveness" or "without result."[15] Clearly that is the critique implied here, hence the translation "futile."[16] The people vigorously assert, based upon their current circumstances, that serving God yields no result, and worse yet, that serving this God appears worthless and futile. This assessment of service to God is reinforced by the structure of the clause itself (in the figure below, each line follows Hebrew order):

אֱלֹהִים		עֲבֹד		—		שָׁוְא
complement	+	infinitive construct	+	[null verb]	+	noun
God.[17]		serving		is		Futile

Typically, in a verbless clause, the subject appears first with the predicate to follow, yet in this instance the predicate (שָׁוְא, "futile") has been fronted with the subject (עֲבֹד אֱלֹהִים, "serving God") following in a verbless clause. As a linguistic phenomenon, focus-fronting typically set the focus-constituent (here, שָׁוְא) over against other elements either from the shared knowledge of the world or the discourse context. Based upon the worldview of the community, although service to God *should* yield benefits, it apparently does just the opposite. The noun שָׁוְא, "futile," is

14. The question of divine justice in light of the apparent prosperity of the wicked appears repeatedly in the Old Testament, but it is most at home in the wisdom traditions (cf. Job 21:7–16; Ps 73:3; Eccl 7:15; 8:10, 14). It is also evident in the prophetic corpus (Jer 12:1; Hab 1:13b).

15. Jerry Shepherd, "שָׁוְא," in *NIDOTTE* 4:53–55. The term also appears in the third commandment (Exod 20:7; Deut 5:11). In those instances, the prohibition is against using YHWH's name in a worthless or cavalier manner, especially in the making of oaths.

16. Other translations capture a similar sense with "useless." Cf. NET, HCSB. See also Petersen, *Zechariah 9–14 and Malachi*, 219; Clendenen, "Malachi," 435.

17. Admittedly, it is linguistically possible to understand the structure of the verse differently: [null subject] + [null copula] + noun + infinitive construct + complement ("[It] [is] futile to serve God"). Two factors, however, warrant against this rendering. First, the occurrences of clauses with a null subject followed by a null copula are exceedingly rare in the Old Testament. As a possible example, see Ruth 3:13, "if he wants to do his duty . . . , *good* [טוֹב]." See the treatment of this verse by Robert Holmstedt, *Ruth*, BHHB (Waco, TX: Baylor University Press, 2010), 168. Second, and more importantly, given the prophet's penchant for fronting, its appearance here seems stylistically consistent with the remainder of the book.

focus-fronted to draw attention to the reality that drives the subsequent claims.

As evidence of the initial claim, the people pose a rhetorical question in v. 14c–e. The interrogative מָה, "what," is frequently used in rhetorical questions that anticipate a strongly negative response, and such a response is clearly anticipated here as well.[18] The question concerns whether there is any "gain" (בֶּצַע) in serving God. The noun בֶּצַע occurs twenty-three times in the Old Testament with repeated references to bribery, dishonest gain, and injustice, especially in the prophetic corpus (Isa 56:11; 57:17; Jer 6:13; 8:10; 22:17; Ezek 22:13; Hab 2:9). Hill suggests that בֶּצַע has "neutral connotations" in this verse and further, that "the issue was one of correctly interpreting the blessings-and-curses theology of the Mosaic legal tradition."[19] While Hill is correct in his second observation concerning blessings and curses, his first observation likely needs revisiting. If בֶּצַע, "gain," elsewhere focuses on self-gain, then perhaps the near universal negative connotation of the term should be taken seriously. To be sure the question posed by the community reflects a deep-seated concern that the blessings and curses theology of the covenant tradition does not appear operative, but more specifically, the question may reflect a darker concern in that they are not benefitting personally from their obedience.[20] Perhaps the appearance of this term (בֶּצַע) is meant to highlight the underlying focus of the community, i.e., their gain.

In the two כִּי ("because") clauses that follow, the community stresses their own fidelity to YHWH.[21] In the first clause, the community contends that they have kept YHWH's "requirements." The Hebrew term מִשְׁמֶרֶת has a wide range of meaning, but here it likely functions in a manner similar to that in Deut 11:1 where both the noun, מִשְׁמֶרֶת ("requirements") and the verb שׁמר ("to keep") appear in tandem, as here in Mal 3:14d: "You shall love YHWH your God, therefore, and keep [שׁמר] his requirements [מִשְׁמַרְתּוֹ], his decrees, his ordinances, and his commandments always." Similar to its usage in Deut 11, מִשְׁמֶרֶת in Mal 3:14 is synonymous with more familiar terms associated with the covenant. The implication is clear: the community asserts that it has been faithful in its covenantal commitments.

The second causal (כִּי) clause is more opaque than the first. The community indicates that they have walked about as mourners (קְדֹרַנִּית) before YHWH. The root קדר means "to be dark, to mourn" and is paired with הלך elsewhere in reference to the act of mourning associated with the dead or contrition for sin (cf. Pss 38:7; 42:10; 43:2). The usage of this collocation (קדר + הלך) here, however, lacks any explanatory reference as to the reason for mourning. Snyman proposes that such mourning may be the result of grief, perhaps due to the failure of sacrifices at the hands of improper priestly instruction (1:6–2:9), or to the failure of mixed marriages and ethical failures related to marriage (2:10–16), or even the failure of crops (3:10–12).[22] While possible, the context may point in a slightly different direction. The phrase may be intended to suggest a posture of piety in the truest sense of the word.[23] Glazier-McDonald proposes that the language here is meant to signal

18. *IBHS* §18.3g.

19. Hill, *Malachi*, 332.

20. Jacobs suggests that the community is asking "What's in it for me?" (*The Books of Haggai and Malachi*, 308).

21. Here the occurrences of כִּי introduce causal subordinate clauses. Cf. *IBHS* §39.3.4e.

22. Snyman, *Malachi*, 165.

23. Cf. Petersen, *Zechariah 9–14 and Malachi*, 219.

"their earnestness, the seriousness with which they have taken their obligations to Yahweh."[24] Thus the image of the person walking about as a mourner is meant to stand in stark contrast to those who walk about arrogantly, testing God (v. 15a–b).

Taken together, both causal (כִּי) clauses reinforce the cognitive dissonance expressed in v. 14b. Not only has the community presumably kept the requirements of YHWH, they have walked about in humble piety and yet there is nothing to show for such commitment; there is no gain. In the minds of the community, the futility of serving God has been on full display.

2. The Apparent Approbation of the Arrogant (3:15a–d)

The argument shifts from the futility of serving God to that of the prosperity enjoyed by those engaged in faithless actions. The beginning of v. 15, וְעַתָּה, "and now," signals this shift. As a discourse marker, וְעַתָּה points to the implications of what has just occurred for the "here and now of the speaker or addressee."[25] In light of the community's confession in v. 14, i.e., faithful service to God is futile, the community considers the plight of the arrogant and concludes that indeed they must be the ones blessed. The verb אשׁר, "to call blessed," appeared in the previous disputation (3:12a) but with one noticeable shift here. According to the fifth disputation (3:6–12), because of the covenantal faithfulness of those in Yehud, YHWH will rain down blessings upon the community. As a result of those blessings and the fructification of the land, the nations will declare those in Yehud as blessed (אשׁר). In this disputation, the community clearly anticipates this type of blessing predicated upon their faithfulness (v. 14), yet it remains lacking. It is the failure of such blessings to materialize that has led to their assertion concerning the futility of faithfulness. The only ones enjoying any type of "gain" (בֶּצַע) are the arrogant ones (זֵדִים), those that the community labels as "blessed" (אשׁר). In the book of Psalms, the arrogant ones (זֵדִים) are the godless who stand in opposition to YHWH (Ps 86:14); they are the presumptuous ones who turn aside from YHWH's instruction (119:21). Moreover, as Hill suggests, they are the ones who "assume in their pride that their behavior is not subject to divine judgment."[26] Although such a claim seems logically impossible based on covenantal expectations, for the community in Yehud, it remains experientially verifiable.

This argument by the community continues in v. 15b–c with two statements that support the initial claim in v. 15a or, to be more precise, the comments made in v. 15b–c provide the *rationale* for the community's assertion that the arrogant are blessed. This type of argumentation is evident in the structure of the two lines. Both lines begin with the particle גַּם, often translated as "even, also." The construction גַּם + X / גַּם + Y is often employed when two or more pieces of information are used to substantiate a preceding argument or claim, as here.[27] Thus, as suggested above, lines b–c serve to support or substantiate the claim made in line a.

24. Glazier-McDonald, *Malachi*, 214. Verhoef proposes that the phrase is in reference to acts of devotion (*The Books of Haggai and Malachi*, 316).

25. *BHRG* §40.39. Verhoef attempts to capture this sense with "henceforth" (*The Books of Haggai and Malachi*, 317).

26. Hill, *Malachi*, 335.

27. *BHRG* §40.20. Cf. Gen 21:36. Contra Glazier-McDonald, *Malachi*, 214, who understands the use of גַּם as introducing "intensive clauses," following GKC §153, thus "indeed, even." See also Clendenen, "Malachi," 438.

Main claim:	We pronounce the arrogant blessed. (v. 15a)
Substantiating claim 1:	Not only have those who have done wickedness been built up. (v. 15b)
Substantiating claim 2:	but they have tested God and escaped. (v. 15c)

Understood this way, the arrogant (זֵדִים) and the evildoers (עֹשֵׂי רִשְׁעָה) are not two separate groups, but in fact the very same. The arrogance of the evildoers is rooted in their presumed success on the one hand and in their ability to escape divine justice on the other. The real concern, however, is not limited to the actions of the evildoers alone, but to the presumed action (and inaction) of YHWH as well. In verse 15b, the people bemoan that the "those who have done wickedness [have] been built up [נִבְנוּ]." The verb ("built up"; בנה) is in the *niphal* and should be rendered in the passive sense. Constructed this way, the claim alleges that the evildoers have been the recipients of YHWH's generosity; they have been built up *by* YHWH. The gain (בֶּצַע) that should belong to those who keep the requirements of the covenant (v. 14) appears to have been given to the evildoers instead, and more problematic still, this seems to be the work of YHWH. This challenge recalls the community's earlier complaint in 2:17.

The second substantiating claim involves the testing of YHWH by the evildoers. Although the verb "test" (בחן) here is the same as the verb employed in 3:10, their connotations differ considerably. As noted in the discussion related to 3:10, בחן ("to test") is quite often used in the sense of judgment, purification, and character formation, and, in that context, the community is challenged to test God in order to prove God's faithfulness and reliability. In 3:15, however, בחן more nearly matches the meaning of נסה, "to test," in the sense of rebellion and unbelief. What proves most egregious to the community is that evildoers have rebelled against God; they have tested God without consequence. Rather than receiving their just rewards for rebellion, they have escaped (מלט) the punishment of YHWH, an assertion that runs counter to the claims made both in the prophetic corpus (e.g., Jer 32:4; 34:3; Ezek 17:15, 18) and in the wisdom literature (Prov 11:21; 19:5; Job 22:30). Those texts firmly assert that evildoers do not escape the gaze of YHWH and his accompanying judgment, and yet for the community in Yehud, reality seems to suggest otherwise.

D. A Narrative Report (3:16)

The initial exchange between YHWH and the community follows the generally established pattern of previous disputations, but in v. 16 the prophetic speech is interrupted by a narrative report, a feature unique to this disputation. The second person ("you") language that dominates the first two verses shifts as both YHWH and "the Godfearers" are referenced in the third person.

1. The Response of Some within the Community (3:16a)

The verse opens with the conjunctive adverb אָז ("then") which signals that what occurs in the report follows sequentially the events mentioned in the preceding verses.[28] What is detailed in the narrative report is subsequent to and presumably a result of the previous exchange between YHWH and the larger community. Among the questions raised by this verse is the precise identity of those who responded in v. 16 (i.e., the Godfearers) and

28. *BHRG* §40.6.2.

their relationship with those who uttered harsh words in vv. 13–15. Some interpreters suggest that the two groups are actually one in the same; those who uttered the "harsh words" in verses 13–15 are in fact the ones who are mentioned in v. 16. The LXX appears to have adopted such a reading: "These things the fearers of YHWH spoke [ταῦτα κατελάλησαν οἱ φοβούμενοι τὸν κύριον]." Read this way, those who fear God in v. 16 are in fact the very ones who said "these things," that is, the harsh words in vv. 13–15.[29] Snyman, among more recent interpreters, has championed this position. He suggests the repeated use of דבר in the *niphal* in both v. 13 and v. 16 identify those who uttered the harsh words with the Godfearers in v. 16.[30] While such an interpretation appears straightforward and simple, subsequent verses in the disputation seem to call this approach into question. For example, in v. 17 the disputation shifts from narrative back to DD where YHWH refers to the Godfearers in the third person while apparently speaking to Malachi's audience in the second person (v. 18), thus suggesting that more than one group seems to be in view.[31] Because of this complexity, other models for understanding the groups involved in this final disputation have been offered.

Several interpreters suggest that as many as three groups may be in view in this final disputation.[32] According to this view the DD that takes place within the disputation (vv. 13–15, 18) focuses on the "in group," i.e., Malachi's larger audience. The second group, the Godfearers, functions as the "inner group," a group of the "pious orthodox," to borrow the language of C. C. Torrey.[33] Those within this group represented a formal sect within Yehud during the Persian period. The third group, often labeled the "out-group," would have included the arrogant evildoers mentioned in v. 15. While intriguing, Scalise's cautionary word that much of the Old Testament does not support such "rigid sociological boundaries," especially between an in-group and an "inner group," is in order and should be heeded.[34]

This leads to a third option for understanding the groups mentioned in this disputation, and the one adopted here. The arrogant evildoers comprise one group (v. 15). The other group may be understood more generally as Malachi's audience, those that he addresses in verses 13–15, 18. The narrative report in verse 16 does not interrupt the disputation in order to turn its attention to an "inner group," but instead to those from Malachi's audience who have responded to his prophetic ministry. As Scalise explains, "The Yahweh-fearers in Malachi 3:16 are not a closed group. They have had an authentic, transformative encounter with God," and through

29. The appearance of ταῦτα has led some to emend אָז, "then," to זאת or זה, "these things."

30. Snyman, *Malachi*, 166. Cf. Jonathan Gibson, *Covenant Continuity and Fidelity*, 204–5; Glazier-McDonald, *Malachi*, 217; Weyde, *Prophecy and Teaching*, 358. Weyde predicates his assessment on the use of narrative reports in Joel 2:18 and Hag 1:12 and suggests that in those contexts the entire community has a change of heart following the information provided in the narrative report. He contends that a similar phenomenon is at work in Mal 3:16. Weyde is correct in his assessment of the texts in Joel and Haggai, but the shifting discourse referents in the subsequent verses in Mal 3 appear to complicate any type of simple correspondence between the texts.

31. Moreover, this approach may presuppose an unlikely level of "social homogeneity." For more on this particular critique, see Jon Berquist, "The Social Setting of Malachi," *BTB* 19 (1989): 122.

32. Berquist, "The Social Setting of Malachi," 121–26; Jon Berquist, *Judaism in Persia's Shadow: A Social and Historical Approach* (Minneapolis: Fortress, 1995), 100–101; Shemaryahu Talmon, "The Emergence of Jewish Sectarianism in the Early Second Temple Period," in *Ancient Israelite Religion: Essays in Honor of Frank Moore Cross*, ed. Patrick D. Miller Jr., Paul D. Hanson, and S. Dean McBride (Philadelphia: Fortress, 1987), 587–616; Taylor and Clendenen, *Haggai, Malachi*, 441.

33. C. C. Torrey, "The Prophecy of Malachi," *JBL* 17 (1898): 1–17.

34. Scalise, "Malachi 3:13–4:3," 573.

that encounter, they have come to fear YHWH.[35] Such a reading aligns with the larger theme of reversal that is at work in this disputation.

According to v. 16a, those who feared YHWH "spoke among themselves, each with his neighbor." Here דבר ("to speak") appears in the *niphal* and has a reflexive sense, similar to v. 13, but a reciprocal idiom has been added in this verse, "each with his neighbor," (אִישׁ אֶת־רֵעֵהוּ). Hill suggests that the idiom should be understood in an emphatic sense, in that it denotes sincerity and purposefulness of this dialogue."[36] A similar usage of a reciprocal idiom is used in Ezek 33:30 but there the hearers are doing just the opposite; they are not listening with sincerity. The addition of "each with his neighbor" in Mal 3:16 may not be intended to highlight the sincerity of the listener, which seems difficult to ascertain at best, but perhaps simply to differentiate the active participants. In v. 13d, the *entire* community asks, "What have we said among ourselves against you?" with the implication that the larger audience has engaged in such discourse. In v. 16a, the focus narrows with the inclusion of the reciprocal idiom: they spoke among themselves, "each with his neighbor." The addition of the idiom signals that whereas the entire community had engaged in the "harsh words" in vv. 14–15, a small subset had spoken together in v. 16 and that they alone had experienced a change of mind concerning YHWH and his work in the world.

2. The Divine Response to the Godfearers (3:16b–f)

Verse 16b–c indicates that YHWH "listened attentively" (קשׁב) and "heard" (שׁמע) the discussion among the Godfearers.[37] The verb קשׁב can be understood simply as a synonym of שׁמע ("to hear") or אזן ("to give ear"), but in this instance, its appearance may be to rebuff the community's allegations concerning YHWH's apparent disinterest in faithful piety (v. 14). In their harsh words, the community contended that YHWH gave little attention to the faithfulness of the people (v. 14d). The narrative report confirms to the contrary that YHWH indeed pays close attention to his people and their acts of faithfulness.

The narrative report explains further that a "book of remembrance" (סֵפֶר זִכָּרוֹן) was written before YHWH.[38] The term "remembrance" (זִכָּרוֹן) functions in at least three different ways in the Old Testament.[39] The noun comes from the verb, "to remember," (זכר) and can simply refer to a memory, i.e., something that is remembered (e.g., Eccl 1:11; 2:16). By far, however, the most frequent use of

35. For a more extensive review of this position, see Scalise, "Malachi 3:13–4:3," 572–74.

36. Hill, *Malachi*, 338. Jacobs argues similarly and suggests that the idiom is meant to suggest that they were "reasoning together" (*The Books of Haggai and Malachi*, 312).

37. Verhoef, *The Books of Haggai and Malachi*, 320, notes that v. 16b–c may in fact be the content of the words spoken by those who fear YHWH. Understood this way, the statement that "YHWH listened attentively and he heard" functions as a confession by the Godfearers and stands in contrast to the complaints uttered by the larger community in vv. 14–15. This view seems unlikely based primarily on linguistic grounds. The verb דבר is typically employed in Hebrew narrative to signal a speech event in a narrative text. Although speech content can follow דבר (cf. Gen 41:9), in the vast majority of texts where דבר appears, the content of the speech itself (i.e., that which is spoken) is introduced formally by the complementizer לֵאמֹר, "saying" (e.g., Gen 17:3; Exod 6:12). The absence of לֵאמֹר here suggests that דבר, "to speak," is intended to offer a terse narrative report concerning the actions of the Godfearers i.e., "they talked among themselves," without any indication of the speech content itself. On the discourse-pragmatics of דבר, see Cynthia L. Miller, *The Representation of Speech in Biblical Hebrew Narrative: A Linguistic Approach*, HSM 55 (Winona Lake, IN: Eisenbrauns, 2003), 373–86.

38. The Hebrew verb כתב, "to write," appears in the *niphal* in v. 16d ("a book of remembrance was written before [YHWH]"). There is no reference to who did the writing.

39. Leslie C. Allen, "זכר," in *NIDOTTE* 1:1100–1106.

זִכָּרוֹן is in reference to something that functions as a memorial or a reminder of something else. For example, twelve stones are placed in the Jordan as a זִכָּרוֹן, a memorial, to Israel's entry into the land (Josh 4:7). The onyx stones and twelve gems on the ephod and breastplate of the high priest were intended as a זִכָּרוֹן, a reminder, of the twelve tribes as the priest entered into God's presence. Even major festivals were labeled as a זִכָּרוֹן. Passover was a memorial of the Exodus (Exod 12:14) and the Feast of Unleavened Bread functioned as a זִכָּרוֹן, a reminder, of YHWH's torah (Exod 13:9).

Beyond these two usages, the term זִכָּרוֹן also appears in reference to a memorandum of records. The closest parallel to Mal 3:16 in the Old Testament is Esth 6:1 where זִכָּרוֹן is also used in tandem with "book" (סֵפֶר) and clearly refers to some type of annal or record book.[40] The books of Ezra and Esther allude to the royal archives in the Persian period where important decisions, decrees, and events would have been recorded. As these texts suggest, when necessary, such archives were apparently consulted (Ezra 4:15, 19; 5:17; Esth 2:23). For example, Ezra 4 reports that Bishlam and other officials from the region Beyond the River sent a letter to King Artaxerxes to report on the rebuilding of Jerusalem. They encouraged the king to look through the "book of records" (סֵפֶר זִכָּרוֹן) to learn of Jerusalem's history as a "rebellious city." The assumption is that such important events would have been recorded within these annals. Similarly, in Ezra 5, a different governor of the region Beyond the River, Tattenai, writes King Darius to ask if the king would search the royal archives to see whether there was a record of the decree by King Cyrus that permitted the rebuilding of Jerusalem. In both instances, the kings respond with letters to confirm that indeed a search had taken place of the royal archives, and further still, that such important events had been noted in the records. Thus, as Nogalski has rightly suggested, the mention of a book here in Mal 3 draws from that Persian tradition of such an annal, one that would have included names, but equally important key events.[41] It is this assurance that the actions of the YHWH fearers have been recorded that proves critical for understanding the purpose of the book and its implications for understanding vv. 17–18.

Beyond the nature of the book as an annal, the larger question concerns the purpose of the book of remembrance within the context of this disputation. The text explains that this book "was written before him [לְפָנָיו] for those who fear YHWH [לְיִרְאֵי יְהוָה]." Several translations render לְיִרְאֵי as "*concerning* those who fear the Lord" (NIV) or "*of* those that respect the Lord" (NET).[42] Commentators translate the phrase similarly. Glazier-McDonald, for example, renders the entire phrase "A book of remembrance was written before him *regarding* those who fear Yahweh."[43] Scalise challenges such translations and contends that this reading "understands the book of remembrance to be *about* those who fear the Lord."[44] As she rightly notes, the *lamed* preposition is better rendered "for" in this instance, i.e., the book of remembrance was written *for* those who feared YHWH.[45] While the book

40. Various types of heavenly "books" (סֵפֶר) are mentioned in the Old Testament. Most famously, perhaps, is a "book of life" (סֵפֶר חַיִּים) mentioned in Ps 69:28, and likely referenced in Exod 32:32.

41. Nogalski, *Redactional Processes in the Book of the Twelve*, 207.

42. Cf. NRSV, ESV.

43. Glazier-McDonald, *Malachi*, 206. Cf. Snyman, *Malachi*, 167; Clendenen, "Malachi," 441.

44. Scalise, "Malachi 3:13–4:3," 577. Italics original.

45. Scalise, "Malachi 3:13–4:3," 577. Cf. *IBHS* §11.2.10d, the *lamed* of interest.

likely included their actions, as suggested above, its purpose was not for YHWH.[46] The report of a "book of remembrance" was intended as a word of consolation and of hope "*for* those who fear YHWH and respect [חשב] his name" (v. 16d).[47]

The verb חשב means to hold something in high regard, to esteem or honor it.[48] In 1:6, the priests (and presumably the community) were roundly rebuked and described as "those who despise my name" (בּוֹזֵי שְׁמִי). The actions of the Godfearers in 3:16 stand in stark contrast to those mentioned in 1:6. Rather than despising the name of YHWH, those who talked among themselves esteemed his name; they held it in high regard. The offense of those who despised the name of YHWH was so great that YHWH longed for the doors of the temple to be closed (1:10). In this final disputation, where the theme of reversal pervades the rhetoric, the faithful are those who hold the name of YHWH in high regard. Rather than being shut out of the temple (1:10), their names are recorded in a book of remembrance "before [YHWH]" but done so "for [them]," i.e., the Godfearers. Such an announcement confirms that their faithfulness had not escaped the watchful eye and listening ear of YHWH, a thought that had apparently haunted the faithful. Moreover, this kind of remembrance served as the ground of their future hope (3:17–21[4:3]).

E. A Second Response: YHWH's Words of Assurance (3:17–21[4:3])

The final verses of the disputation are intended not simply as words of assurance but of invitation, culminating in a declaration about the coming day of YHWH. The Godfearers mentioned in v. 16 are described (in third person) as God's "special possession" (v. 17). While the Godfearers are mentioned, they are not the intended audience in the remainder of the disputation. In v. 18, second-person language returns ("you") making explicit the shift in the prophetic discourse back to the larger audience addressed in vv. 13–15. What follows in this final section is intended to convince the audience that their earlier "harsh words" remain invalid and that there is hope for all who should choose to fear the name of YHWH (v. 20a). In this, there is both assurance and invitation; assurance that God remains faithful to his people and an invitation for those within the larger audience to join those who fear YHWH (v. 16).

1. The Godfearers as a Special Possession (3:17a–e)

The Godfearers are described in v. 17 as a "treasured possession" (סְגֻלָּה). Drawing from parallels with the Akkadian cognate *sikiltum* ("private

46. Nogalski, followed by Scalise, argues that what was written for the Godfearers was likely some form of the book of Malachi, or perhaps even the Book of the Twelve itself. For the particulars of this line of argumentation, see Nogalski, *Redactional Processes*, 207–9; Scalise, "Malachi 3:13–4:3," 578–79.

47. On the implications of the "book of remembrance," Weyde argues similarly and connects v. 16 with the "announcement of salvation" in v. 17. He notes that several late texts (Ps 139:16; Dan 10:21; 12:1, 4) refer to books that appear to give information about the future of a person or about that which is to come. This leads to his conjecture that the book of remembrance contained a report of the YHWH fearers' future (*Prophecy and Teaching*, 361–62). In Ezra and Esther, however, such books of remembrance were intended as records of the past, but clearly, they had implications for the present. This seems to be the operative view in Mal 3 as well. The record of faithfulness reported in 3:16 confirms YHWH's attentiveness to the pious while also providing the justification for the announcement of salvation that follows in v. 17.

48. On חשב, see the larger discussion in Glazier-McDonald, *Malachi*, 222–23.

hoard, accumulation"), Moshe Greenberg argues that סְגֻלָּה could be understood as an economic term meaning "a personal possession, a treasure."[49] Although the term occurs infrequently in the Old Testament (eight times), its usage seems to bear out Greenberg's claim. Ecclesiastes 2:8 and 1 Chr 29:3 mention סְגֻלָּה alongside references to gold and silver, a clear indication that סְגֻלָּה is associated with the notion of treasure, i.e., something this is special. Within the book of Deuteronomy, the term takes on additional, covenantal overtones. In its three appearances in that book (7:6; 14:2; 26:18), סְגֻלָּה appears within the following clause: they "shall become for him a people, a special possession" (היה + לוֹ + לְעָם + סְגֻלָּה). The subsequent phrase in Deut 7:6 and 14:2 reads, "from all the peoples who are upon the face of the earth" (מִכֹּל הָעַמִּים אֲשֶׁר עַל־פְּנֵי הָאֲדָמָה). The implication is clear: YHWH has created a treasured possession, his people (i.e., the entire nation of Israel), from among all the peoples of the earth. Throughout the book of Malachi, the prophet has leaned heavily upon the language of Deuteronomy, and this is no less the case in verse 17, but in this instance, Malachi has appropriated this Deuteronomic claim with some alteration.[50] Two elements are missing, עַם ("people") and the longer prepositional phrase mentioned above ("from all the peoples who are upon the face of the earth"). The identity of the סְגֻלָּה, the "special possession," has been narrowed considerably in Malachi. The focus no longer rests upon Israel (עָם, "people") writ large, but upon the Godfearers. They are the ones who alone will be YHWH's treasured possession. In addition, the contrast is not between Israel and the nations as in Deuteronomy, but more narrowly, between the Godfearers and the larger community in Yehud. Only those who have turned back to YHWH will be his special possession and the recipients of renewed covenantal promises.[51]

The structure of verse 17a–c confirms this reading. In the Hebrew, the noun סְגֻלָּה, "special possession," is the final word in this lengthy line. Its unusual location has prompted a number of suggested readings, including Smith's contention that the word is best understood as a later gloss appended to the end of the sentence.[52] Beyond Smith's suggestion, some English translations have understood the noun סְגֻלָּה, "treasured possession," to function as the complement to the verb עשׂה, "to make, act," thus "in the day when I make up my treasured possession" (ESV; cf. NET; NASB). Yet when עשׂה is used similarly elsewhere, it is in reference to acquiring property (cf. Gen 31:1; Deut 8:17; Isa 19:10). In Mal 3, however, the focus is not on acquiring property; it is on recognizing the status of those who belong to YHWH, i.e., a special possession. The preferred reading is to understand סְגֻלָּה as part of the modified phrase from Deuteronomy (היה + לוֹ + לְעָם + סְגֻלָּה) as suggested above, and to recognize that the placement of סְגֻלָּה at the end of the clause is an example of extraposition of the verbal complement.[53] The clause concerns what will become of the Godfearers on the day YHWH acts. The first part of the clause signals that the Godfearers belong to YHWH, but the precise na-

49. Moshe Greenberg, "Hebrew Segulla: Akkadian Sikiltu," *JAOS* 71 (1951): 172–74.

50. Gibson, *Covenant Continuity and Fidelity*, 205–12; Weyde, *Prophecy and Teaching*, 362–66.

51. Hill, *Malachi*, 361.

52. Smith, "Malachi," ICC, 84.

53. *BHRG* §34.5.4; Holmstedt, "Critical at the Margins," 109–56. In this type of construction, a "cognitive tension is produced by delayed articulation." Extraposition differs from right-edge dislocation in that the latter requires a resumptive element to be present earlier in the clause. Further, as with fronting, exposition sets one alternative over against another. In this instance, either the Godfearers will be YHWH's special possession, or they will be destroyed like the wicked ones.

ture of that relationship is not known until the end of the full line. Those who belong to him will not be forgotten; they in fact will become his special possession.

In explaining his relationship to the Godfearers, YHWH invokes the father-son metaphor, which was employed earlier in Mal 1:6. In that context, YHWH lamented that the community failed to show him the honor a son would show a father.[54] In Mal 3, however, YHWH pledges that on the day he acts he will demonstrate compassion on the Godfearers even as a father would on his son. In selected texts, the collocation חמל עַל can mean more generally "to spare" (Jer 50:14), but in a number of instances there is a more emotive sense implied.[55] In Exod 2:6, for example, the Pharoah's daughter sees the crying baby Moses in the basket and חמל עַל, "has compassion upon" him. In Jer 15:5, Jerusalem's impending destruction is announced and the prophet asks who will חמל עַל, "have compassion," upon the city and who will grieve for her. In Mal 3:17c–d, there appears to be a clear amalgamation of the two ideas. Indeed, YHWH will spare the Godfearers, but it seems driven by the kind of compassion expressed in the familial metaphor of father and son.[56] The reference to the son is qualified, however, by the appositional phrase, "the one who serves him" (הָעֹבֵד אֹתוֹ).[57] This appositional phrase explicitly addresses the charges levied by the community against God in verse 14b. There the community bemoaned that "to serve [עבד] God is futile." In response to that corporate complaint, YHWH offers the assurance that those who serve him, that those who are his special possession (v. 17c), upon them he will pour out his compassion and spare them in the day that he acts.

2. The Reversal of Communal Assumptions (3:18a–c)

In light of this assertion concerning the status of the Godfearers, YHWH turns to address directly those who were making harsh statements in verses 13–15. The use of the second person plural ("you") replicates the language used in the earlier verses and confirms the intended audience. In those verses, the community (i.e., "you") understood themselves as separate from the arrogant and evildoers. Yet based upon their own experience, they concluded that God no longer differentiated between the righteous and the wicked. In verse 18, YHWH declares that on the day that he acts (v. 17c) such clouded vision will become clear once more. This sobering announcement is intended to do more than convince the community to drop their complaint; it is an invitation to choose the way of the Godfearers (vv. 16–17).[58]

The opening verb, וְשַׁבְתֶּם, comes from the root שׁוב, which is normally rendered "to turn, return,"

54. Father imagery is also employed in Mal 2:10. The larger familial context is invoked in that instance. The father-son metaphor is seemingly ubiquitous in the Old Testament. Cf. Exod 4:22–23; Deut 32:6; 2 Sam 7:14; 1 Kgs 17:13; 22:10; 28:6; Pss 2:7; 68:6[5]; 89:27[26]; 103:13; Isa 63:16; 64:8; Jer 3:4, 19; Hos 11:1.

55. Clendenen asserts that חמל does not carry as much "emotional freight" as related terms like נחם or רחם, thus justifying his suggested rendering of the verb as "spare" (Clendenen, "Malachi," 447). Whether חמל has as much "emotional freight" as other terms seems difficult to adjudicate. The fact that חמל is employed alongside the father-son metaphor, however, does seem to suggest something more than "spare" is intended.

56. Petersen captures this nuance nicely with his suggested translation of "act favorably" (*Zechariah 9–14 and Malachi*, 218).

57. The relationship between the anchor and the appositive is best understood as a "restrictive apposition." In such instances, the anchor creates a set of possible referents (here בְּנוֹ, "his son"), but "the anchor alone does not render the intended referent identifiable; the appositive is needed to make the referent specific and identifiable" (Holmstedt and Jones, "Apposition in Biblical Hebrew," 27). Thus, in Mal 3:17e, the phrase הָעֹבֵד אֹתוֹ, "the one who serves him," makes the referent specific by distinguishing it from other sons who in fact may not serve the father.

58. Scalise, "Malachi," 360.

but שׁוּב can also function as an auxiliary verb when paired with another verb as here (ראה, "to see, discern"). In those instances, the verb functions adverbially and typically denotes repetition, i.e., "again," "once more."[59] YHWH declares that "once more" the community will be able to see, or distinguish, between the just (צַדִּיק) and the wicked (רָשָׁע). This word pair appears repeatedly in the Old Testament, especially in the books of Psalms and Proverbs, as a means of contrasting the two groups. While the two terms can refer more generally to character (upright vs. guilty), the terms can also refer to conduct and action.[60] For example, the book of Proverbs warns that the actions of the wicked (רָשָׁע) are deceitful (12:6) and often lead to violence (10:6, 11), whereas the righteous are those who embody God's instructions (Ps 1:2; Prov 10:11). While this distinction between the just and wicked likely has its roots within the larger wisdom tradition, Malachi has appropriated that tradition specifically for the context of his own audience. In Mal 3:18, the contrast in conduct is narrowly defined by the two appositional phrases that follow: "those serving [עבד] God and those who do not serve [עבד] him." The use of "serve" (עבד) echoes its earlier use in this disputation, once on the lips of the community and once in the spoken discourse of YHWH. In verse 14b, the community complains that it is futile "to serve [עבד] God," while in verse 17e, YHWH describes the Godfearers as like a "son who serves [עבד] [his father]." While those within the larger community assume serving God is futile, YHWH invites them to become like the Godfearers, in full confidence that in due season the difference between the two groups will become apparent.

3. The Coming Day of YHWH (3:19–21[4:1–3])

The concluding verses to the final disputation provide the most extensive reflection on the day of YHWH in the book of Malachi. Although this "day" was mentioned first in 3:2, the treatment of this theme reaches its crescendo in these three verses. Together, they announce that on that day, YHWH will mete out judgment on the arrogant and evildoers while bringing restoration and joy to those who fear YHWH.

Although 3:19[4:1] begins a new chapter in English (see Structure and Literary Form above), the language and imagery in 3:19–21[4:1] points to the overall continuity and cohesiveness of the disputation. The brief reference to "day" earlier in the disputation (3:17; "on the day that I act") is revisited here in 3:19–21[4:1–3], but with its implications explained and amplified. YHWH announces, "Behold, the day is coming." The collocation הִנֵּה ("behold") followed by a participle frequently signals the immediacy of the future event being described; this kind of announcement typically has foreboding overtones and Mal 3:19[4:1] is no exception.[61] The coming day is described metaphorically as "burning like an oven" (בֹּעֵר כַּתַּנּוּר). The noun "oven" occurs in only a handful of other texts (15x) in the Old Testament and typically refers to a literal oven, a place used for cooking (e.g., Exod 8:3; Lev 2:4; 7:9; 11:35; Neh 3:11; 12:38). The prophets employ the term metaphorically in varying fashion (Isa 31:9; Hos 7:4, 6), but the closest analog to its use in Mal 3:19[4:1] appears in Ps 21:10[9]. The psalmist declares of YHWH, "you will make them like a fiery oven [תַּנּוּר] when you appear. [YHWH] will swallow them up in his wrath [אַף], and fire

59. *IBHS* §32.2.3c.

60. More generally, as. Smith, *Micah-Malachi*, 339, explains, the just person is described as one who is faithful to covenant relationships while the wicked are those who break their covenant with others and with God, and thus are the "ungodly."

61. *IBHS* §40.2.1b.

[אֵשׁ] will consume them" (NRSVUE). Similar to Mal 3:19[4:1], the images of a blazing oven and fire become the operative image in signaling divine judgement. Although Mal 3:19[4:1] does not include the Hebrew noun for fire (אֵשׁ), the prophet does employ two verbs that imbue the text with a similar meaning, בער, "burning," and להט, "set ablaze, burn."[62] This image of fire and burning appears regularly in the Old Testament in connection with the divine judgment of the wicked (e.g., Isa 10:16; 30:27; Jer 4:4; 7:20).[63]

In verse 15, the arrogant and evildoers were first mentioned, and as explained above, these are not two separate groups, but instead two terms that refer to the same group. The community lamented over that group's success and seeming prosperity, not to mention its apparent capacity to avert divine reprobation. That image of an obdurate and enduring group shifts dramatically, however, in verse 19b where they are labeled as קַשׁ, "stubble, chaff." Verhoef suggests that the operative idea associated with this label is that of "flammability."[64] Without question, several texts compare evildoers to stubble or chaff that will be quickly consumed by fire (Exod 15:7; Isa 47:14; Joel 2:5; Obad 18; Nah 1:10).[65] As worthless stubble, they will be powerless to save themselves from the ravages of fire (Isa 47:4). Beyond these texts, however, other texts describe the wicked as קַשׁ, "stubble," that is driven by the wind (Isa 40:24; Jer 13:24; Ps 83:13; Job 13:25). In these latter examples, the ephemerality and impermanence of the wicked is stressed. In Mal 3:19[4:1], both meanings appear operative. The arrogant and evildoers will not escape their testing of God forever (v. 15c). They will be no match for the coming judgment of YHWH; they will be consumed like stubble in a fire. Their apparent constancy and durability are little more than an illusion; their ephemerality and impermanence will come into full focus on that day. This is the fate that awaits those who once seemed "blessed" and "built up." So great will their destruction be that neither "root or branch" will remain.[66]

In verse 20[4:2], the prophet turns attention

62. The latter verb, להט, "set ablaze," appears in Joel 1:19, 2:3 in reference to events associated with the Day of YHWH. The image of fire (אֵשׁ) was also employed earlier in the fourth disputation, but in that instance the "refiner's fire" is the operative image (3:2). Even as the priests will be affected on that day, so too will be the arrogant and evildoers. The former will be refined so that worship may once more be "pleasing to YHWH" (v. 4), while the arrogant and evildoers will be destroyed so that injustice and wickedness might be eradicated. With both acts, YHWH lays claim to his position as the one worthy of worship.

63. On development of the "fire as judgment" theme in Israel's prophetic literature, see the brief comments in Weyde, *Prophecy and Teaching*, 367–68. Weyde suggests that the notion of a "burning day" in Mal 3:19[4:1] reflects a "rather late stage in an assumed growth of the 'day' traditions in post-exilic prophecy" but does not reflect the types of features associated with even later prophetic traditions (Zech 12) or apocalyptic material (Dan 10).

64. Verhoef, *The Books of Haggai and Malachi*, 325.

65. Whereas the foreign nations are the objects of destruction, i.e., קַשׁ, "stubble," in several texts, the condemnation is more narrowly focused in the book of Malachi to those within the Yehudite community.

66. The function of the אֲשֶׁר clause in verse 19e[4:1e] requires further assessment. Grammarians typically understand אֲשֶׁר as either introducing relative clauses or complement clauses, but then hasten to add that אֲשֶׁר can also function as a subordinating conjunction which introduces causal, purpose, result, and conditional clauses (Cf. JM §169.f; *IBHS* §38.3; *BHRG* §36.3.1). Most translations render verse 19e[4:1e] as a result clause, "so that." Rather than creating a third category for אֲשֶׁר, i.e., a subordinating conjunction, it may be preferable to limit אֲשֶׁר to its binary function as introducing either relative or complement clauses. Clauses such as the one in verse 19e[4:1e] are then understood as examples of relative clause extraposition, that is, the relative clause has been moved further down in the sentence structure. The relative clause ("which shall not leave them root or branch") is separated from its head ("the coming day") by an intervening clause ("says YHWH Sabaoth"). Weyde has observed that there are a number of texts where "roots" and "branches" (or "fruit") are mentioned in association with the destruction of the wicked, quite often in reference to roots drying up (Hos 9:16) or branches withering (Job 18:16; Weyde, *Prophecy and Teaching*, 368–69). In Mal 3:19[4:1], the extraposed relative clause explains the nature of the coming day. Like many other references to judgment, this

back to the Godfearers, "those who fear my name." In verses 13–15, the entire community is referenced with the plural "you"; they were the ones offering harsh words against YHWH. The narrative report in verse 16 indicates that "those who fear YHWH" (יִרְאֵי יְהוָה) apparently reversed course and changed their view of YHWH. As a result, YHWH declares that they will be his "special possession" on the day that he acts. Precisely what this means for those who fear YHWH is outlined in verses 20–21[4:2–3].[67] On that day, a "sun of righteousness [שֶׁמֶשׁ צְדָקָה] will rise with healing in its wings" (NRSVUE). The phrase "sun of righteousness" appears only here in the entire Old Testament, which complicates the determination of its meaning. While this phrase remains unique to the Old Testament, the image of a winged solar disc is ubiquitous in ancient Near Eastern cultures (Egyptian, Assyrian, Babylonian, Persian). The Egyptian god Ra and the Babylonian god Shamash are closely associated with the sun and Persian iconography repeatedly employs the image in reference to Ahuramazda.[68] In the book of Malachi, the prophet has employed this traditional, and likely familiar image, in an attempt to capture what will happen "on that day."

Interpreters have posited at least four different understandings of this image. Because solar imagery occurs repeatedly throughout the Old Testament in association with YHWH, some have suggested that the phrase "sun of righteousness" refers explicitly to YHWH.[69] In Ps 84:11, for example, the psalmist refers to YHWH as a "sun" (שֶׁמֶשׁ) and

day will leave them without root or branch. The verbal clause "shall set them ablaze," however, explains the instrument of that destruction. Holmstedt cautions that "any English rendering other than a relative or complement analysis is better understood as a reflex of translation technique and English grammar, not as the structure of Biblical Hebrew" (Robert D. Holmstedt, "Headlessness and Extraposition: Another Look at the Syntax of אשר," *JNSL* 27 [2001]: 15). In the example from Malachi, the absence of a root or branch is in fact the "result" of what happens "on that day," which likely explains why a number translations create a "result clause" (NRSV, NASB, ESV). Other translations simply create an independent statement with verse 19e[4:1e] (NIV, CEV, NET). Both options are the result of "translation technique and English grammar," to borrow from Holmstedt, "Headlessness and Extraposition," 15, but they do not necessarily reflect what is occurring in the structure of Hebrew text itself. For further discussion on extraposition and relative clauses, Holmstedt's entire article, "Headlessness and Extraposition," 1–16. See also the earlier observations of Moshe Goshen-Gottstein, "Afterthought and the Syntax of Relative Clauses in Biblical Hebrew," *JBL* 68 (1949): 35–47.

67. The language in 3:20[4:2] stands in stark contrast to the opening verses of the second disputation. In 1:6, the priests (and presumably the community) were roundly chastised for their failure to fear God. Rather than fearing and honoring God, there were described as "those who despise my name" (בּוֹזֵי שְׁמִי).

68. On the larger ancient Near Eastern context, Mark S. Smith, "The Near Eastern Background of Solar Language for YHWH," *JBL* 109 (1990): 29–39. See also Bernd Janowski, "JHWH und der Sonnengott. Aspekte der Solarisierung JHWHs in vorexilischer Zeit," in *Pluralismus und Identität*, Veröffentlichungen der Wissenshaftlichen Gesellschaft für Theologie 8, ed. Joachim Melhausen (Gütersloh: Gütersloher Verlagshaus, 1995), 214–41; Joel M. LeMon, *Yahweh's Winged Form in the Psalms: Exploring Congruent Iconography and Texts*, OBO 242 (Göttingen: Vandenhoeck and Ruprecht, 2010). LeMon, 191–92, notes that

> there are many types of winged disk in Syro-Palestinian art, owing to this trope's long history of use throughout numerous ancient Near Eastern cultures (e.g., the 'militarized' winged disk, the 'anthropomorphized' winged disk, the winged sun disk issuing streams of water). Hence, claims about the correspondence between this biblical image and iconographical motif require refinement. To which type of winged disk does the image of Yahweh correspond? Indeed, many forms and aspects of the winged disk seem to be refracted in depictions of the winged Yahweh. . . . Hence, one may conclude that no single image stands behind portrayals of Yahweh in winged form. As the literary contexts change, the meaning and significance of the motif of Yahweh's wings change.

69. Glazier-McDonald, *Malachi*, 234–36. Cf. William P. Brown, *Seeing the Psalms: A Theology of Metaphor* (Louisville: Westminster John Knox, 2003), 89. On the connection of solar imagery to YHWH, see his larger discussion (81–103). Richard R. Deutsch argues similarly for the association of this image with YHWH. He contends for a particularly strong Egyptian influence in the use of this image, suggesting that both the "sun of righteousness" and healing wings "are good examples of the extent of Egyptian influence on people living in Palestine"

"shield" and in Isa 60:19–21, the prophet declares that "the sun will no longer be your light by day," but instead YHWH will be an "everlasting light." Other references to YHWH's presence as a "light" (אוֹר), especially in the psalms, appear to invoke solar imagery as well (e.g., Pss 27:1; 43:3; 104:1b–2a). A second option is to understand "sun of righteousness" in light of Israel's royal ideology. In selected texts, human kingship and solar imagery appear together. (2 Sam 23:3; Ps 72:5). Interpreted along these lines, the reference to "healing in its wings" in Mal 3:20[4:2] would refer to the monarch's obligation to the well-being of his people. These connections lead Mark Smith to conclude that the label "sun of righteousness" operates as a reference to a future royal figure, "Israel's future savior."[70] A third option is to understand "sun of righteousness" more generally as a "figurative description of the eschatological day."[71] As Kessler has noted, the connection between the morning sunrise and the creation of righteousness has a long history of tradition in the ancient Near East and certainly would have been familiar to Malachi's audience.[72] The fact that "sun of righteousness" (שֶׁמֶשׁ צְדָקָה) is indefinite, i.e., "*a* sun of righteousness" rather than "*the* sun of righteousness," might provide additional support for this reading. Understood accordingly, the emphasis would be on a dawning of a "new day" that will usher in the righteousness of God and result in a "complete reversal of current circumstances."[73]

A fourth option, and the one preferred here, is a combination of the first and third.[74] The image refers to the eschatological day that is coming, but clearly implies that YHWH is the active agent. In verse 19c[4:1c], the prophet announces the "coming day" which will set the arrogant and evildoers ablaze. A closer inspection of verse 20a[4:2a] suggests that the latter verse is meant to stand in parallel to the former.

> וְלִהַט אֹתָם הַיּוֹם הַבָּא
> The coming day shall set them ablaze. (v. 19c[4:1c])
>
> וְזָרְחָה לָכֶם יִרְאֵי שְׁמִי שֶׁמֶשׁ צְדָקָה
> The sun of righteousness shall rise for you who fear my name. (v. 20a[4:2a])

The parallel structure is even more apparent in the Hebrew text. The word order is nearly identical: verb (*weqatal*) + complement/adjunct + subject.[75] Moreover, the events described contribute to the contrast. The coming day of judgment will leave the arrogant and evildoers "without root or branch" whereas the rising of the "sun of righteousness" will produce "healing in its wings" (בִּכְנָפֶיהָ) for those who fear YHWH's name. The one brings destruction, the other life. The noun "healing" (מַרְפֵּא) only occurs three other times in the prophetic corpus, all in the book of Jeremiah (8:15; 14:19; 33:6). In each instance, the notion of healing

(Graham S. Ogden and Richard R. Deutsch, *Joel and Malachi*, ITC [Grand Rapids: Eerdmans, 1987], 112). As LeMon's work suggests, however, the use of the image is likely more complex than Deutsch intimates.

70. See Mark S. Smith, *The Early History of God: Yahweh and the Other Deities in Ancient Israel*, 2nd ed. (Grand Rapids: Eerdmans, 2002), 149–59.

71. Hill, *Malachi*, 349; Gibson, *Covenant Continuity and Fidelity*, 211; Snyman, *Malachi*, 173.

72. Kessler, *Maleachi*, 290.

73. Hill, *Malachi*, 349.

74. Nogalski appears to lean in this direction (*The Book of the Twelve: Micah–Malachi*, 1066).

75. An exact parallel is not possible because the verb זרח, "to rise," is monovalent, meaning that it never takes a complement. In the other seventeen occurrences of the verb, the construction is either simply subject + verb, or as in Mal 3:20[4:2], an adjunct prepositional phrase is included. This feature likely explains Hill's labeling of the *lamed* in the prepositional phrase לָכֶם as a *dativus ethicus* (Hill, *Malachi*, 349). Cf. *IBHS* §11.2.10d.

(מַרְפֵּא) refers to YHWH's salvation for his people and stands in contrast to the disastrous judgment that befell Jerusalem in 587 BCE.[76] In Jer 33:6, YHWH pledges "Behold I am going to bring [Jerusalem] recovery and healing [מַרְפֵּא]; I will heal [רפא] them." This raises the question, "What does Malachi mean by healing in this context?" The answer lies back in the phrase "sun of righteousness" (שֶׁמֶשׁ צְדָקָה). Although most translations render צְדָקָה as "righteousness" (NEB; NIV; NRSV), Hill is correct in that "the sense is really that of 'justice' as a characteristic of God, the divine judge."[77] In this sense, when the sun of righteousness arises, when the new day dawns, God will restore "right order" to the community.[78] Those who had once asked "Where is the God of justice?" (2:17) will now experience the fullness of YHWH's צְדָקָה in their midst.

The healing derived from the outpouring of YHWH's justice will cause them to "skip about" (פוש) like "calves from the stall" (v. 20d[4:2d]). The construct phrase "calves from the stall" (עֶגְלֵי מַרְבֵּק) has the connotation of calves that are tied up and fattened in preparation for slaughter (cf. 1 Sam 28:24; Amos 6:4). Yet these "fattened calves" will be set free; they will "go out" (יצא). Snyman notes that "to be free, not only from a stall, but also from imminent death is indeed reason for joy."[79] While those in Malachi's audience may not have worried about imminent death, they despaired about reality as they construed it. The image of a stall-fed calf set free and skipping about is meant to signal the considerable reversal that will take place when YHWH's justice is poured out and that which seems wrong is made right. Rather than believing service to God is futile and walking about as mourners (v. 14), those who fear YHWH's name will be released to live a new way of life, one filled with exuberant joy.

Verse 21[4:3] concludes this disputation with the announcement that those who fear YHWH's name will "trample [עסס] the wicked ones."[80] This declaration, however, does not suggest that those who fear YHWH's name will "act as YHWH's co-workers in the destruction of the wicked."[81] Quite the contrary, the righteous ones will actually benefit from the judgment already wrought upon the "wicked ones" as the causal clause (כִּי clause) in verse 21b[4:3b] suggests.[82] Those who fear YHWH's name will tread upon the wicked *because*

76. In similar fashion, "healing" (מַרְפֵּא) appears in opposition to the wrath of YHWH in 2 Chr 36:16.

77. Hill, *Malachi*, 350.

78. Glazier-McDonald, *Malachi*, 240.

79. Snyman, *Malachi*, 174.

80. Although it is possible that the verb עסס is meant to continue the idea of animals romping about in the pastures, the imagery appears to shift. At minimum, it suggests dominance of one party over the other. Glazier-McDonald proposes that the verb עסס means "to tread down, crush" but then notes that from this verb comes a derivative, עָסִיס, "sweet wine," i.e., wine derived from the treading down of grapes. Because עָסִיס, "sweet wine," appears in texts that refer to the Day of YHWH (Joel 4:18; Amos 9:13) and because divine judgment is often compared to drinking a cup of wine that will cause people to "reel and stagger" (Ps 60:5; 75:9; Jer 25:15), Glazier-McDonald contends that Malachi is appropriating the imagery of treading grapes in the winepress as part of the Day of YHWH imagery (*Malachi: The Divine Messenger*, 242). Glazier-McDonald's argument concerning the linkage between wine and the day of YHWH is valid. Whether or not the fullness of her argument can be supported only by the verb עסס remains questionable. The reference to "ashes" in v. 21b[4:3b] (rather than grapes) further problematizes her proposal.

81. Weyde, *Prophecy and Teaching*, 377. Jacobs offer a similar reading, calling the righteous the "instruments of YHWH's judgment" (*The Books of Haggai and Malachi*, 323).

82. On the non-participation of the Godfearers in the destruction of the wicked, cf. Snyman, *Malachi*, 174; Scalise, "Malachi," 361; Verhoef, *The Books of Haggai and Malachi*, 332; Petersen, *Zechariah 9–14 and Malachi*, 226. Glazier-McDonald suggests Godfearers will "participate indirectly" by treading down the ashes of the wicked (*Malachi*, 243).

the wicked are now nothing more than אֵפֶר, "dust, ash."[83] The striding over the ashen remains of the wicked is not intended as a spiteful or vengeful act, but rather an indication of their status as YHWH's special possession (סְגֻלָּה; v. 17) on the day that YHWH acts.[84]

Canonical and Theological Significance

The complaints uttered by the community in 3:14–15 revisit the concerns of the community uttered previously in the fourth disputation (2:17). In that disputation, the "wearisome words" uttered by the community focused on two related issues. The apparent success of the evildoers prompted the community to assume that "all who do evil are good in the eyes of YHWH." For the community, the evildoers were the apparent beneficiaries of divine favor even though such a claim ran counter to the covenant. This observation led the community to question the very justice of God. That disputation focused on the actions of the evildoers and the inaction of a just God. In the sixth disputation, similar theodicy-related observations emerge as it relates to the actions of the evildoers (v. 15b) and the inaction of YHWH (v. 15c), but a third—and more troubling assertion—is added. The community claims that "to serve God is futile" (v. 14b). Such service is futile because there is no apparent gain (בֶּצַע) in serving this God (v. 14c).

In the sixth disputation, the question of the theodicy remains on the table but at a much deeper level, the question being posed is whether this God remains worthy to be served. As suggested in the Explanation of the Text section, the question raised by the community in verse 14b reflects a deep-seated concern that the blessings and curses theology of the covenant tradition no longer appears operative and worse yet, that the community is not benefitting directly from their obedience. As a result, the community toys with the unthinkable conclusion that perhaps this God no longer merits their service and devotion.

In many ways the questions being probed in the final disputation are somewhat similar to that in the book of Job. The opening verses of that wisdom book describe a person who was "blameless and upright, one who feared God and turned from evil" (1:1). The subsequent description of his considerable wealth accords well with a full-orbed blessings and curses theology. The blameless and upright Job is labeled "the greatest of all the people of the East" (1:3 NRSVUE). The assumption is that faithful service to YHWH yields gain. The conversation between YHWH and the accuser in the subsequent verses, however, seeks to test that claim. In rather pointed

83. Given the references to "burning ovens" and the use of the verb להט, "to set ablaze," in v. 19, the idea of burned ash is clearly in view.

84. The phrase "on the day that I will act" (בַּיּוֹם אֲשֶׁר אֲנִי עֹשֶׂה) in 3:21b[4:3b] repeats the same phrase that appeared earlier in 3:17c. In that verse, those who feared YHWH are declared YHWH's "special possession" (סְגֻלָּה). The implications of that status are made explicit in 3:21b[4:3b].

fashion, the accuser poses a question to YHWH, "Does Job serve God for nothing?" If Job was not the "greatest man in all the East," if wealth, success, and prosperity had not fallen to him, would he still choose to be faithful to this God? The presumed answer to the accuser's rhetorical question is "no." The underlying assumption is that the only reason Job (or anyone) would serve this God is because of the benefits to be accrued. While Mal 3:14–15 does not provide such a rich "backstory" and its language is far more terse and succinct than that of Job, the assertion made by the community seems to have much in common with the question posed by the accuser in Job 1:9. The accuser ponders whether Job would serve God in return "for nothing," while the community in Mal 3:14b seems to assert that a God who offers "nothing" is not worthy of service. The seemingly intrinsic connection between service and gain is operative in both.

Following an encounter with the Divine in a whirlwind (Job 38–42), Job changes his mind concerning this God (42:6) and the human condition.[85] The earlier question uttered by the accuser concerning whether Job would serve God "for nothing" receives a jarring "yes." The encountered God *is* worthy of service, benefits and gains aside. In Malachi, it appears that the Godfearers had reached a similar conclusion. They jettisoned the larger community's claim that this God was not worthy to be served due to the perceived absence of "gain." This makes the label applied to them, "those who fear God," i.e., the Godfearers, all the more apt. Rather than covering their mouths like Job in a visible sign of change, they assumed the posture of one who revered this God. Period. They spoke among themselves words of assurance, and while the book of Malachi does not record the content of their dialogue, the remainder of the disputation offers the reader a clue. The subsequent verses suggest that the absence of any perceived benefits is not suggestive of the absence of this God. Lest they think otherwise, those who serve this God are reminded that they will not be forgotten. Quite the contrary, they are remembered by this God (v. 16) and they remain "before him." They will be his "special possession" on the day that he acts (v. 17c), and on that day, people will be able to distinguish once more between "those serving God and those who do not serve God" (v. 18a).

Such hope, however, is not rooted in escapism or some type of "pie in sky" theology that avoids reality, but in something far greater. As Helmut Thielicke explains, "I do not believe in the future life because of some dream of the hereafter. I believe in it because I am already the companion of him who has begun a history with me and will never let me fall away from his faithfulness."[86] This final disputation suggests that hope is not rooted in the accrual of perceived benefits; it is rooted in the undeniable faithfulness of this God, both now and on the day in which he acts.

85. Dale Patrick, "Translation of Job 42:6," *VT* 26 (1976): 369–71.

86. Helmut Thielicke, *The Evangelical Faith III*, trans. Geoffrey W. Bromiley (Macon, GA: Smyth & Helwys, 1997), 410.

As suggested in the introduction to this disputation, these concluding verses do not deny the realities that confronted that community (and us), but instead, they suggest that present experiences do not fully define all of reality. These verses argue that our anguished faith will find its hope in a renewed commitment to a faithful God whose in-breaking will set all things right.

CHAPTER 8

Malachi 3:22–24[4:4–6]

VIII. An Exhortation and a Looming Curse

Main Idea of the Passage

The final three verses of Malachi are comprised of two appendices (3:22[4:4] and 3:23–24[4:5–6]). Both additions return to familiar themes from earlier in the book (i.e., torah and the coming day of YHWH), but with notable expansion of both, including the mention of Moses and Elijah. Together the appendices provide a concluding word of instruction, but even more, they provide an invitation for the community to adopt a particular posture of faith that informs the present in light of that which is yet to come.

Literary Context

The relationship of 3:22–24[4:4–6] to the larger book has prompted considerable discussion. These verses are often seen as an addition due primarily to the absence of any features associated with the disputation form that has dominated the book, and perhaps more importantly, the seeming lack of continuity with the larger prophetic message found in 1:1–3:21[4:3]. In addition, the absence of the speech formulas that appear repeatedly in the book, i.e. "says YHWH (Sabaoth)," are often cited as further evidence of its dissimilarity with the preceding passages as are the syntactical variations present in the final verses.[1] Taking these matters into account, Paul Redditt goes so far as to suggest that the final three verses lack any real sense of meaningful

1. On the "syntactical dissimilarities," see Hill, *Malachi*, 377–78. By way of example, Hill notes that while גָּדוֹל, "great," and נוֹרָא, "fearful," both appear in 1:14 and in 3:23[4:5], the two terms are used as predicate adjectives in the first instance and attributive adjectives in the second. Similarly, the use of יוֹם, "day," and בּוֹא, "to come," in 3:2 (יוֹם בּוֹאוֹ, "the day of his coming") differs from its use in 3:23[4:5], בּוֹא יוֹם, "the coming of the day."

continuity with the preceding disputations.[2] By contrast, Michael Floyd contends that "the claims of thematic discontinuity between [the epilogue] and the preceding parts of the book have been greatly overstated."[3] Floyd explains that the reason for this continuity is because the final three verses were not appendices added separately, but in fact a product of the prophet himself. In addition to Floyd, a number of other scholars have suggested that these verses should be understood as part of the original book of Malachi and are intended to function primarily as a conclusion to that book alone.[4]

As noted above, the prevailing view is that the final verses were added as an appendix to the book. To suggest that the final three verses were a subsequent addition, however, is not to suggest an absence in continuity with remainder of the book, as suggested by Redditt. Rainer Kessler, for example, argues that the verses represent secondary additions, but ones that demonstrate considerable continuity with the larger book. Chief among his arguments is that these verses "take up what dominates the second half of the book of Malachi, namely, a view of the future."[5] As mentioned in the introduction, the book of Malachi shifts in orientation following the third disputation. Beginning with the fourth disputation (2:17–3:5) and continuing in the fifth and sixth (3:6–12; 3:13–21[4:3]), a future horizon moves to the fore. That which is to come is mentioned in each disputation: the coming of the messenger and then YHWH (3:1–2); the coming of a renewed land predicated upon faithfulness (3:10–12); and the coming of a day when YHWH will act (3:17–21[4:3]). In addition to the thematic continuity (i.e., the future horizon), important lexical connections bind the secondary additions to that which precedes them. Most notably is the near verbatim link between 3:1 and 3:23[4:5]. In the former text, YHWH declares, "Behold, I am about to send my messenger" (הִנְנִי שֹׁלֵחַ מַלְאָכִי), while in the latter, he announces, "Behold, I am sending to you Elijah the prophet" (הִנֵּה אָנֹכִי שֹׁלֵחַ לָכֶם אֵת אֵלִיָּה הַנָּבִיא).

In addition, 3:2 and 3:19[4:1] make reference to the day (יוֹם) that comes (בּוֹא); that same vocabulary appears in 3:23[4:5] but with added descriptors, "before the great and awesome Day of YHWH comes" (לִפְנֵי בּוֹא יוֹם יְהוָה הַגָּדוֹל וְהַנּוֹרָא).

Beyond the thematic and lexical links to the book, there are clear allusions to the torah and torah expectations in several of the disputations (1:6–2:9; 2:10–16; 2:17–3:5; 3:6–12), as well as explicit references to the prophetic tradition (e.g., the coming day of YHWH) in 2:17–3:5 and 3:13–21[4:3]. The mention of Moses and Elijah in the

2. Redditt, *Haggai, Zechariah and Malachi*, 185.

3. Floyd, *Minor Prophets, Part 2*, 568.

4. Floyd, *Minor Prophets, Part 2*, 568–69. Most recently, see Gibson, *Covenant Continuity and Fidelity*, 220–35. He argues that there is considerable overlap between the vocabulary found in 3:22–24[4:4–6] and that in the remainder of the book. Based on his calculations, approximately 80 percent of the terms in the final three verses appear elsewhere in Malachi. While such evidence is not conclusive, Gibson admits, he does argue that it does make a strong case for the "originality and integrality" of Mal 3:22–24[4:4–6] with the remainder of the book. For a similar reading of the final three verses, cf. Baldwin, *Haggai, Zechariah, and Malachi*, 251; Glazier-McDonald, *Malachi*, 243–45; Verhoef, *The Books of Haggai and Malachi*, 337–38; Clendenen, "Malachi," 455.

5. Kessler, *Maleachi*, 302–3.

final three verses reinforces these intended connections.[6] The reference to these two figures from Israelite history also serves another purpose. More than an attempt to connect with the allusions and traditions embedded within the book of Malachi, these appendices suggest that at minimum "a developing sense of canon" appears at work.[7] In this sense, the final three verses represent connections to a larger body of literature in the Old Testament. Consequently, most interpreters argue that these verses likely have a "double-duty" function, to borrow Hill's language, in that they serve as an appropriate conclusion to the book of Malachi, but also to a larger corpus of literature.[8] The question that remains is which corpus? Some interpreters, for example, expand the scope to the Book of Twelve, suggesting that Mal 3:22–24[4:4–6] operates as the conclusion to that entire collection.[9] Greater still, others argue that these verses serve as a conclusion to the entire prophetic corpus or even as a conclusion to the Law and the Prophets as a whole.[10] In the Explanation of the Text section below, attention to these verses as a conclusion to the book of Malachi will be considered as well as intertextual and canonical connections.

I. Superscription (1:1)
II. YHWH's Relentless Love (1:2–5)
III. Dishonoring the Divine King (1:6–2:9)
IV. An Unfaithful Community (2:10–16)
V. The Coming of the God of Justice (2:17–3:5)
VI. The Call to Return to YHWH (3:6–12)
VII. The Hope of Those Who Fear God (3:13–21[4:3])
➡ **VIII. An Exhortation and a Looming Curse (3:22–24[4:4–6])**
A. Appendix 1: An Exhortation to Remember the Torah of Moses (3:22[4:4])
B. Appendix 2: An Announcement of the Coming of Elijah (3:23–24[4:5–6])
1. The Intended Action of Elijah (3:23[4:5])
2. An Ominous Curse (3:24[4:6])

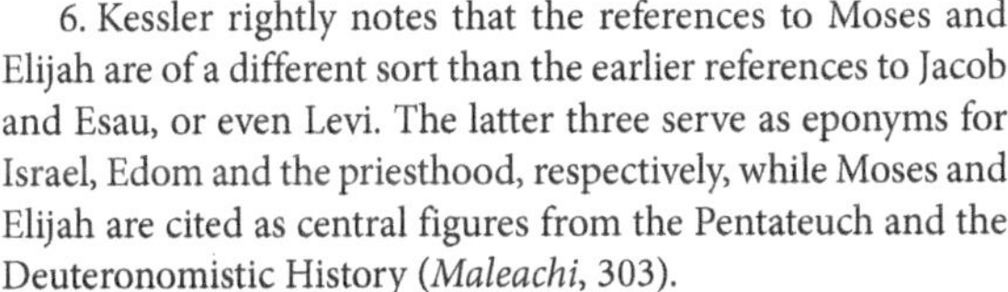

6. Kessler rightly notes that the references to Moses and Elijah are of a different sort than the earlier references to Jacob and Esau, or even Levi. The latter three serve as eponyms for Israel, Edom and the priesthood, respectively, while Moses and Elijah are cited as central figures from the Pentateuch and the Deuteronomistic History (*Maleachi*, 303).

7. Nogalski, *The Book of the Twelve: Micah-Malachi*, 1068. Similarly, Kessler suggests that the three verses are making "explicit reference to Torah and prophecy as textual corpora" (*Maleachi*, 303).

8. Hill, *Malachi*, 364–65.

9. Petersen, *Zechariah 9–14 and Malachi*, 233; Hill, *Malachi*, 364. Petersen observes that the only other book in this collection with an epilogue is that of Hosea (14:10). Because that verse appears to have resonance with selected texts in the Psalter and the wisdom literature and because Mal 3:22–24[4:4–6] has resonance with the Pentateuch and former prophets, Petersen proposes that the epilogues in the two books "act as a canonical envelope," with the purpose of integrating the Book of the Twelve with the remainder of the canon.

10. As a conclusion to the prophetic corpus and in particular, as an allusion to the transition from the end of the Torah (Deut 34) to the opening lines of the prophetic corpus (Josh 1), see Rudolph, *Haggai, Sacharja 1–8, Sacharja 9–14, Maleachi*, 291. Rudolph makes a compelling case. He observes that the reference to Moses as "my servant" in 3:22[4:4] occurs in both Deut 34:5

Translation and Exegetical Outline

(See page 179.)

Structure and Literary Form

As noted above under Literary Context, the final three verses lack the elements of the disputation form that has dominated the six sections in the book. Rather than a verbal exchange between the community and YHWH, as present in the other pericopes in Malachi, YHWH alone speaks. In these three verses, other forms are operative. The opening imperative in 3:22[4:4] signals the shift to exhortation; YHWH exhorts the community to torah faithfulness. In the final two verses, the particle הִנֵּה, "behold," plus a participle signals an announcement formula intended to communicate that "divine action will take place in the immediate future."[11] Coupled with the announcement of the coming of Elijah is the mention of a curse. The reference to covenant curses as a result of disobedience appears repeatedly in the book of Malachi (e.g., 1:4–5; 1:14; 2:2–3; 3:5; 3:7–11). With this final collection of verses, the book ends with the announcement of a potential curse upon the entire land (3:24[4:6]). In so doing, the announcement provides yet another thematic link between the book and the appendices. The final three verses may be understood as two appendices likely added at different times. Although brief, the final appendices do provide a logical structure to the end of the book.

Some LXX manuscripts reverse the order of the appendices so that the exhortation to remember the Torah concludes the book. Typically, this is explained as an attempt to ensure that the book of Malachi does not end in a curse. Rainer Kessler argues differently. He suggests that given the considerable number of lexical links between 3:23–24[4:5–6] and the final disputation (3:13–21[4:3]), however, it is likely that the appendix associated with Elijah's coming was connected directly to the final disputation.[12] In this way, even as the final disputation focused on the coming day of YHWH, so did that which immediately followed in the appendix.

and Joshua 1:2, 7 (and only appears one other time in the Hebrew Bible (Num 22:18). For a similar view, see also Kessler, *Maleachi*, 307–8). As a conclusion to the entirety of the Law and Prophets, see Redditt, *Haggai, Zechariah and Malachi*, 185. Snyman and Weber have even noted the links between Mal 3:22[4:4] and Ps 1, and in particular, the reference to תּוֹרָה (Torah) in Mal 3:22[4:4] and Ps 1:2. Snyman contends that "the reference to the Torah at the end of the prophetic book and at the beginning of the Writings likewise creates a link between the second and third part of the Hebrew canon" (Snyman, *Maleachi*, 186). See also Beat Weber, "Psalm 1 and Its Function as a Directive into the Psalter and Towards a Biblical Theology," *OTE* 19/1 (2006): 237–60.

11. Nogalski, *Interpreting Prophetic Literature*, 23. Although Hill labels this as a "type of messenger formula" (*Malachi*, 375–76), Nogalski classifies it as a distinct category.

12. Kessler, *Maleachi*, 308.

Malachi 3:22–24[4:4–6]

Verse	Hebrew	English	Outline
			VIII. An Exhortation and a Looming Curse (3:22–24[4:4–6])
			A. Appendix 1: An Exhortation to Remember the Torah of Moses (3:22a–b[4:4b–b])
3:22a[4:4a]	זִכְרוּ תּוֹרַת מֹשֶׁה עַבְדִּי	"Remember the Torah of Moses, my servant	
3:22b[4:4b]	↑ אֲשֶׁר צִוִּיתִי אוֹתוֹ בְחֹרֵב עַל כָּל יִשְׂרָאֵל חֻקִּים וּמִשְׁפָּטִים	↑ that I commanded him on Horeb for all Israel—the statutes and judgments.	
			B. Appendix 2: An Announcement of the Coming of Elijah (3:23–24c[4:5–6c])
3:23[4:5]	הִנֵּה אָנֹכִי שֹׁלֵחַ לָכֶם אֵת אֵלִיָּה הַנָּבִיא לִפְנֵי בּוֹא יוֹם יְהוָה הַגָּדוֹל וְהַנּוֹרָא	Behold I am sending to you Elijah the prophet before the coming of the great and awesome day of YHWH.	1. The Intended Action of Elijah (3:23[4:5])
3:24a[4:6a]	וְהֵשִׁיב לֵב אָבוֹת עַל בָּנִים וְלֵב בָּנִים עַל אֲבוֹתָם ↑	And he will turn the hearts of fathers to children and the hearts of children to fathers ↑	2. An Ominous Curse (3:24a–c[4:6a–c])
3:24b[4:6b]	פֶּן־אָבוֹא	lest I come	
3:24c[4:6c]	וְהִכֵּיתִי אֶת־הָאָרֶץ חֵרֶם	and strike the land with utter destruction.	

Subsequently, the appendix related to the Torah of Moses would have been added with the intent of connecting the first two parts of the canon.[13] Similar to the view of Kessler, Russell Fuller argues that the LXX likely represents the original (and older) sequence. The appendix referring to Elijah would have followed the sixth disputation and the appendix focused on the Torah would have appeared last. In this way, Fuller argues, the mention of the Torah in 3:22[4:4] creates an *inclusio* with Josh 1, thus creating a frame around the entire prophetic corpus (Former and Latter Prophets).[14] Fuller suggests that at some point, the scribes moved 3:22[4:4] to its current position in the MT to place emphasis on the Elijah tradition and the coming day of YHWH.[15] This move may have also been prompted by the larger canonical sequence (i.e., Pentateuch then Prophets).

At a synchronic level of reading the configuration of appendices in the MT creates something of a "chronological sequence." The exhortation to remember the Torah is intended to shape the community's view of the present while the announcement of the coming of Elijah and the Day of YHWH was meant to point to the future and the expectations associated with it.

Explanation of the Text

A. Appendix 1: Exhortation to Remember the Torah of Moses (3:22[4:4])

The first appendix exhorts the community to return to the Torah, and more specifically, to torah faithfulness. This exhortation is not an afterthought appended to the entirety of the book but a response to all that preceded it. Throughout the book of Malachi, the community's waywardness has received considerable attention and now, as the book closes out, the community is invited to return back to torah and the God who gave it (cf. Mal 3:7).

The rhetoric in the first appendix makes considerable use of Deuteronomistic language.[16] The opening imperative זִכְרוּ, "remember," invokes a key theme from the book of Deuteronomy. In that book the verb occurs fifteen times and frequently links remembering with covenant fidelity; the community is enjoined to remember what YHWH did for them so that they might respond in kind with

13. Kessler, *Maleachi*, 308.

14. Fuller contends that the LXX reflects a separate Hebrew *Vorlage*. Russell E. Fuller, "The Sequence of Malachi 4:4–6[3:22–24] in the Greek and Hebrew Textual Traditions: Implications for the Redactional History of the Minor Prophets," in *Perspectives on the Formation of the Book of the Twelve: Methodological Foundations, Redactional Processes and Historical Insights*, ed. Rainer Albertz, James Nogalski, and Jakob Wöhrle, BZAW 433 (Berlin: de Gruyter, 2012), 371–79. See also Fuller's earlier assessment in "Hebrew and Greek Biblical Manuscripts: Their Interpretations and Their Interpreters," in *The Dead Sea Scrolls in Context: Integrating the Dead Sea Scrolls in the Study of Ancient Texts, Languages, and Cultures*, vol. 1, eds. Armin Lange, Emmanuel Tov, Matthias Weigold and Bennie Reynolds III (Leiden: Brill, 2010), 1–10. See also S. D. Snyman, "Malachi 4:4–6 (Heb 3:22–24) as a Point of Convergence in the Old Testament or Hebrew Bible: A Consideration of the Intra and Intertextual Relationships," *HTS Theological Studies* 68 (2012), 4–5.

15. Fuller, "The Sequence of Malachi 3:22–24," 375.

16. Vocabulary typically identified as Deuteronomistic includes: "Torah of Moses" (תּוֹרַת מֹשֶׁה), "Horeb" (חֹרֵב), "all Israel" (כָּל־יִשְׂרָאֵל), and "statutes and judgments" (הַחֻקִּים וְהַמִּשְׁפָּטִים). Hill, *Malachi*, 369.

their own covenant fidelity.[17] To remember in the Old Testament is not simply a recollection of the past, although it certainly includes that, but instead such recollection of the past is meant to inform and guide. In short, one remembers in order to act rightly. In Deut 8:2, for example, Moses exhorts the community to remember (זכר) God's faithfulness to his people through the desert which, in turn, should compel them to "keep the commandments of YHWH your God," by walking in his ways and by fearing him (v. 6). A similar connection between remembrance and action appears in Ps 103:18b. The line reads literally, "those who remember (זכר) his commandments in order to do (עשׂה) them." It is with this same intent that the writer of Mal 3:22 [4:4] exhorts the community to "remember the Torah of Moses."

This explicit association of Moses with the Torah dominates the book of Deuteronomy and further connects this appendix with Deuteronomic traditions. From the opening verses of Deuteronomy (1:5) until its final chapters (33:4), Moses appears as both scribe and teacher of the law to God's people (31:19).[18] Outside of the book of Deuteronomy, this close association between Moses and Torah is often found embedded within a much larger construction, "the book of the Torah of Moses" (סֵפֶר תּוֹרַת מֹשֶׁה). This phrase appears fourteen times in the Old Testament, both in the former prophets (Josh 8:31, 32; 23:6; 1 Kgs 2:3; 2 Kgs 14:6; 23:25) and in several post-exilic texts (Dan 9:11; 13; Ezra 3:2; 7:6; Neh 8:1, 2; 2 Chr 23:18; 30:16). As Scalise astutely observes, the references within the former prophets tend to occur at significant moments within the life of Israel.[19] In those instances, the "Torah of Moses" was deemed authoritative for shaping both the actions and the identity of those involved. Post-exilic texts are even more explicit in their reference to an authoritative "book" (סֵפֶר), as evident especially in Neh 8:1–2. In the same vein, the reference to the "Torah of Moses" in Mal 3:22[4:4] appears to invoke an authoritative text, which Hill understands as "an organic unity comprising the covenant stipulations, civil and ethical instruction, and narrative traditions associated with Moses as lawgiver."[20] This emphasis on the law of Moses represents a significant shift away from earlier attempts by Haggai to focus attention on the Davidic covenant and its contemporary iteration (2:20–23). Malachi, by contrast, orients the community to the Mosaic covenant, as does Ezra and Nehemiah sometime later. Hill argues that "this shift from person-based authority to a document-based authority in the Hebrew religious community was necessary given the reality of the Persian suzerainty and the uncertainty of reinstating the Davidic dynasty."[21] Two other terms appear at the end of the verse and confirm the focus on torah. On the meaning and function of "statutes and judgments" (הַחֻקִּים וְהַמִּשְׁפָּטִים) within this verse, see below.

Grammatically, the relative clause in this verse can be translated in one of two ways depending on which noun is identified as the clausal head; neither option fundamentally alters the understanding of the verse, however. If "Moses,

17. Deut 5:15; 7:18 [2x]; 8:2, 18; 9:7, 27; 15:15; 16:3, 12; 24:9, 18, 22; 25:17; 32:7.

18. Kessler, *Maleachi*, 305.

19. Scalise, "Malachi," 363–64.

20. Hill, *Malachi*, 371–72. For those who align generally with Hill's assessment, cf. Gibson, *Covenant Continuity and Fidelity*, 231–32; Glazier-McDonald, *Malachi*, 247; Redditt, *Haggai, Zechariah, Malachi*, 185. Others have proposed that the phrase "Torah of Moses" may be more limited in scope, perhaps referring to the book of Deuteronomy alone (Floyd, *Minor Prophets, Part 2*, 624) or to some form of the "law book" of Ezra (cf. Ezra 3:2; Neh 8:1). Verhoef suggests that the context in Mal 3 is insufficient for making an exact determination as to its scope and content (*The Books of Haggai and Malachi*, 338).

21. Hill, *Malachi*, 372.

my servant," is understood as the noun head, then the relative clause would be translated as "to whom I commanded (him) on Horeb." In this instance, the object marker (אֵת) + third masculine singular pronoun is understood reflexively.[22] This would suggest that the verb "to command" (צוה) has a double complement: אוֹתוֹ ("him") and חֻקִּים וּמִשְׁפָּטִים ("statutes and judgements"). The NET attempts to capture this reading: "Remember the law of my servant Moses, to whom at Horeb I gave rules and regulations for all Israel to obey." By contrast, if the head of the relative clause is understood as "Torah" (תּוֹרָה), then the phrase would be rendered, "Remember the Torah of Moses my servant which I commanded him on Horeb for all Israel—the statutes and judgements."[23] This reading is the reading adopted here and the preferred reading for three reasons. First, Hill correctly notes that the reflexive construction (as proposed in the first option) of the relative (אֲשֶׁר) + the object maker (אֵת) is "uncharacteristic" of Deuteronomy and the larger Deuteronomistic history.[24] Second, when the relative (אֲשֶׁר) + "to command" (צוה) + the object maker (אֵת) does appear in Deuteronomy and the Deuteronomistic history, quite often the clausal noun is תּוֹרָה, or a related synonym.[25] Third, this reading makes better sense of the final two words in the clause, "statutes and judgments." In the book of Deuteronomy, the two terms appear together frequently as "summary terms," or parallel terms, for the Torah of Moses.[26] As a result, the two terms are better understood as a form of apposition with "Torah" (תּוֹרָה) functioning as the anchor.[27] A number of English translations have attempted to reflect this construction by moving the final two Hebrew words closer to the anchor noun. The NIV, for example, renders the verse "Remember the law of my servant Moses, the decrees and laws that I gave him at Horeb for all Israel" (Cf. NRSV; ESV).

The mention of Horeb in this appendix also invokes yet another strong association with the Deuteronomistic tradition. An alternate name for Sinai, "Horeb" occurs seventeen times in the Old Testament with more than half of the occurrences in the book of Deuteronomy, with another two later in the Deuteronomistic history.[28] More important than simply its frequency, however, is its significance. Horeb is the place where the covenant with YHWH was established ("YHWH our God made a covenant with us at Horeb," Deut 5:2). In that act of covenant making, the entire nation "stood before YHWH" (Deut 4:10, 15). It was there that they encountered God and were called to remember his "laws," "statutes," and "ordinances"

22. Glazier-McDonald, *Malachi*, 250. Glazier-McDonald is following the earlier suggestion of Alexander von Bulmerincq, *Der Prophet Malachi*, vol. 2 (Tartu: J. G. Krüger, 1932), 556.

23. Although relative clauses are typically located adjacent to the nouns they modify (i.e., their head), they can be extraposed or separated from the head. Here the absolute noun ("Moses") plus the appositive ("my servant") separates the clausal head ("torah") from the relative clause.

24. Hill, *Malachi*, 367. There are repeated examples in both collections of a relative (אֲשֶׁר) + "to command" (צוה) + the object maker (אֵת), and in each instance the construction is not reflexive. Cf. Deut 31:5, 29; Josh 1:13; 7:11.

25. Cf. Deut 6:1, 20; 8:1; 11:13, 22; 31:5; 2 Kgs 17:13. Note especially the lexical and syntactical similarities between Mal 3:22[4:4] and Josh 22:5. In the Joshua text, the relative clause appears in the same form, with the clausal noun being "Torah." In addition, Moses is referred to as the "servant of YHWH" (עֶבֶד־יְהוָה).

26. Kessler, *Maleachi*, 307; Gibson, *Covenant Continuity and Fidelity*, 233. See also Verhoef, *The Books of Haggai and Malachi*, 340. Cf. Deut 4:1, 2, 8, 14; 5:1; 11:32.

27. Utilizing the taxonomy of apposition posited by Holmstedt and Jones, Mal 3:22[4:4] represents a particular form of apposition that they identify as "Equivalence: Identification" ("Apposition in Biblical Hebrew," 33–34). In such instances, quite often the anchor and the appositive are separated by other constituents, in this instance, a relative clause.

28. Cf. Deut 1:2, 6, 19; 4:10, 15; 5:2; 9:8 18:16; 29:1; 1 Kgs 8:9; 19:8. The remaining texts include Exod 3:1; 17:6; 33:6; 2 Chr 5:10; Ps 106:19.

(Deut 4:8). All of this language and imagery from Deuteronomy informs the carefully crafted appendix in Mal 3:22[4:4]. The call to "remember the Torah of Moses" is a call to a renewed identity. At Horeb, their identity was rooted in the laws, statutes and ordinances associated with the covenant (Deut 4:12–14), and at Horeb, they encountered their God. What happened at Horeb stands in stark contrast to the life experienced by the present community in Yehud. Throughout the book of Malachi, the community is chastised for its failure to maintain covenant faithfulness and throughout the book of Malachi, the community complains about the seeming absence of the Divine. The first appendix exhorts the community to remember what happened at Horeb, but not as an act of sentimentality, but instead as an act of renewal so that the past might become the present once more. The community is invited to remember (and to do) the Torah of Moses so that they too might be a people who stand before God once again.[29]

The reference to Horeb in the first appendix also provides a link to the second appendix. Only one other time in the Old Testament does the biblical narrative report of a person going to Horeb. In an effort to flee the wrath of Jezebel, Elijah treks through the wilderness for forty days and forty nights as he made his way to "Horeb, the mountain of God" (1 Kgs 19:8). Like the community gathered at Horeb in Deuteronomy, Elijah also heard the voice of God (Deut 4:12; 1 Kgs 19:13); both parties experienced a theophany on that mountain. Thus, Horeb was more than just a place for the dispensing of law or a place of refuge, it was "a place of revelation."[30]

B. Appendix 2: Announcement of the Coming of Elijah (3:23–24[4:5–6])

In the second appendix, attention returns to a theme found in the fourth and sixth disputations (i.e., the day of YHWH), but with considerable expansion.

1. The Intended Action of Elijah (3:23[4:5])

The opening line in 3:23[4:5] replicates that found earlier in 3:1. Both lines begin with the particle הִנֵּה, "behold," followed by a first-person singular pronoun plus the participial form of שׁלח, "to send." In 3:23[4:5], the form of the first-person pronoun utilized is אָנֹכִי. Elsewhere in the book, the form is אֲנִי (cf. 1:4, 6, 14; 2:9; 3:6, 17; 3:21[4:3]).[31] There is another text in the Old Testament that provides a near *exact* parallel to the construction in the second appendix, a parallel even closer than Mal 3:1. Not only does Exod 23:20 parallel Mal 3:23[4:5] lexically and syntactically, but its subject matter proves particularly illuminating. The line reads

הִנֵּה אָנֹכִי שֹׁלֵחַ מַלְאָךְ
Behold, I am sending a messenger.

As Petersen has noted, the verbal parallels between 3:23[4:5] and Exod 23:20 (הִנֵּה אָנֹכִי שֹׁלֵחַ מַלְאָךְ, "behold I am sending") coupled with what is being sent ("a messenger;" "Elijah") are "too striking to be accidental."[32] In announcing the coming of Elijah in 3:23[4:5], Malachi appears to draw from a previous text in which YHWH sent another messenger.

29. "Israel's faith in the present tense and hope in the future tense was always conditioned by her ability to 'remember' the words and deeds of YHWH in the past" (Hill, *Malachi*, 374).

30. Kessler, *Maleachi*, 306.

31. Some have pointed to this difference in the appendix as further evidence that these verses were subsequent additions to the book, likely by another author. In 3:1, the first-person pronoun appears as a pronominal suffix attached to the particle. The collocation הִנֵּה ("behold") followed by a participle frequently signals immediacy. *IBHS* §40.2.1b.

32. David L. Petersen, *Late Israelite Prophecy: Studies in Deutero-Prophetic Literature and in Chronicles*, SBLMS 23 (Missoula, MT: Scholars Press, 1977), 43.

This appropriation of the Exodus text in the second appendix is likely intended as a literary construction meant to bridge the Torah and the Prophets.[33] Even more, this connection suggests that just as YHWH sent a messenger to his people before, he will do so again.

The intent in 3:23[4:5] is in part to clarify the identity of the messenger mentioned earlier in 3:1. In that text, the person to be sent is simply labeled as מַלְאָכִי, "my messenger," but in the second appendix, "Elijah, the prophet" is mentioned. The name utilized here, אֵלִיָּה, is a shortened form of the longer theophoric name, אֵלִיָּהוּ. The latter name appears by far with greater frequency in the Deuteronomistic history (62x), at times with the appositive "the Tishbite" (e.g., 1 Kgs 17:1) or "the prophet" (only in 1 Kgs 18:36), but most commonly without any appositional element to follow.[34]

The mention of Elijah as the forerunner to the coming day of YHWH was likely grounded in several key aspects of the prophet's life. Most notably is the report in 2 Kgs 2:11 that Elijah did not die, but instead ascended into the heavens. If Elijah was with God then he certainly could be sent out on mission again on behalf of God. There are other features of equal importance, however. Elijah may have been invoked as well because of his success in turning the people of Israel back to YHWH, as evident in his battle with the prophets of Baal at Mount Carmel (1 Kgs 18). The language in that text proves particularly striking, given the remainder of the second appendix. Malachi 3:24[4:6] reports that Elijah the prophet will turn the hearts (לֵב) of the people lest a curse come upon them. In 1 Kgs 18:37, Elijah prays that through his appearance and his actions the hearts (לֵב) of the people will be turned back to YHWH.[35] Elijah's success in 1 Kgs 18 may have been interpreted as harbinger of his success as the forerunner to the Day of YHWH.

In his analysis of 3:24[4:6], Snyman also points to the story of Naboth's vineyard in 1 Kgs 21.[36] In that text, Elijah calls out Ahab for his unjust treatment of Naboth. This text signals that Elijah was not only a prophet committed to calling out theological and cultic abominations, but also a prophet concerned with matters of justice. While the book of Malachi spends considerable time on the cultic infractions of the community, social injustice remains clearly in view as well. In the face of injustice, Elijah announces that Ahab's household will be "burned up" or "consumed" (בער). In the sixth disputation, Malachi explains that the arrogant and evildoers will be set ablaze on the day that will come "burning [בער] like an oven." While the lexical similarities are suggestive, the thematic connection is critical.

The figure of Elijah also serves as an apt counterpart to the mention of Moses in the first appendix (3:22[4:4]). Even as Moses was the dominant figure in the Torah, so too was Elijah the dominant figure within the corpus of the Former Prophets.[37] Within the larger narrative framework of Israel's history, both figures demonstrated absolute fidelity to YHWH even as they both worked signs and wonders in the sight of God's people, and as suggested above, both experienced a theophany on Horeb, the only ones to do so in the Old Tes-

33. Hill, *Malachi*, 375. Clendenen, who argues that appendices to the book were written by the prophet, contends that this citation from Exod 23:20 better explains the alternate form of the first-person pronoun (אָנֹכִי). For Clendenden, the alternate form of the pronoun need not be explained by a subsequent editor ("Malachi," 461).

34. The LXX adds the appositional phrase found in the opening verse of the Elijah cycle, τὸν Θεσβίτην, "the Tishbite."

35. Although the verbs for "turn" differ in the two texts (1 Kgs 18:37, סוּר; Mal 3:24[4:6], שׁוּב), the two verbs remain within the same larger semantic domain.

36. Snyman, *Malachi*, 189.

37. Snyman, *Malachi*, 189.

tament.[38] In addition to these similarities, Jacobs suggests that both figures were likely included in the appendices due to their respective functions, "one as a law-giver and one as the voice of YHWH to a sinful people who had broken the law."[39]

Even though the text does not indicate how Elijah will come, it does offer a temporal reference with the final prepositional phrase, "before the great and awesome Day of YHWH" (3:23[4:5]). Although mentioned explicitly here, the notion of a "coming day" was referenced earlier in the book. The idea is mentioned somewhat obliquely in 3:2, and then with greater elaboration in 3:17, 19[4:1], and 21[4:3]. In searching for an apt and descriptive label for this day, the editor turned to another book with a strong cultic orientation and borrowed the language utilized there: "the great and terrible Day of YHWH" (cf. Joel 2:31b). The cosmological and meteorological phenomena mentioned in Joel 2 that will precede the coming of this day are indeed terrifying and fear-inducing: blood, fire, and columns of smoke will appear in the heavens and the earth (Joel 2:30), with the sun turning to darkness and the moon to blood (Joel 2:30–31). Such an event "constitutes the ultimate theophany."[40] Joel announces that on that day only those who call upon YHWH will be saved, while the nations will be gathered in the valley of Jehoshaphat for judgement. In Malachi, however, such imagery is altogether missing. In place of the terrifying cosmological and meteorological phenomena is Elijah, the messenger, the one who will presage the coming Day of YHWH. Moreover, as Mal 3:13–21[4:3] explained, the coming day of judgement will be less about Israel and the nations, as much as it will about "the just and the wicked, . . . those serving God and those who do not serve him" (3:18).[41]

2. An Ominous Curse (3:24[4:6])

Although the final verse in the book is clearly meant to explain the purpose of Elijah's arrival, its interpretation has proven difficult due to the somewhat enigmatic and perplexing language in the first half of the verse. The opening verb, שׁוּב, "to turn back," appears regularly throughout the larger prophetic corpus and often connotes repentance or restoration. Similar usage appears regularly in the book of Malachi as well (1:4; 2:6; 3:7 [3x], 24[4:6]). The more precise question concerns the relationship of the verb to the phrase that follows: "hearts of fathers to sons and heart of sons to fathers." Who is turning back to whom and for what reason? In an attempt to offer some clarity to this phrase, the LXX emended the verse. The translator apparently understood the first half of the phrase in reference to the restoration of the immediate family. To this end, the plural forms in the MT were made singular: Elijah will turn the "heart of a father to a son" (καρδίαν πατρὸς πρὸς υἱὸν). In the second half of the line, the LXX expands the work of Elijah to include the larger community, "the heart of a man to his neighbor" (καρδίαν ἀνθρώπου πρὸς πλησίον αὐτο). In short, with the coming of Elijah, the entire community will enjoy a renewed unity as the covenant people of YHWH.

More recent interpreters have offered an array of interpretive solutions. Some have suggested that the use of the plural אָבוֹת, "fathers," and בָּנִים, "sons," is intended to function as a merism, and thus should be understood idiomatically as

38. Hill, *Malachi*, 384.

39. Jacobs, *The Books of Haggai and Malachi*, 328.

40. Hill, *Malachi*, 386.

41. In reference to the coming Day of YHWH, Jacobs offers an important cautionary word for interpretation. She writes that "while the formulation manifests an eschatological framework for the depicted actions or events, that time is remote but not necessarily at the ultimate end of time" (*The Books of Haggai and Malachi*, 328). Cf. Hill, *Malachi*, 376.

"everyone." With this proposed reading, the preposition עַל is rendered as "with:" "he will turn the hearts of fathers together with sons [to YHWH]." The final prepositional phrase (i.e., "to YHWH") is implied.[42] Elijah will cause everyone to return to YHWH. Others have suggested that the language in this verse is highly metaphorical and meant to refer to the covenantal relationship between God and Israel. Understood this way, בָּנִים, "sons," is meant to refer to Israel while אָבוֹת, "fathers," refers to YHWH.[43] The father-son metaphor appeared earlier in the book (1:6) and is typically cited as support for this position. Assis explains that "the prophet will return the heart of God to Israel and he will return the hearts of Israel to God."[44] While the parent-child metaphor is used repeatedly among the prophets, and notably in the first book in the Book of the Twelve (Hos 11:1), the plural form אָבוֹת, "fathers," is never used in reference to YHWH.[45] A third proposal looks at possible discord within society, particularly between the older and younger generations, as an explanation. Assuming that this appendix was added quite late, interpreters propose that the conflict is the result of a younger generation enamored with the Hellenistic culture and parents (אָבוֹת) longing for their children to remain faithful to their heritage.[46]

A fourth interpretation, and the one followed here, suggests that the reconciliation envisioned in this verse concerns the אָבוֹת, "fathers," (i.e., the ancestors who first established a covenant with YHWH) and the present generation.[47] Rather than a reference to the rectification of a right social order, as the third option suggests, this verse calls for a wholesale renewal of the covenant. Verhoef explains that "When Elijah comes he will restore the covenant relationship. In this process, he will turn about the hearts of the wicked posterity [i.e., בָּנִים, "sons"] to the hearts of them with whom God has entered into a covenant at Horeb."[48] Previous mention of אָבוֹת, "fathers," within the larger book is instructive and suggests that such renewal remains necessary. In the third disputation (2:10), the prophet chastises the people for their behavior and alleges that they have profaned the covenant with their forefathers, אָבוֹת. In the fifth disputation, YHWH declared that "ever since the days of your forefathers [אָבוֹת], you have turned aside from my statutes and not kept them" (3:6). The assumption is that the current generation has failed in its covenantal commitment and stands at odds with the generation at Horeb, the one that entered into covenant with YHWH. In response to the present generation's waywardness, YHWH invites the community to "return [שׁוּב] to me so that I may return [שׁוּב] to you" (3:7). This language of turning back or returning (שׁוּב) appears once more in this appendix. This covenant renewal will not be at the initiative of the community, but rather as a result of the work of God who will send Elijah.

42. W. Emery Barnes, *Haggai, Zechariah, Malachi*, CBSC, 2nd ed. (Cambridge: Cambridge University Press, 1934), 135. The NET, more recently, has adopted this reading: "He will encourage fathers and their children to return to me."

43. Caryn. A. Reeder, "Malachi 3:24 and the Eschatological Restoration of the 'Family,'" *CBQ* 69 (2007): 695–709; Elie Assis, "Moses, Elijah, and the Messianic Hope: A New Reading of Malachi 3, 22–24," *ZAW* 123 (2011): 207–20.

44. Assis, "Moses, Elijah and the Messianic Hope," 212–13.

45. Assis admits as much, but then counters this challenge by noting the use of the plural אֲדוֹנִים for "lord, master" in 1:6 as evidence in support of his proposal. Assis fails to mention that the plural construct form of אָדוֹן occurs repeatedly and regularly elsewhere in the Old Testament in reference to YHWH, which likely explains its usage in 1:6, but the same cannot be said of אָב, "father."

46. Rudolph, *Haggai, Sacharja 1–8, Sacharja 9–14, Maleachi*, 292; Kessler, *Maleachi*, 311; Snyman, *Malachi*, 191. Glazier-McDonald offers a similar proposal but argues that the tension exists during the Persian period, likely over the matter of foreign wives mentioned in 2:10–16 (*Malachi*, 255).

47. To stress the identity of the אָבוֹת, Hill properly renders the term "forefathers" (*Malachi*, 388).

48. Verhoef, *The Books of Haggai and Malachi*, 342.

In many ways, the work of Elijah parallels the work of another figure mentioned from Israel's past. Even as Levi "he turned [הֵשִׁיב] many from iniquity" and to return to covenantal faithfulness (2:6), so too will Elijah cause many to "turn back" (הֵשִׁיב) to the covenant.

The final clause begins with the subordinating conjunction פֶּן, "lest." This conjunction typically expresses some form of contingency as it relates to the matrix clause, and more often than not, refers to the prevention of some action or event, as is the case here.[49] YHWH will send Elijah to turn hearts back to the covenant *lest* YHWH comes and strike the land (הָאָרֶץ) with a curse (חֵרֶם).[50] Although some interpreters have understood "land" (הָאָרֶץ) to be more cosmic in scope, particularly given the appropriation of Joel 2 ("the great and terrible Day of YHWH") and the cosmic references mentioned in that text, the mention of "land" in Mal 3:24[4:6] is likely more modest in scope and refers more particularly to the province of Yehud and those living within that land. The book of Deuteronomy repeatedly claims that covenantal faithfulness is meant to be lived out within the land itself (4:5, 14; 5:31; 6:1; 12:1), but even more, that such fidelity has an impact upon the land. This suggests that there is "an intimate connection between the nature of the land" and those who dwell within it.[51] Such a connection was already on display in the fifth disputation. YHWH invited the people to return (שׁוּב) to him (3:7) and test him (3:10). If they will do so, YHWH declares, then the land will be blessed and the community will be known as a "land of delight" (3:12). The final line in the book employs this same logic but in reverse. If the community fails to return to YHWH, then the land (and those who inhabit it) will face the consequences of covenantal unfaithfulness; they will face utter destruction (חֵרֶם).[52]

Rather than understanding this final line simply as an ominous warning, or worse yet, a lingering threat, it could be understood as a word of hope. As Gibson has suggested, "in promising to send Elijah, [YHWH] is working behind the scenes to save his people from the curse. The curse is real but so too is YHWH's initiative to rescue."[53] Even as the book of Malachi opened with a strong affirmation of YHWH's covenantal commitment so too does it conclude.

Canonical and Theological Significance

The Coming of Elijah

The reference to the return of Elijah before "the great and awesome day of YHWH" (Mal 3:23[4:5]) received considerable attention in later Jewish tradition.[54]

49. *IBHS* §31.6.1c; *BHRG* §41.11.

50. Although some grammarians borrow "case" language and identify this construction as a "double accusative" (*IBHS* §10.2.3), the clause הִכֵּיתִי אֶת־הָאָרֶץ חֵרֶם is best understood as a verb + complement (הָאָרֶץ) + adjunct (חֵרֶם).

51. Glazier-McDonald, *Malachi*, 258.

52. Kessler acknowledges that the challenge presented by having חֵרֶם ("destruction, ban") as the final word in the verse merits our attention: "We must take note of the fact that Malachi (and with it the prophetic corpus) ends with a word of destruction. It is indeed an annihilation that is not supposed to occur because of Elijah's work of reconciliation beforehand. But if this too were rejected, would not the threat still remain in force. *We cannot avoid the gravity of this*" (*Maleachi*, 313; italics added).

53. Gibson, *Covenant Continuity and Fidelity*, 256.

54. By way of overview, see Joel A. Weaver, *Theodoret of Cyrus on Romans 11:26. Recovering an Early Christian Elijah*

Elements of this claim were appropriated in varying ways, but generally speaking they reflected the central role that Elijah played in subsequent Jewish eschatological thought.

The earliest such appropriation likely appears in Sirach, a wisdom text written in Hebrew in the early second century BCE, and then translated into Greek several decades later. In the panegyric frequently labeled "Praise of the Ancestors" (44:1–50:24), the author acknowledges and extols the fidelity of key figures from Jewish history. In Sirach 48:1–11, Elijah is mentioned, along with a list of laudable events from his life. In verse 10, the author explains that "At the appointed time, it is written, you [Elijah] are destined to appease wrath before [the time of God's] anger, to turn the hearts of parents to their children and to restore the tribes of Jacob."[55] Sirach's rendering of this verse closely parallels that of Mal 3:23–24a[4:5–6a] with a few notable exceptions. Instead of mentioning the "day of YHWH," the author refers to "wrath," perhaps a reference to the potential divine curse upon the land mentioned in Mal 3:24c[4:6c].[56] The Malachi text mentioned that Elijah would return the hearts of the fathers to the sons and the hearts of sons to their fathers. In Sirach, however, the second line of Mal 3:24[4:6] has shifted considerably. According to Sirach, the Elijah figure will "restore the tribes of Jacob" implying that the arrival of Elijah will not only stave off the curse, but also will serve as the precursor to the restoration of the nation.

Similar themes appear in two texts from the Dead Sea Scrolls. In 4Q558, Elijah is mentioned by name. The fourth lines reads "to you I will send Elijah be[fore . . .]" and then it breaks off. The fifth line includes the word "lightning" leading Collins, among others, to postulate that the line is in reference to the Day of YHWH.[57] Although quite brief (and fragmentary), the text does appear to invoke the notion of an Elijah figure that will precede the coming Day of YHWH, a claim that clearly aligns with Mal 3:23[4:5].

The eschatological hymn 4Q521, sometimes labeled "a messianic apocalypse," speaks of a coming "messiah" (משיח) that will act as God's agent in ushering in the kingdom of God. Although the name "Elijah" does not appear in the text, 4Q521 2 III, 2, does cite Mal 3:24a[4:6a] in an apparent invocation of the larger Elijah tradition. Additionally, 4Q521 2 II, 12–13, mentions that the one who comes will "heal the wounded, give life to the dead, and preach good news to the poor and he will [sat] isfy the [weak] ones and lead those who have been cast out and enrich the hungry."

Redivivus Tradition, American University Studies 249 (New York: Peter Lang, 2007), 99–148. For a more detailed analysis of selected texts, see Brenda Jean Shaver, "The Prophet Elijah in the Literature of the Second Temple Period: The Growth of a Tradition," (PhD diss., The University of Chicago, 2001), 124–223.

55. The phrase "the time of God's" is lacking in the Hebrew text. The translation suggested above by David Miller follows the LXX. For a brief review of this phrase in both textual traditions, see David M. Miller, "The Messenger, the Lord, and the Coming of Judgement in the Reception History of Malachi 3," *NTS* 53 (2007): 7n23.

56. Weaver, *Theodoret of Cyrus on Romans 11:26*, 103.

57. John J. Collins, "The Works of the Messiah," *DSD* 1 (1994), 106. Cf. Shaver, "The Prophet Elijah in the Literature of the Second Temple Period," 164–66.

Shaver, following Collins, notes that Elijah was well-known for the performance of numerous miracles, which included healing the sick, feeding the hungry and even resurrecting the dead, the "very same miracles which are to be performed in the end-time."[58] The point remains, however, that an anointed one (משיח), like Elijah, will come prior to the arrival of God's kingdom.[59]

Other texts from the first century allude to the tradition associated with the return of Elijah, but perhaps few so explicitly as those found in the New Testament.[60] Elijah is the fourth most frequently mentioned Old Testament figure in the New Testament, behind Moses, Abraham, and David. His name occurs some twenty-nine times with twenty-five of the appearances in the Synoptic Gospels and another two in the Gospel of John.[61] Throughout the Synoptics, the Gospel writers equate John the Baptist with the returning Elijah figure. In Luke's birth account of John the Baptist, for example, the angel announces that "with the spirit and power of Elijah, [John] will go before [Jesus], to turn the hearts of parents to their children and the disobedient to the wisdom of the righteous, to make ready a people prepared for [YHWH]" (1:17 NRSVUE). The language in the announcement borrows heavily from Mal 3:23–24[4:5–6] to ensure the association between the two figures is clear, as is its implication (i.e., John is the harbinger of the coming of YHWH). The opening chapter of the Gospel of Mark highlights the centrality of this theme. Verse 2 begins with a citation from Mal 3:1, "See, I am sending my messenger ahead of you, who will prepare your way" (NRSVUE), and, although the name of Elijah is not mentioned explicitly in this chapter, the description of John's attire (i.e., cloth of camel hair and leather belt) recalls that of Elijah in 2 Kgs 1:8. Mark leaves little doubt that John's arrival should be viewed through the lens of Mal 3:23–24[4:5–6], and this is confirmed further by John's actions: he was "calling Israel to repentance and to preparation for the coming day of God's manifestation of salvation and judgement."[62] On Jesus's recognition of John as "Elijah who is to come," see Matt 11:14.

In all three Synoptics, Elijah appears alongside Moses and Jesus in the episode of the transfiguration (Matt 17:1–8//Mark 9:2–8//Luke 9:28–36). Although some might suggest that the appearance of Moses and Elijah simply confirm that Jesus is the fulfillment of the Law and the Prophets, such an explanation fails to address the rich

58. Shaver, "The Prophet Elijah in the Literature of the Second Temple Period," 182. See also the treatment of 4Q521 in Miller, "The Messenger, the Lord, and the Coming of Judgement," 8–10. Miller challenges this reading and contends that these actions will be performed by the coming Lord (אדני), not the Elijah figure (10n37).

59. Collins has made this case most forcefully. See his assessment of 4Q521 in John J. Collins, *The Scepter and the Star: The Messiahs of the Dead Sea Scrolls and Other Ancient Literature*, ABRL (New York: Doubleday, 1995), 117–22, and Collins, "A Herald of Good Tidings. Isaiah 61:1–3 and its Actualization in the Dead Sea Scrolls," in *The Quest for Context and Meaning: Studies in Biblical Intertextuality in Honor of James A. Sanders*, ed. C. A. Evans and S. Talmon (Leiden: Brill, 1997), 225–40.

60. Allusions to Elijah appear in 1 Enoch 89:51–52; 90:31; 4 Ezra 6:26; 7:28.

61. The remaining two appearances occur in Rom 11:2 and James 5:17.

62. Larry W. Hurtado, *The Gospel of Mark* (New York: Harper and Row, 1983), 4.

theological confession that is at work in the text. The Markan account is particularly intriguing in that Elijah is mentioned first ("And there appeared to them Elijah with Moses" [9:4 NRSVUE]). This is likely because of Elijah's role as the forerunner, as Hooker has suggested, or similarly, that the coming of Elijah is meant to inaugurate the end times, as proposed by Gnilka.[63] Garland offers the most promising explanation, however, for the appearance of the two figures together. He cites Deuteronomy Rabba 3:17: "God told Moses: when I will send Elijah, the prophet, you are to come, both of you together" and then concludes that the appearance of these two together "is a sign that the end is drawing near."[64] Understood this way, the coming of Elijah in the transfiguration account stands within the larger tradition associated with Mal 3:23–24[4:5–6] and functions as yet another sign within the Gospels that the coming of Jesus carries with it eschatological overtones of the in-breaking of God into the world.

Hope Engendered Faithfulness

While the final verses in the book apparently have a canonical function, they also integrate the claims of the entire book into a final overarching theological confession. The themes associated across the six disputations in the book of Malachi can be reduced to two primary arguments. Schart suggests that Mal 1:6–9, 2:10–16 and 3:6–12 "tries to motivate the hearers/readers to wholeheartedly fulfill the torah, especially in cultic matters," while Mal 2:17–3:5 and 3:13–21[4:3] "defends the argument that righteous behavior in the present will be rewarded with overwhelming blessing in the future."[65] The two appendices reflect these dual emphases. The exhortation to "remember the torah" points to the former while the reference to Elijah and the coming day of YHWH recalls the latter. Together they signal a posture of faith that is focused on the present but grounded in the future.

In the sixth and final disputation, the people complained that serving God was "futile" (שָׁוְא) and that there is nothing to be gained (בֶּצַע) from being faithful to this God. The two appendices seek to upend that claim by asserting that covenantal

63. Morna D. Hooker, "What Doest Thou Here, Elijah?," in *The Glory of Christ in the New Testament: Studies in Christology in Memory of George Bradford Caird*, eds. L. D. Hurst and N. T. Wright (Oxford: Oxford University Press, 1987), 62–67; Joachim Gnilka, *Das Evangelium nach Markus (MK 8:27–16:20)*, EKKNT (Neukirchen-Vluyn: Neukirchener, 1978), 37.

64. David E. Garland, *Reading Matthew: A Literary and Theological Commentary* (Macon, GA: Smyth & Helwys, 2001), 184. In the Markan and Matthean accounts of the transfiguration, Jesus explains that "Elijah has already come" (Matt 17:11// Mark 9:13), with the disciples understanding this as a reference to John the Baptist (Matt 17:13).

65. Aaron Schart, "Putting the Eschatological Visions of Zechariah in the Place: Malachi as a Hermeneutical Guide for the Last Section of the Book of the Twelve," in *Bringing out the Treasure: Inner Biblical Allusions in Zechariah 9–14*, ed. Mark J. Boda and Michael H. Floyd, JSOTSup 370 (Sheffield: Sheffield Academic Press, 2003), 342. I would slightly amend Schart's argument to suggest that 3:6–12 actually crosses into both categories and perhaps, given its location in the book, the emphasis might actually be on the second argument more than the first.

faithfulness remains the expected norm but commitment to that norm is not predicated on what happens in the present moment. Instead, such commitment is borne out of anticipation for that which is yet to come. In 3:17, YHWH announces that on "the day" that he acts, those who fear him will belong to him; they will be his "special possession" (3:17). The coming of Elijah functions as a precursor to the day that YHWH will act, a day in which those who have turned to YHWH will avoid utter destruction and instead, belong to him.

A similar expression of faith appears in Paul's admonition to the community at Thessalonica. In his first letter to the Christians there, Paul makes reference to the "coming of [YHWH]" in 4:13–5:11 but, as Nijay Gupta has noted, the emphasis in this letter "is on life shaped in light of the hope of the *parousia*" (emphasis added).[66] Or, put differently, it is on hope-engendered faithfulness.[67] In the opening chapter of the book, Paul praises them for serving "a living and true God" while they "wait for his Son from heaven, whom he raised from the dead—Jesus, who rescues us from the wrath that is coming" (1:9b–10, NRSVUE).[68] Gupta observes that "rather than prognosticate about the eschatological timeline, Paul shifts the concern to right living as people of day and light (5:6–8)."[69] In short, Paul calls the community to live in faithfulness even as they wait in anticipation.

The final verses of Malachi provide more than just an apt conclusion to a prophetic book. In many ways, they join with the larger witness of Scripture in calling believers to a particular embodiment of faith: an expressed faithfulness that is predicated upon an assured faithfulness of the one that we serve. In this way, hope is intended to engender faithfulness even as faithfulness is an expression of that hope.

66. Nijay Gupta, *1 and 2 Thessalonians*, ZCINT 13 (Grand Rapids: Eerdmans, 2019), 90.

67. Gorman terms this as "anticipatory participation in the future" (Michael Gorman, *Becoming the Gospel* [Grand Rapids: Eerdmans, 2015], 100).

68. Just prior to the lengthy passage on the coming of the Lord, Paul writes, "We ask and urge you in the Lord Jesus that, as you have learned from us how you ought to live and please God (as, in fact, you are doing), you should do so more and more. For you know what instructions we gave you through the Lord Jesus" (1 Thess 4:1–2 NRSV).

69. Gupta, *1 and 2 Thessalonians*, 91.

Ancient Sources Index

Old Testament

Genesis

Exodus

Leviticus

Numbers

Deuteronomy

Joshua

Judges

Ruth

Proverbs

Ecclesiastes

Isaiah

Jeremiah

Lamentations

Ezekiel

Daniel

Hosea

Joel

Amos

Obadiah

New Testament

Matthew

Mark

Luke

Romans

2 Corinthians

Galatians

1 Thessalonians

James

1 Peter

1 John

Deuterocanonical Books

Sirach

Pseudepigrapha

1 Enoch

4 Ezra

Dead Sea Scrolls

Subject Index

Author Index